John Henrik Clarke

AFRICANS *at the* CROSSROADS

Notes for an *African World Revolution*

Africa

P.O. Box 18
Trenton, N

D0869661

Africa World Press, Inc.

P.O. Box 1892
Trenton, New Jersey 08607

Book design and typesetting by Malcolm Litchfield
This book is composed in Goudy and Galliard Bold

Cover Illustration by Carles J. Juzang

Library of Congress Catalog Card Number: 91-74121

0-86543-270-8   Cloth
0-86543-271-6   Paper

CONTENTS

▼

iii

Three: Different Roads to Freedom

Four: Africa, Zionism, and Friends Without Friendship

Five: Colonialism and the Conquest of the Mind

DEDICATION

▼

To my children, Nzingha Marie Clarke and Sonni Kojo Clarke, and
their generation who will inherit the responsibilities of the
African World Revolution.

PREFACE

What's the Hour of the Night?

▼

After four score years of freedom
Our so-called leaders say
That the race has made great progress
And we face the dawn of day
But the day is not quite dawning
Millions of my peoples stand
Pleading at the bars of justice
For reparations and land
We're not free in this country
And the truth is the light
So I turn to ask my watchman
What's the hour of the night?

We died fighting for democracy
I admit this to be true
Yet countless African men & women
Have no homes or work to do
If we wish to see the daylight
Or the rising of the sun
We need our self-determination
Our own affair to run
Since only reparations will
Put freedom in our sight

Let us turn to ask the watchman
What's the hour of the night?

We fought with the mighty armies
When they battled with the Huns
Faced the fierce pangs of combat
Heard the roar of mighty guns
But no change came in our condition
When the smoke had cleared away
For the blood we shed in battle
Did not bring the dawn of day
All of our suffering and service
Left us in the same old plight
So I turn to ask my watchman
What's the hour of the night?

The whites are celebrating their freedom
A bicentennial whose praise they sing
But Africans are also jumping on board
Although we didn't get a thing
We're still struggling for Integration
As though it was a glorious fight
So I've got to ask my watchman
What's the hour of the night?
Music is an art or science
In which African men reign supreme
But the story of our progress
Is still a vision or a dream
But we have great voices for singing
But we have no voice in court
Imagine being attacked by police dogs
Just to register and vote
With self-determination
We would have our perfect right
So we turn to ask our watchman
What's the hour of the night?

African men boast of their religion
Though I wonder if they should
When you take an inventory
You'll find them not so good
We build thousands of fine churches
With the dollars that we give
Yet masses of our people
Have no decent place to live
We say God is our rich father
Yet we're always in a tight
Watchman strike a match and tell me
What's the hour of the night?

Civil rights laws just for us
Is proof that we're not free
How could we be fooled to think
We had a share in this democracy
When foreigners come here
They're made citizens by choice
Citizenship was imposed upon us
We never had a voice
The passage of the 14th amendment
Took away the right
So you better ask your watchman
What's the hour of the night?

Time is running out for us
A deadline we must meet
To file reparation petitions
And make politicians earn their seats
If we're to win this battle
Every organization must join the Fight
Then we'll tell our watchman
What's the hour of the night.

Queen Mother Audley Moore, July 27, 1950

INTRODUCTION

▼

THE WELL-KNOWN AFRICAN American poet Countee Cullen began his famous poem "Heritage" with the question, "What is Africa to me?" In this book of political essays I have expanded the question by asking, "What is Africa to Africans, and what is Africa to the world?" Professor Ivan Van Sertima of Rutgers University has stated that African history has been locked in a 500-year-old room and, figuratively speaking, there is a need to open that room and look for Africa, its peoples, and their significance for the whole world.

All mankind has met African people at the crossroads of history at one time or another.

The greater portion of the Roman Empire rose and fell in Africa. In the early persecution of Christians, more Africans were killed in the amphitheaters of North Africa than in the Roman arenas. Because African history, political or otherwise, has been seen mainly through the eyes of conquerors, missionaries, and adventurers, whose interpretation of Africa and its people in most cases is a kind of sick fantasy, it is time that Africans tell their own African story. In looking at African history from the Africancentric point of view, my honest attempt is to correct some of the prevailing misconceptions about Africa and its people in order to see the global significance of Africa. It must be remembered that more than one-half of human history had occurred before the people now referred to as Europeans played any significant part in the shaping of world history.

Africa has been under siege for over 3000 years, being preyed upon by one foreigner or the other. None of these foreigners came to Africa to do any good for Africans. Need and greed brought them to Africa.

Need and greed kept them there.

In looking at the invaders of Africa there is a need to look at invaders in general and their mission.

Most invaders, being masters of propaganda, generally depict themselves as civilizers with a mission. And contrary to their rhetoric, their impact on the invaded country is generally negative.

For over a thousand years the invaders of Africa came from Western Asia, now referred to as the Middle East. These invaders first declared war on African culture. They had no respect for African religious customs, and they looked with disdain on all African ways of life alien to their understanding. These invaders made every effort to destroy the confidence of African people and the image of God as Africans originally conceived God to be. In large areas of Africa, Africans stopped worshipping a god of their own choosing and stopped speaking of God in a language of their own making. This was the greatest achievement of the Europeans in Africa: the insidious conquest of the minds of the African peoples.

The Arab slave trade and Arab oppression of the Africans came a thousand years before the European slave trade. The Arab slave trade, unfortunately still spoken of in hushed tones or rarely spoken of at all, has as disastrous an effect on African people as the European slave trade.

The Arab slave trade drained Africa of its land power and organization to the extent that Africans did not have the organized strength to totally resist the European slave trade. I repeat: No European ever came into Africa to do Africans any good.

In these political essays, the main focus of my attention is the politics and resistance movements in the African world from the latter part of the nineteenth century to the latter part of the twentieth century. I am aware that there is a need to analyze the main currents in African history from the eve of the slave trade in the fifteenth and sixteenth centuries to the present. But in his book, *How Europe Underdeveloped Africa*, the Guyanese scholar Walter Rodney has made this kind of analysis and more.

Since the beginning of the European invasion, Africa and its people have been struggling against three tragedies of European design: slavery, colonialism, and neo-colonialism, i.e., the aftermath of slavery and colonialism. Before and after the African Independence Explosion, which began in 1957 in Ghana, a nation then referred to as The Gold Coast, the colonizers of Africa made a hasty retreat that would only be temporary; they would return to Africa under a new guise, neo-colonialism. The Africans had been living under an illusion of independence, because no African state existed where Africans were totally in charge of their economic destiny.

From early twentieth century to the present, African scholars have been producing a highly select and significant body of political literature about the plight of African peoples. It is unfortunate that most of this literature is seldom read and poorly circulated. In the United States, serious consideration should be given to Chancellor Williams' book, *The Rebirth of African Civilization* and his master plan for African redemption, *The Destruction of African Civilization*. Professor Ronald Walters of Howard University's Department of Political Science has said: "Capitalism has no flags and no national loyalty." By extension I believe it is important to add that communism also has no national flag or national loyalties. If either of these systems is to be used for Africa's salvation, African scholars, thinkers, and politicians must reshape these systems and Africanize them to the point where they are applicable to Africa's situation.

Perhaps the greatest political mistake that has been made in Africa in relation to the Independence Explosion is the European training of the African heads of state and their respective supporters, whose ideas of the state are negatively influenced by this very training. Whatever system the Africans use for themselves must be reshaped by the concept of Africans for Africa. Neither the communists nor the capitalists have a master plan for African freedom. While there are strong ideological differences between the capitalists and the communists, their intention in Africa is the same. Both of them would like to rule over African people and their resources by any means necessary.

The salvation of Africa must be designed by the collective mind of the African world. The imitation European states now in existence throughout the African world have no long-range future. If Africans want capitalism, they will have to develop their own concept and approach to it, and they will have to do the same thing in regard to communism or socialism. Any African who thinks he can come to power in Africa and share it with a European is extremely naive. Europeans did not come into Africa to share power with Africans.

They came to rule, and they intend to rule or ruin. There is nothing in Africa that Europeans need that they cannot obtain through honorable trade. Europe and the Western world in general have many things that Africans need, while Africa has much of what they need.

I know no case in history where the Europeans shared power with Africans. When Africans look toward their future, they must envision an Africa that is as African-ruled as France is French-ruled and England is English-ruled. No one needs to apologize ever for wanting to be the master in his own house. The total liberation of Africa must involve a commitment from all the Africans on the face of the earth.

A Pan-African skills bank needs to be established so that the Africans in Africa have access to the training and the technical talent developed by Africans living abroad. Most Africans living abroad who are serious about Africa have a holistic loyalty toward all Africans across the border lines of African states that, in most cases, were drawn to facilitate the Europeans.

Part of what I often refer to as the "evil genius" of Europeans is their ability to create states so they could fall apart. This is the invisible and sometimes visible hand of neo-colonialism.

The late Dr. Kwame Nkrumah explains neo-colonialism in the following manner: "The essence of neo-colonialism is that the State which is subject to it is, in theory, independent and has all the outward trappings of international sovereignty. In reality its economic system and thus its political policy is directed from outside."[1]

The significance of Africa, and of the Caribbean Islands, has not been properly assessed. The African presence in what has been mistakenly referred to as the New World began in the Caribbean Islands. And in this area and in parts of South America, especially Brazil, the Africans planned and successfully brought into being some of the greatest slave revolts in history. There is a literature on this subject and on African people in general in the Caribbean that is still shamefully neglected. C.L.R. James' book, *Black Jacobins*, and two books by the late Prime Minister of Trinidad, Eric Williams, *Capitalism and Slavery* and *The Caribbean from Columbus to Castro*, are examples.

---

[1] Kwame Nkrumah, *Neo-Colonialism: The Last Stage of Imperialism*, International Publishers, New York, 1966, Introduction, p. ix.

Pan-Africanism, which has sometimes been referred to as an idealistic African child living away from home, was developed in the Caribbean Islands, mainly by three Trinidadians: H. Sylvester Williams, C.L.R. James, and George Padmore, whose book, *Pan-Africanism or Communism*, is as relevant now as it was when he wrote it more than two decades ago. The Jamaican Marcus Garvey and his ideas for African redemption did not get the serious attention that was due to him in his lifetime and is not being given that attention now, when the message of his program is needed throughout the African world.

Until Africans throughout the world begin to tell their own story, the story will not be properly told.

Africa and its people are figuratively and symbolically knocking at the door of the twenty-first century. Africans caught in the crossfire of the struggle for world power are learning some painful lessons they should have learned long ago: Mainly, freedom is not free. Freedom is something you take with you own hands. You maintain it with your own hands. Freedom is not handed down from one generation to another. Each generation must assume the responsibility of securing their manhood, their womanhood, the definition of their being on earth that in the final analysis is nationhood. In knocking at the front door of the twenty-first century, the Africans of the world are saying the progression of circumstances has changed us from being a people begging and pleading to a people insisting and demanding. It is futile for anyone to say that African people are not ready to rule themselves. They are as ready as any people in the world. But ready or not here they come.

John Henrik Clarke

One

NOTES FOR AN AFRICAN WORLD REVOLUTION

▼

COMMENTARY I

▼

MY APPROACH TO THE SUBJECT, an African World Revolution, might sometime sound like a fantasy, but please bear in mind that sometimes the fantasy of today is tomorrow's reality. In addition to a need for a total reconsideration of Pan-Africanism, a cultural revolution is needed within the whole of the African world. The most important aspect of this revolution will occur within the geography of the continent of Africa, which is almost 12 million square miles, endowed by nature with some of the greatest mineral wealth in all the world. I believe the technical and scientific aspects of this revolution will begin with the Africans living outside of Africa who have been exposed, through education, to the kind of technological education that Africa needs in order to renew its old societies and make them workable within the modern world. It is important for us to learn who our friends are and who our enemies are and how to make the best use of both of them. The principal concepts of nation structure, nation formation, and nation building have been taken away from us as well.

The ability to examine our adversaries, to move among them, and still to advance while learning something of their technique has also been taken away from us. We have been rather naive in our interaction with people and we have overlooked too many items in relationship to our freedom. We have not developed a technique for dealing with our own traitors. But if we cannot do anything else, we can at least isolate them.

Why do we let so many known traitors to the African cause walk among us, unharmed? One of those traitors advocated that blacks should join UNITA and South Africa against Angola. I was the first

3

person to take a public stand against it and to say that by no means should an African ever lift arms against another African. Yet, except for a brief inept reply in the *New York Amsterdam News*, that was just about the end of it. But we have not looked closely at Angola. We haven't even looked at Savimbi's {1990} present visit. Why is it that Savimbi is having some success there? He's passing himself off as a Black Nationalist and getting away with it. In the name of national liberation, he permitted crimes against his own people while in the pay of the enemies of the Angolan people. Why is he getting away with it in Angola? When are we going to face up to the truth about what happened in Angola? He would not be able to get away with it had Angola's alleged political Left done a good job of communication with the people. But who came to power in Angola? Not Angolans. A bunch of assimiladoes, Europeanized blacks, and over half of them in the government have white Portuguese wives. Most of them are Catholics. Most of them have never worn indigenous African dress nor eaten indigenous African food. They cannot communicate with the people when they live a life alien to the people's culture.

This is not a main item—Savimbi himself is not a main item—on the agenda, but it is important that we study the Savimbis of the world. We have to concede that some people have made their separate peace, and they're no longer part of us.

Since we missed so many vital items that relate to us and twenty years later wish we had dealt initially with them, I'm going to pick up an item now and deal with it because this item relates to the kind of revolution that we need among ourselves. We need to do what all people do, that is, ask the question: *Who is loyal to this house?* Too many people walk among us, live among us, but declare no loyalty to us. They eat our bread and sleep in our beds. No one asks whether they are loyal to the cause of our liberation. Africans throughout the world must begin to practice the essential selfishness of survival. Our open-mindedness and our hospitality to strangers have been turned against us.

Current Opposition to Self-Determination

The United States Census Bureau is experimenting with an idea that could be disastrous for African Americans. There will be a new classification on the census form. If you're racially mixed, you can put down mixed. Now there are a whole lot of retreating blacks looking for their Dutch uncles and their Irish grandfathers. And there are a whole lot of blacks of Indian descent related to Seminoles and related to everything except Africa. These "mixes" can be used as a buffer. Then a lot of us will overlook something that we need to know about our history in this country, about the role of certain mixed people in our history who are blacker than the blacks in their actions.

Before we deal with mixes, let's ask the question: Who mixed them? Inasmuch as they were all African people and all black when they left Africa, they arrived here all African and had African names that their oppressors could not understand. The slave ships didn't bring any West Indians, East Indians, or black Americans, didn't bring any AKAs or Deltas, didn't bring any high yellows or low yellows. Those who mixed them are now going to put the mixes against the so-called unmixes. Where will that put most of us? Within our own families, most of us have every color gradation under the sun. A cousin who is mixed is just as much a cousin as one who is unmixed. What these enemies of African people understand at last is something the Karl Marx did not understand. While European life is based principally on economics and class, non-European life is base principally on religion and culture. If they can split African Americans along these lines, they can pit one against the other.

In South Africa the coloreds discovered something: They discovered that they were being used. When the apartheid government took them off the voting rolls, took them off the housing consideration roll, they got the point. Now some of them prefer to be called African and live in the African neighborhoods and don't distinguish themselves from other Africans because they are equally oppressed.

But the American government that intends to create the census classification of "mixed" is not prepared to accept the mixes into their social order. You will see the mixes at work for the white American social order, but you will not see the mixes in their living room or at their dining room table. They have just begun to discover that once you put all the purely African people or people of African descent together, including the African people of Asia (100 million people called Untouchables)—once you put all of that together, you've got a formidable force in the world. And what keeps them from greatness is their inability to unify their culture and make a connection with Africa.

Look at the African people in the Pacific. Some are mixed with Polynesians; some not mixed at all. In India, some mixed with East Indians, some not mixed at all. If all mixed people of the world were classified as such, they might constitute a major portion of the world's population. Now the white established order is against us, and we have to consider what are we going to do when they ask for these kinds of classifications for many of us will fall for it without knowing that it is a trap.

Mulattoes in History

Part of our total revolution in the world is the revolt against other people's classification of us: The writer and social critic, Lerone Bennett, has said, "We have been named ... we must be namers; we have to decide the name and the category." We have to look at our history in this country and in Africa itself. What did the mix do in Ghana—those mixed sons of German missionaries, the Randolphs and the like? In Ghana—and this is a case where serious study is needed—along the coast, among the Fanti people, where there are a lot of these mixtures in public life, not a single mixed person ever turned on Africa in favor of his father's people. Out of these mixes came some of the finest politicians that Ghana and Africa in general are to know. People like Casely Hayford, Horton Mills, the Kwesi Brew family, all committed mixed people, who laid down the foundation for modern political Ghana.

Are we going to ignore all of that? Can we deal with the fact that Gordon in Jamaica was a mixture? He's a national hero. He was the one who began to call attention to the fact that the emancipation of slavery in Jamaica had been a sham. It was sham everywhere. So there's no point in saying that Jamaican emancipation came thirty years ahead of emancipation in the United States. All that you are saying is that your sham is greater than our sham. Slavery still exists only in a different form. Slavery has not been abolished; it's been transformed.

Let's look at the United States. Let's look at some mixes that we need to take into consideration. Frederick Douglass was mixed. Are we going to give him up? Bishop {Henry McNeil} Turner was mixed.

Frederick Douglass may be the finest leader to come out of the nineteenth century. Bishop Turner was the forerunner of the radical ministry, starting in the nineteenth century and living until the early part of the twentieth century. Are we going to stop going to Tuskegee because Booker T. Washington was mixed? What kind of trap are we going to get ourselves into?

When we look at public servants, what would we have done without Adam Powell? Arrogant, big mouth? He could pass for white anyplace, but he lived blackness, smearing it in people's faces and building a political career out of it. Look at Walter White of the NAACP—smug, arrogant, blue-eyed blonde, but always acting as though he were doing us a favor because he passed for black. But let's look at the good and the bad. Let's look at the mixed cop-outs. Then we should look at some black cop-outs, too, because color really isn't the main factor; it is commitment and an understanding of the nature of our cause.

Now what are we going to do when the census taker asks are you mixed? You've suffered as a black person, you lived as a black person and American law says one drop of us makes you a whole of us. Are we ready to deal with the stupid racial laws of the United States? I thought I'd call this to your attention because there is trouble still to come. The nature of this trouble sometimes is the inability to stay in struggle.

Some years ago I went out to Milwaukee and helped to set up a Black Studies program which was going pretty well. When I returned, three years later, most of the black fellows had white girls and some of the black girls had white men. I turned to one of the girls who was very active in all of this and I asked what happened. She said, "The brothers left us alone, and after all we're human." Then turned toward this white man (she was married to him) and said, "To tell you the truth, I don't love him.... I don't even like him." I asked, "Why? Why the marriage? Why the relationship?" And she answered, "Professor Clarke, the struggle is so lonely, and people need people."

I think we missed taking care of some vital things in our struggle. We failed to do some housekeeping. She should not have been so lonely that she would marry a man she not only didn't love, but didn't even like. We should produce a caliber of young people who can take on the loneliness of struggle. A lot of people struggle in loneliness and a lot of people do what they do out of choice.

I have often said that I've met a number of rich men in my life, and I never met one who had a better mind than mine. All right then, so if it were my choice to be rich, I think I could have made it. I have the mentality to bring it off and yet I do not regret having walked down this course of action. I haven't regretted the nature of the commitment, for it has made me total as a human being. It has locked me into struggle in such a way that struggle becomes a way of life, becomes a birthright. We leave, as best we can, our stamp on a generation in a partial message through our truthful participation in struggle. These are some preface notes. I shall go deeper into the subject now.

Dreams and the Spiritual Revolution

How are we going to make complete changes? Dream a little bit and hope a little bit and know that if a people can have the will to bring off any monumental scheme, *they've got to dream, then they've got to make it so.*

We should start with the making of a spiritual revolution. Most of us, one way or the other, some place or the other, associate with some form of religion and some form of church. I am not asking anyone to believe anything. I'm saying that everything that touches your life should be an instrument of liberation and that making your spirituality an instrument of liberation does not make you one mite less religious, but more so.

We might have to step back in order to step forward. We might have to ask some questions. What kind of religion did African people have before Judaism, Christianity and Islam? How did African people determine right and wrong before these religions appeared in Africa? These religions, all made from elements of our own spirituality—dressed up, garnished and brought back to us and sold to us as something original—when there's nothing original in any of the three. How do we get back? And how do we transform what we've got into an instrument of liberation? How do we understand that we can be religious without being spiritual and be spiritual without belonging to any religion? Because the spiritual came first, before the formation of the religion itself. The religions came out of the spirituality that already existed.

How do we go back, and pick up, and utilize some of these values—values of self love, self appreciation, appreciation for the family, a concept of unity, and a concept of distribution of goods and services that was purely socialist before Europe? How do we go back to ourselves and find the mechanism of our own salvation?

Perhaps we need to look at other people and how they take systems from the outside and transform them into something they need inside. The Chinese tried Stalin's concept of communism, i.e., Marx and Engels' concept of communism. It didn't fit their soul; it didn't fit their cultural being. Did they become lesser communists? No. They *Chinesized* their communism to the point where they altered it and made it fit the Chinese psyche and the Chinese soul.

In our own revolt, in the establishment of a new spirituality of liberation, can we make these alterations without the assumption we're trying to destroy their faith when in actuality we are strengthening and building their faith?

We have never said or agreed that religion was the opiate of our people. That could come from none but a European, because he's made it the opiate. Religion or spirituality (the more correct term) was part of the totality of our life. It wasn't a Sunday occurrence; it was a total occurrence. It determined much of our life.

How can we have a revolt, a spiritual revolt, without the assumption that we're trying to destroy the church when in actuality we're trying to strengthen the church, trying to give it a new mission, a new destiny and a new will?

Study of Reaction To Oppression

I do not think we study enough how other people reacted to forms of oppression. I don't think we study enough the rise of modern Japan. We do not need to imitate Japan. I personally think the Japanese capitalists will ultimately back themselves into a corner where they won't be anything but brown-skinned or yellow-skinned Europeans if they don't stop at a given point. But what gave them the ability to rise and to organize are things that they still have. They still have a basic religion of their own design and choice. They still have the fervor of a Japanese nationalism, a love of nation and self that cuts down on the friction between Japanese and Japanese. And, they believe in themselves as thinkers.

A recent news item reports that a twenty-four year-old trainee on Wall Street learns enough information to feed it to someone else where they would engage in a $19 million stock swindle. Do you know we've got twenty-four year-old people who don't think that they have the ability to handle $1000? The structure of one man's brain is not radically different from another. These young people merely peeped the system and made it work in their favor. If they can peep the system and make it work in their favor, there's something radically wrong with the system itself. Because I am so uncapitalist and because I know, as a teacher, that the modern capitalist rose on slavery and exploitation of all people (black and white), I have no vested interest in its survival. If it goes, it goes, Yet, I know that you cannot live in a capitalist society with any degree of safety and comfort without having capital.

It seems that I'm engaged in a contradiction. If I believe in socialism (and I do), why do we believe just as much in black ownership of black communities, which seems like communism? To me, black ownership of the black community places in the hands of black people the economic means to effect social change in our favor. We can build a private school if we don't like the public school; use our politics to bring more pressure on the public school. Remember, always look back in order to look forward. How did African people rule states before this encroachment? They're as African as you, and if they did this, they had something you do not have, and that is self-confidence—self-confidence based on an understanding of both your culture and your religion. And your understanding should be that your religion and your politics are all one and the same and that all of these things have to come together to advance you in total. This practically is all the Japanese understand.

Remember, 200 years ago they didn't have a good wheelbarrow, and look at them now. They committed themselves to mastering Western technique. But in mastering these techniques, they did not make the mistake we made over integration. They mastered Western techniques and held on to their basic culture and their basic religion and their basic customs and way of life. They altered them to suit themselves. But we thought that by being integrated we had to put aside our customs and our religion. We even stopped eating cornbread or some of us did. Some of us who love watermelon will eat watermelon no more. [We] live in pain without watermelon.

In looking at a spiritual revolution, we have to make our spirituality a part of our totality and not a weekend matter for getting dressed up and going out on Sunday. It must be a part of our total approach to life: how we treat our children, how we treat our wives, how we treat our uncles, or we deal with the evil ones, how we deal with the drunken ones.

If we're going to have a spiritual revolution, we're going to have to have a commercial revolution. Why is a socialist talking about a commercial revolution? Because I know without the mastery of the techniques of commerce, no country can function well no matter what kind of governmental system. We must master our community, control the basic wealth in our communities and see that a dollar turns over eight times before it leaves the community (and sometimes make sure it doesn't even leave at all). Every time we need a shoe repaired we go to another brother, get the shoe repaired. Another brother is fixing the car, etc. It's a built-in economic system in our own community based on confidence in ourselves and based on making sure that the techniques, the basic skills and the basic crafts in the community are forever sharp. You've got to do a job if you want to keep the job.

Look back and see. When we (as Africans) had all these skills for running nations and running them well and weren't asking for any outsiders to educate our children, how did we lose it and how will we regain it? Because—no matter how we look at it, no matter if we try to avoid it—our next assignment in history is nation management and nation structure. No matter how we try to avoid doing so, we have to look again at Booker T. Washington, Marcus Garvey, W.E.B. DuBois and Elijah Muhammad. These men were all saying the same things, using different vantage points, different words, different organizational structure.

The Vision of Nation Building

People rise and fall within the context of the nation institution. When they lose the ability to master and control the nation institution they lose their freedom. This is where we are: a nation within a nation searching for a nationality. This is why we can say American and not add African to it. No one of German descent would ever say American without adding German to it, prefacing it in fact: I'm a German who was born in America.

What did we do when we had states of our own? Let's look at the last cluster of states. For the moment I am not dealing with the first great states, the Nile Valley states. Let's deal with those other rivers for a while and the great states on these other rivers, i.e., the Niger River states of Ghana, Mali and Songhai. The handling of the gold trade by Ghana, literally controlling the Trans-Saharan Trade in gold, created a monarchy so democratic that it was the role model for the democratic monarchies of the world. Let's see what happened when Africans went into Spain with the Berbers and the Arabs.

Spain, a sleepy, poorly administered country (then and now) was put on its feet, given a university and sidewalks with lights, its financial institutions controlled mainly by the Grandees, the Spanish Jews. This would last for 800 years with Africans administering a country far away from home. In the meantime, at home there would be over a thousand years of great structures of states in Inner West Africa. Ghana being the best known was assumed to be the first. But, the state of Mali had its great emperors: Mansa Musa, Roman Sekouru and Sundiata (the youth who started it all). Then, finally, the greatest of all the African states emerged, one larger than the continental limits of the United States: Songhai, with its university at Sankore, its great scholars, its finest rulers, Sonni Ali and Mohammed Abu Bekr Itoure. Can we look back at examples of African magnificence in the ruling of the state and can we look at the records of what other people said about them when foreigners came into these countries? What did they say about what they saw? They would call the last of these great rulers, Mohammed Abu Bekr Itoure, the greatest civil administrator of all times.

If concurrent with the existence of slavery in the United States (1493-1528), a ruler existed who was called the greatest civil administrator of all times, why is it that we have so little knowledge of him now? Why do we pull so little on the greatness that we have been in order to understand the greatness we still have to be? We've made such poor use of our history and our heroes.

Heinrich Barth says of Mohammed Abu Bekr Itoure, "He was the greatest ruler of state of his time." What were the other rulers of state at this time: The emperors of China, Europe getting off its feet, after the Dark Ages? There were many great rulers. Why is it that this

African was called the greatest of them all, barring none, having examined all of them? And why can't we today look at his life, look at his rule and look at his state and begin again the whole concept of state formation? I don't mean someone else came to collect the taxes; he did it himself. No one else came to develop his army; he developed it himself. No one else developed his marketplaces; he did it himself. And, he revolutionized the whole concept of weights and measures.

As a people, we must pull on the total good, yesterday's good, in order to create today's nation structure, in order to shape the kind of people we will have to be tomorrow. We will have to learn that the carbon copy of our oppressor's originality is wearing out, if indeed, he ever had any originality at all.

We have to study yesterday in order to create today. Now these states existed concurrent with the beginning of the slave trade. These states in Inner West Africa existed concurrent with the coast of West African slave trade. Let's examine what went wrong with our family communication. If we're going to have a whole revolution for social change, we have to look at when we had it as against when we lost it. We have to draw on the past in order to make the present and the future. What can we learn from how we got into this trap? What can we learn about the Europeans of that day and their intentions towards us that have not radically changed in this day? Europeans have not changed.

Today, when the Russians and United States meet, they're not talking about liberation; they're not talking about liberating anyone. At their summit conferences, they decide which of them will control what part of the world and how to stay out of each other's way so that the conflict between them won't weaken them to the point where people can escape from their control. They are discussing power: who will have it and who will dispense it. They do not envision the world free of the domination of the West, i.e., the United States, Russia and Europe.

The Vision of Self-Determination

If we are going to free the world from Western domination, we have to envision ourselves as having the ability to do so. If we envision ourselves as having the ability to do so, we have to have some understanding of the world when it was not under the domination of Europe. European domination has nothing to do with the European having a superior mind, of having ability that you do not have. It has to do with the fact that the European believed he could do it and gained enough confidence to do it. We can do the same if we make up our minds to do it.

Now, as a result of the Europeans' rise to power, a revolution began in the world, one we must now revolt against. To revolt against it, we must understand how it began. How then did we lose our Africanness? What will we have to do to regain it? How did we lose the concept of nationness and develop a concept of dependency? The most dangerous of all dependencies is to depend on your powerful oppressor to free you and share power with you, because powerful people never train powerless people to take their power away from them. So, we're dealing with a contradiction in terms.

It's a contradiction to go into schools and to expect education; there is only a form of indoctrination. There are certain basic curricula that we can use to educate ourselves. Therefore, for us, most of our education must happen in the home, in the community and the church. You think the church is a less spiritual institution when it is engaging in education? It is not; it is a more spiritual institution. There are many ways of praying and there are many ways of serving whatever deity you happen to choose. What I'm concerned about now is how we got into this trap so I can at least estimate how we're going to get out of it.

Losing The Concept of Nation

The major loss in the fifteenth and sixteenth centuries was the concept of nation, the attaching of Africans onto other nations: some to England, some to France, some to Portugal, and then some to the worst of the element to come out of Europe—the United States.

Europe was getting rid of its human waste matter. It sent some to Australia; it sent some to the Pacific. And here we have to look again at what happened to the Africans in the Pacific. What happened to the Africans in Tasmania? The entire island was destroyed. The British sent a lot of Irish prisoners, oppressed white people, to Tasmania, the islands near Australia, where every man, woman and child was destroyed. The British knocked one year to five years off an Irish prison-er's sentence, depending on how many Tasmanians he killed. And bringing two matching ears to the British authorities to show that you had killed a Tasmanian would mean one year to five years off of your sentence.

The Essential Selfishness of Survival

Here is something we do not understand today: *the nature of oppressed people preying on other oppressed people in order to resist oppression.* When we use the term "Third World," we better use it carefully. Because there are a whole lot of people in the Third World who, in order to ingratiate themselves to the oppressor, would gladly become an "honor-ary" oppressor where we are concerned. Some have already done so.

Yet, with our goodness (our built-in hope), our beautiful humanity, our belief in justice for all people, we fall into their traps. One of the traps we fall into is mostly made by Hispanics. They watch to see you fight for something, and the minute you win they come in and ask for half of it, when they were never even in the fight. And many times they get it, especially the Puerto Ricans. They weren't even near the fight. You give them half of your pie, and they want parity, which means half.

Because we have not learned to practice, figuratively speaking, the essential selfishness of survival, we should give no piece of the pie until every member of our family has a piece of the pie. If you fight for a pie, then you fight for it for your family, and I wish you well. But I fought for this for my own kith and kin, and they take priority in its distribu-tion.

When we began to lose these nation lessons we began to move deeper and deeper into a trap, into a trap of dependency. And yet into that same trap came the ingredients of liberation. We have not studied enough how the slaves in the Caribbean took advantage of the poor quality of the British craftsmanship. How many times, especially in places like Jamaica, did the British bring over furniture from England and this furniture, made from softwood, became dessert for termites who just ate it up? The local craftsmen used that hard Jamaican wood. They had good mahogany then; they don't have it now because they overcut it. They have to wait another twenty to forty years for it to grow again before they'll have enough mahogany for furniture distribution. But they had it then, a good forest, good mahogany.

So, they remade the British furniture using local wood, as against the wood brought over from England. These craftsmen, not only learned to make furniture, they learned to repair the sugar mills. They were great blacksmiths and subsequently worked their way out of servitude and communicated with the black American freemen who had also learned similar crafts in New England.

The Resurgence of Revolt

This is where the real revolt began; this is where the whole concept of "let us be a nation again, let us be a people again, let us build institutions again" began, in Jamaica. We need to draw some impetus on what we have already done in order to understand what we still must do. These brothers in Jamaica and in other islands came together and began to form organizations not based on who was from what island, but based on the fact that all of them (those in America and those on the islands) had the same problem. That problem was oppression. This is why the Barbadian Prince Hall came to the United States and built the first masonic order but did not call it that because it wasn't about socializing and drinking. It was about social uplift; it was about trying to free the slaves still not free, so he called it the African Lodge. Peter Ogden, from Antigua, would take a similar approach to the Odd Fellows.

If we're going to revolt today, we have to look back at a time when able African people pulled themselves out of dominance. Then we have to study how it was that these black rebels, on the eve of the Civil War, forced the issue. I'm not saying that the Civil War was fought over slavery; we all know better than that. We know that no white man has ever fought any wars over any black people; we don't even have to argue about that. But the emotional fervor around slavery had helped to solidify the whole issue and the whole concept, i.e., African people searching to be whole again and searching to be a nation again.

After the Civil War—and after the British emancipation, when they discovered it was a phony, when they discovered they hadn't been emancipated—the black people had no jobs, had no housing, and they still had to go back to the same plantations to live. Then another revolution and another revolutionary period began in the Caribbean Islands. That's when we discovered over here that the so-called Reconstruction had been betrayed by the Tilden-Hayes election (1876). We had to fight for freedom all over again, and the African-American at the latter half of the nineteenth century was far more committed than those of the twentieth century, far clearer on what he had to do and had no illusions about freedom. Because he knew that in spite of emancipation, he had no freedom and he had no nation. This initiated a form of Pan-Africanism, migration Pan-Africanism, that we need to study.

Blacks tried to migrate to Africa. Martin Delany with the great Jamaican Robert Campbell searched for a place for settlement. Their respective reports are still worth reading, especially Campbell's report, *Pilgrimage to My Motherland*. I'm saying that if we want to revolt—and we should be in constant revolt against our condition—there are examples in Europe and elsewhere that we could use, but there are better examples among ourselves.

We do not need to leave home to understand the concept of revolt or the concept of a social order, different from the economic system that we have lived under. These men, in Africa, in the Caribbean Islands and in the United States were very clear on this concept. Where did we get fuzzy? At what point did we give up the original approach to revolution and begin to try to integrate into the house of the oppressor?

The Mechanics of State Formation

Early in the twentieth century, African nations began to emerge. A special study should be made of Ghana, especially early twentieth century politics in Ghana and the revolt against colonialism. Casely Hayford fathered modern Ghanaian politics. He converted his fight for the return of the exiled kings into a fight for independence. This was in the early part of the century as the British began to exile the Ghanaian kings, Prempeh and Yaa Asantewa. They began to build a youth movement (essential to every revolution). When near his death in 1931, Hayford wanted to turn over the mantle of responsibility to another Ghanaian, he turned it over to a young man he had trained: Joseph P. Danquah. Hayford said, when he was fully aware that he was dying, "Send for J.P." Then, according to one report, he said to the young lawyer, "The mantle of responsibility now is yours. Lead this nation to independence."

Working under J.P. Danquah, was a young student, who then went by the name of Francis K. Nkrumah. He began to train Nkrumah to take the mantle of responsibility. They did not do as we do today— leave things to chance. They planned them. They came out of a society that we need to reproduce today in order to bring about our revolution. *Our children should be picked out and trained for leadership from birth. You can watch how that child handles a fork; watch that child's ability to share with the group; watch that child's ability to protect the group and to accept the training that will make that child improve. We should spot leaders early and begin to train them.* We should make a priesthood of this effort.

Let's examine how the Japanese were trained to create modern Japan. So many were directed to go into oceanography, so many go into the sciences, into chemistry, and so many to go into higher mathematics, into industrial mathematics, into scientific mathematics. And they roamed the earth to see how other people did things. They came home not so much to imitate them, but they ultimately did it their way. They didn't produce things just to show that they could do it. Until recently, the Japanese had no skyscrapers; they don't have too many now. They didn't think they needed them and didn't begin to build them until the island became so crowded they knew that was one way of saving space. Africa has a number of skyscrapers. If Africans build skyscrapers to show that they can build them, then all right, build them; but spatially they don't need them. They build them just to imitate other people.

What I'm trying to look into is how people maintain certain techniques that make them believe enough in themselves and become less dependent on other people in order to be whole again. And that the nature of oppression robs us of our wholeness, a lot of our confidence, and, if we're going to have a cultural revolution, this cultural revolution must first be based on regaining our confidence in our ability to handle everything in a nation.

This is why I've always disagreed with the current approach to South Africa; that we need to fight more than apartheid. Apartheid is a real issue. Apartheid has caused misery to millions of people. We need to fight it all the way; but, while fighting it we need to prepare to take over that nation. A nation needs railroads. Who's going to build them? But if we buy steel from someone else, we've got to pay a high price. Who's going to develop an internal steel industry? Who's going to master the mines? Who's going to market what comes out of the mines? All of this is part of the restoration of self-confidence, and all of this involves a return to things that we've already done at a previous time in history.

This is why, especially in New York City and New York State, we are literally kept from our history. If you expect the present day school system to give history to you, you are dreaming. This, we have to do ourselves. The Chinese didn't go out in the world and beg people to teach Chinese studies or let them teach Chinese studies. The Japanese didn't do that either. People don't beg other people to restore their history; they do it themselves. They learn something about freedom that we have to learn. Freedom is something we must take with our own hands and secure it with our own hands. If other people's hands secure it for us, other people's hands can take it away from us. Our main ally and our most dependable ally in the fight for freedom is ourselves.

When we look again at Ghana in the 20s, we will understand why that nation would come into being before other West African nations. Why didn't Nigeria become independent ahead of Ghana? Ghana had something Nigeria still doesn't have, a homogenous structure. Their people have had conflicts among themselves, but they never had conflicts that were so lasting they would fight unto death. Everything would stop short of destruction. There are no wars in Ghana that parallel the Yoruba Wars, Yoruba against Yoruba, or the Hausa and Fulani Wars, Moslem against Moslem.

Because the wars in Ghana were short lived, they did not build up a lot of bitterness, one against the other. In a political set-up they could operate one to the other. They did something that we have not noticed (and would do well to notice). Not only did they create politicians of substance, they created the greatest body of political literature in any African country, before or since.

African Political Literature

Look at [John] Mensa Sarbah's work, *Fanti Customary Laws*, a book about how the Fanti people use the laws to uplift the nation. *Fanti National Constitution*. In another book, entitled *Toward Nationhood in West Africa*, a Ghanaian, J.W. deGraft Johnson, wrote and laid out a bluprint for a nation. These books are not hiding from anyone. They can still be read; most of them have been reprinted.

Casely Hayford wrote the first nationalist novel, *Ethiopia Unbound*. Then another little classic work, worth re-reading now because it explains the difference between East Africa (where the whites took the land) and West Africa (where the whites could not take the land). It's called *The Truth About the West Afrikan Land Question*.

Danquah, Nkrumah's schoolmaster, looks at the religion, in *Akan Doctrine of God*. And then there is his little classic pamphlet, "Obligations in Akan Society," which he personally gave me one evening while scolding me at the same time. Study Akan society and study Yoruba Society, the two African cultures that have sustained themselves longer away from home than any other African cultures that I have seriously studied. It is the Yorubas and the Akans who have brought off most of the slave revolts.

What I'm saying is that if we are going to change anything today, we must understand the nature of change that we have already effected and how this nation, Ghana, created not only a political apparatus for political change and revolution but created a literature to explain it, and that literature is still in existence.

Some Nigerian literature—especially the early works of Nnamdi Azikiwe, on the settlement of Liberia—is still worth reading. His work *Renaissance Africa*, is still worth reading. In Southern Africa, there's another great body of literature by John Tingo Dubabayu and his son Don Dubabayu; Sol Plaatje's excellent work on the native problem in Southern Africa; Apollo Cagwa's work on the culture of Uganda, which literally stopped the wars between the Arabs, the Protestants and the Catholics and brought about a peace in Uganda at the turn of the century.

African Identity

What I've been alluding to is this: If there's going to be a world revolution among African people, we have to locate African people and connect with African people. No matter what we call ourselves and what island we came from or what part of Georgia or Alabama, we can still identify with these regions, but the overall identification should be with Africa and with African people wherever they are on the face of this earth.

We need to study how Pan-Africanism came into being in the closing years of the nineteenth century. We need to study H. Sylvester Williams again and examine this Pan-African League begun in Trinidad at a time when the East Indians and the Chinese were encroaching on the African population. What solidified Pan-Africanism on those islands? What were the early dreams of Marcus Garvey, and why did a Marcus Garvey emerge from Jamaica rather than some other place? Why did he have so little success in Jamaica and so much success outside of Jamaica? Why is it likely that if Marcus Garvey were walking down the streets of Jamaica right now, alive, some confused Jamaican might stone him to death? Why did he have more success in the United States? It's not because we have a better level of intelligence than others; not because we are more loyal or committed than others. Because the nature of our oppression in the United States has told us clearly: You are not wanted here; you were brought here to labor. Now that machines have made your labor obsolete we want to get rid of you.

In Jamaica, they still had the semblance of nation. They still thought they belonged to something: They belonged to an empire that was controlling the world. The sun never set on it. They assumed that they were a part of it; they still do.

It is not a matter of one master being more committed than the other. Different kinds of masters use a different nature of oppression. The British have an expression: *It is not only in the administration of justice it must be so, it must also appear to be so.* The British created a colony that gave the illusion of nation. But the crude white man in the United States wouldn't even give you the illusion. They even put signs on the water fountains: "Black," "Colored," "White." Look at the utter ridiculousness of it: water—Black, Colored, White! So we had no illusions about him. The white man left us with no illusions of nation.

When Marcus Garvey began preaching nation, if black Americans responded to it more than others, it was because we needed it more than others. Yet when we study the structure of the movement, the Garvey movement was strictly a Caribbean movement, administratively; but his followers and his supporters, financially, were almost solely black Americans. The ministers of the movement, the clerical workers, were basically Caribbeans. Yet this caused no conflict, then or now.

We're not going to have to guess about Garvey's movement now. One thing Professor Robert Hill's ten-volume history (six volumes are already in print) of Garvey's movement has already done is to locate the documents that end any argument. So now we can examine the documents, and we don't have to debate how the movement was structured and who ran the movement.

It is important that it existed because part of our future revolution, part of our move towards nationness, part of our move toward self-reliance in our community would have to be based on a serious study of this movement and to what extent it explained the concept of nationhood.

The Continuity of Self-Reliance

Once again we have to look at self-reliance as advocated by the educational program of Booker T. Washington, political reliance as advocated by W.E.B. DuBois and national and international reclamation and the redemption of Africa as advocated by Garvey. Then look at their other students, the spin-off from the movement, the heirs to movement, the inheritors of the entire concept: Elijah Muhammad and Malcolm X.

When you look at this in total context you will come to a Jesse Jackson and partly see what he's doing. Before going to South Carolina to lecture someone asked me what I thought of the future for Jesse Jackson's Rainbow Coalition. I replied, "It has a great future in awakening people to realize that the political mechanism is not serving them to the extent that it needs to. It can wake up both blacks and whites to come together politically who are not going to come together socially."

I saw this happen in San Antonio, Texas, during my Army days. These were poll tax periods and the black policy (numbers) man paid the poll tax for the blacks and the Mexican policy (numbers) man paid the poll tax for the Mexicans. Together they had 30,000 votes in their hands before the election started. They could decide who would or would not be mayor of that town. This went on for years until someone convinced the Mexicans they were white. This broke it up.

Now my point in alluding to Jesse Jackson is that he is awakening in this country a concept that if poor whites and poor blacks have the same oppressor, they can put their political strength together and perhaps both of them can overcome their oppressor. He's not asking us to marry, he's not asking us to live next door to each other. He's not even asking us to like each other. He's showing us political mechanism.

When my friend who called me from South Carolina asked me about the Rainbow, and I said, "I grew up in the South where I saw rainbows after almost every rain, but have you ever seriously looked at a rainbow? Where is the black color in the rainbow? All right, you see a streak of grey, you see a blue, sometimes a red ... and yet the symbol is good. But the blackness of the rainbow is missing. I'm talking about an actual rainbow now. I'm not talking about conversation. I'm talking about a rainbow. Because I've looked in the sky and seen enough of them to know ... that black is not there. Yet I believe that Jackson, as well as King, is a part of our revolution. Part of the revolution that will lock into our political revolution and our spiritual revolution. That if we think that we can advance and claim those things that belong to us in this world without a drastic change that we call a revolution then we are dreaming."

I do not mean that you have to kill people, that you have to shoot at anybody (although that's a part of it, but not all of it). A revolution means social change; it means a total change. In revolution you don't patch up old clothes, you find new clothes. Many times you don't patch up old ideas, you find completely new ideas. We are such an imaginative people that we have survived by innovation. We are people on this stage of the world without a script. Many times we have to make up the script, right in front of the audience. So, I have not been talking about anything that we cannot do, or have not been doing all along.

Summation

I'm suggesting that we take a serious look at ourselves. We must rehearse for nation building by controlling our community. By controlling the input into our education. By examining the curricula used in the school to train our children. If it's not good, we have to either make it good or have it eliminated by having political control over our community (and political control leads to other kinds of control) and by learning some form of self-reliance which can employ large numbers of African people in service with other African people.

If we could understand the nature of our mission in the world, if we could understand that Africa is a continent of 12 million square miles, we wouldn't have any unemployment for the next thousand years. With all those railroads to be built, all the steel foundries to be built, the refineries to be built, the oil to be discovered, do you think there's less oil in the body of Africa than there is in other places? Probably more.

We have to make the connection with African people outside of Africa, especially with the large number in India and the Pacific. We need a political apparatus that will stretch around the whole world, bringing African people together.

The ultimate answer is Pan-Africanism. What needs to feed into Pan-Africanism is a new kind of spirituality. In total liberation, religion cannot be left out, commerce cannot be left out, culture cannot be left out. How we think, how we walk, how we act; everything we do must be part of a totality. We have to learn how to relate to African people everywhere. Wherever they are on the face of the Earth.

Africans who have one kind of product on one side of Africa need to send it to another part of Africa, all that they can't use. So, if we're going to do this, what are we going to have to do? Stretch a railroad system across Africa. It has to be done by African engineers; African planners. If someone else does it for us, they're not really going to charge us for it, they're going to control us doing it.

Part of the success of the raid at Entebbe, in Uganda, is that the Israelis had built that airport and had trained that army. It was no achievement to get in there and knock out that airport and "rescue" those people who weren't that captive in the first place. But when someone else makes your roads, trains your army (they also control the mentality of our army). Our army is less valuable to us because we did not train it and we did not indoctrinate it. I'm talking about some things that have to be universal and have to relate to the totality of our history. We have to understand how history (as I've said before) is still a clock that people use to tell their time of day. It is a compass that people use to locate themselves on the map of human geography.

When we bring about the total revolution it will be the ultimate unity of all of our people through a Pan-African concept. When we start taking pride in what islands we came from without making a cult of it, when we can take pride in being a Georgian—I hope to speak of myself as a Georgian and an Alabamian, not so much with pride, but the fact that I survived both of them. I survived two hells and two frying pans. I got double strength to live through that.

In returning to the South, I saw the same thing: a spirit that I didn't find in other places. What I'm talking about is this: We can be different. Yet while being different, we're all the same people, with the same destiny.

Marcus Garvey said, "One God, One Aim, One Destiny." And that is true. But what we have to understand—no matter what we plan to be, no matter where we are in life—that it's whom we relate to that we begin to examine history: where we've been, where we are in order to understand where we still have to go. I maintain that the first step in liberation is self-discovery and that history in the final analysis is the same as the relationship of a child to his or her mother's breast.

The African revolution will have to be technical, spiritual and cultural. It will have to preserve and enhance the best of old Africa, which will be the main ingredient for the Africa still to come. At the heart of the solution will be the concept of Pan-Africanism—a dynamic program of Pan-Africanism—working for the unity of African people throughout the world.

COMMENTARY II

▼

THE PEOPLE OF THE African world entered the twentieth century searching for a definition of themselves and their relationship to the rest of the world. In the United States they were recovering from the betrayal of the Reconstruction following the Civil War and looking for new directions in the midst of the Booker T. Washington period (1895–1915). African-American laborers, instrumental in the founding of the Knights of Labor, were now being denied membership in the craft unions. Previously, they had championed the rights of immigrant craftsmen to enter these unions. These craftsmen did not return the compliment and joined other whites in barring Black Americans from these unions. It was less than fifty years after the Emancipation Proclamation. New schools and institutions were being built at a rapid pace. Black Americans were trying to regain what slavery and colonialism had taken away. Their African Consciousness Movement had started early in the nineteenth century, mainly by free New England blacks such as William Wells Brown, the first African-American novelist; Martin Delany, often called the father of Black Nationalism; and David Walker, whose famous *Appeal to the Colored People of the World* is still worth serious consideration. In the United States the finest nineteenth century leader had been Frederick Douglass. From the Caribbean Islands the best-known leader was Edward Wilmot Blyden, whose Inaugural Address at Liberia College in 1881, called for Africans throughout the world to reclaim their Africanness. In the twentieth century this effort was reflected in the first Pan-African Congress called in London by H. Sylvester Williams, a Trinidadian lawyer, in 1900.

The Caribbean activists in the African Consciousness Movement, who would later influence Marcus Garvey, were Abbot Thorne and Robert Love. Slave revolts in the Caribbean Islands had been massive and more successful than in the United States because of the maintenance of an African culture continuity that was a basic communications system among slaves.

Africa was at the end of more than 100 years of anticolonial wars. The politics of exile and assassination, literally invented by the British, was frustrating the Africans' attempt to reclaim their lost sovereignty. Embryonic political movements had developed in large areas of Africa, mainly in the West African states of Nigeria and Ghana and in South Africa.

One of the sadder aspects of the plight of African people is that there are too many times when they search for an ideology for their salvation without first looking among themselves. Too many times their ideology is borrowed from their former slave masters and is not applicable to their case. We often forget what Dr. ben-Jochannan has asked us to remember: that religion and ideology are the deification of a people's culture. Therefore the religion, culture, and ideology of our oppressor will not suit our case without serious alteration and rethinking. The ideas that were dreamed and created in Europe by Europeans were created to maintain European power and domination. These ideas are not applicable to our case. Therefore, in the search for an ideology we need to be original and creative, and we need to recognize the fact that powerful people never educate powerless people in how to take their power away from them. Therefore an ideology for our salvation will have to be created by us to suit our case, and we need not be apologetic about it.

A world upheaval in the fifteenth and sixteenth centuries created slavery in the colonial system that followed. It would take a similar world upheaval, initiated by African people, to destroy the aftermath of these two evil systems.

People who oppress other people generally create a rationale to justify this oppression. They deny their victims anything that is called culture and history because they know that a consciously historical people cannot easily be oppressed and by saying or inferring that the people you oppress are without history or culture, they are also saying that we are without humanity and not deserving of human consideration.

Pan-Africanism is a reoccurring theme among African people the world over. The search for unity is really the search for the restoration of their total human beingness. It is also a search for the restoration of the state under their rule. The enemies of Pan-Africanism and African nationalism know that the success of this movement will lead to a higher concept called an African World Union, and this concept will in turn make African people a factor in the political and commercial power of the world.

I think that a teacher lives through whatever results he gets from his students. I remember one of my great teachers, strangely, or I guess not too strangely, a black Puerto Rican with a German-sounding name, Arthur Schomburg. I remember when I went into his office in New York, having read his essay "The Negro Digs Up His Past" while doing chores in a high school in Columbus, Georgia. I wanted to know the whole history of African people. I wanted to know it within the hour. But he told me something that is still really viable. He said, "Son, go study the history of Europe, for when you know the history of your oppressor, you will know why you were misplaced in history." He then emphasized what we're calling African history and African-American history is nothing more than the missing pages of world history.

Once we begin to look at history from the backdrop of world history, I think that we are going to get some of our history straight. We are the most historic of people because we are the oldest of people. We are the father and the mother of mankind. And when we study our oppressor, we're going to get angry for what he got away with in telling us that the world waited in darkness for him to bring the light, because we're going to discover that for most of man's existence, not only did he not bring the light, but that he, in fact, had no light to bring.

I'm really talking not just about Pan-Africanism. I'm talking about the possibility of an African World Union. it's a favorite theme of mine because as I look at the geography of the world, I see African people all over that geography, including large numbers of African people in Asia and the Pacific Islands, whom the world seems to have forgotten. We are the most strategically located people on the face of the earth considering that we are in Asia, in the West Indies, in North and South America, and in Africa itself. I'm trying to convey the fact that we are not a minority people and that properly looked at, we are the third, if not the second, largest ethnic group on the face of the earth. And the most expensive piece of geography on the face of the earth is ours, and I mean all of it, including the north of Africa.

Now statistically, what I am talking about is this. Between South America, the Caribbean, other scattered islands, and the United States, you have in excess of 200 million people of African descent. And if you count the mixtures of people, what then? We made no laws governing racial classification, but according to some unwritten laws, the millions of people with at least one drop of African blood are considered all African. All of these laws were made against us, but we made none. In fact, we played no role in the development of this concept called race.

Now, if we look at the African population in Africa, we find it has been counted as 500 million for the last fifty years. How could the population of a people be so stagnated unless their men are sleeping away from home, and this you know is not true. So if we count Africans properly, you might have 400 to 500 million people. For example, in Nigeria the British counted the population at 36 million census after census. The Nigerians participated in the census to keep from paying taxes—if they know how many there are then they know how much taxes to charge—the Nigerian census takers came up with an excess of 50 million. But the last census in Nigeria came up with nearly 80 million people. Now I know that the brothers are fertile, but they can not reproduce themselves that fast.

What we are saying is that once Africans are properly counted, we're going to come up with a much larger number. And what we have to understand is that the population of the whole continent of Australia was entirely black before the British almost destroyed the entire population. New Guinea was entirely black, the Hebrides Islands, the Solomon Islands, were entirely black. All of these are black areas. Once we count the number of blacks in other parts of Asia, numbering into the millions, how can we be counted as a minority people? So when I say beyond Pan-Africanism, I'm trying to put together the picture of the possibility of an African World Union. And when I talk about alliances, I am talking about the major alliances that black people have to make, and that is with ourselves. Once we make an alliance with ourselves, then we can decide which other alliance we need.

I received a letter before coming here {in Atlanta University's Main Lecture Hall, ca. 1978, 1979} that disturbed me but told me a lot about the trend of development. It was from one of the outstanding black literary figures, who heads three organizations. He was taking me to task because he heard that in a speech in Atlanta I had said that black people should make no alliances with people other than black people. That's not what I said. I said that blackness or "Africanity" should be our first allegiance or our first allegiance should be to ourselves, and we had better begin to understand something about the essential selfishness of survival. What I was trying to get at was this debate over Marxism-Leninism that is tearing Black organizations apart. What they are doing in many respects is arguing someone else's case and neglecting the ideology and the needs of home.

Now most of us here are active in some aspect of Pan-Africanism and know how important an African World Union is at this juncture in history. When the Sixth Pan-African Conference took place in Dar Es Salaam, other problems that African people had not anticipated came to the surface. The delegates to this conference did not come to deal with the problems of different ideologies within the Pan-African camp, the terrible conflict between Left and Right and the conflict among the political Left itself. Further, they were not prepared to deal with the problem of language and its relationship to politics and culture. They did not expect that they would have to deal with the presence of Arabs or Arab-oriented blacks insisting on using Arabic as the official language of the conference. At one point in the conference the white translators of French literally went on strike and brought the conference to a temporary close. Had the delegates been sufficiently alert, they would have known there is a large number of professionally known and trained French-speaking Africans who can translate French into English and English into French.

Those who wanted to impose the Arab language on the conference merely wanted to impose the political will of the Arabs not only on the conference but on Africa itself in spite of the fact that the Arabs are ambivalent towards Pan-Africanism.

The crisis with the delegation coming from the United States was that the Africans could not recognize them as coming from an African state though they were the largest delegation. What the Africans did not understand then and now is that the African population in the United States is, in essence, an African nation away from home and the most politically active of all the Africans who live outside of

Africa.

Brazil, of course, with its more than 60 million Africans, is the largest African nation away from home; but, unfortunately, the Africans in Brazil are only mildly politically active. While there have been courses of study and great interest in Africa by Africans living outside of Africa, the Africans at home, within Africa, have not shown similar interest in their brothers and sisters who were forced out of Africa in that catastrophe called the slave trade. True Pan-Africanism will be when these various branches of the African family can meet with one main objective in mind: the total liberation of African people everywhere they live on the face of the earth.

Why have we had so little discussion on the Sixth Pan-African Conference, and why was it the least successful of all the Pan-African congresses? This was the first Pan-African congress that met on African soil. They met in a free African state with the sanction of the head of that state—President Julius Nyerere. The ingredients for success had been assembled. Too many different political groups pulling in different directions killed the possibility and literally reduced this congress to shambles. We need to study this congress so that this catastrophe can never happen again.

Now once we get at the bottom of the reason for the failure of this congress, we will find that this is part of the crisis in leadership and the crisis in communications between Africans and Africans. And what we need as much as we need a conference on Pan-Africanism is a Pan-African communication system that would get things across to our people.

We need to look at something that we have played around with, without properly examining it for a number of years and that is the nature of leadership and what kind of leadership people need at different times in history. Sometimes the leadership of one time in history is inadequate for another period in history.

What kind of leadership do we need right now? I think folks in Africa and in America, in looking at the Pan-African concept, had better start rethinking the kind of leader that we need. Maybe we need a soft man and a hard man, too. Maybe we need a composite of several kinds of personalities, but we need a person who can hold his {or her} program apparatus together and relate African people all over the world to each other. Maybe we need a man who is something of a saint or something of a tyrant. Maybe we need a man who is a mixture of personalities, kind of a cross between a tiger and a child. I'm fishing for answers just like you, but I know one thing for sure—we don't need most of those that we've got right now.

Leadership

There are some strange people appearing now in leadership positions. They are people with some personal problems over and above what I think we need to be solving at this time. I think that they need to be relegated to some place where these problems can be solved. What they have forgotten is that I met many of these present-day leaders thirty-five years ago under different circumstances. They weren't black then. But they are blacker than the night now. I met one of these black leaders thirty years ago, and he said at that time that no one shares his bread or sleeps in his bed but a white woman and her sister. He is now considered to be one of the outstanding black leaders. Now what happened to him in the journey from whiteness to blackness, when I have been black all of my life, every day all of my life? What transformation did he have to go through to get what I was born aware of? And how genuine is he now? He wasn't genuine thirty years ago when there was no commerce in blackness.

I think that we need to examine all of these ego-starved people now on the scene of leadership talking about Pan-Africanism with one breath and spreading dissension between people with the other. I think we need to come down a little harder, and we need to examine people a little more thoroughly. If they cannot take the examination, they don't deserve the job of leadership. In the years since our forced exile from Africa we have been in one crisis after another over leadership. We stand at the crossroads of history engaged in a sad debate over direction and definition in political leadership.

We are not beginning to feel the effects of being excluded from power for so long. If a people are out of power for a long period of time, they long desperately for power; and when they come close to power, they panic. Being out of power so long makes you hungry for power, and when you come close enough to touch it, it frightens the hell out of you. The presence of power eliminates all of your excuses. Figuratively speaking, if you are steering the car you can't blame whitey because you are in charge now. The one thing oppression does to a people is to kill in them the mind and the will to assume responsibility. When you get on the edge of power you experience a critical moment of self-discovery and that is the tragic separation from having lost power, and this is part of what our conflict is about. A people out of power long desperately for power and when they get close to it, they panic. Many times people want power, but they do not want responsibility. Too many times we have looked outside of ourselves for leadership and political development. This essentially is what is happening right now in this destructive argument over Marxism and Leninism.

African Socialism

Now before going any further, let me make myself clear. I do not believe that there is any solution for African peoples/problems outside of the world arena of socialism. But when I say socialism I mean something much different from those who are arguing over Marxism and Leninism. So hear me out on this. I approach socialism through my African nationalism. Socialism interests me to the extent that my people are served; to the extent that my people are not served—to hell with it!

Let's look at Pan Africanism. I am talking about commitment. I am talking about the option open to African and poor people in their fight for liberation. I am trying to look at some past mistakes that we have made and how we will have to avoid these mistakes in future. Today some of our new and much needed organizations are being torn apart in an argument over Marxism and Leninism. The brothers are repeating a mistake that we have been making down through the years. They are looking outside of the family for a solution to the family's problems. The ideals that went into the making of the concept of the term called socialism were already old in Africa not only before Karl Marx was born but also before Europe itself was born. So when we say that our problems would have to be solved as the world's problems must be solved, within the arena of socialism, we do not necessarily mean that we have to go to Europe to find the solution.

An African king, Akhenaton, preached that concept from the throne 1300 years before the birth of Christ. That was over 3000 years ago. This man, who thought so much about life that he would not crush a flower, gave to the world the concept of monotheism or the oneness of God, out of which would come Christianity. His greatest and most famous convert was a young prince in the royal family of Egypt named Moses, and we need not go too deeply into that here. I was at a conference some years ago on black and Jewish relationships, and the Jews are still trying to recover from the onslaught of the excellent black scholarship that they did not know existed.

We discussed Moses and tried to locate him and both the Africans and the Jews on the map of human geography, only to discover that the Jews were some of the children that came out of our house. We dealt with Moses, who was first and foremost an African. The main point is that we dealt with Moses first as an African and secondarily as a Jew, and *this* is a matter open to question.

Threshold

What we need to do is deal with the main currents of history and how so much history has been distorted and how many of our theoreticians' ideas from an early era in history have been credited as other people's ideas. I am talking about the best ideas of the socialist concept that came out of African society and survived throughout the years when Europe itself was in darkness. In the debate over Marxism and Leninism, some of our brothers are following people like hungry garbage collectors picking up their ideological leavings and neglecting the political food at home. I think what we need to do is look into our lives and see what we have to offer as solutions. The saddest thing about these brothers is that they are ignorant about our history in particular and world history in general.

Let's now look at some of the main currents of history that brought us to this time and place. *We are a people standing at the threshold of freedom arguing whether to cross that threshold with our right foot or left.* In this case the solution is simple. The step that gets you across the threshold is the correct step.

We need to examine our fear of freedom and our longing for freedom. We need to examine these societies we created that gave man so many of the ideas that still govern man and so much of the basics we have.

These other African societies were mainly communal. They were neither rich nor poor. These societies were collectively owned by all of the people. People could neither be bought nor sold because people belong to everybody. There were no orphanages because no one discarded their children. There were no old people's homes because no one discarded their mothers and fathers. There was no welfare as such because the entire state was a welfare state, welfare for all people. I maintain that these societies at their best had the purest form of socialism ever known to man and that we, in our search for socialism as a means to get away from capitalistic society that imprisoned and exploited us through the years, need to look back at these societies and the impact of change on them.

Christianity had its early development in Africa and in Western Asia and the most tragic thing that happened to Christianity occurred when the Romans, who had been burning people alive for being Christians, became Christians. When Christianity left Africa and came to Europe it was not Christianity any more but Christendom.

Now there is a difference between Christianity and Christendom. Christianity is a religion, Christendom is a political instrument. All Christianity has ever been to white people is a political instrument. It has been the political apparatus of their world-wide expansion and the rationale for every crime that they ever committed against anybody at any time, including two World Wars. Now, this religion is a stranger among them because they lack the temperament and the capacity to practice it. The European could neither practice Christianity nor democracy, not even for twenty-four hours, because if he practiced one of the commandments, "Thou shalt not steal," he would have to return all stolen property starting with us. How could he possibly have built capitalism, with three hundred years' free labor, unless the missionaries justified his action? Christianity and democracy are two things he could not afford to practice, not even for twenty-four hours, because he would have to dismantle his entire society.

When we look at the impact of Christianity on African society, the impact was not bad; in fact, it was rather good, so long as the Africans were in charge of the society. It became bad when the European interpretation of Christianity, which is anti-Christian, began to be accepted by the Africans. The Africans also played a major role in the creation of Islam, and the Islamic impact on Africa wasn't bad, at first. Yet, it went through many manifestations that the brothers don't want to deal with because we have a romance around Islam that we need to examine.

When Islam rose and spread into the Western Sudan, the Africans seized Islam and under its inspiration became the original conquerors of Spain in the year 711 A.D., and the whole Mediterranean area as well. They held it for 800 years. But internal disputes began to develop between Moslems and Moslems and sometimes between the Africans and the Arabs, and these internal disputes weakened Africa ultimately to the point that they did not have the reserve strength to take on Europe when Europe rose and began its enterprise in the slave trade.

We need to examine all of our relationships with people, all of our encounters in the years outside Africa, particularly in the area called the New World. We need to understand that this concept of socialism has been with us in some form in these communal societies in the years away from Africa. In the so-called New World, Africans rebelled in Jamaica, the Maroon Revolt; in Brazil, any number of revolts, in particular the revolt at Palmares; in the Guyanas, the famous Berbice Revolt; and in Haiti, the revolt led by Toussaint L'Ouverture, Christophe, and Dessalines.

Black Theoreticians

These short-lived estates established by the previously mentioned rebellions, were principally African socialist states. Later, another mistake occurred when a group of French-oriented African Haitian aristocrats took over; and they did not make an African state in Haiti. They do not have an African state now. They made a pseudo-European state that did not fit the purpose then and does not fit the purpose now. My point is that when Africans created independent states outside of Africa, these states, until they were destroyed were basically socialist states.

There are a number of black nationalists now and others who are in a quandary about the nature of political commitments. They argue Marx and Lenin because this is available, and I am not against Marx or Lenin. Karl Marx had some interesting things to say about the Europe of his day. But he wasn't talking about us at all. Very often we hear people say liberty and justice for all, and we run to where the all is being given out only to discover that nobody was talking about us.

Karl Marx wasn't talking about us. He might have incidentally said something that was relevant to us, but he was talking about the feudal Europe of that day, and when he spoke of African and Asian societies, he said that they were primitive communes, which proves that he did not understand those societies. Those societies were so complicated that they would challenge your imagination trying to understand them, and nobody called primitive could put together societies of this nature.

So all right, Karl Marx, speaking to the Europe of his day, had some relevant things to say about the Europe of his day and some but not all these things were relevant to the whole world. Now, the Africans had no such feudalism, and therefore their society functioned differently. A new kind of message was needed for those societies. What the brothers need to do is to address themselves, after reading them, to the African socialist thinkers and theoreticians who existed concurrent with Karl Marx and who addressed their message directly to us. In this country (the United States), Martin Delany; in the British (now the American) Virgin Islands and the West Indies, Edward Blyden; in Ghana, John Masa Sarbah, mentor of the Ghanaian political activist, Casely Hayford, the father of international West African nationalism. Let's discuss these men, because they are so neglected in our lives and we do not know that at the same time Karl Marx was preaching his theory of socialism we had people preaching similar theories to us because we have neglected the literature.

Edward Blyden left the West Indies in the 1850s, went to Africa, rose high in the Liberian government of that day, wrote on African communal societies in his book on African customs, which is the greatest defense of taking indigenous African ways of life and updating them in order to compliment the Africa of the day. His great classic work, *Islam, Christianity and the Negro Race*, should be compulsory reading for all Black Christians and Muslims, because he had resolved before the nineteenth century so many of the things in dispute now. Placing a lot of his emphasis on West Africa, Blyden wrote a small classic work on the land question in Africa, and he had much more to say abut it than Karl Marx had to say about the land question in Europe. He addressed himself to the concept of land tenure. What we need to do is look at home and look abroad concurrently. We need to get out of our minority psychosis and realize that we are international people.

On Alliances

I'm not against alliances and allegiances so long as we understand that Africanity or blackness is our first allegiance, because every time we forget this we are in serious trouble. I'm not against alliances, but I am against all alliances in which I do not control the apparatus of the alliance. I could go back a long way and show you the kind of mistakes we've made in making alliances with other people. The early alliances between blacks and whites against slavery were mostly paternalistic, though we did not have much of a choice at the time. There were alliances between black and white farmers in the United States after the Civil War, but once these whites became sold on their whiteness, they turned on the black and joined the Ku Klux Klan.

The blacks laid the foundation for the Knights of Labor and then invited the immigrant craftsmen (from Europe) into it. One of the best functioning chapters of it was in Chicago. These immigrant craftsmen became more American than other Americans and drove the blacks out of the Knights of Labor and founded the American Federation of Labor. The black craftsmen who invited them in were now out.

We are veterans at making alliances with people who betray us, and the only reason that they betray us is that we do not control the apparatus of the alliances nor do we punish people who betray us. We should enter into no other alliances where we do not control the apparatus of these alliances. Make whatever alliances that are to our benefit, but understand that the first alliance we must make is to ourselves.

Let me give you a case in point that is very telling. Fifteen years ago about thirty-two African nations broke diplomatic relations with Israel, partly over the Arab-Israeli dispute. They broke with Israel over the Arab-Israeli conflict relative to Zionism. There was no indication that the Arabs rewarded the Africans for favoring them. The Arab nations told the African nations that they would have to pay the same price for oil as the other nations. Now, what the African nations should have done before they broke with Israel was to strike a bargain. How much would it be worth to you for me to make a break? Then, if it's worth nothing to you, I won't break. They forgot to bargain before they moved, and they found the Arabs, in spite of the support that they had gotten from the Africans, playing the same white game. Just like all of the rest, the Arab hopes to dominate. Once we begin to bargain, we will deal with situations like this much better.

Let me make it clear, however, that I do not think that the conflict between the Africans and the Arabs, which as it exists is not much of a conflict, can be thrown into the arena of the Arab-Israeli conflict. One thing that we have to learn strategically is to choose the time and the arena of the conflicts that we have to deal with and not let our conflicts be used by others.

In conclusion, I think that the young African-American woman poet Carolyn Clark Fowler Gerrard in her poem on Pan-Africanism has encapsulated what I have been trying to say. She said, "Pan-Africanism is an inner need to know ourselves. We need to keep looking at each other until we annihilate our own suspicious moves and recognize the same enemy looking back at all of us, over all the seas and all the centuries."

THE NINETEENTH CENTURY ORIGINS OF THE AFRICAN AND AFRICAN-AMERICAN FREEDOM STRUGGLE

▼

I N THE OPENING CHAPTER of his book *Africa, The Roots of Revolt*, Jack Woddis writes:

> The history of Africa's relations with the West has been a history of robbery—robbery of African manpower, its mineral and agricultural resources, and its land. Even though direct slavery no longer exists, labor, resources and land remain the three dynamic issues over which the struggle for the future of Africa is being fought out. The form of this struggle, it is true, is a political fight for national independence; but the abolition of foreign control of labor, resources and land is the substance for which this independence is being sought.

In spite of what may seem to be an exaggeration, this statement is basically true, and it has a direct relationship to the plight of the people of African descent in the United States. Africans and African-Americans are victims of the same historical experience. One was enslaved; the other was colonized.

The respective freedom movements of Africans and the African-American are as old as their initial contact with the Europeans who came into Africa as guests and decided to stay as conquerors. There was

41

nothing in the Africans' previous experience that had equipped them to deal with the Europeans who started to prey on Africa in the fifteenth and sixteenth centuries. The Europeans had awakened from their medieval lethargy, and with embryonic technology, mainly the gun, they started their era of exploration and exploitation. They were searching for a new supply of energy, more land and raw materials and now markets for their goods. They found a new supply of energy in the slave trade and more land in the discovery of what they have called the New World.

The European slave trade, initiated by the Portuguese, was soon challenged by other hungry European nations. Robert I. Rotberg gives the following description of how the slave trade started in his book, *A Political History of Tropical Africa*.

> From the early years of the seventeenth century, the merchants and navies of other European nations successfully challenged the supremacy of Portugal along the costs of the Atlantic and Indian oceans. The Dutch, the English, the Scots, the French, the Danes, the Swedes, and the Prussians all assumed a part of the lucrative commerce that Portugal has hitherto largely monopolized. The great national companies superseded the "interlopers" or buccaneers who had raided Portuguese and Spanish shipping for private gain during the sixteenth century and began, despite the antagonism of Spain, to trade directly with the New World. The newer naval powers were thus able to halt a long-term drain on the finances of the trade and to reverse an unfavorable balance of payments position that, at the expense of France, England, and the cities of northern Europe, at first had benefitted Portugal and Spain and, during the seventeenth century, the United Provinces of the Netherlands. Thereafter, England and France both tried to turn their American and African colonies into exclusive, protected markets and sources of raw materials. By so doing, they, like the earlier colonial powers, became committed economically to a system of tropical production that relied upon supplies of slave labor.
>
> The Spaniards had been the first to take Africans to the New World. After learning that the indigenous inhabitants and their own settlers would not or could not successfully work the

mines or the plantations of tropical America, they turned increasingly to Africa for assistance. The labor of African slaves thereafter enabled Spanish and, eventually, Portuguese, Dutch, English, and French settlers to exploit the virgin lands and mineral riches of the Americas and to grow sugar, tobacco, coffee, indigo, cotton, and a host of other crops profitably. Thus, Europe's exploitation of America presupposed an abundance of unskilled African laborers that naturally gave to the slave trade the status and the style of big business. During the seventeenth and eighteenth centuries, the nations of Europe competed among themselves for the black cargoes of Africa; they built forts or otherwise established themselves on the shores of Africa; they befriended indigenous middlemen or chiefs and encouraged them to enslave their fellows for shipment overseas.

The hunger for slave labor became an addiction to the Europeans. Now the Africans were trapped into the cruelest bind in history. Many African nations had to either capture and sell slaves to the Europeans or become slaves themselves.

The British came late and furious into the slave trade, led by Captain John Hawkins and his "good" ship *Jesus*. John M. Weatherwax, in a pamphlet on this subject, refers to John Hawkins as "The Man Who Stole A Continent." The essence of his description of Captain Hawkins and the collective European slave trade is as follows:

> There was a man who stole a continent.
>
> Being cruel as well as greedy, and possessing power, he enslaved twenty million of its people, sending them over the ocean—ten million to the Eastern Hemisphere and ten million to the Western Hemisphere.
>
> In the process of capturing the twenty million people whom he sold, eighty million other people died—some during slave raids (for when a village was raided, often the very young and very old and the sick were killed), some from exposure, disease and grief during shipment abroad, and some by suicide at the water's edge or in transit.
>
> The sale of twenty million human beings as slaves gave the man hundreds of millions of treasure. But this was the only the

start of his enrichment.

He and his children and grandchildren and those to whom they sold slaves received much, much more (many billions more) through the unpaid labor of whole generations of slaves. But this, too, was not at all the end of their enrichment.

And so, from these three sources—(1) the sale of slaves, (2) the unpaid labor of generations of slaves, and (3) the practice of paying (on the average) a half-wage to descendants of slaves—there was, over the years, a tremendous, almost un-countable, accumulation of wealth.

The quantity of this stupendous treasure is now so immense that banks in every city of the land, and underground vaults for the storage of gold, are required to house and guard it.

Although this treasure—every penny of it—has been squeezed from the very hearts of blacks, absolute control and disposition of it is in the hands of whites.

The accumulation of this fabulous wealth made it possible for The Man Who Stole a Continent and his children and grandchildren to build railroads and bridges and tunnels, mines and oil wells and lumber mills, power plants and office buildings and factories, farm machinery and grain slices and canneries which made the exploitation of other continents and other peoples easier.

Besides, all of the favored managers of these enterprises, and especially the owners thereof, were able to have many homes, even palaces, many servants, and the luxury of travel at the dictate of a whim.

The finest hotels, the most able doctors, the best office suites, were at their command.

By the end of the eighteenth century the wealth obtained from African slave labor made the European Industrial Revolution possible and also created the basis for modern capitalism.

In the United States, South America, and in the West Indies the contribution of slave labor to the development of the so-called New World differed only by degree. It should be stated here that the people of African descent contributed to the making of the Americas in many ways other than as slaves.

Africans participated along with Europeans in the discovery and exploration of the New World not only as slaves, but also as free men, retainers, and servants. Nuflo de Olano, who accompanied Balboa in 1513, was one of thirty Africans in the expedition. Varying numbers of Africans participated in the expeditions of Cartes, Velas, Coronado, De Soto, and Pizarro. Ayllon had Africans in his troops in 1526 when he marched from the Florida peninsula northward to establish San Miguel in what is now Virginia. The most famous person of African descent of this era was Estevanico, or little Stephen, who, in 1539, blazed the way for the Spaniards into what is now New Mexico. Africans arrived in the area that later became Jamestown, Virginia, as explorers, nearly a hundred years before they reappeared as slaves in 1619.

By the end of the seventeenth century this picture had changed completely. The Europeans saw in African manpower the means to secure free labor for the building of the Americas. The Africans, upon entering into the slave system of the Americas, became exposed to the most diabolical and consistent application of mental and physical torture the world has ever known. As the Africans reflected on their miserable state, and the strange and brutal hell surrounding them, they became creatures of conflicting emotions caught in the throes of nostalgia. Very often the Africans would recklessly gamble their lives away in suicidal attempts to destroy the entire slave system. These attempts only had limited success—but enough to drive fear into the hearts of the slave-owning hierarchy. The prime targets of the Africans during these attempts were the slave masters and their families.

As a consequence of these spasmodic attacks, the slave owners soon realized that they were losing face and money, and sometimes their lives. They decided that a full course of action spiritual and physical, as well as psychological, must be implemented if the Africans were to be transformed from proud rebellious men to docile servants. The plans of the slave owners entailed some of the most extreme forms of torture. Despite the atrocities inflicted on the Africans as a means of breaking their spirit, the slave masters soon realized that this alone would be useless as long as the Africans retained their proud spirit. The Christian Church came up with a design to bring about complete subversion of the Africans to the desired slave code of conduct demanded by the feudal society of the Americas.

Reverend Kyle Haselden, editor of the magazine "Christian Century," makes the following comment (*New York Times*, August 2, 1964) on the role of church in the planting of racism in the United States:

The religious community in American society produced and sustained—sometimes on Biblical grounds—the anti-Negro bias which has permeated the American mind from the beginning of the nation until the present day. Out of the nation's religious community come Biblically and doctrinally supported theories of racial inferiority, and from this same source came immoral ethical codes which justified the exploitation of the Negro and demanded that the white man hold himself in sanctifying aloofness from the Negro.

Moreover, the patterns of segregation which divide the common life of the country racially had their beginning in the church before they found their perfection in the secular society. It was not the secular world which infused the church with its contemptuous views of the Negro and imposed a segregated life on the Christian community. These offenses appeared first in the religious community, even if we view the religious community in its narrowest definition.

The white man distorted the Bible into a defense for slavery and taught the Negro the passive virtues of Christianity, partly in the hope of making him tractable and content with his servile life. The white Christian, in developing American culture, confused Christianity with morality, morality with gentility, and gentility with aloofness from the Negro. As early as 1630, a bare ten years after the arrival of the first Negro slaves, white Christians condemned the crossing of the racial line as a "abuse to the dishonor of God and shame of Christians."

In 1663, a group of slaves joined white indentured servants to plan a rebellion. Some slaves took the Christian version of the Bible literally and believed that God meant all men to be free. Such a slave was Gabriel Prosser of Virginia who felt that he was divinely inspired to lead his people out of bondage. Over 40,000 slaves were involved in his revolt of 1800 before it was betrayed.

All that I have said has been leading to this single point: While different manifestations of resistance to slavery and colonialism existed throughout the seventeenth and eighteenth centuries, the best organized resistance came in the nineteenth century. The nineteenth century freedom movements in Africa, in the West Indies, and in the United States made the present-day twentieth century movement possible. In fact, the whole of the nineteenth century for us can justifiably be called the "century of resistance." Concurrent with the slave revolts in the United States there were anticolonial revolts in Africa. The new Western capitalist class was demanding more profits from the slave system while the British were going through the motions of abolishing it. The British were actually changing from one form of slavery to another. In the United States there was no such pretense.

In his essay, "A Brief History of the Negro in the United States," John Hope Franklin gives us this picture of that period:

> By the beginning of the nineteenth century there were unmistakable signs of profound economic and social change taking place in the United States. The commercial activities of the new nation were expanding; and there were those who already were beginning to think in terms of promoting industrial development similar to that which was occurring in England and on the Continent. Beyond the areas of settlement, rich new land was beckoning settlers who could plant staple crops and enjoy the freedom offered on the frontier. In 1803 the United States purchased the vast Louisiana Territory, and although it would be many years before the entire area would be settled, Americans and European immigrants were rapidly moving beyond the mountains. The greater portion of the people who moved from the Atlantic seaboard were committed to the institution of slavery, and if they had any slaves they took them along. Not even the War of 1812, in which several thousand Negroes fought, halted the march of Americans and slavery into the new West.

There were two distinct freedom movements among African-Americans during the first part of the nineteenth century. One represented by continuous slave revolts and the other by "free" black men and women who were engaged in a concerted effort to free their enslaved brothers and sisters. The movement, led by free black petitioners for freedom, was started during the latter part of the eighteenth century by men like John B. Russwurm and Prince Hall.

When Prince Hall arrived in Boston, that city was the center of the American slave trade. Most of the major leaders of the revolutionary movement of that day were, in fact, slaveholders or investors in slave-supported businesses. Hall, like many other Americans, wondered: What did these men mean by freedom?

The condition of the free black men, as Prince Hall found them, was not an enviable one. They were free in name only. Discriminatory laws severely circumscribed their freedom of movement.

By 1765 Prince Hall saw little change in the condition of blacks, and though a freeman, at least in theory, he saw his people debased as though they were slaves still in bondage.

In 1788 Prince Hall petitioned the Massachusetts Legislature, protesting the kidnapping of free Africans. This was a time when American patriots were engaged in a constitutional struggle for freedom. They had proclaimed the inherent rights of all mankind to life, liberty, and the pursuit of happiness. Hall dared to remind them that black men in the United States were human beings and as such were entitled to freedom and respect and respect for their human personality.

Frederick Douglass was the noblest of all American black men of the nineteenth century and one of the noblest of all Americans. This great abolitionist's civil rights views are as valid today as they were a century ago. Samuel E. Cornish and John B. Russwurm started a newspaper in order to tell the black man's story from his point of view. John B. Russwurm, talented editor and politician, is generally credited with being the first African graduate of an American college (Bowdoin in 1826). Among the white men who helped to create the first freedom movement, Wendell Phillips and William Lloyd Garrison are outstanding. Henry Highland Garnet, a fiery Presbyterian minister, was a leader of the militant abolitionist wing. Sojourner Truth, the first black woman to become an antislavery lecturer, was also a strong leader in the feminist movements of the nineteenth century. Harriet Tubman was a pioneer rebel and slave activist who later served as a nurse, scout and spy in the Civil War. John Brown, called "God's angry man," was the first white martyr to die for African freedom.

The African slaves never accepted their condition passively. In his book, *American Negro Slave Revolts*, Dr. Herbert Aptheker records 250 revolts and conspiracies, and in placing them in their historic and social context, he very astutely throws new light on the operation of the slave system itself.

In 1857, the famous Dred Scott Decision theoretically opened all territories to slavery. But before any considerable number of slaves could be taken to them the Civil War began and Congress, in 1862, prohibited slavery in the territories.

After four years of conflict, Northern victory in the Civil War resulted in the emancipation of the slaves. The slaves had played an important part in the achievement of their freedom. Some 186,000 black troops took part in 198 battles and skirmishes and suffered 68,000 casualties. The total number of Africans, including servants, laborers, and spies, amounted to more than 300,000. President Lincoln had acknowledged that the war could not have been won without the help of black troops.

In the opening chapter of his book, *Black Reconstruction*, Dr. W.E.B. DuBois states: "Easily the most dramatic episode in American history was the sudden move to free four million black slaves in an effort to stop a great Civil War and forty years of bitter controversy, and to appease the moral sense of civilization."

The appeasement, if it was an appeasement at all, was short-lived. For eleven years following the end of the Civil War African-Americans participated in the political life of the nation on both state and national levels. For the first time in the nation's existence it seemed as if its democratic promise was going to be kept. By 1875, the tide was turning against the African in the South and in the rest of the country. Some Southern whites actually attempted to reestablish slavery. The Republican party had bargained away the political rights of the African people in order to pacify the brooding white south. Some black politicians held on for a few more years but their heyday in American politics was over.

The period African-American history from 1877 to 1901 is called the nadir—the lowest point—the time of the great depression. This is the period when Africans lost the right to participate in the government of this country. In this period lynching became the order of the day. Most of the Jim Crow laws that still shame this nation in the eyes of the world came into being during this period.

Until near the end of the nineteenth century the African Freedom Struggle was a military one. This aspect of African history has been shamefully neglected. I do not believe the neglect is an accident. Africa's oppressors and Western historians are not ready to concede the fact that Africa has a frightening heritage. The Africans did fight back and they fought exceptionally well. This fight extended throughout the whole of the nineteenth century. This fight was led in most cases, by African kings. The European referred to them as chiefs in order to avoid equating them with European kings. They were kings in the truest sense of the word. Most of them could trace their lineage back to more than a thousand years. These revolutionary nationalist African kings are mostly unknown because the white interpreters of Africa still want the world to think that the African waited in darkness for other people to bring the light.

In West Africa the Ashanti Wars started early in the nineteenth century when the British tried to occupy the hinterland of the Gold Coast, now Ghana. There were eleven major wars in this conflict. The Ashanti won all of them, except the last one. In these wars Ashanti Generals—and we should call them Generals, because they were more than equal to the British generals who failed to conquer them—stopped the inland encroachment of the British and commanded respect for the authority of their Kings.

In 1844, the Fanti Kings of Ghana signed a bond of agreement with the English. This bond brought a short period of peace to the coastal areas of the country. In the eighteen sixties, King Ghartey, the West African reformer, advocated democratic ideas in government at a time when the democratic institutions of Europe were showing signs of deterioration. King Ghartey ruled over the small coastal Kingdom of Winnebab in pre-independent Ghana. He was the driving spirit behind the founding of the Fanti Confederation, one of the most important events in the history of West Africa.

There were two freedom struggles in pre-independent Ghana. One was led by the Ashanti in the hinterland and the other was led by the Fanti who lived along the coast. The Ashanti were warriors. The Fantis were petitioners and Constitution makers. The Fanti Constitution, drawn up in conference between 1865 and 1871, is one of the most important documents produced in Africa in the nineteenth century. In addition to being the constitution of the Fanti Confederation it was a petition to the British for the independence of the Gold Coast.

In 1896 the British exiled the Ashanti King Prempeh and still was not able to completely take over the hinterland of the Gold Coast. Fanti nationalists, led by Caseley Hayford, started the agitation for the return of King Prempeh and soon converted this agitation into a movement for the independence of the country.

The stubborn British still did not give up their desire to establish their authority in the interior of the country and avenged the many defeats that they had suffered at the hands of the Ashantis.

In 1900 the British returned to Kumasi, capital of Ashanti, and demanded the right to sit on the Golden Stool. Sir Frederick Hodgson, who made the demand on behalf of the British, displayed his complete ignorance of Ashanti folklore, history, and culture. The Ashanti people cherished the Golden Stool as their most sacred possession. To them it is the Ark of the Covenant. Ashanti kings are not permitted to sit on it. The demand for the Stool was an insult to the pride of the Ashanti people and it started the last Ashanti War. This was is known as "The Yaa Asantewa War" since Yaa Asantewa, the reigning Queen Mother of Ashanti, was the inspiring spirit and one of the leaders of this effort to save the Ashanti kingdom from British rule. After nearly a year of heroic struggle Queen Yaa Asantewa was captured along with her chief insurgent leaders. At last the British gained control over the hinterland of the Gold Coast. To accomplish this they had to fight the Ashanti for nearly a hundred years.

In other parts of West Africa resistance to European rule was still strong and persistent. While the drama of Ashanti and other tribal nations was unfolding in the Gold Coast, an Ibo slave rose above his humble origin in Nigeria and vied for commercial power in the market places of that nation. In the years before the British forced him into exile in 1885, he was twice a King and was justifiably called the "Merchant Prince of West Africa." His name was Ja Ja. The story of Ja Ja is woven through all the competently written histories of Nigeria. His strong opposition to British rule in the eighteen eighties makes him the father of eastern Nigerian nationalism.

In the French colonies the two main leaders of revolts were Behanzin Hossu Bowelle, of Dahomey, and Samory Toure, of Guinea. Behanzin was one of the most colorful and the last of the great kings of Dahomey. He was one of the most powerful of West Africans during the closing years of the nineteenth century. After many years of opposition to French rule in his country he was defeated by a French mulatto, General Alfred Dodds. He was sent into exile and died in 1906.

Samory Toure, grandfather of Sekou Toure, President of Guinea, was the last of the great Mandingo (Manding) warriors. Samory is the best known personality to emerge from the Mandingoes in the years following the decline of their power and Empire in the Western Sudan. Samory defied the power of France for eighteen years and was often referred to by the French who opposed him as the "Black Napoleon of the Sudan." He was defeated and captured in 1898 and died on a small island in the Congo River in 1900.

In the Sudan and in East Africa two men, called Dervish Warriors, Mohammed Ahmed, known as the Mahdi, and Mohammed Ben Abdullah Hassen, known as the Mad Mullah of Somaliland, were thorns in the side of the British Empire. Mohammed Ahmed freed the Sudan of British rule before his death in 1885. The country stayed free for eleven years before it was reconquered. Mohammed Ben Abdullah Hassen started his campaigns against the British in Somaliland in 1899 and was not defeated until 1921.

Southern Africa has furnished a more splendid array of warrior Kings than any other part of Africa. Shaka, the Zulu king and war lord, is the most famous, the most maligned and the most misinterpreted of all South African Kings. By any fair measurement he was one of the greatest natural warriors of all times. He fought to consolidate South Africa and to save it from European rule. When he died in 1828 he was winning that fight.

Shaka's fight was continued with varying degrees of success and failure under the leadership of Kings like Moshesh of the Basutos, Khama of the Bamangwato, Dingan, Shaka's half-brother and successor, Cetewayo, nephew and disciple of Shaka, Lobengula, whose father, Maselikatze, built the second Zulu Empire and Bambata, who led the last Zulu uprising in 1906.

What I have been trying to say is this: For a period of more than a hundred years African Warrior nationalists, mostly kings who had never worn a store-bought shoe or heard of military school, out maneuvered and out generaled some of the finest military minds of

Europe. They planted the seeds of African independence for another generation to harvest.

Near the end of the nineteenth century some of the personalities in the African and the African-American people had produced an intellectual class that was in revolt against the second-class citizenship that had been fastened upon all their people. This revolt, led by the great scholar W.E.B. DuBois, did not stop the solidification of disfranchisement and segregation in the South. Southern politicians and Northern philanthropists had already anointed Booker T. Washington of Tuskegee Institute, and declared that he was the leader of the Black American people. The people themselves were not consulted in this matter.

The African-American journalist, Loren Miller, in a speech, "The Call for Leadership," delivered at Stanford University in California, 1962, makes the following appraisal of Dr. DuBois for this period:

> When W.E.B. DuBois won the battle for the minds of Negroes in his historic conflict with Booker T. Washington, his victory signalized the triumph of his concept of the talented tenth as the leaders of, and the spokesmen for American Negroes. He believed that members of this Talented Tenth—educators, ministers, lawyers, editors, doctors and dentists, political leaders—would, in the very process of securing an education to fit them for their professions, furnish pragmatic proof of the invalidity of the then current doctrine of racial inferiority. He was confident that this educated and select minority would lead the masses in a sustained and purposeful assault on the restrictions that doomed the Negro to poverty and degradation; it was an essential aspect of the DuBois credo that the talented tenth would accept its role as servants of the other 90 percent, just as he believed he had done.... DuBois and his contemporaries fashioned the NAACP as the chosen instrument of the elite to whom he believed the masses should look for guidance and salvation.

The concept of the Talented Tenth failed because the black elite did not assume the responsibility expected of them. They were too busy imitating the white middle class and retreating from their own people.

W.E.B. DuBois, without their assistance, embarked upon a more radical course of action. During the early part of this century he became the intellectual father of his people. After the death of Booker T. Washington in 1915, his leadership was unchallenged until the emergence of Marcus Garvey in the early twenties. Dr. W.E.B. DuBois, more than any other person, sowed the seeds of what is now being called the "Black Revolution."

In summation, both the African and the African-American freedom struggles have their roots in the nineteenth century. In our present struggle we would do well to look back at this period in order to look forward more clearly. Our present freedom struggle goes far beyond the liberation of ourselves. Concurrent with this struggle we must join other people and make our contribution toward creating the new age of man.

EDUCATION FOR A NEW REALITY IN THE AFRICAN WORLD

▼

THE CRISIS IN AFRICAN EDUCATION is really a crisis in African self-confidence. Most of us who have thought seriously about this matter know that our former slave masters cannot afford to educate us. Powerful people never educate the victims of their power in how to take their power away from them. This simple fact eludes most of us, especially those African-Americans who call themselves scholars and leaders.

The subject for this paper, "Education for a New Reality in the African World," is old and new. It is both topical and historical. What we are dealing with here is the power and politics of history.

In his essay, "The Basis of African Culture," the Caribbean writer, Timothy Callender, has said: "What we do for ourselves depends on what we know about ourselves and what we accept about ourselves."

We have not made the best use of the power and politics of history because we have, in all too many cases, accepted the European definition of who we are and our place in history. We follow after people who do not know where they are going. In our search for an ideology, we need to search first among ourselves. The ideology of our former slave masters cannot save us. We will not be truly liberated until we are the main instruments of our liberation. The liberation that I am mainly concerned with here is the liberation of our minds from being dependent on other peoples to do our thinking.

Africa is our center of gravity, our cultural and spiritual mother and father, our beating heart, no matter where we live on the face of this

55

earth.

In a speech entitled: "The American Negro and the Darker World," delivered in New York on April 30, 1957, Dr. DuBois, the Elder Statesman among African-Americans, made the following comment that I consider relevant to this paper. He said:

> From the fifteenth through the seventeenth centuries, the Africans imported to America regarded themselves as temporary settlers destined to return eventually to Africa. Their increasing revolts against the slave system, which culminated in the eighteenth century, showed a feeling of close kinship to the Motherland and even well into the nineteenth century they called their organizations "African," as witness the "African Unions" of New York and Newport, and the African Churches of Philadelphia and New York. In the West Indies and South America there was even closer indication of feelings of kinship with Africa and the East.

Dr. DuBois is referring to our first attempts to regain the African culture, ideology and history that we lost in slavery and the slave trade and in the colonial system.

This fight to hold on to our Africanness started in Africa, as the slaves captured in the hinterland fought to keep from being taken to the coast of West Africa, where the slave ships were waiting. They also fought to keep from being put on the ships and continued to fight when they were forced on the ships to start the journey to the so-called New World.

The distinguished African-American poet, Countee Cullen, began his famous poem, "Heritage," with the question: "What is Africa to me?" In order to understand Africa and its place in world history, we must extend the question by asking, "What is Africa to the Africans and what is Africa to the world?" There is a need to locate Africa and its people on the map of human geography. In his article, "The African Root of the War," in the *Atlantic Monthly*, our own great historian, W.E.B. DuBois, tells us:

> Always Africa is giving us something new .... On its Black bosom arose one of the earliest, if not the earliest, of self-

protecting civilizations, and grew so mighty that it still furnishes superlatives to thinking and speaking men. Out of its darker and more remote forest fastnesses came, if we may credit many recent scientists, the first welding of iron, and we know that agriculture and trade flourished there when Europe was a wilderness.

Dr. DuBois tell us further:

Nearly every human empire that has risen in the world, material and spiritual, has found some of its greatest crises on this continent of Africa. It was through Africa that Christianity became the religion of the world. In Africa the last flood of Germanic invasions spent itself within hearing of the last gasp of Byzantium, and it was again through Africa that Islam came to play its great role of conqueror and civilizer.

Especially in independent African institutions, the mission should be to see African people as a part of world history and to make the best use of the contribution of African people to the world. We must reclaim the minds of our children.

The greatest teachers of African children, and also for African adults, are the silent teachers all around called images. These silent images are more effective than the spoken word. There is a need to examine the effect of images on the minds and future conduct of African children. I will begin with a quote from a speech by a great African nineteenth century educator, Dr. Edward Wilmot Blyden. This was Dr. Blyden's inaugural address when he became the president of Liberia College. This speech is as timely now as when Dr. Blyden made it in 1881. He said:

The people generally are not yet prepared to understand their own interests in the great work to be done for themselves and their children. We shall be obliged to work for some time to come not only without the popular sympathy we ought to have, but with utterly inadequate resources.

In all English-speaking countries, the mind of the intelligent Negro child revolts against the descriptions of the Negro given in elementary books—geographies, travels, histories. . . .

Having embraced or at least assented to these falsehoods about himself, he concludes that his only hope of rising in the scale of respectable manhood is to strive for whatever is most unlike himself and most alien to his peculiar tastes. And whatever his literary attainments or acquired ability, he fancies that he must grind at the mill which is provided for him, putting in material furnished to his hands, bringing no contribution from his own field, and of course, nothing comes out but what is put in.

That was our great sorrow then. This is our great sorrow now. Blyden was speaking for the ages. Until we free ourselves from dependence on other people, we will never be free.

Day by day, we must deal with the images that influence and control us.

What we do for ourselves depends on what we know about ourselves and what we are willing to accept about ourselves. When other people control what we think about ourselves, they will also control what we do about ourselves. We must reclaim our heritage in order to be a total people.

We can confront the world if first we confront ourselves. We can change the world if first we change ourselves.

With the independence of Ghana, in December 1957, which signalled the beginning of the African Independence Explosion, a reassessment should have been made to all approaches to African education both in Africa and abroad. Most of what passed for education in Africa prior to this time had been missionary indoctrination, a form of containment using the educational concepts of their colonial masters. The Africans used the same basic textbooks as their colonial masters and arrived at some of the same conclusions. Africans had been trained to serve alien powers that did not have their long-range interests at heart. In the British territories there were facsimiles of university training in a few places, no well-developed technical schools in any places. The examinations in these schools were made up in England and subsequently forwarded to England for correction. These schools were in no way African, proving again that the powerful never train powerless people in how to take their power away from them. On the eve of this Independence Explosion and in the years immediately following, Africans did not have people adequately trained in the basic skills, such as plumbing, electronics, road-building, harbor maintenance, airport building and airport maintenance. Some were hurriedly trained, using European materials and European technique. Before Europe, Africans were trained by Africans to maintain themselves based on methods and an understanding of the existing environment.

The invasion of Africa by foreigners, first from Western Asia then from Europe, threw African societies out of balance. Some of the African methods that were workable before the invasion and the disruptions were no longer workable afterwards. Therefore, immediately following the Independence Explosions the Africans in Africa were on the horns of several dilemmas. They had forgotten much of their own methods of maintaining themselves, and they had not completely mastered the methods of maintenance of their colonial masters.

The large number of Africans who went to Western schools immediately following the Independence Explosion studied ideologies and political science and different aspects of the humanities. Some of them realized, belatedly, that Africa's greatest need was students skilled in the nation-building sciences, such as metallurgy, mining engineering, chemical engineering, electrical engineering, water purification, and every aspect of the medical profession. Too many Africans went abroad and studied at the expense of their government and came home with an education that was of no use to that government. In both developed and undeveloped mineral wealth, Africa is the world's richest continent. Africans have not been trained in how to harness that richness and use it for Africa's benefit as against the benefit of foreign powers and investors. To do this, Africans must be trained to face this new reality in being educated in the basic skills essential to the technical management of a nation.

Until his untimely death a few years ago, Africa's greatest historian and social thinker, Cheikh Anta Diop, wrote extensively on this subject, mainly in his book, *Africa: The Politics of a Federated State*. In his book he analyzed the already known and potential wealth in Africa and what the Africans would have to do to preserve it. He also decried the fact that a large amount of this wealth had already been taken out of Africa and deposited in other countries. Both as a historian and social thinker, Cheikh Anta Diop was a clear voice crying out in a political wilderness. In spite of this condition of despair, some responsible people and alert students heard his voice, read his monumental writings and, as a result, slowly began the political process that will eventually deliver every aspect of Africa to African people.

Cheikh Anta Diop, who was a trained scientist as well as a historical and political thinker and prophet, collectively called for the reeducation of African people so that they could master those educational and political tools essential to the reclaiming of Africa and the unification of African people the world over.

When we turn to another important part of the African world—the Caribbean Islands and South America—the process of being educated for a new reality is both different and the same. The Africans away from home present a problem in education that is frustrating and challenging because here we are talking about the same problems with different dimensions. The forced migration of Africans out of Africa in the fifteenth and sixteenth centuries began with the settlement of the Caribbean Islands and subsequently South America. African labor, which maintained the plantation system in this area, renewed the economy of Europe and helped to lay the foundations for the civilization that is referred to as the New World. If the Africans were educated at all, they were educated to serve the plantation system and its extensions. Some Africans developed skills—blacksmithing, small boat maintenance, housing construction, basic design and maintenance. Some were furniture and leather craftsmen, indispensable to the maintenance of the plantation system. Because they maintained some African cultural continuity, they also brought off some of the most massive slave revolts in history. Starting in the years before the American Revolution and lasting until the middle of the nineteenth century, they entered the twentieth century still carrying the spirit of these revolts and a lot of the skill they had developed while maintaining the plantation system.

Before and after the spirit of African Independence had spread to the Caribbean Islands, large numbers of Caribbeans had been educated in the basic skills of small-nation maintenance. The theme of Africa reverberated through these islands throughout the eighteenth and nineteenth centuries. By the end of the nineteenth century, this theme, and a theory to match, had been brought together. It was then called Pan-Africanism. Pan-Africanism was not only a new form of thinking in the African world, it was a new approach to education and the possibility of African world unity.

In the first half of the nineteenth century, the African-American had experienced massive slave revolts and radical thinking in the beginning of the growth of independent African institutions, mainly the African Methodist Episcopal Church. During the second half of the nineteenth century, they experienced both progress and a rebirth of the old oppression, concurrent with the end of the massive anti-colonial wars in Africa. Therefore, the African world came into the twentieth century fighting, bleeding, looking for a new way of life, trying to regain the nationhood lost during slavery and colonialism, trying to find that form of education that would prepare them to once more be the masters of themselves.

In the United States, a new process of education was started at Tuskegee Institute by Booker T. Washington. This was education for self-reliance. Though he strategically never said this is education for nationhood, in the final analysis this is what it is. At Tuskegee, African-Americans or any other Africans from any other part of the world were being trained in the nation-building, the nation-mainte-nance sciences. Students were also being trained to be producers as well as consumers. In many practical ways, Booker T. Washington was saying if you live in a brick house, you should also own a brick factory. And if you wear shoes, you should learn how to make shoes. The cooks and bakers school at Tuskegee became so exceptional that the Ameri-can Army sent some of their cooks to Tuskegee for training. There were also schools for plumbing, electronics, both rural and urban, and the general builders' trade. There was a need then and now for a proliferation of the Tuskegee-type school throughout the whole of the African world. Other schools using the Tuskegee model did flourish throughout some of the southern states until, on the eve of the second World War, African education was mistakenly turned towards the liberal arts—the same mistake that was made in Africa and in the Caribbean Islands.

Education for a new reality must take one thing into consideration: To maintain a nation there is a need to train large numbers of people, consistently, in the basic skills of nation maintenance. W.E.B. Dubois' alleged opposition to Booker T. Washington is still grossly misunder-stood. Booker T. Washington and W.E.B. DuBois had a difference of opinion on educational methodology. DuBois also believed in education for self-reliance with major emphasis on political responsibility. Marcus Garvey, a Jamaican, was attracted to the United States by the teachings of Booker T. Washington. Because Marcus Garvey came out of a class of craftsmen, he too believed in education for self-reliance. It is this aspect of the Booker T. Washington program that attracted him. The debate over what manner of education is best needed for the African world began early in the twentieth century, continued throughout the century, and is not over to this day.

I see no way for this dilemma to be resolved except throughout the framework of a Pan-African approach to education. Africans must be educated for self-reliance, nation maintenance, nation management in every regard. Eventually, Africans must learn how to design and make every needed facility used in the African world from a safety pin to a locomotive and to an aeroplane.

The new reality in the African world is that with the 300 million Africans living outside Africa in the Western world, with the millions of people of African descent in the Pacific Islands, with nearly 100 million blacks in India called Untouchables, mostly of African descent, and with the continent of Africa estimated to have 500 million Africans, there could be, if there aren't already, a billion African people on the face of the earth during the first half of the twenty-first century. There's a need to build a network of educational systems to train a billion people to face this reality. We can create an economic system furnishing goods and services to each other. To do this, we must stop answering to the word *minority*, no matter where we are, in or out of Africa. We must stop asking other people to do for us what we need to learn to do for ourselves with great skill and consistency. By a serious study of our historical past, we might have a more correct bearing on the present and a more confident view of the future. In reclaiming our own humanity, we will enhance the humanity of the entire world. This is the basis of our education for a new reality.

AFRICAN-AMERICAN HISTORIANS AND THE RECLAIMING OF AFRICAN HISTORY

Some Neglected Origins of the African World Revolution

▼

THE AFRICANS WHO CAME to the United States as slaves started their attempts to reclaim their lost African heritage soon after they arrived in this country. They were searching for the lost identity that the slave system had destroyed. Concurrent with the black man's search for an identity in America has been his search for an identity in the world, which means, in essence, his identity as a human being with a history, before and after slavery, that can command respect.

The African-American connection with Africa is not new. In fact, this connection was never completely broken. "Africa-consciousness," in varying degrees, good and bad, has always been a part of the psyche of the African people, in forced exile in South America, the Caribbean Islands, and in the United States. There has always been a conflict within the black American's Africa-consciousness. This conflict was created early and was extended beyond all reasonable proportions by the mass media of the twentieth century through jungle movies, elementary textbooks on geography and history, and travel books written to glorify all people of European extraction—in essence, white

63

people. These distorted images have created both a rejection of Africa and a deep longing for the Africa of our imagination, the Africa that was our home and the first home of what man has referred to as "a civilization."

Contrary to a still prevailing opinion, most of the literate Africans in forced exile have always had a positive image of Africa. They have rejected the image of Africa as a backward and barbarous land. To the extent that the information was available, the early black writers and thinkers made every attempt to locate Africa on the map of human geography. They soon discovered that Africa and her people had a history older than the history of their oppressors. They also learned how and why the Christian church had to read the Africans out of the respectful commentary of human history. While the pretense was that Africans were being civilized and Christianized, this was really the beginning of what Walter Rodney has called "The Under-development of Africa." In his book on the subject, Rodney analyzes the first European impressions of the people and cultures on the west coast of Africa. "Several historians of Africa," he points out, "after surveying the developed areas of the continent in the fifteenth century, and those within Europe at the same time, find the difference between the two in no way to Africa's discredit."

He quotes a Dutch account of the city of Benin in west Africa to prove that, at first, the Europeans compared African cities and cultures favorably to their own:

> The town seems to be very great. When you enter into it, you go into a great broad street, not paved, which seems to be seven or eight times broader than the Warmoes Street in Amsterdam.
>
> The King's palace is a collection of buildings which occupy as much space as the two of Haarlem, and which is enclosed with walls. There are numerous apartments for the Prince's ministers and fine galleries, most of which are as big as those of the Exchange at Amsterdam. They are supported by wooden pillars encased with copper, where their victories are depicted, and which are carefully kept very clean.
>
> The Town is composed of 30 main streets, very straight and two hundred and twenty feet wide, apart from an infinity of

small intersecting streets. The houses are close to one another, arranged in good order. These people are in no way inferior to the Dutch as regards cleanliness; they wash and scrub their houses so well that they are polished and shining like a looking glass.

In his essay, "The African Roots of the War," written for the *Atlantic Monthly*, May 1915, the great African-American scholar, W.E.B. DuBois, decried the fact that:

There are those who would write world history and leave out this most marvelous of continents. Particularly today most men assume that Africa lies far afield from the center of our burning social problems and especially from our present problem of world war.

Yet in a very real sense, Africa is a prime cause of this terrible overturning of civilization.... In Africa are the hidden roots, not simply of war today but of the menace of war tomorrow.

Always Africa is giving us something new or some metempsychosis of a world-old thing. On its black bosom arose one of the earliest if not the earliest, of self-protecting civilizations, and grew so mightily that it still furnishes superlatives to thinking and speaking men. Out of its darker and more remote forest vastness came, if we may credit many recent scientists, the first welding of iron, and we know that agriculture and trade flourished there when Europe was a wilderness.

Nearly every human empire that has arisen in the world, material and spiritual, has found some of its greatest crises on this continent of Africa, from Greece to Great Britain. As Mommsen says: "It was through Africa that Christianity became the religion of the world." In Africa the last flood of Germanic invasions spent itself within hearing of the last gasp of Byzantium, and it was again in Africa that Islam came to play its great role of conqueror and civilizer.

In the reestablishment of the connection with Africa and in the search for a more enlightened image of that continent and its people, the early black writers in the United States soon learned that Africa was an important factor in world history and that in the great human drama of the rise and fall of nations, Africans had played every role from saint to buffoon.

These writers, preachers, and self-educated men of affairs, referred to themselves mainly as Africans—not "coloreds," nor "Negroes" nor "blacks," but as Africans. Nearly all their organizations bore the name "African," and they thought of themselves as African people. This small group of black freedmen and escaped slaves began to develop during the latter half of the eighteenth century. By the end of that century, their presence was being felt as petitioners, antislavery speakers and pamphleteers. Their writings and their place in history is well recorded in *Early Negro Writing 1760-1837*, by Dorothy Porter, giving the following information.

The first literary talent of African-Americans began to develop in the years between 1760 and 1837, concurrently with mutual benefit organizations expressing their social consciousness. In most cases these organizations bore African names and their leaders referred to Africa as their homeland. Mrs. Porter tells us:

> This early disposition to associate together for mutual improve-
> ment provided a training ground for the half-educated as well as
> for the educated and ambitious among the sons of Africa in the
> United States. The very titles of these organizations suggest that
> they were directed in the main to the improvement of the social
> and political status of blacks.

The Free African Society was organized by the black Methodists in 1787. This society under the leadership of Richard Allen and Absalom Jones brought into being the first independent black church in the United States—the African Methodist Episcopal Church. The early black churches were more than religious organizations. They performed the services of social agencies, publishers, community centers, and occasionally hiding places for escaped slaves. The first historical protest and literary writings of the black freedmen in the New England states found an outlet in the church or organizations affiliated with the church. In the "Essay on Freedom with Observations on the Origins of Slavery," written by a member of the Sons of Africa Society that was formed in 1798, the writer outlines some of the difficulties blacks were encountering in seeking freedom and expressed appreciation to the people of the city of Salem, Massachusetts, for showing signs of "approbation of the Africans' freedom." These pamphlets, broadsheets, and monographs continued to appear throughout the first half of the nineteenth century, and their writers helped to establish the early black press in the United States. Some of these writers became editors of such papers as *Freedom's Journal, The North Star* and *The Anglo-African Magazine*.

The spiritual and cultural return to Africa is reflected in the names of early black institutions, especially in the churches. In his book, *The Redemption of Africa and Black Religion*, St. Clair Drake draws this picture of the black church during its formative years:

> Black people under slavery turned to the Bible to "prove" that Black people, Ethiopians, were so powerful and respected when white men in Europe were barbarians. Ethiopia came to symbolize all of Africa; and throughout the 19th century, the redemption of Africa became one important focus of meaningful activity for leaders among New World Negroes. "Ethiopianism" became an energizing myth in both the New World and in Africa itself for those pre-political movements that arose while the powerless were gathering their strength for realistic and rewarding political activity. Its force is now almost spent, but "Ethiopianism" left an enduring legacy to the people who fought for Black Power in the 20th century, and some of its development needs to be understood.

In closing years of the nineteenth century, the Africans in the Caribbean Islands, South America, and in the United States continued to object to the distorted pictures of Africans in elementary school books, geographies, travel books and histories. As far back as 1881, the renowned Dr. Edward Wilmot Blyden, on the occasion of his inauguration as president of Liberia College, sounded the note that called for a new approach to the teaching of African history and culture. Dr. Blyden is the best known of the Caribbean scholars who returned to Africa. Of his many books, *Christianity, Islam and the Negro Race*, first published in 1887 and reprinted in 1967, is an enduring classic.

In the United States, W.E.B. DuBois continued some of the work of Dr. Blyden and carried it into the twentieth century. The unity and liberation of all Africa was the main mission of the life of W.E.B. DuBois. He did not pursue this mission in isolation, and he sought allies wherever he could find them. His interest in Africa began during his student days at Harvard University. As a result of this interest, he wrote his first major work, *The Suppression of the African Slave Trade to the United States* (1896). This interest was continued in two other works, *The Souls of Black Folks* (1903) and *The Gift of Black Folks* (1924). During his editorship of the *Crisis Magazine*, 1910-1934, he introduced Africa as a subject of concert for black Americans. *The Negro*, published in 1915, was his first attempt to write a survey history of the African world. His little-known, yet important essay, "The African Roots of the War," was published the same year. In this essay, he dared to deal with the imperialist origins of the First World War and Africa in general.

After World War I new men and movements rose to challenge the old social order and to ask for a new one. The best-known movement of this period was the Universal Negro Improvement Association (UNIA). The best-known personality was its dynamic founder, Marcus Garvey. Concurrent with the rise of the Garvey movement a literary and cultural awakening called the Harlem Renaissance brought more attention to the world's most famous ethnic community. The Harlem Renaissance, in its own way, was an African-consciousness movement, accentuated by Marcus Garvey and his program that asked Black Americans to consider a return to their motherland.

Among black writers, artists, and thinkers like W.E.B. DuBois, James Weldon Johnson, J.A. Rogers, Arthur A. Schomburg, and William Leo Hansberry, the period of the Harlem Renaissance was a time of African rediscovery. In their writings these scholars affirmed that Africans were great storytellers long before their first appearance in Jamestown, Virginia, in 1619. The rich and colorful history, art and folklore of West Africa, the ancestral home of most African-Americans, present evidence of this, and more.

Contrary to a misconception that still prevails, the Africans were familiar with literature and art for many years before their contact with the Western World. Before the breaking up of the social structure of the West African states of Ghana, Melle (Mali), and Songhai, and the internal strife and chaos that made the slave trade possible, the forefathers of the Africans who eventually became slaves in the United States lived in a society where university life was fairly common and scholars were beheld with reverence.

There were in this ancestry rulers who expanded their kingdoms into empires, great and magnificent armies whose physical dimensions dwarfed entire nations into submission, generals who advanced the technique of military science, scholars whose vision of life showed foresight and wisdom, and priests who told of gods that were strong and kind. To understand fully any aspect of African-American life, one must realize that the black Americans are not without a cultural past, though they were many generations removed from it before their achievements in American literature and art commanded any appreciable attention. I have been referring to the African origin of African-American literature and history. This preface is essential to every meaningful discussion of the role of the African-American in every major aspect of American life, past and present. I want to make it clear that the African people did not come to the United States culturally empty-handed.

I will elaborate very briefly on my statement that the forefathers of the Africans who eventually became slaves in the United States once lived in a society where university life was fairly common and scholars were beheld with reverence. During the period in West African history—from the early part of the fourteenth century to the time of the Moroccan invasion in 1591, the city of Timbuktoo and the University of Sankore in the Songhai Empire was the intellectual center of Africa. Black scholars enjoyed a renaissance that was known and respected throughout most of Africa and in parts of Europe. At this period of African history, the University of Sankore, at Timbuktoo, was the educational capital of the Western Sudan. In Felix Dubois' book, *Timbuktoo, the Mysterious* (1895), there is a fitting description of ancient Timbuktoo:

> The scholars of Timbuctoo yielded in nothing to the saints in their sojourns in the foreign universities of Fez, Tunis and Cairo. They astounded the most learned men of Islam by their erudition. That these Negroes were on a level with the Arabian Savants is proved by the fact that they were installed as profes-

sors in Morocco and Egypt. In contrast to this, we find that the Arabs were not always equal to the requirements of Sankore.

I will speak of only one of the great black scholars of ancient Timbuctoo. Ahmed Baba was the last chancellor of the University of Sankore. He was one of the greatest African scholars of the late sixteenth century. His life is a brilliant example of the range and depth of West African intellectual activity before the colonial era. Ahmed Baba was the author of more than forty books, nearly every one of which had a different theme. He was in Timbuctoo when it was invaded by the Moroccans in 1591, and he was one of the first citizens to protest the occupation of his beloved home town. Ahmed Baba, along with other scholars, was imprisoned and eventually exiled to Morocco. During his expatriation from Timbuctoo, his collection of 1,600 books, one of the richest libraries of his day, was lost.

Now, West Africa entered a sad period of decline. During the Moroccan occupation, wreck and ruin became the order of the day. When the Europeans arrived in this part of Africa and saw these conditions, they assumed that nothing of order and value had ever existed in these countries. This mistaken impression, too often repeated, has influenced the interpretation of African and African-American life in history for over 400 years.

The essence of the African-consciousness of the writers who were a part of the Harlem Renaissance is contained in the book, *The New Negro*, edited by Alain Locke. Essays like "The Mind of the Negro Reaches Out," by W.E.B. DuBois, "The Legacy of the Ancestral Arts," by Alain Locke, and "The Negro Digs Up His Past," by Arthur A. Schomburg, show a creative concern for Africa. When the book, *The New Negro*, was published in 1925, the Association for the Study of Negro Life and History, under the leadership of its founder, Carter G. Woodson, was ending the first decade of its existence. In 1926 he founded what we now know as African-American or Black History Week.

The terms, Black History Week or African-American History Week, taken at face value or without serious thought, appear to be incongruous. At the time, the question did arise, why is there a need for a Black History Week when there is no similar week for the other minority groups in the United States? The history of the United States in total consists of the collective histories of minority groups. What we call "American civilization" is no more than the sum of their contributions. The African-Americans are the least integrated and the most neglected of these groups in the historical interpretation of the American experience. This neglect has made Black History Week a necessity.

Most of the large ethnic groups in the United States have had, and still have, their historical associations. Some predate the founding of the Association for the Study of Negro Life and History (1915). Dr. Charles H. Wesley tells us, "Historical societies were organized in the United States with the special purpose in view of preserving and maintaining the heritage of the American Nation." In 1944 there were a total of 904 ethnic historical societies in the United States and Canada, an increase of 46 percent over the number listed in 1936, 583. Among these societies were those representing groups whose origins were German, Irish, French, Jewish, Dutch, Spanish, Russian, Norwegian, Scandinavian, Swedish, Swiss, and Finnish. The leaders of these historical societies were of the opinion that the history of the United States could not be written from the point of view of "adaptation and assimilation" but that the "cultural riches brought to the Western world, in what has been termed the elements composing the national whole, must be studied and appraised before a complete understanding of American history and American civilization is possible."

In "Racial Historical Societies and the American Tradition," included in his book, *Neglected History* (1965), the African-American historian, Charles H. Wesley, describes the work of ethnic historical societies in this manner: "They must gather up precious records and interpret them. Both in language and in that subtle understanding that they have absorbed by natural circumstances of the way of life of their own folk, they possess keys to unlock doors that bar the way to a full comprehension of the social history of America."

Within the framework of these historical societies, many ethnic groups, black as well as white, keep alive their beliefs in themselves and their past as a part of their hopes for the future. For black Americans, Carter G. Woodson led the way and used what was then called "Negro History Week" to call attention to his people's contribution to every aspect of world history. Dr. Woodson, then Director of the Association for the Study of Negro Life and History, conceived this special week as a time when public attention should be focused on the achievements of America's citizens of African descent. Black History Week comes each year about the second Sunday in February, the objective being to select the week that will include both February 12, the birth of Abraham Lincoln, and February 14, the date Frederick Douglass calculated to have been his natal day. Sometimes the celebration can include only one day, in which case the Douglass date gets preference. The aim is not to enter upon one week's study of black people's place in history. Rather, the celebration should represent the culmination of a systematic study of black people throughout the year. Initially, the observance consisted of public exercises emphasizing the salient facts brought to light by the researchers and publications of the association during the first eleven years of its existence. The observance was widely supported among black Americans in schools, churches and clubs. Gradually, the movement found support among other ethnic groups and institutions in America and abroad.

The acceptance of the facts of black history and the black historian as a legitimate part of the academic community did not come easily. Slavery ended but left its false images of black people intact. In his article, "What the Historian Owes the Negro," the noted African-American historian, Benjamin Quarles says:

> The Founding Fathers, revered by historians for over a century and a half, did not conceive of the Negro as part of the body politic. Theoretically, these men believed in freedom for everyone, but actually they found it hard to imagine a society where Negroes were of equal status to whites. Thomas Jefferson, third President of the United States, who was far more liberal than the run of his contemporaries, was nevertheless certain that "the two races, equally free, cannot live in the same government."

Early white American historians did not accord African people anywhere a respectful place in their commentaries on the history of man. In the closing years of the nineteenth century, black historians began to look at their people's history from their vantage point and point of view. "As early as 1883 this desire to bring to public attention the untapped material on the Negro prompted George Washington Williams to publish his two-volume *History of the Negro Race in America*." The first formally trained African-American historian was W.E.B.

DuBois, whose doctoral dissertation, published in 1895, *The Suppression of the African Slave Trade to the United States 1638-1870*, became the first title to be published in the Harvard Historical Studies. Carter G. Woodson, another Harvard Ph.D., advanced African world history and became a defender who could document his claims. Woodson was convinced that unless something were done to rescue black people from history's oversight, they would become "a negligible factor in the thought of the world." Woodson in 1915 founded the Association for the Study of Negro Life and History. During the preceding twenty years, an American Negro Academy had been founded in Washington, D.C., and a Negro Society for Historical Research had appeared in New York. These organizations were short-lived because they lacked a historian of Woodson's ability, someone who was also a leader of men and an organizational administrator.

Carter G. Woodson was born of former slaves, Annie and James Woodson, in 1875 in New Canton, Virginia. He suffered all the hardships of poverty while growing up. Only a five-month district school was available to him, and he was unable to attend it on a regular basis. He studied at home while working on the family's farm. Already he had established a lifetime habit—studying at home. In his early years he was mostly self-taught. He mastered all the fundamentals of common school subjects by the time he was seventeen, then went to Huntington, West Virginia, where he worked in the coal mines. He later entered Douglass High School and earned a teaching certificate in less than two years; pursued further education at Berea College in Kentucky, where he received the Litt. B. degree. He continued his education at the University of Chicago, where he was awarded the B.A. and M.A. degrees. His travels in Europe and Asia and graduate studies at the Sorbonne in Paris enriched his cultural background and prepared him for graduate work at Harvard University, where he was awarded the Ph.D. in 1912. After Harvard he had an extensive career as an educator: principal of Douglass High School, teacher of languages and history in high schools of Washington, D.C., dean of the School of Liberal Arts, Howard University, and supervisor of schools in the Philippines. This varied experience made Carter G. Woodson see the need for a special time each year to call attention to his people's contribution to the history and culture of this country and the world. Thus, Black History Week.

After serving many years as a teacher in public schools, Woodson became convinced that the role of his people in American history and in the history of other cultures was being either ignored or misrepresented. The Association for the Study of Negro Life and History was founded to conduct research into the history of African people all over the world. The next year he began publication of the *Journal of Negro History*, which has never missed an issue.

A chronicle of Woodson's far-reaching activities must include the organization in 1921 of the Associated Publishers, Inc., which had as one of its purposes the publication of books on African people not usually accepted by most publishers; the establishment of Negro History Week in 1926; the initial subsidizing of research on black history; and the writing of many articles and books on African-American life and history.

Woodson believed that there was no such thing as "Negro history." He said what was called "Negro history" was only a missing segment of world history. He devoted the greater portion of his life to restoring this segment. He also realized that once this segment was integrated into school textbooks and taught with respect and understanding, there would no longer be a need for a Negro History Week.

In the U.S. Civil War, Blacks fought bravely and died in great numbers for their own freedom. The idea that the black man played an insignificant role while white men fought and died to set him free is not supported by official records. Materials related to the black Americans are available in official Civil War records, but unfortunately are completely omitted in most school textbooks.

Africa came into the Mediterranean world mainly through Greece, which had been under African influence; and then Africa was cut off from the melting pot by the turmoil among the Europeans and the religious conquests incident to the rise of Islam. Africa prior to these events had developed its history and civilization, indigenous to its people and lands. Africa came back into the general picture of history through the penetration of North Africa, West Africa, and the Sudan by the Arabs. European and American slave traders next ravaged the continent. The imperialist colonizers and missionaries finally entered the scene and prevailed until the recent reemergence of independent African nations.

Africans are, of course, closely connected to the history of both

North and South America. The African-American's role in the social, economic, and political development of the American states is an important foundation upon which to build racial understanding, especially in areas in which false generalizations and stereotypes have been developed to separate peoples rather than to unite them.

The spiritual and intellectual journey to Africa was continued by many black scholars other than Carter G. Woodson. At Howard University, William Leo Hansberry, considered to be the greatest Africanist to emerge from the black American community, trained a generation of students to learn and respect African history. His articles, monographs and conference papers on the subject appeared in leading journals throughout the world.

In the period of the Italian-Ethiopian War, the streets of Harlem were an open forum, presided over by master speakers like Arthur Reed and his protege, Ira Kemp. Young Carlos Cook, founder of the Garvey-oriented African Pioneer Movement, was on the scene, also bringing a nightly message to his street fellows. Part of every message was about Africa.

A revolution in thinking about Africa occurred after World War II. The revolution was most widespread among black Americans, who are the most estranged and alienated African people in all the world.

In 1947, J.A. Rogers published his most outstanding work, *World's Great Men of Color*, in two volumes. This is the enduring masterpiece in African world biography. Before his death in 1966, at the age of eighty-five, he had devoted at least fifty years of his life to researching the lives of great African personalities and the roles they had played in the development of nations, civilizations and cultures.

In 1958, the American Society of African Culture published the book, *Africa as Seen by American Negroes*. The editors of this book had creatively compiled some of the best essays that black American scholars had written on Africa during the preceding ten years.

In 1964, *Ebony* Magazine published a series of articles on the ancient and medieval history of Africa by William Leo Hansberry. This was the most extensive series of this nature ever to appear in a black publication. The articles were extracted from a projected four-volume history of Africa that Hansberry had been writing for nearly a genera-tion. Unfortunately, this larger work was not finished before he died in 1965. However, two of his books, edited by Joseph E. Harris, head of the History Department of Howard University, were published in 1974 and 1977: *Pillars in Ethiopian History* and *African and Africans as Seen by Classical Writers*.

During the Civil Rights movement, called the "American Black Revolution," interest in Africa led to a massive demand for Black Studies, mostly by black students at predominantly white universities. A number of books by black American scholars helped to place Africa in proper historical focus during this period. In my opinion, some of the most important of these books are: *The African Presence in Asia* by Joseph E. Harris (1971), *Introduction to African Civilizations* by John G. Jackson (1974), *The Destruction of Black Civilization: Great Issues of a Race From 4500 B.C. to 2000 A.D.* by Chancellor Williams, and three books by Yosef Ben-Jochannan, *Black Man of the Nile* (1970), *Africa: Mother of Western Civilization* (1970), and *African Origins of the Major Western Religions* (1971).

African-American and African-Caribbean scholars from the early part of the nineteenth century to the present made a personal mission out of the effort to reclaim African history. They repudiated the often repeated charge that Africans have no history.

They found that we cannot place African humanity and history in proper perspective until we deal with the distortions of African history. The hard fact is that what we call "world history," in most cases, is only the history of Europe and its relationship to non-European people. The Western academic community, in general, is not yet willing to acknowledge that the world did not wait in darkness for European people to bring the light. The history of Africa was already old when Europe was born.

Two

FIVE AFRICANS AND THEIR UNCOMPLETED REVOLUTIONS

▼

COMMENTARY

▼

KWAME NKRUMAH WAS Africa's political light of the twentieth century. He was a light that may shine in some way for centuries to come. He inherited the political impotence that came from Ghana and Africa's physical struggle against colonialism in the nineteenth century. He was fortunately born in an African country that never accepted the assumption that foreigners had the right to rule over them. Therefore, from the beginning of European encroachment, as reflected in King Asa's speech to the Portuguese in 1482, the indigenous rulers of this country suspected foreign rule and found different ways to fight against it through nearly 500 years of its presence, from 1481 to 1957. In the closing years of the nineteenth century, the Ghanaians had already fought a number of wars against the British, who were trying to seize control of the hinterland. The British thought they could break the spirit of the Asante people by seizing the Golden Stool, the equivalent to the Ark of the Covenant to Africans of Ghana. Fought in the closing years of the nineteenth century, the last of these wars was led by a woman named Ya Asantewa, then Queen Mother of the Asante people after the exile of her relative, King Prempeh. She was defeated with the help of the famous West Indian regiment, mainly from Jamaica, and sent into exile. The politics of exile is an aspect of African political history still waiting for a scholar equal to its importance.

E. Casely Hayford and other young Ghanaian politicians converted the demand for the return of their exiled royalty into a demand for their independence. This demand was worded in the form of a plea for educational improvement and the preparation for Ghanaians to manage

79

their own affairs. After the death of Casely Hayford in 1931, the mantle of responsibility was passed to Joseph B. Danquah, a brilliant local lawyer who was Kwame Nkrumah's teacher. Dr. Danquah's books and pamphlets, especially *The Akan Doctrine of God* and *Obligation in Akan Society*, which relate to pre-independent Ghana, then called the Gold Coast, were an intellectual preface to Ghanaian independence, along with the works of Casely Hayford, the father of early twentieth-century Ghanaian politics.

Joseph B. Danquah was considered this country's primary intellect on the eve of independence and after. He was head of the United Gold Coast Convention, the quasipolitical party that was permitted to exist before independence. It was Danquah who invited Kwame Nkrumah, then a student in London, back to Ghana to be the secretary to the United Gold Coast Convention. Nkrumah subsequently broke with his old schoolmaster, Danquah, and formed the Convention Peoples Party. This break between the schoolmaster and his former student was unfortunate for Ghana on many levels, because had they found a way to combine their respective talents, Ghana could have emerged a better and stronger nation with a special kind of unity that the future enemies of the state would not have been able to destroy.

Joseph B. Danquah was an African traditionalist. He believed in making the best use of the traditions that Africa had before the coming of the Europeans, while also making the best use of the thing brought by the Europeans. He was clear in projecting the idea that African traditionalism should prevail in a modern state and was no contradiction to a modern state.

Kwame Nkrumah, who had been away from Africa well over ten years in schools in the United States and in London, seemed to have forgotten these traditions, if ever he took them seriously in the first place. Some of his values and much of his political ideology was European-based. In spite of what might seem to be a political drawback, Nkrumah, soon after his return to Ghana in 1947, began to emerge as a new light and spirit restoring Africans' confidence in themselves and convincing them that they could rule a modern state. Loyal young politicians around him and some older ones, too, helped him convince a population that this previously unthought of possibility could be true. Kwame Nkrumah became the light of the Africa still to be. His former schoolmaster, Danquah, now among the opposition, did not oppose the independence of Ghana; he opposed some of the radical methods being used to bring independence into being.

Dr. Danquah was unfortunately vilified by a large number of people who had not read any of his volumes of writing or made any attempt to understand his principled position in relationship to Ghana.

After Kwame Nkrumah came to power, March 1957, he immediately set in motion ideas and projects leading to the unification of Africa. He would call for a conference of the independent states in Africa, then only eight. Many of the ideas Nkrumah and Trinidadian George Padmore worked out for the Fifth Pan-African Congress in Manchester, England in 1945 were now resurfacing in Ghana. Organizationally, Padmore was one of Nkrumah's advisers. Some of the ideas credited to Nkrumah were originally George Padmore's. Padmore-Nkrumah political teamwork did not last long after independence, but while it lasted it took Africa a giant political step forward. Ghana became the political beating heart of the African world. Nkrumah had taken a continent for its symbolic walk in the sun. The confidence of the Ghanaian people with their independence began to reverberate throughout most of Africa, and other nations began to petition for independence. This small African nation had set in motion some political changes that would eventually affect the whole world. The enemies of Ghana, and Africa in general, decided this celebration of freedom would not last. As new nations came into being, elements of disruption also came into being within these nations. The brief rise and fall of the Congo, now Zaire, is a case in point.

In the meantime, Kwame Nkrumah had made Ghana the political convention center of Africa. He had founded the African Ideological Institute, which was strong in studying the ideologies of Europe and weak in studying the ideologies of Africa itself. Many Western-educated Africans did not believe that Africa had anything to offer for its own salvation. That was the major flaw in Africa's political program at that time. And it is the major flaw in Africa's political program now. They still have not taken into consideration that Africa built a number of civilizations lasting over 1000 years without a network of jails and without a word in their vocabulary that meant "jail." They had no orphanages because no one discarded children. They had no homes for the aged because no one discarded their mother, father, or grandparents. What Westerners would later call social agencies were built into the society itself. They also had no psychiatrists of the European type. A society can be measured by how it takes care of the very old and the very young. By this standard African societies hold up quite well against other societies of the world. There were periods when African societies in their humaneness were far ahead of European societies. This is what Joseph B. Danquah, in his attempt to call attention to the value of African traditionalism, failed to get across because most Western-educated Africans failed to listen to him and other men of his persuasion. Had the people of Ghana been able to combine the values of African traditionalism with modernism, they would have built the kind of state strong enough to endure the wrath of its enemies.

It is noble, ambitious, and yet unfortunate that Nkrumah tried to be an international man before he became a national Ghanaian. He attempted to participate in the unity of Africa before he had achieved the unity of Ghana. His marriage to the Egyptian woman who was a Coptic Christian might have symbolically achieved something for African unity, but it achieved nothing for Ghanaian unity. After the death of George Padmore, Nkrumah unfortunately surrounded himself with too many back-scratchers, back-patters, and professional flatters, who inflated his ego and neglected his reasoning. He lost some of the communication he originally had with the people, especially the market women, the ordinary worker, and the street people who generally get the political news long before it reaches the newspapers. Too many people willing to help him—who could have saved him—were kept away from him. Some of the South African communists who worked their way into his staff were political Zionists looking after their own interests. When his government fell in 1966, they fled like rats on a sinking ship. His government was overthrown while he was abroad trying to make some sense out of the tragic situation in Vietnam. He was still trying to be an international man. The salvation and unification of Ghana should have been his primary goal. Ghana should have been his window on the world. To some extent I think it was. I do not, for a moment, question that he loved that country and its people, but I do pause to wonder whether he thoroughly understood them, their moods, and their temperament. His years in exile in Guinea were obviously years of rethinking and planning. From his messages from Cankry and his books written after the overthrow of his government, it is clear that Nkrumah was one of the finest political minds produced in twentieth-century Africa. He was a human being with many virtues and some faults, but it is important to say of him that he was that African who, in the middle of the twentieth century, took Africa for its political walk in the sun, made Africa believe in itself again, and made Africans throughout the world proud of being African. He took African people throughout the world for a brief and all-important walk in the political sun. For that reason his name in African history deserves to be remembered with admiration forever.

The short and unhappy political career of Patrice Lumumba is an African tragedy that was not solely created within Africa. He was the victim of conflict and competitive international forces over which he had no control and little knowledge of their intent. The Western enemies of Africa never intended for a rich and stable Congo to exist in the heart of Central Africa. To destroy the Congo, they had to forget or pretend to forget all they had previously known about this vital part of the African continent.

The area of Africa then called the Congo, now Zaire, has not always been wracked with conflict. The Africans in the Congo built a great indigenous civilization before the first appearance of the Europeans, particularly the Portuguese, and after the expulsion of the Portuguese in the 1590s. They built a number of large and stable kingdoms, roads and transportation systems, modern for that day. Driven out of the West African slave trade with the entry of the British, the Portuguese found a new colonial home in the Congo and subsequently Angola. In the Congo they entered into a partnership with the Africans. This partnership lasted over one hundred years before the Africans discovered that the Portuguese wanted to turn their country into a slave-trading colony. Prior to this discovery, Congolese kings had changed their names to sound Portuguese, had started wearing Portuguese clothes, and had developed a taste for various Portuguese food. The Africans were genuine in wanting a partnership with the Portuguese. This partnership fell apart because the intentions of the Portuguese were not honorable. After the expulsion of the Portuguese in the 1590s, most of the kingdoms came together in a protective alliance, and the Congo enjoyed a high degree of sovereignty from the 1590s until the Berlin Conference in 1884.

There had been many serious attempts to take over the Congo. There were many attempts by the Arabs. In the 1600s the Congo had a rebirth of its sovereignty and national pride under a great king, Shamba Bey Lingongo. In the closing years of the nineteenth century, Belgium and other European powers began to make claims on the last territories in Africa not then under European control. These claims and counterclaims led to the Berlin Conference of 1884 and subsequently the Brussels Conference the following year. The Congo came under Belgian control, and Belgian atrocities in the Congo became an international disgrace. With justification, this can be called an African Holocaust. The number of Africans murdered in the Congo more than exceeded six million. It was more than twice that number. European writers like E.D. Morel (in his work, *Black Man's Burden*) and Roger Caseman (in his diaries) exposed these atrocities to the world. The American writer Mark Twain wrote a small book, *King Leopold's Soliloquy*, that was widely circulated.

For Belgium, the Congo became a colonial jewel furnishing a multiplicity of minerals and other resources. To a great extent it was an isolated colony. The Congolese were not encouraged to visit other Africans who lived next door, and other Africans were not encouraged to visit them. Patrice Lumumba broke this pattern by attending a meeting in Ghana. He came back to his country enlightened, with his spirit enhanced by meeting Africans from other parts of the continent. He had built the only political party in the Congo, cutting across all cultural and tribal lines. He was a politician who did not live long enough and observe other politicians well enough to become skillful in this ancient craft. His political moves were too obvious and were often checked or frustrated before he could execute them. He had good intentions, but in a position of power good intentions are not enough. He asked the United Nations for help, and the help they gave him made the situation worse.

The Congo crisis was a test for the United Nations. Dag Hammerskjold, then United Nations Secretary-General, wanted the U.N. to pass this test. The eventual arrest and detainment of Patrice Lumumba heightened the Congo crisis and U.N. forces, brought there to solve the problem, were like too many cooks in a kitchen. For weeks the whereabouts of Lumumba was unknown. During these weeks he became a living martyr. Black-American activists disrupted a meeting of the United Nations General Assembly demanding to know what had happened to Patrice Lumumba. His death, still shrouded in mystery, confirmed what these activists had suspected all along. After his death the Congo saw the rise of a number of pretenders for power, the most noted being Moise Tshombe of Katanga Province. Dag Hammerskjold lost his life, in an airplane crash, in an attempt to solve this problem. The Ghanaian troops, who tried to rescue Patrice Lumumba, were not permitted to do so by their white English commander, General Alexander. The Congo situation, on all sides, was full of paradoxes and contradictions. What was at issue was not the people of the Congo, but European control over the vast mineral and agricultural wealth of the Congo. Books, articles, and pamphlets written on the Congo situation are equivalent to the volumes in a major library. The following poem by Patrice Lumumba is a summary of the Congo Situation:

A Morning in the Heart of Africa
by Patrice Lumumba

For a thousand years you, Negro, suffered like a beast,
    your ashes strewn to the wind that roams the desert.

Your tyrants built the lustrous, magic temples
    to preserve your soul, preserve your suffering.

Barbaric right of fist and the white right to a whip,
    you had the right to die, you also could weep.

In your totem they carved endless hunger, endless bonds,
    and even in the cover of the woods a ghastly cruel death
    was watching, snaky, crawling to you like branch from
    the holes and heads of trees
    embraced your body and your ailing soul.

Then they put a treacherous big viper on your chest,
    on your neck they laid the yoke of fire-water,
    they took your sweet wife for the glitter of cheap pearls,
    your incredible riches that nobody could measure.

From your hut, the tom-toms sounded into the dark of night

carrying cruel laments up mighty black rivers
about abused girls, streams of tears and blood,
about ships that sailed to the country where the little man
wallows in an ant-hill and where dollar is the king,
to that damned land which they called a motherland.

There your child, your wife were ground day and night
by frightful, merciless mill, crushing them in dreadful pain.

You are man like others. They preach you to believe
that good white god will reconcile all men at last.

By fire you grieved and sang the moaning songs
of homeless beggar that sings at strangers' doors.

And when a craze possessed you and your blood boiled through
the night
you danced, you moaned,

Like the fury of a storm to lyrics of a manly tune
a strength burst out of you for a thousand years of misery
in metallic voice of jazz, in uncovered outcry
that thunders through the continent in gigantic surf.

The whole world, surprised, woke up in panic
to the violent rhythm of blood, to the violent rhythm of
jazz,
the white man turning pallid over this new song
that carries torch of purple through the dark of night.

The dawn is here, my brother, dawn! Look in our faces,
a new morning breaks in our old Africa.

Ours only will now be the land, the water, the mighty rivers
which the poor Negro was surrendering for a thousand years.

And hard torches of the sun will shine for us again
they'll dry the tears in your eyes and the spittle on your face.

The moment when you break the chains, the heavy fetters,
the evil, cruel times will go never to come again.

A free and gallant Congo will arise from the black soil,
a free and gallant Congo—the black blossomed, the black
seed!

Reprinted from Link (India)

Among the notable personalities of African descent who became
known in the twentieth century, Marcus Garvey is the most written
about and the least known. Unfortunately, he is the victim of many
people who, without reading one word that he wrote or any of the
numerous books written about him, became instantaneously over-
opinionated about him. They think that the main objective of his
movement was to take African Americans back to Africa. This was
only part of his objective. His main objective was the redemption of
Africa and the restoration of pride in Africa by all the African people
on the earth. In spite of the fact that he rarely ever used the word
"Pan-African," he was the ultimate Pan-Africanist. This fact is best
reflected in the monumental documents compiled by Professor Robert
A. Hill, University of California at Los Angeles, and in the works of
Professor Tony Martin of Wellesley College. The importance of
Professor Hill's work is that he has located the original documents
pertaining to the Garvey movement that eliminates some of the
excuses for the misinterpretation of what Marcus Garvey said and what
his movement was about.

Professor Hill's introductions to the volumes are scholarly and show
great insight into the movement and the period of its existence. I do
not personally always agree with his conclusions. However, I applaud
his work for its monumental contribution to Garvey scholarship and
the assistance it will bring to all serious scholarship on this subject for
the future.

I have found the single volume, *Marcus Garvey Life and Lessons,* of
more value in understanding Garvey's thought process than some of the
larger volumes and their important documents. In this volume Robert
Hill lets Marcus Garvey speak for himself, and Marcus Garvey speaks
very well. Professor Hill's contribution in compiling documents relating
to the neglected aspects of Marcus Garvey and his movement, United

Negro Improvement Association, stands astride the field of Garvey scholarship in such a way that no serious scholar can ignore it.

In its own way, the works of Professor Tony Martin are equally important, but not as extensive as those of Professor Hill. He has unearthed and analyzed still more missing dimensions of the Marcus Garvey saga. His book, *Race First* (1983), should not be ignored. He presents a Marcus Garvey that is close to the people that followed him and shows us a Marcus Garvey who found language and the method to make African-Americans listen to a message that had been propagated in another way one hundred years before he arrived in the United States from Jamaica in 1916. The timing of his arrival and the planting of the seeds of his movement were perfect. He arrived before the end of World War I and began to build his movement in the tragic aftermath of the war, when the nation was plagued with riots and racial disorders following the war.

The Secretary of War had told black soldiers that their position in America would not be changed because of the war. Riots against black soldiers and black people in general had begun before the war ended, coming to a tragic climax called the Red Summer in 1919.

Marcus Garvey toured some of the riot areas, telling the black riot victims that they were not wanted in America; that we should not only prepare not only to go back to Africa, but that we should prepare to buy our own ships, the Black Star Line. If this was an impossible dream, it was at least a complimentary dream. By 1920 his movement had communicated with Africans in Africa, in the Caribbean Islands, and in South and Central America, and he called his famous convention in 1920 at the old Madison Square Garden.

For a brief few years in history Marcus Garvey was the best known figure of African descent in the whole world. There were movements rising to support him and movements rising to destroy him. He had both internal and external enemies, one as vicious as the other. It is not often mentioned, but Marcus Garvey also had a large number of Caribbean enemies, some from his home island of Jamaica.

The administration of the Garvey movement was basically Caribbean. The followers of the Garvey movement in the United States were basically black Americans.

The Back-to-Africa redemption concepts were born over one hundred years before the arrival of Marcus Garvey. They, however, did not achieve the wide following that Garvey's movement was fortunate enough to achieve because the earlier ideas were propagated mainly among an elitist group that did not find a method and the language to reach the common working people. From 1920 until his imprisonment in Atlanta, Garvey's paper, *The Negro World*, attracted some of the most able black writers of the day. The paper was widely circulated and secretly smuggled into the colonial areas of Africa. In addition to regular news, the paper contained poetry, literature, and various essays on different aspects of African history. It was the best-known African publication in the world at that time.

Garvey tried to change the images that influence the minds of African people, e.g., he taught respect for the color black (the natural color of most African people) by taking pride in things of this color. He founded the Black Star Line [shipping] and the Black Cross Nurses, as opposed to Red Cross Nurses. Some number of his members began to open factories and produce black dolls. Others opened grocery stores and basic service stores like tailoring and basic dressmaking. Marcus Garvey was preparing his people to resume the responsibility of nationness. The enemies of his people did not want them to understand nationness then, and their position in this regard has not changed one iota in the more that sixty years since the deportation of Marcus Garvey and the gradual decline in the effectiveness of his movement.

The three major Back-to-Africa Movements before Garvey's, never received the following or the attention as his because they did not attract a mass following. Thanks both to the works of Professor Hill and Professor Martin we can reappraise certain aspects of the Garvey movement that we previously thought we had the answer to.

Marcus Garvey's Liberian scheme needs a reassessment based on the old facts we did not know and the new facts we have not thoroughly examined. In 1921, the bunch of American lackeys in control of Liberia led Marcus Garvey to understand that they were going to let him start his experiment in that nation. By 1924, after he had made all preparations, sent thousands of dollars in equipment and personnel to Liberia, they made it plain to Garvey that this would not be so. The lackeys were still obeying their American masters. This betrayal is often blamed on W.E.B. DuBois. This is a mistake because DuBois did not have that kind of power or connection in Liberia.

There is no need, at this time, to raise the career of Marcus Garvey by lowering the career of W.E.B. DuBois, an intelligent giant of his time, who would also have been an intelligent giant at any time. The fact that DuBois occasionally erred does not disprove my point. He lived long enough not only to realize some of his errors, he also had the courage to correct some of them. This, in essence, is the true measure of the man.

As I have called for a careful examination of the documents and introduction to the documents compiled by Professor Robert A. Hill, I am equally insistent in calling for an examination of the work of Tony Martin, whose work has a different tone and a different dimension. In his books, *The Poetry of Marcus Garvey* and *Literary Garvey*, he has called attention to an aspect of Garveyism that goes beyond the Back-to-Africa Movement and the concept of African redemption. Marcus Garvey was holistic in his approach to African people. I consider Professor Martin's book *The Pan-African Connection* second in importance to his first major work on the subject, *Race First*. This book reflects the fact that African people never gave up the idea of returning to Africa, at least in spirit if not in body. Though we were scattered throughout the Western world and had to take on names and national identity based on the needs of slave buyers and colonial masters, some of us always knew that we were essentially an African people— wherever we were on the face of this earth—and that a large number of us left Africa on the slave ship. When that slave ship came to the Caribbean Islands, some slaves were dropped off at different islands and became Barbadians, Trinidadians, or Jamaicans and the African people took on the names of smaller islands.

In the United States we took on the name of the country that had purchased us. We knew that the slave ships only brought African people out of Africa who had never heard of Trinidad, Barbados, Jamaica, or the British colony that became the United States. We were all African people when we left Africa, and we were all one color. This was before the massive bastardization of African people that gave us colors from extreme black to white and almost white.

Marcus Garvey tried to deal with this issue of the conflict in color, which he interpreted as a conflict in loyalty. He assumed that the internal racial conflict in the United States was the same as the one in Jamaica. On this point he was wrong. This assumption was one of the few negating factors in his relationship to the black American community.

The court trials of Marcus Garvey are too extensive to be repeated here. After his conviction for charges of misuse of the United States mails to defraud investors of the Black Star Line, he was sent to a federal prison in Atlanta. In 1927, he was pardoned by President Calvin Coolidge and deported to his home, Jamaica. Slowly his movement began to fragment and decline. The late C.L.R. James has said, in effect: Considering his slender resources and the amount of propaganda and personalities arrayed against him, the building of Garvey Movement was one of the great propaganda miracles of all times.

His return to Jamaica was return to struggle. He had previously tried to start the movement in Jamaica but without success. He was elected to public office and served one term before the forces of reaction made it impossible for him to continue in public service. Deeply in debt, he returned to his trade as a master printer, paid off most of his debts, and went to London, where for a number of year he edited *The Blackman* magazine and corresponded with his numerous followers throughout the world; his wife and two sons returned to Jamaica. These last London years seemed like a contradiction, unlike the early London years of learning, years of inquiry, years of broadening the scope of his dream of a unified African world.

Interest in Marcus Garvey, his movement, his hopes, and dreams were renewed during the Italian-Ethiopian War because so many of the things he had previously said had come to pass. This is best reflected in the magazine he edited, *The Blackman.* The issues of this magazine in bound or single volumes are a political education that goes beyond anything learned in a classroom. Marcus Garvey was well-informed on world affairs. He was absolutely ruthless in the criticism of the conduct of the Italian-Ethiopian War, especially from the Ethiopian side. He had said that the Ethiopian ruling class had spent so much time being an elitist ruling class that they didn't take time out to train the kind of army that could defend the country. He implied that the Ethiopia of 1935–36 was not the same Ethiopia of 1896 when the Emperor Menelik defeated the Italians in their first attempt to take over Ethiopia. When Haile Selassie left his country and settled in England briefly after the defeat of his army, Marcus Garvey was his severest critic. Marcus Garvey's criticism and appraisal of the African world through *The Blackman* would continue until his death in 1940.

For the next decade and far beyond, interest in Marcus Garvey declined. There were a number of doctoral theses written on Marcus Garvey that were not known outside of the university library where they were written. Edward David Cronon's book, *Black Moses, The Story of Marcus Garvey and the Universal Negro Improvement Association*, renewed interest in Marcus Garvey and his movement in spite of its many errors in fact and in interpretations. This book whetted the appetite of a number of scholars who had not previously known of Marcus Garvey and his movement. These scholars now began independent research. Some of them corrected Cronon's errors. Some of them introduced new errors. In the black community white interpretations of Marcus Garvey began to be challenged across the board. Whatever Mr. Cronon's intentions, he did stir up a new generation of Garvey scholars and researchers who set in motion a new inquiry into this most remarkable African figure.

Most of the governments in Africa were in some way influenced by Marcus Garvey and his teachings. He was the unseen teacher at the Fifth Pan-African Congress in Manchester, England in 1945. The ideas that came out of this congress helped to set the African Independence Movement in motion. Nearly every present-day country in Africa is an imitation of their former colonial masters. In my opinion, none of them will be truly free African independent nations until they look at values within themselves and develop an African methodology of ruling the state. These states and their rulers from 1940 to the present should have and must consider a lesson that Marcus Garvey taught repeatedly when he said at his mass rallies, referring to the whole of the African world: "Up, up, you mighty race, you can accomplish what you will."

One day in the not-too-distant future, Malcolm X will be honestly referred to as a prophet and a master teacher, because that is exactly what he was. He was both a religious and political activist. He appeared in the life of black America and in the life of the world like a bright star that faded before its full luster could be shown.

In the book that I edited, consisting of a series of articles about Malcolm X, entitled *Malcolm X: The Man and His Time*, I prefaced several articles with the following commentary.

Soon after his assassination on February 21, 1965, Malcolm X became the subject of a number of articles appraising his career and his effect on the black freedom movement. Most of these articles were too hastily written and showed no understanding of what Malcolm X and his mission meant to his people. The evaluation of Malcolm X is related to the evolution of black America in the great human drama now being called "the Black Revolution in the United States."

After the death of Malcolm X, a number of writers discussed how well they "knew" him. Some of these new "authorities" on Malcolm X would not come near him when he was alive. Black writers, however, with few exceptions, did not rush to print with hurriedly written articles on Malcolm X. They seem to have been recovering from the shock of his death. When their articles did begin to appear, they were generally better than the large number of articles by white writers that were published on Malcolm X soon after his death.

Malcolm X was forced out of the Black Muslim movement and into a dangerous wind current of history. Figuratively speaking, he did not have the time to balance himself in this wind current before he was swept off his feet and into his death. His challenge to mid-twentieth century America is both simple and complicated. He merely asked America to keep its promise of democracy to his people.

After leaving the Black Muslim movement he immediately put himself in danger by attempting to organize the black community for self-defense. He called upon all sections of the black community to formulate a solution to the problems facing Black Americans. Out of this coalition of various elements in the black community came the Organization of Afro-American Unity. His trips to Africa are significant because they took the black Americans' struggle out of the confines of the continental United States and linked it with the non-white world. The civil rights problem, to him at least, became a human rights problem and he attempted to internationalize it.

No matter how much is said about what Malcolm X was, the speculations about what he could have been will go on for a good number of years. The triumph and tragedy of his short-lived leadership have their mystique, which is, on reflection, both intriguing and sad, like the memory of lost love.

His dream of a world where his people will walk in freedom and dignity was temporarily deferred by his assassination. The assassin killed the dreamer but not the dream. This dream is the legacy he left us.

Malcolm X was easy to meet and difficult to know. He listened to all and learned from many, while being careful not to mistake the trivial for the profound. The article "The Last Days of Malcolm X" by Earl Grant was extracted from a much larger work.

Grant is one of the few people who can say that he was a personal friend and associate of Malcolm X. All of the contributors to my book knew Malcolm X personally.

Other contributors—including Betty Shabazz (Mrs. Malcolm X)—present a picture of a Malcolm X not generally known to the public. What comes through in these articles is the profound humanness of the man himself.

Malcolm X and his activities got some of the best and worst press coverage of any personality of our time. Fortunately, Malcolm X was the master of press conferences, and he always got the best out of them. Many writers arrived at sweeping conclusions about Malcolm X without ever confronting him or seriously trying to understand the nature of the movement that his personality, almost solely, brought into being. Those who viewed him at close range got a different picture than others who attempted to view him from a distance with detachment and what some people call objectivity.

The many dimensions in the personality of Malcolm X made him a difficult person to understand and interpret. He was a person always in the process of growth and change. He had outgrown the Black Muslim movement led by Elijah Muhammad long before he was forced out of it. It was inevitable that Malcolm X would see the major weakness of this movement and try to grapple with it. The major weakness is the escapist method it uses to offer identity and dignity to black Americans.

In an attempt to bolster its appeal by identification with Islam, the Black Muslim movement advocates complete withdrawal from American society—either by the concentration of all blacks (apparently to the exclusion of whites) in a part of the territory of the United States or by a mass return to Africa. This approach is not feasible under prevailing circumstances. The main consideration is this: Withdrawal from American society is most decidedly not what most black Americans want. First and foremost they want justice in a country that promises justice and dignity to all of its citizens.

The personal evolution of Malcolm X brought him to an understanding of this fact. The United States, the country that made him, was his special vantage point—his window on the world. From this vantage and from this window he attempted to see how the struggle of the Black man in the United States related to Africa, Asia, and the other parts of the so-called Third World. This was the essence of his evolution and growth.

The best interpreter of Malcolm X is Malcolm X. He was a man in transition. In his short and eventful lifetime, he made many changes because he learned many things. Most important of all, he learned how to correct himself. He was principally a speaker and his style was one of the most effective of any orator of this century. His language was direct and to the point and could be understood on all educational levels. His speech "Message to the Grass Roots," delivered in November 1963, is a perfect example of his mastery of language and the projection of ideas. It was this kind of creativity in Malcolm X that literally built the Black Muslim movement in the United States. This speech also proves that Malcolm X was an astute revolutionary theoretician.

The speech "God's Judgment of White America" set in motion or brought to the surface the difficulties precipitating the forces and circumstances that caused him to be forced out of the Black Muslim movement.

The speeches of Malcolm X in Africa are bridge building efforts that were partly successful. The fact that these speeches were made at all is remarkable. Even more remarkable is the fact that they were listened to respectfully by most of the heads of state in Africa, who responded quite favorably to the message of Malcolm X.

The African projection of Malcolm X and his brief travels in Africa, on behalf of the plight of black Americans, showed that he had an insight into the worldwide struggle of black people that was over and above that of any other designated leader. His speech to the domestic Peace Corps, made in December 1964, proves again how effective Malcolm X was in getting his message across to young people. To them he was more than a public orator; he was a great teacher and an intellectual father.

The article "Some Reflections on 'Negro History Week' and the Role of the Black People in History" is an excerpt from the pamphlet *Malcolm X on Afro-American History*. Malcolm X clearly understood that history is an instrument of both enslavement and liberation, and he was trying to tell his people, especially the young, how to use history affirmatively.

While the untimely death of Malcolm X is tragic and unfortunate, the positive aspect is that he left behind a philosophy of liberation. When seen in total context, it will effect his emergence as the finest revolutionary theoretician and activist produced by America's black working class in this century.

The life of Malcolm X was shaped by social and political forces over which he had no control. We have to examine his life in retrospect in order to understand how these forces shaped his destiny from early childhood until his untimely death. He was born in the midwest section of the United States that had never boasted of a large black population. He had a black American father who was a Garveyite and a mother from the island of Grenada. His father was killed by the Northern version of the Ku Klux Klan early in his life before Malcolm X could understand the meaning of such atrocities. His mother slowly began to lose her mental balance which would subsequently cause her to lose her children. This scar on the mind of Malcolm X would later influence his early manhood and his search for direction in the definition of his people on this earth.

When a white teacher tried to discourage him from pursuing professions beyond menial labor, he suspected that there was something wrong with the society itself that put a limitation on his ambitions. His best education was outside of the classroom. In order to survive, he had to do many things that he would later teach others to avoid. He was a waiter in a restaurant in Harlem, a hustler, a dope-taker and a dope dealer, and, to some extent, a petty gangster. He lived with his sister for a while in Boston, where he was arrested on a robbery charge and spent some time in jail. He did not know it at the time, but the jail was his university, the place of dramatic change and awakening. He was introduced to the Islamic faith and began to exercise some discipline over his own action. He was always a man whose physical bearing commanded respect. He read literature pertaining to Islam and became fascinated with words. To pursue this fascination, he began to seriously study the dictionary, starting with the meaning of the letter "A." This was a crude approach to self-education, yet it was thorough. When released from jail, he was introduced to Elijah Muhammad, who became for him the father he had been wanting all of his life. His loyalty to Elijah Muhammad and his interpretation of Islam influenced his life like a purifying ritual.

Malcolm X became the representation of the Nation of Islam in New York and gradually, through his speeches and his challenge to non-Moslems, gave that religion and its followers a public presence they otherwise would never have had. He was liked by both Moslems and non-Moslems, who respected and followed him. He became a most sought-after speaker and a merciless debater. Very often, when he was prefacing his remarks with the statement, "the Honorable Elijah Muhammad teaches us that . . . , " he was teaching original lessons of his own over and above anything the Honorable Elijah Muhammad had ever thought about. On the eve of the March on Washington in 1963, he requested permission from Elijah Muhammad to participate in this activity. Permission was not granted. The occasional illness of Elijah Muhammad made a lot of the male members of the group—especially those in the Fruit of Islam, an organization that Malcolm X had helped to develop—jealous of Malcolm's influence and position in the Nation. They assumed that in the event Elijah Muhammad died, Malcolm X would be his logical successor.

Malcolm X's speech at Manhattan Center in New York, when he referred to the death of President Kennedy as "chickens coming home to roost," seemed to be the flaw that his detractors were looking for. Malcolm X was suspended from the Nation soon after the speech. This was announced as a thirty-day suspension. When the thirty days were almost up, and Malcolm had not heard from Elijah Muhammad, he founded his own organizations, Muslim Mosque Inc. and the Organization of African-American Unity, modeled after the Organization of African Unity.

His trips to Africa were of historical importance. His interpretation of what he saw while in Mecca is terribly distorted and misused. The essence of what he said is that he saw Moslems of every color, from white to extreme black, worshipping in the same religion and showing respect for one another. Too many times this has been interpreted as meaning that Malcolm X had suddenly turned into an integrationist. Nothing is further from the truth.

Malcolm X understood the forces in the world that had oppressed his people. He never forgave them. He never forgot them. His speech,

"A Message to the Grass Roots," was one of the clearest revolutionary documents of the twentieth century. In this speech Malcolm X deals with the land as a part of nation. He also deals with nationalism as the cohesive force that holds a nation together. This and others of Malcolm's speeches need to be carefully and seriously read. Malcolm X was ahead of his time. In the more than twenty years since his death, he continues to be ahead of most of the progressive thinkers on black liberation. His autobiography, written with Alex Haley, needs to be read by the generation that did not know him personally. An in-depth analysis needs to be made of his trip to Ghana and his meeting with Nkrumah. Alice Windom, of St. Louis, Missouri, has written a graphic account of his days in Ghana.

I have said elsewhere that in another country, under other circumstances, Malcolm X might have been a king and a great one. By extension, in a country that is true to its Christian and democratic promise, he might have been anything he wanted to be if his talent gave him the ability to be it. The black community of Harlem was Malcolm's window on the world. From this window he saw the world and became, in his own time, a man of international significance.

Unfortunately, nearly all African revolutions in the twentieth century were aborted because the monumental international forces that had been controlling most of African economic wealth, through control of the mineral and human resources, had no intention of letting Africa fall into African hands. To assure their hold on Africa, they cleverly programmed African people into a form of dependency that gave them access to the development of Africa's wealth. After the independence of Ghana in 1957, the Independence Explosion began to spread throughout the rest of Africa; many Africans were prepared to rule the state apparatus but were not technically prepared to rule the wealth.

Unfortunately again, most Africans had lost from their historical memories all they ever knew about the ages in history when they ruled their respective countries without foreign assistance or foreign interference. Because the African people of the world have not seriously studied the last one thousand years of African history *before* the slave trade, they are not prepared to prophesy and plan the one thousand years *after* the slave trade. Therefore it can be said sadly that the Independence Explosion in Africa came both too soon and too late.

Most of the Africans who became heads of state were European-educated. Their style and methodology for running a state was a poor carbon copy of the European original, because the traditional African method of running the state had been lost from their memory. Many Africans assumed that they were freeing themselves from colonialism while sadly being trapped into another form of colonialism. This is what I have often referred to as the evil genius of Europe. No invader came to Africa to train Africans to be independent and free of their influence. This is just as true of the Arabs, who are also invaders, having been in Africa for only a little over a thousand years.

Tom Mboya was a product of East Africa, the most invaded part of the continent. On this subject we need to consult Reginald Copland's work, *East Africa and Its Invaders*, and another book by Sir Harry Johnston, *The Colonization of Africa by Alien Races*. This is a part of Africa where another slave trade drama unfolded that is well-documented and still comparatively unknown. I am referring to the Arab slave trade that started a thousand years before the Atlantic, or European, slave trade in West Africa and for a period just as devastating. The Arabs have not been called on to answer for their crimes in Africa, because their crimes are not well-known and because the millions of Africans who became Muslims in Africa are willing to excuse or to forget their crimes.

The coming of the European to East Africa had as its rationale the stopping of the Arab slave trade. To some extent this was achieved, but the Europeans began another form of slavery called colonialism. At the turn of the century, European settlers began to seize the best land in East Africa, sometimes referred to as the White Highlands. Kenyan Jomo Kenyatta dealt in part with this situation in his book *Facing Mount Kenya* but more directly in a pamphlet, *Kenya, Land of Friendship*. The documentation of the history like the history of Africa in general, is the history of invaders and the clash of cultures as well as the African's attempt to survive and prevail in the midst of this political storm.

Tom Mboya came to public attention in the midst of a political storm referred to as the Mau Mau uprising. When I first wrote about him in 1960, I referred to him as the "world's youngest statesman," which indeed he was at the time. He was one of the three shining lights in Africa during that period; the other two Abdel Nasser of Egypt and Kwame Nkrumah of Ghana. He had one of the sharpest minds of his day. Though he was not fully university-trained, he had a quick and ready facility in dealing with world politics in general and African politics in particular. At press conferences, he never panicked or lost his composure or failed to have an intelligent answer for any question that was put to him.

We will never know where the five African revolutionists mentioned in this section could have gone or what they could have been had their lives continued. They were all cut down while they were still growing.

Their lives tell us something about what African people will have to know in the future about the preparation for leadership and the protection of their leaders.

It is clear that the powerful and evil forces intent on controlling Africa and its resources will not allow a strong leader to appear in Africa who will explain to Africa the true nature of power and what to do with it. It is also clear that the next cadre of leaders in Africa must prepare African people to assume a position in world power. Therefore, responsibility to protect them from the forces whose intent is to control Africa and its resources by any means necessary.

This is a problem and a responsibility not only for the Africans who live in Africa but for all of the African people of the world. We must realize symbolically and figuratively, no matter where our bodies are geographically, our political and cultural heartbeat is in Africa.

It is Pan-African nationalism or nothing! African people must make an alliance with themselves before they seriously think of making an alliance with other people.

The greatest memorial we can have for the five revolutionists mentioned here and their incomplete revolutions is to complete the revolutions they started, because in different ways using different methods all of them were working toward the liberation of all African people on the face of the earth. Our mission should be to complete their revolution and the completion should be the legacy that we leave for our people and for all people.

KWAME NKRUMAH

The Political Rehearsal:

His American Years

▼

THERE IS NO WAY to understand the late Dr. Kwame Nkrumah, or any other man, without also understanding the country in which he was born and to what extent that country and the circumstances of his birth did influence the total of his life.

The Gold Coast (now Ghana) was a colony whose people never acknowledged their colonial status. They engaged the British in a series of wars, known as The Ashanti Wars, that lasted over a hundred years. In these wars the people let it be known that they would never live peacefully under foreign domination.

When Kwame Nkrumah was born in 1903, these military wars were over, and a new kind of leader emerged in this country. E. Casely Hayford was the most outstanding of these new men.

Kwame Nkrumah grew to manhood while the agitation against the restrictions of colonial rule was being converted into the agitation for eventual independence. When he left Ghana for additional education in 1935, the great E. Casely Hayford had died and the mantle of leadership had fallen on the shoulders of Dr. Joseph B. Danquah, former schoolmaster of Kwame Nkrumah.

Nkrumah now began what can be referred to as his American years. In the writings about this period in the life of Kwame Nkrumah the significance of these years is grossly underrated. The influence of the

101

ten years spent in the United States would have a lingering effect on the rest of his life.

He began his preparation to continue his education in the United States early in 1935. In the late summer of that year his plans were completed. First, he visited a relative in Lagos, Nigeria, in order to raise some funds. In his journey to the United States he stopped in Liverpool and in London, where he learned that the dictator, Mussolini, had invaded Ethiopia. This added to his depression and awakened his nationalism. His first lessons in the working of international colonialism and how it operates were now being learned. This learning was later reflected in his pamphlet, *Towards Colonial Freedom*, published in London in 1947, two years after the historic fifth Pan-African Congress in Manchester, England. This sadly neglected early work by Kwame Nkrumah is a key to his thinking and a clear indication of what his future development and direction would be. In the foreword to the 1962 reprint of this pamphlet he said: "When I was a student in the United States I was so revolted by the ruthless colonial exploitation and political oppression of the people of Africa that I knew no peace. The matter exercised my mind to such a degree that I decided to put down my thoughts in writing and to dilate on the results of some of my research concerning the subject of colonialism and imperialism."

He now began to organize his long essay "Africa in the Struggle Against World Imperialism," which was published years later as a book under the title *Towards Colonial Freedom*. He was unable to find anyone who would undertake to publish this work at this time. The important point that I am trying to make here is this: That from the vantage point of the United States, with its large internal colony of exploited black people, the student and later teacher, Kwame Nkrumah, saw a picture of world imperialism that he could not have seen in any other country. This vantage point and what he saw set the thought pattern in motion that resulted in the writing of *Towards Colonial Freedom*. This little book reflects the basis of the political and philosophical thought of Kwame Nkrumah.

He had arrived in the United States during the fall of 1935. He had been accepted at Lincoln University in Pennsylvania. The acceptance had not come easily. On March 1, 1935, he had sent an urgent letter to the Rev. G. Johnson, dean of students at Lincoln reminding him that over a year had passed since he had applied for permission to enter the school. His admission card came in August. This application blank that was sent to him by Lincoln University stated among other things that the applicant should write a brief story of his life and his reasons for wanting to attend this school. The following is the essence of what he wrote:

> I neither know where to begin nor where to end because I feel the story of my life has not been one of achievements. Furthermore, I have not been anxious to tell people of what may have been accomplished by me. In truth, the burden of my life can be summarized into a single line in "The Memorandum" quoted by Cecil Rhodes—"so much to do so little done . . . ." In all things I have held myself to but one ambition and that is to make necessary arrangements to continue my education in a university in the United States of America, that I may be better prepared to serve my fellowman . . . .

The statement sums up Nkrumah's philosophy of life-service to his fellowman.

He arrived in New York toward the end of October and proceeded to Lincoln University, where he enrolled without having enough funds for one semester's tuition. This was the beginning of his American years.

Black Americans were becoming more Africa conscious. The Italian-Ethiopian War was responsible for this new interest and anger about Africa. A number of study groups showed interest in African history. The best known of these groups was the Blyden Society, named after the great nationalist and benefactor of West Africa—Edward Wilmot Blyden. (I personally remember Kwame Nkrumah attending several meetings of this society.)

He was also active in the Ethiopian Students Union and other African student associations. In these years there were very few white people who were interested in African students. Most of the African students who were going to colleges in New York City lived in Harlem. In the summers away from Lincoln University, Kwame Nkrumah lived in Harlem. The first summer that he spent in Harlem was the most difficult. Jobs were hard to find and so were decent inexpensive places to stay. He soon discovered that his investment in fish far exceeded his profit. Now he was without a job again and without a place to stay.

In his autobiography *Ghana*, he writes about this difficult period in the following manner:

> I was wandering down Seventh Avenue in Harlem wondering where I could turn next when I suddenly ran into a fellow student from Lincoln who came from Demerara in British Guinea. I told him of my difficulties: no money, no job and nowhere to go. "Don't worry, old chap," he said encouragingly, "I think I can solve the accommodation problem as a start." He explained that he knew a West Indian family who were extremely kind and sympathetic and that if he went along and put my case before them, he felt they might help me out. Sure enough, by the time I had told my story tears were in the eyes of the womenfolk who offered me this small spare room, and added that I was not to worry about the payment until I managed to find a job.

In spite of the hardships he had some kind of social life. He tells us further that:

> It was through a doctor friend of this family that I was introduced to my first girl friend in America. This was Edith, a nurse at Harlem Hospital. I must have been a great disappointment to her. I was quite penniless so, apart from taking her for walks and gazing into shop windows, I could not offer her much in the way of entertainment. And I must have been a bit of a bore because my favorite amusement at that time was to stand and listen to soap-box orators at the street corners. I was quite happy to spend my evenings there either quietly listening or, as was more often the case, provoking arguments with them.

These evenings were a vital part of Kwame Nkrumah's American education. He was going to a university—the university of the Harlem streets. This was no ordinary time and these street speakers were no ordinary men. This was the period during, and immediately after, the Italian-Ethiopian War. The streets of Harlem were open forums, presided over by master speakers like Arthur Reed and his protégé Ira Kemp. The young Carlos Cook, founder of the Garvey-oriented African Pioneer Movement was on the scene, also bringing a nightly message to his street followers. Occasionally, Suji Abdul Hamis, a champion of Harlem labor, held a night rally and demanded more jobs for blacks in their own community. He had started the movement for community jobs in Chicago in 1930, where he was then known as Bishop Conshankin. He was a powerfully built black man and he often dressed himself up in a bright colored cape, high Russian boots, and a Hindu-like turban. His slogan was, "More Jobs for Negroes: Buy Where You Can Work."

This is part of the drama that was unfolding on the Harlem streets as the student, Kwame Nkrumah, walked and watched. Another part of this drama was the rebirth of interest in "The Philosophy and Opinions of Marcus Garvey."

During these depression years Nkrumah began to learn how hard it was for black people in this country just to stay alive and support their families. Once more in his own words he says:

> It was around about this time that I found a job in a soap factory. I had imagined that I would leave work each day exuding that scent of roses or honeysuckle, but this was far from the case. It turned out to be by far the filthiest and most unsavory job that I ever had ... at the end of two weeks I was almost fit to be transformed into a bar of soap myself. My limbs ached so much at the day's end that I to rub myself nightly with liniment before I could hope to get any sleep and build up enough energy to tackle the next day. A doctor friend of mine advised me strongly to leave the job. If I did not, he said, I would certainly never complete my education in America.

In order to survive in America he still needed a job. He joined the National Maritime Union and every summer thereafter, until the outbreak of the Second World War in September 1939, managed to get employment at sea.

The Blyden Society, the Ethiopian World Federation, and other organizations attracted a number of African supporters. Some of them were students like Kwame Nkrumah. The American Black Press improved its coverage of news about Africa. In the reporting on the Italian-Ethiopian War this press was fortunate in having in its service at least two reporters who had been well-schooled in African history in general. The reporters were J.A. Rogers, an historian and journalist and Dr. Willis N. Huggins, historian, teacher, and community activist. In his dispatches from Ethiopia, J.A. Rogers gave an astute analysis of the war to the *Pittsburgh Courier*. He was the only reporter on the scene who was looking at the conflict from a black perspective. Rogers also commented on the political intrigues in Europe that led to this conflict. Later, in a small book, *The Real Facts about Ethiopia*, he digested his reports and produced the most revealing document about the Italian-Ethiopian War that had then appeared in print.

Dr. Willis N. Huggins, a high school history teacher and founder of the Blyden Society for the Study of African History, went to Geneva and reported on the League of Nations meetings concerning the Italian-Ethiopian War for the *Chicago Defender*. Dr. Huggins had already written two books on Africa: *A Guide to Studies in African History* and *Introduction to African Civilizations*.

In the collective talent of J.A. Rogers and Dr. Huggins the Afro—American press was fortunate enough to have two keen observers who could see through the subterfuge and pretenses of the European powers and their frantic schemes to keep their African colonies. Both Rogers and Huggins saw behind and beyond the headlines and foretold the future repercussions of Ethiopia's betrayal. Their reports were a high-water mark in black American journalism.

Kwame Nkrumah came to America during this period and into this atmosphere. The "Back-to-Africa" teaching of Marcus Garvey was now being reconsidered. The Harlem Literary Renaissance had died. The black urban communities, especially in the North were entering a renaissance of African consciousness and nationalism. The first nation-wide black student unions were formed. The unions included African students from all over the continent. The attack on Ethiopians and the reemergence of Garveyism and the hardships of the depression years had created a semblance of unity among black Americans.

Kwame Nkrumah's plans for the eventual independence of his country were formulated during his student years in the United States. In his book *Kwame Nkrumah*, Bankole Timothy writes that Nkrumah dreamed of organizing all Africans in the United States so that they might return and perform useful services for Africa. He was the moving force behind the organization of the first General Conference of Africans in America in September 1942. At the same time he dreamed of a West African Federation and together with Nuamdi Arikiwe of Nigeria and Durosimi Johnson of Sierra Leone, planned on returning to their respective countries to start political agitation toward this objective.

An analysis of the colonial situation and the essence of the objective is contained in the following statement of purpose taken from Kwame Nkrumah's book *Towards Colonial Freedom:*

What Must Be Done

We have demonstrated that the imperial powers will never give up their political and economic dominance over their colonies until they are compelled to do so. Therefore, we suggest the following general plan, theory and method, leaving the details to be filled in by the truly enlightened leadership that will carry out the colonial liberation.

The growth of the national liberation movement in the colonies reveals:

(1) The contradictions among the various foreign groups and the colonial imperialist powers in their struggle for sources of raw materials and for territories. In this sense imperialism and colonialism become the export of capital to sources of raw materials, the frenzied and heartless struggle for monopolist possession of these sources, the struggle for a redivision of the already divided world—a struggle waged with particular fury by new financial groups and powers seeking new territories and colonies against the old groups and powers which cling tightly to that which they have grabbed.

(2) The contradictions between the handful of ruling "civilized" nations and the millions of colonial peoples of the world. In this sense imperialism is the most degrading exploitation and the most inhuman oppression of the millions of peoples living in the colonies. The purpose of this exploitation and oppression is to squeeze out super-

profits. The inevitable results of imperialism thus are: (a)
the emergence of a colonial intelligentsia, (b) the awakening of national consciousness among colonial peoples,
(c) the emergence of a working class movement, and d)
the growth of a national liberation movement.

In present-day historical development, West Africa represents the focus of all these contradictions of imperialism.

Theoretical Basis

The theory of the national liberation movement in colonial
countries proceeds from three fundamental theses:

The dominance of finance capital in the advanced capitalist
countries; the export of capital to the sources of raw materials
(imperialism) and the omnipotence of a financial oligarchy
(finance capital) reveal the character of monopolist capital
which quickens the revolt of the intelligentsia and the working
class elements of the colonies against imperialism and brings
them to the national liberation movement as their only salvation.

He continued the development of his plan against colonialism in
this manner:

The duty of any worthwhile colonial movement for national
liberation, he says, however, must be the organization of labor
and youth; and the abolition of political illiteracy. This should
be accomplished through mass political education which keeps
in constant contact with the masses of colonial peoples. This
type of education should do away with that kind of intelligentsia
who have become the very architects of colonial enslavement.

These thoughts were developed in the United States, five years
before Kwame Nkrumah returned to Ghana. His political thought
reached maturity during his "American years." The influence of these
years extended through his entire political career.

The African Students Association in America continued to grow
both in strength and in numbers. The association magazine *The African*

Interpreter contained many analytical and angry articles about Africa. Among the Gold Coast students who were regular contributors to the magazine were: Ako Adjei, who later became minister of the interior in the first government after the independence of Ghana, and K.A.B. Jones-Quartey, who later headed the Institute of Extra-Mural Studies at the University College, Achimota.

In his autobiography *Ghana*, Kwame Nkrumah says:

> My ten years in America had been happy and eventful, but at the same time they had been remarkably strenuous. Life would have been so much easier if I could have devoted all of my time to study. As things were, however, I was always in need of money and had to work out ways and means of earning my livelihood.

In 1945, Nkrumah, now living in London and associated with George Padmore, was one of the conveners of the Fifth Pan-African Congress. Most of the ideas that led to the African Freedom explosion came out of this Congress. George Padmore's report on the formation of this Congress is as follows:

> The Pan-African idea died, apparently, until fifteen years afterwards, in the midst of the second World War, when it leaped to life again in an astonishing manner. At the Trades Union Conference in London in the winter of 1945 there were black labour representatives from Africa and the West Indies. Among these, aided by coloured persons resident in England, there came a spontaneous call for the assembling of another Pan-African Congress in 1945, when the International Trade Union had their meeting in Paris.
>
> After consultation and correspondence a Pan-African Federation was organized.
>
> On August eleventh and twelfth there was convened at Manchester, the headquarters of the Pan-African Federation, a Delegate Conference representing all of the organizations which have been invited to participate in the forthcoming Congress. At that ad hoc meeting a review of the preparatory work was made. From the reports it revealed that the position was as

follows:

> A number of replies had been received from Labour,
> Trade Union, Co-operative, and other progressive organiza-
> tions in the West Indies, West Africa, South and East
> Africa, in acknowledgment of the formal invitation to
> attend the Conference. Most of these bodies not only
> approved and endorsed the agenda, making minor modifica-
> tions and suggestions here and there, but pledged themselves
> to send delegates. In cases where either the time is too short
> or the difficulties of transport at the present time too great
> to be overcome at such short notice, the organizations will
> give mandates to the natives of the territories concerned
> who are traveling to Paris to attend the World Trades
> Union Conference. Where territories will not be sending
> delegates to the Trades Union Conference, organizations will
> mandate individuals already in Great Britain to represent
> them.
>
> In this way we are assured of the widest representation,
> either through people traveling directly from the colonial
> areas to Britain, or individuals from those territories who are
> already in the British Isle. Apart from these overseas dele-
> gates, more than fourteen organizations of Africans and
> peoples of African descent in Great Britain and Ireland will
> participate in the Conference.

This Pan-African Congress brought together the greatest diversity
of African people since the heyday of Marcus Garvey. The political
development of Kwame Nkrumah, which had been accentuated by his
ten years in the United States, went into the making of this Congress.
Dr. W.E.B. DuBois, who was a participant in the Congress makes this
statement in the booklet, "History of the Pan-African Congress"
(1963).

> I especially remember that great Pan-African Congress of 1945,
> held in Manchester, England, whose co-secretaries were those
> who have gone on to become Founder of the Republic of
> Ghana, Dr. Kwame Nkrumah, and that valiant, intrepid leader,

Jomo Kenyatta, who will not stop until Kenya has attained its full independence. George Padmore was the organizing spirit of that congress. There were many others there with whom I have worked through the years and whom the world should remember. For that was a decisive year in determining the freedom of Africa.

Kwame Nkrumah returned to his country in 1947 and worked for a while for the United Gold Coast Convention, then the prevailing political party. Having returned home after more than ten years abroad he was restless and impatient with the slow pace of progress and the lack of commitment on the part of the British on the demands for independence. The people of the Gold Coast were fired with the idea of nationhood.

But it was not until 1949, after the impact of the second world war, that this movement received a fresh and powerful impetus from the formation of the Convention People's Party under the leadership of Dr. Kwame Nkrumah. The new party, which was founded following a split in the United Gold Coast Convention (hitherto the leading nationalist body in the country) proved to be immediately popular and new members, attracted by its insistent demand for "Self-Government Now," flocked to join its rank.

Popularity is not, however, necessarily synonymous with success, and the road to self-government and eventual independence was long and arduous. In 1950, Nkrumah and several other leading CPP members were imprisoned in James Fort, Accra, on charges that arose as a result of pursuing a policy of "positive action" against the government.

Meanwhile, an All-African committee had been appointed to inquire into constitutional reform. As a result of its findings, a general election was held in January 1951, and for the first time, an African majority was granted a considerable measure of responsibility. This majority was held by the CPP, which had won 34 out of 38 seats in the Legislative Council. In jail with Kwame Nkrumah at the time of these elections was Kojo Botsio, one of his leading lieutenants, as well as many other of his close associates. It fell therefore to K.A. Gbedemah, another leading lieutenant, who had himself been released from jail a few months earlier, to act as chairman of the CPP at this time and to organize the victorious election.

Immediately after Dr. Nkrumah was released to become leader of government business, and later by a constitutional amendment, Prime Minister. But half-measures were not enough to satisfy the party's demands for freedom. Thus in September 1951, Dr. Nkrumah issued a broadsheet emphasizing that, despite the recognition they had received, he and his fellow CPP ministers were working according to plan for the attainment of full independence. The broadsheet took the form of a challenge to the pary's political opponents:

> We of the Convention People's Party have made it plain that we are working according to plan but we are nevertheless prepared to re-adjust or even change our tactics and strategy if our detractors and opponents accept the challenge to join us in declaring Positive Action for Self-Government Now. My colleagues and I are prepared to resign from the Government immediately if the so-called opposition parties ... join me and my Party in staging Positive Active for full SG now.

The state of Ghana came into existence on March 6, 1957, when the former Gold Coast colony, Ashanti, the northern territories of the Gold Coast, and the Trusteeship territory of Togoland attained Dominion status and independence. The name of the country recalls a powerful monarchy that from the fourth to the thirteenth centuries A.D. ruled the region of the middle Niger. The Ghana Independence Act received the Royal assent on February 7, 1957. The General Assembly of the United Nations, in December 1956, had approved the termination of British adminstration in Togoland. Togoland became an integral part of Ghana.

Kwame Nkrumah's greatest achievement was in the area of Pan-Africanism. He made his country the rallying point and the inspiration for African countries who had to win their freedom. He was the first universal African hero of this century. He, more than any other person, figuratively took Africa and its people for their "walk in the sun." He extended his aspiration beyond Pan-Africanism and introduced the possibility of an African World Union.

As a result of Kwame Nkrumah's understanding of the plight of African-Americans and of his awareness that so much of their skill was unused in this country, he established a better relationship with black

Americans that no other African head of state has done before or since. During the period when he was in power, he employed more black Americans than all of the other African states combined. This is one way that he used to spell out his Pan-African concept and his belief in the eventuality of an African World Union.

He was Africa's magnificent dreamer. He dared to believe that African people could be the masters of their destiny. In an editorial in the magazine, *Africa*, the writer Ralph Uwechme has said: "The death of Kwame Nkrumah in exile in a foreign land and in political disgrace may remain forever a dark spot on the conscience of the entire African world.... Whatever else he was, Nkrumah was by his words and works the leading African citizen of our generation."

He was the best example of dynamic African leadership to emerge in this century. Nearly ten years before his death, in his book *Africa Must Unite*, he said what the new African citizens and their leaders would have to be.

"Africa needs a new type of citizen," he said, "a dedicated, modest, honest, informed man. A man who submerges self in service to his nation and mankind. A man who abhors greed and detests vanity. A new type of man whose humanity is his strength and whose integrity is his greatness."

PATRICE LUMUMBA AND THE UNFINISHED REVOLUTION IN THE CONGO (ZAIRE)

▼

THE LIFE OF PATRICE LUMUMBA proved that he was a product of the best and worst of Belgian colonial rule. In more favorable circumstances, he might have become one of the most astute national leaders of the twentieth century. He was cut down long before he had time to develop into the more stable leader that he was obviously capable of being. When the Congo emerged clearly in the light of modern history he was its bright star.

His hero was Dr. Kwame Nkrumah, and the model for his state was Ghana. "In a young state, " he had said, paraphrasing a similar statement made by Dr. Nkrumah, "you must have strong and visible powers."

At the beginning of his political career he was pro-Western in his outlook. "Mistakes have been made in Africa in the past, but we are ready to work with the powers which have been in Africa to create a powerful new bloc," he said at the beginning of 1960. "If this effort fails, it will be through the fault of the West."

As a reformer he was somewhat of a republican in his approach. "Our need is to democratize all our institutions." he had said on another occasion. "We must separate the Church from the State. We must take away all power from the traditional chiefs and remove all privileges. We must adapt socialism to African realities. Amelioration of the conditions of life is the only true meaning independence can have."

His resentment of Belgian authority was unyielding in most cases. Mostly because he believed that paternalism was at the base of this

115

authority. This by-product of colonialism never failed to stir a rage within him. On the other hand, his reaction to the Belgian Missionary attempt to enforce Christianity on the Congo was one of indifference. He had been subjected to both Catholic and Protestant mission influence, without showing any particular affection for either. His parents were devout Catholics. Being neither an atheist nor anti-Christian, he yet considered submission to a religion to be a curb to his ambitions. Rebellion was more rewarding and less wounding to his pride. During his long and lonely rise from obscurity to the Congo's first Prime Minister, he taught himself never to completely trust power in the hands of others. This attitude is reflected in the suspicion that developed between him and the UN forces in the Congo.

His conflicts with the other Congo politicians was due mainly to his unyielding belief in the unitary state and partly to his lack of experience in explaining, organizing, and administering such a state. Nevertheless, he was the only Congolese leader with anything like a national following, a point too often overlooked. His greatest achievement in the early difficult months of Congo independence was in maintaining, with only a few defections, the solidarity of his widely disparate coalition government.

Lumumba belonged to the company of Kwame Nkrumah, Julius Nyerere in Tanganyika, Tom Mboya in Kenya, and Sékou Touré. These leaders believed that the only way to build an effective modern state free from the shackles of narrow tribal loyalties is to create a single, strong central government. This firm stand joined the issues in the Congo and created both the supporters and the opposition to Lumumba.

He argued his case at the Round Table Conference that gave the Congo its independence in 1960. He laid it before the electorate in June 1960, and won an indecisive victory. Finally, he tried to force it on his Federalist opponents when he took control of the first independent government. Most of Lumumba's critics considered this to be his greatest error. He tried to cast the Congo into the tight mould of Ghana, rather than into the larger, more accommodating mould of Nigeria. The argument is interesting though useless now.

Patrice Lumumba's body now lies a-moldering in some unmarked and inglorious Congo grave ... both his truth and spirit go marching on, much to the discomfort of his murderers.

No other personality in African history has leaped so suddenly from death to martyrdom. In death he might have already made a greater contribution to the liberation and understanding of Africa than he could have made had he lived. In his short lifetime the stamp of his personality was pressed firmly into the African continent. He was purely an African of the mid-twentieth century. No other place and no other set of circumstances could have charged his life and caused his death in the same unique and tragic way. In death, he cast forth a spirit that will roam the African land for many years to come.

For a long time the Congo appeared to be a peaceful island untouched by African anticolonialism. In the twelve brief years between 1946 and 1958, the Belgians began to lose what had appeared to be an impregnable position. Some important events occurred in Africa and the rest of the world, and broke up the trinity (peaceful arrangement) in Belgium's alleged "perfect colony." A change of political direction in Brussels and mounting nationalist pressure coming from within Africa helped to end the illusion that all was well and would stay well in the Congo. At last the Belgians began to have some second thoughts about their policy in the Congo. The missionary-trained evolved, the supposedly emancipated, Westernized middle class had found their voices.

Certain fundamental problems formed the core of the colonial dilemma in Africa; although Belgian colonists chose to ignore this fact. The same problems existed in the Congo as elsewhere in Africa. Freedom, self-determination, hatred of racial discrimination, and white settlement without assimilation made the Congo people feel unwanted in their own country, except as servants for white people.

It was within this order of ideas that the Belgian Socialist Party attempted to change the trend of Belgium's colonial policy and devise a more humane approach to the problems of the Congo people. The accelerated economic development in the Congo during the war and after the war had changed the structure of the Congolese community. The black population of Leopodville rose from 46,900 to 191,000 between 1940 and 1950. By 1955, the black population of Leopoldville had reached some 300,000. The mass exodus of Congolese from rural areas and their concentration in urban centers created new problems. The detribalized workers did not return to their respective villages when the city no longer afforded them employment.

It was incumbent upon the Belgian Socialist Party to define its position in relation to the Congo. As far as basic premises were concerned, the party did recognize "the primacy of native interests; and the aim of its activity will be to prepare the indigenous population gradually to take charge of its own political, economic, and social affairs, within the framework of a democratic society." Further, the party expressed its "uncompromising opposition to any kind of racial discrimination" and advised a raise in the standard of living of the people of the Congo. Only those whites who are prepared to work for the realization of these aims and who constitute the administrative personnel of the indigenous population are to enjoy the support of the government. This preparation for self-government presupposes the political organization of the Congo, i.e., the initiation of the native into citizenship. With this proposal the Belgian Socialist Party admitted that the Congolese were not accepted as citizens in their own country. This fact had been the cause of a broadening dissatisfaction among the Congolese since the early part of the twentieth century. With the relaxing of political restriction this dissatisfaction began to manifest itself in a form of embryo nationalism. The future Congolese leaders had already begun to gather their first followers. All of the early political parties in the Congo were the outgrowth of regional and tribal associations. Patrice Lumumba was the only Congolese leader who, from the very beginning of his career, attempted to build a Congo-wide political organization.

During his short-lived career Patrice Lumumba was the first popularly elected Congolese Government Prime Minister. Like a few men before him, he became a near-legend in his own life time. The influence of this legend extended to the young militant nationalists far beyond the borders of the Congo, and it is still spreading.

Of all the leaders who suffered imprisonment at the hands of the Belgians before 1960, Lumumba had the largest number of followers among the Congolese masses, mainly because he had more of the qualities of character with which they liked to identify, i.e., the ability to communicate, naturalness, and an identification with family. As a speaker he was equally effective in French, Ki-Swahili, or Lingola. The devotion of the rank and file of his party, Movement National Congolairs (MNC), to Patrice Lumumba was not a unique phenomenon. More significant is the fact that he was able to attract the strongly expressed loyalties of a tribally-heterogeneous body of the Congolese. This made him the only national political leader. While other politicians tended to take advantage of their respective associations as the path to power, Lumumba took the broader and more nationalistic approach and involved himself in other movements only indirectly related to politics.

In 1951, he joined the Association des Evolves de Stanleyville, one of the most active and numerically important of all the clubs in Orientale Province. He was in the same year appointed Secretary-General of the Association des Postiers de la Province Orientale—a professional organization consisting mostly of postal workers. Two years later he became vice-chairman of an Alumni Association consisting of former mission students. In 1956, he founded the *Amicle Liberale de Stanleyville*.

Patrice Lumumba was a member of the Beteteta tribe, a Mongo subgroup. He was born on July 2, 1925, in Katako-Kombe in the Sunkuru district of the Kasai Province. In growing up he only received a primary school education. Very early in life he learned to push himself beyond the formal limits of his education. He made frequent contributions to local newspapers such as *Stanleyvillois* and the more widely read publications, *Voix du Congolais* and *Crois du Congo*. Unlike the vast majority of Congolese writers of the period who placed major emphasis on the cultural heritage of their own tribes, Lumumba's early writings emphasized—within the limits of Belgian official restrictions—problems of racial, social, and economic discrimination.

On July 1, 1956, the career of Patrice Lumumba was temporarily interrupted when he was arrested on the charge of embezzling 126,000 francs ($2,200) from the post office funds. He was sentenced to serve a two-year prison term. On June 13,1957, the sentence was commuted on appeal to eighteen months, and finally to twelve months after the "wolves" (supporters) of Stanleyville reimbursed the sum in question. Subsequently, Lumumba left Stanleyville and found employment in Leopoldville as the sale director of the Bracongo (polar beer) Brewery.

Leopoldville became a good vantage point for Lumumba's Congo-wide activities. He had now entered into the crucial phase of his political career. In 1958, while combining the functions of vice-chairman of a liberal friendship society, the *Circle Liberal d'Etudes et d'Agreement*, with those of the president of the *Association des Batetela*, of Leopoldville, he joined a Christian Democratic Study Group, the *Centre d'Etudes et de Recherches Sociales*, created in 1955 by the Secretary General of the *Jeunesses Ouvriéres Christiennes*, Jacques Meert. Among the more prominent members of this organization were Joseph Ileo (now Prime Minister in the Kasavubu government) and Joseph Ngalulu.

Joseph Ileo was editor in chief of the bimonthly *Conscience Africane*. He had already acquired a wide reputation among Congolese when he decided, in July of 1956, to publish a nationalist inspired manifesto that contained a daring thirty-year plan of emancipation for the Congo.

Both Ileo and Ngalula were eager to broaden the bases of the *Movement National Congolais* moderate nationalist organization created in 1956. Patrice Lumumba, then regarded as one of the eminent spokesmen of liberal ideas, joined the (MNC), the group.

Once affiliated with this and other groups, Lumumba readily asserted himself and became the dominant figure. Shortly after proclaiming himself chairman of the MNC's Central Committee, he formally announced on October 10, 1958, the foundation of a "national movement" dedicated to the goal of "national liberation." His action at this moment was prompted by two important developments affecting the Congo. One was the forthcoming visit of a parliamentary committee appointed by the former minister of the Congo, Mr. Patillion, for the purpose of "conducting an inquiry concerning the administrative and political evolution of the country." Another was the creation of a *Movement Pour le Progrés National Congolais* in late November 1958, by the Congolese delegates to the Brussels Exposition. Lumumba moved in and around these groups and quickly projected himself into the role of a dynamic and radical nationalist leader.

A high point in his political development came in 1958, when he was permitted to attended the Pan African Conference in Accra, Ghana. Here he became a member of the Permanent Directing Committee. Patrice Lumumba had now projected himself upon a political stage of international importance. In addition to whatever personal counsel he might have received from Ghana's Prime Minister Nkrumah, there is little doubt that the Accra Conference was an important factor in shaping Lumumba's long-range objectives and further sensitizing him to the philosophy of Pan-Africanism.

When he returned home, the emancipation of the Congo from

Belgium's tutelage assumed first priority among his activities. In March 1959, when Belgium had already announced its intention to lead the Congo "without fatal proclamation and without undue haste" toward self-government, Lumumba went to Brussels, where he delivered several lectures under the auspices of *Presénce Congolese*, a Belgian organization dedicated to the promotion of African culture. On this occasion, Lumumba indiscreetly turned on his host and sponsors and deplored the "bastardization and destruction of Negro-African art," and "the depersonalization of Africa." He reaffirmed his party's determination to put an end to the "camouflaged slavery of Belgian colonization" and elect an independent government in 1961. With this act of boldness, Patrice Lumumba had set the stage for most of his future troubles and probably his future death.

After the target-date for independence had been approved by the *Movement National Congolais*, new troubles began for Lumumba and his supporters. Now that the contestants for power were close to their goal, the competition between them became fiercer. Delegates to the Luluabourg Congress, in April 1959, ran against the demands of other nationalist groups eager to put themselves forward as the standard-bearers of independence. Several of Lumumba's earlier supporters withdrew from the MNC and formed their own parties. With the date for Congo independence practically rushing upon him, Lumumba set out to rebuild the MNC. He involved himself in every phase of his party's activities, organizing local sections of the MNC and recruiting new supporters.

On November 1, 1959, a few days after his wing of the MNC held its congress in Stanleyville, Lumumba was arrested for the second time and charged with having made seditious statements. He was sentenced to six months in jail. After serving nearly three months of his sentence he was released when a delegation of officials from the MNC notified the Belgian government that they would not participate in the Brussels Roundtable Conference unless Lumumba was set free. Soon after his release, Lumumba's party was victorious in the December elections. As expected, Stanleyville proved to be the main Lumumba stronghold in the Congo. In Stanleyville his party won ninety percent of the votes.

Lumumba's status and influence continued to rise. As a representative of Orientale Province, he was appointed to the General Executive College, an interim executive body established after the Brussels

Roundtable Conference. Trouble continued to brew within the ranks of his party. Victor Nendeka, vice-chairman of the MNC, broke with Lumumba for what he termed the "extreme left wing tendencies" of the party leader. In 1960, he organized his own party. Once again Lumumba reshuffled the party personnel and strengthened his position. The MNC emerged from the next electoral struggle as the strongest party in the House of Representatives, with 34 out of 137 seats. In the Provincial Assembly of Orientale, Lumumba's party held 58 out of 70 seats. In the assemblies of Kiva and Kasai Provinces, 17 out of 25 seats were secured.

Lumumba employed several techniques to mobilize his support and activate the rural masses. First, there was the careful selection of party officials and propagandists at the Lodja Congress, held March 9–12, 1960. The delegates of the Bakutshu and Batetela tribes agreed that they would entrust the defense of their interests to the political party that held a prominent position in the region, namely Lumumba's party, the MNC. The party's success among the Bakutshu and Batetela tribal associations was mainly due to Lumumba's tribal origin and the anti-Belgian orientation acquired by these tribes in resisting the penetration of Western rule.

Lumumba and the MNC improved their techniques of building up functional organizations, in order to unify the political actions of the MNC. These organizational networks embraced a variety of interest groups and cut across tribal lines. Through a tactical alliance with minor parties, Lumumba tried to transform the MNC into an integrating structure, where both sectional and national interests would be represented. This program received formal sanction at the extraordinary congress of the MNC, held in Luluabourg on April 3–4, 1960. This was a major landmark in the history of Lumumba's party. Once more he had proven to be the most able of all Congolese leaders.

As the Congo crossed the threshold of independence, new troubles developed within the ranks of the MNC. Communication between Lumumba and some of the leaders of the party broke down. The Congo's most vital instrument of stability, the *Force Publique*, collapsed. The number and complexities of the issues now confronting Lumumba absorbed most of the time he formerly devoted to party activities. Now that the pomp and ceremony of the Belgians' handing over power to elected Congolese leaders was over one struggle for Lumumba was over, but a new and bitter one was beginning.

His devotion to the idea of a united Congo was now more firm. He was one of the few Congolese politicians who had any concept of the Congo as a strong centralized state. Tshombe thought first of carving out of Katanga a state for himself where he could be the boss, with Belgian help. Kasavubu cherished the dream of restoring the ancient empire of Bakongo. Other Congolese politicians were still absorbed in their own tribal ideas and hostilities.[1]

Lumumba had been neither kind nor cautious toward the Belgians. During the independence ceremony, he publicly announced too many of his future plans which included not only the uniting of the Congo but assisting the nations around him (especially Angola) that were still under European rule. This might have been one of his greatest mistakes. The decision to kill Lumumba probably was made that very day. He had crossed the path of the unseen power manipulators who intended to control the Congo economically even if they were willing to allow Lumumba to control it politically. Instead of saying, "Thanks very much for our independence. We appreciate all you Belgians have done for our country," Lumumba said in effect, "It's about time, too! And it's a pity that in a half-century you didn't see fit to build more hospitals and schools. You could have made much better use of your time."

Lastly, when the *Force Publique* revolted in the first days of July, Lumumba tried earnestly to be equal to this and other emergencies exploding around him. He faced the risks of his high position with courage. He moved frantically over his large country trying to restore order escaping death several times by inches. Once he was saved by a Ghanaian officer; another time his car was stoned by a mob. This did not deter him from trying to restore order to his troubled country. In the middle of July, when the structure of order was deteriorating into chaos, Lumumba flew off for a grandiose tour of the United States, Canada, North, and West Africa. This was another one of his unfortu-

---

[1] The Force Publique was the internal police force and the instrument of information in the labor movement. This set in motion a chain reaction tapping those in key positions, who in turn informed others among the populace.

nate mistakes. In his absence the confusion worsened.

In his dealings with the United Nations he never knew exactly what he wanted; showing no steady policy toward the UN, he confused both friends and enemies who grew impatient with his erratic behavior. When the disintegration within his country reached dangerous proportions, he asked for military help from the United Nations. Within three days the UN troops landed. When Lumumba realized that UN troops could not be used as a private army to put down his political opponents, he became disenchanted with their presence in his country.

By now Lumumba had quarreled with nearly every leading politician in the Congo. His continued erratic action shook the confidence of the outside world and of many of the African leaders who had wished him well and hoped that he would restore order rapidly. But a power struggle had erupted in the Congo. Concurrent with this struggle Belgians were working behind the scenes to reconquer the Congo economically; their Congolese puppets, bought and paid for in advance, were deeply engrossed in their self-seeking ventures.

In the last weeks of his life, when he was being dragged around with a rope around his neck, while his captors yanked up his head for the benefit of newsreel cameras, he still carried himself with great dignity as well as courage. When he was beaten up on the plane that carried him to be handed over to his arch enemy Tshombe, he did not cry out nor plead for mercy. When Tshombe's troops beat him again, in the Elizabethville airport, he asked no one for help or pity. He was carried off by Tshombe's troops and their Belgian officers on a journey from which he was certain never to return alive. Lumumba's conduct in the midst of these scenes will always stand to his credit in history. These traits of independence and courage went into the making of his martyrdom—a strange and dangerous (for his adversaries) martyrdom that makes Lumumba a more effective African nationalist in death than he was in life.

Some of those now most vocal in their praise of the dead Lumumba include many who in the past criticized some of his actions and speeches most savagely while he was still alive. Patrice Lumumba was pulled from powere mostly by his own people, who were being manipulated by forces of change and power alien to their understanding.

In the killing of Lumumba, white neo-colonialists and their black African puppets frustrated the southward spread of independence movements. Lumumba had pledged to give assistance to the African nations to the east and the south of the Congo who are still struggling to attain independence, particularly Angola. Lumumba was a true son of Africa, and in his short unhappy lifetime, he was accepted as belonging to all of Africa, not just the Congo.

The important point in the Lumumba story, briefly related, is this: He proved that legitimacy of a postcolonial regime in Africa relates mainly to its legal mandate; but even more, legitimacy relates to the regime's credentials as a representative of a genuine nationalism fighting against the intrigues of neo-colonialism. This is why Lumumba was and is still being extolled as this "best son of Africa," this "Lincoln of the Congo," this "Black Messiah," whose struggle was made noble by his unswerving demand for centralism against all forms of Balkanization and rendered heroic by his unyielding resistance to the forces of neo-colonialism which finally killed his body, but not his spirit. This man, who now emerges as a strange combination of statesman, sage, and martyr, wrote his name on the scroll of African history during his short and unhappy lifetime.

MARCUS GARVEY AND THE
AFRICAN DREAM DEFERRED

▼

I T SEEMS TO ME that the symbolic antecedents of Marcus
Garvey in the Caribbean Islands and the United States started
on the shores of Africa when some of the slaves being forced
onto the ships picked up handfuls of African earth and held it
in their mouths as they were being forced onto the slave ships. They
strained their necks looking back at their homeland until it disappeared
from view. Some of them never lost hope that one day they would
return, unaware of the slim possibilities of such a hope. Europeans were
recovering from their 'Middle-Ages', at Africa's expense, and they came
out of this crisis land poor, resource poor and people poor. This was an
important two-hundred-year turning point in world history, 1400-1600
A.D.

Marcus Garvey emerged from an historical setting that began to
develop early in the fifteenth century. The European awakening that
had begun with the Crusades, had by this time led to a movement to
explore and exploit large areas of the world outside Europe. For the
great states of West Africa, it was a time of tragedy and decline.
Europe's era of exploration and the internal strife in Africa were
contributing factors to the slave trade; the slave trade, in turn, was a
contributing factor to the development of the philosophy of mercantil-
ism that would dominate political and economic thought for the next
three hundred years.

The story of the African slave trade is essentially the story of the
consequences of the second rise of Europe. In the years between the
passing of the Roman Empire in the eighth century and the partial

127

unification of Europe within the framework of the Catholic Church in the fifteenth century, Europeans were engaged mainly in internal matters. With the opening of the New World and the expulsion of the Moors from Spain during the latter part of the fifteenth century, Europeans began to expand into the broader world. They were searching for new markets, new materials, new manpower, and new lands to exploit. The African slave trade was created to accommodate this expansion.

In the fifteenth century, using religion as an excuse, the slavers began to set up myths that nearly always read the African out of human history, beginning with the classification of the African as a lesser being. The Catholic Church's justification for slavery was to bring the African under the guidance of Christendom so that he would eventually receive its blessings.

There were several competing slave systems in the New World. In order to understand the effects of these various systems on the psyche of the Africans, we have to look at each one individually. In Cuba and Haiti, the Africans were often a majority population. This is also true of certain portions of Brazil. Therefore, the system operated differently in these areas, and although it was still slavery, the African had some cultural mobility.

In South America and in the Caribbean Islands, the slave masters did not outlaw the African drum, African ornamentations, African religions or other things dear to the African, remembered from his former way of life.

In the Portuguese areas, in the Caribbean Islands and often in South America, plantation owners would buy a shipload or half a shipload of slaves. These slaves usually came from the same areas in Africa, spoke the same language, and had the same basic culture. Families, in the main, were kept together. If a slave on an island was sold to a plantation owner at the end of the island, he could still walk to see his relatives. This freedom permitted a form of cultural continuity among the slaves in South America, the Caribbean Islands, Cuba and Haiti that did not exist in the United States and that later made their revolts more successful than revolts in the United States.

It can be said that these revolts, and personalities involved, were the Caribbean antecedents of Marcus Garvey. It is against this historical background that he can best be understood. In an article, "A *Birth of Freedom,"* by the Guyanan writer, Sidney King, this point is graphically made when he reminds us that "The Caribbean tradition, taken as a whole, is a revolutionary tradition. It is the stage on which acted Cudjoe and Cuffe, Accabreh and Accra, Toussaint, Quamina and Damon, Adoe and Araby; all leaders of slave revolts in 1750 and in 1850 served to shake that system sometimes to its foundations and to cause it to make democratic concessions as a price of recovery. It was never the same again. Although financial exploitation became more intense and complicated a constitutional superstructure was raised for dealing with human anger and for side-tracking revolution into peaceful awe-inspiring chambers."

The revolts referred to here were epitomized by the Berbic Revolution of 1763. This revolt, Sidney King observes, "struck the first blow for Guyanese independence. It was a blow that the theoreticians of human subjugation will never forget. It was part and parcel of the Caribbean Movement begun by the Caribs against European penetration and domination."

The Berbice slave revolts began when the slaves in Guyana made their first massive attempt to throw off the yoke of their masters and they realized that they would have to kill a large number of white people in order to do so. These killings are spoken of as rebellions and scores of them are recorded. But the Berbice slave rebellion was more than an attempt to abolish slavery; it had the germ of a true revolution—it was an attempt to establish a nation. The importance of this slave rebellion is in the fact that it went far beyond a revolt against prevailing conditions.

The 1763 rebellion came in spite of the Dutch penal code that was set up to prevent it, and it came at the time Spanish slave traders were challenging the Dutch traders both in South America and in the Caribbean Islands. (Between 1624 and 1654 the Dutch had lost their vast slave empire in Brazil.) Other nations—France, Britain and Portugal—were also trying to secure their spheres of influence in the New World.

The Dutch had established themselves in Berbice in 1624. During the years 1624 and 1763, they were the cruelest of slave masters. The Dutch slave code was much harsher than the Spanish code (the savagery of the Dutch code is shown by one provision of calculated cruelty: the burning alive of mutinous slaves over a slow fire). The

Dutch had no institution comparable to the Spanish *Audiencia*, a tribunal that included four judges. Dutch ruthlessness created the situation that came to a climax in the Berbice slave rebellion.

A number of minor uprisings had occurred in 1762, a year before the February Revolution. In his book, *Revolution to Republic*, the Guyanan writer P.H. Daly states that these uprisings, "were not exclusively black against white. In the outbreak of 1762, the rebels had killed many Africans who were fighting on the side of the whites. The prelude to the February Revolution, as seen in the minor uprisings in 1762, had shown many of the nationalist characteristics of the February Revolution itself.

Fundamentally a war of black against white, the February Revolution gradually escalated into a class conflict, still fundamentally against the whites, but internally between the house-gang slaves and the field-gang slaves in the revolutionary leadership." In this conflict over leadership lay the dangerous seed that would grow and destroy the effectiveness of the Revolution.

Cuffe, the leader of the revolt, was a house servant who had been brought to the colony very young and because of his intelligence had been taught carpentering by his master. When the rebellion started in February 1763, at Megdelenenburg on the Canje in Berbice, Cuffe had some misgivings about the outcome and the methods being used. He had hoped to secure better conditions for the slaves without having to resort to war.

The war of the Maroons of Jamaica predated the Berbice rebellion and is better known in history. The word Maroons (usually escaped slaves and their descendants, rarely freed slaves) once spread terror along the skirts of the Blue Mountains of Jamaica. The Maroons, whose revolt started in 1655, were never completely conquered.

Modern Jamaican history, in brief, and the events that led to this famous slave rebellion, started with the coming of the Spaniards in 1494. Jamaica was a Spanish colony for one-hundred-forty-nine years. During this time, the original inhabitants, the Arawak Indians, were literally destroyed and replaced by African slaves. The British took over the island in 1655. Two years later, the Maroons in the hills of jamaica gave some assistance to Don Cristobal Arnaldo de Yssassi, the last appointed Spanish Governor of Jamaica, in his desperate attempt to hold on to the island for Spain. The Maroons were troublesome to

British authorities in Jamaica for the next fifty years. Open warfare between the British and the Maroons, under the leadership of a man referred to as Captain Cudjoe, who had united several settlements under his leadership, broke out in 1728 and lasted for ten years.

A British colonist, Guthrie by name, conceived the plan of making the Maroons "friends" of the government. According to "The Gleaner Geography and History of Jamaica," Guthrie's idea was accepted by the Governor of Jamaica, and a treaty of peace and friendship was drawn up between the Maroons and the Government. The Maroons were given land in different parts of the country, free of taxes. They were allowed to govern themselves and were to be tried and punished by their own chiefs, but no chief could pass a sentence of death on any of them. They were to capture all runaway slaves and take them back to their owners, and also to assist in suppressing any rebellion among the slaves.

Some present-day radical Black Nationalists are still critical of the Maroons for making this agreement in the first place. There is no evidence to prove that they were, in effect, carrying out this agreement. The Maroon revolt, and Caribbean revolts in general, especially the Haitian revolt, can be collectively called the Caribbean antecedents of Marcus Garvey. His legacy in the Caribbean Islands led, in part, to the concept of a Caribbean Federation and the independence movement. The Federation idea was shortlived—a dream deferred, but not forgotten. These, in essence, are the Caribbean antecedents of Marcus Garvey.

It is no accident that Marcus Garvey had his greatest success in the United States among African-Americans. There is an historical logic to this occurrence that seems to have escaped most of the interpreters of Garvey's life and the mass movement that he built, for in many ways, the scene was being prepared for Marcus Garvey for over one-hundred years before he was born. There is no way to understand this without looking at Marcus Garvey's American antecedents; that is, the forces, people and movements that came before him.

Prior to the Civil War, the Caribbean contribution to the progress of African-American life was one of the main contributing factors in the fight for freedom and full citizenship in the northern United States during the eighteenth and nineteenth centuries, and the most outstanding of them saw their plight and that of the African-American as being one and the same.

In eighteenth century America, two of the most outstanding fighters for liberty and justice were the Caribbean Islanders Prince Hall and John B. Russwurm. When Prince Hall came to the United States, the nation was in turmoil. The colonies were ablaze with indignation. Britain, with a series of revenue acts, had stoked the fires of colonial discontent. In Virginia, Patrick Henry was speaking of liberty or death. The cry, "no taxation without representation," played on the nerve strings of the nation.

Prince Hall, then a delicate-looking teenager, often walked through the turbulent streets of Boston, an observer unobserved. A few months before these hectic scenes, he had arrived in the United States from his home in Barbados, where he had been born circa 1748, the son of an Englishman and a free African woman. He was, in theory, a free man, but he knew that neither in Boston nor in Barbados were persons of African descent actually free.

At once, he questioned the sincerity of the vocal white patriots of Boston. It never seemed to have occurred to them that the announced principles motivating their action made stronger argument in favor of destroying the system of slavery. The colonists held in servitude more than a half-million human beings, some of them white; yet they engaged in the contradiction of going to war to support the theory that all men were created equal.

When Prince Hall arrived in Boston, that city was the center of the American slave trade. Most of the major leaders of the revolutionary movement were, in fact, slaveholders or investors in slave-supported businesses. Hall, like many other Americans, wondered: what do these men mean by freedom? The condition of the free black men, as Prince Hall found them was not an enviable one. Emancipation brought neither freedom nor relief from the stigma of color. They were free in name only. They were still included in slave codes with slaves, indentured servants and Indians. Discriminatory laws severely circumscribed their freedom of movement.

By 1765, through diligence and frugality, Hall became a property owner, thus establishing himself in the eyes of white and black people. But the ownership of property was not enough. He still had to endure sneers and insults. He decided then to prepare himself for a role of leadership among his people. To this end he went to school at night and later became a Methodist preacher. His church became the forum for his people's grievances. Ten years after his arrival in Boston, Massachusetts, he was the accepted leader of the black community.

In 1788 Hall petitioned the Massachusetts Legislature, protesting the kidnapping of free blacks. This was a time when American patriots were engaged in a constitutional struggle for freedom. They had proclaimed the inherent rights of all mankind to life, liberty and the pursuit of happiness. Hall dared to remind them that the black men in the United States were human beings and as such were entitled to freedom and respect for their human personality.

It was racial prejudice that made Hall the father of African secret societies in the United States—now known as the "Black Masonry." Hall first sought initiation into the white Masonic Lodge in Boston, but was turned down because of his color. He then applied to the Army Lodge of an Irish Regiment. His petition was favorably received, and on March 6, 1775, Hall and fourteen other black Americans were initiated in Lodge Number 441. When, on March 17th, the British were forced to evacuate Boston, the Army Lodge gave Prince Hall and his colleagues a license to meet and function as a Lodge. Thus, on July 3, 1776, African Lodge No. 1 came into being. This was the first lodge established in America for men of African descent. Later in 1843, a Jamaican, Peter Ogden, organized, in New York City, the first Odd Fellows Lodge for Blacks.

The founding of the African Lodge was one of Prince Hall's greatest achievements. It afforded Africans in the New England area of the United States a greater sense of security and contributed to a new spirit of unity among them.

Hall's interest did not end with the Lodge. He was deeply concerned with improving the lot of his people in other ways and sought to have schools established for the children of free Africans in Massachusetts. Of prime importance is the fact that Prince Hall worked to secure respect for his people and that he played a significant role in the downfall of the Massachusetts slave trade. He helped to prepare the ground-work for those freedom fighters of the nineteenth and twentieth centuries whose continuing efforts have brought the African-American closer to the goal of full citizenship.

In his book, *The Souls of Black Folk*, Dr. W.E.B. DuBois points to the role of the Caribbean in the African-American struggle. They, he says, were mainly responsible for the manhood program launched by the race in the early decades of the nineteenth century. An eminent instance of such drive and self-assurance can be seen in the achievement of John W.A. Shaw of Antigua, who in the 1890s, passed the Civil Service Tests and became Deputy Commissioner of Taxes for the County of Queens in New York State.

On Friday, March 26, 1827, the first issue of *Freedom's Journal*, the first 'Negro Newspaper,' in the Western world, appeared on the streets of New York City. In their ambitious first editorial, Russwurm and Samuel Cornish struck a high note of positiveness that still has something to say to the African-American in his present plight. It read in part:

> We wish to plead our own cause. Too long have others spoke for us. Too long has the republic been deceived by misrepresentations, in things which concern us dearly, though in the estimation of some mere trifles; for though there are many in society who exercise toward us benevolent feelings; still (with sorrow we confess it) there are others who make it their business to enlarge upon the least trifle, which tends to discredit any person of color; and pronounce anathema and denounce our whole body for the misconduct of this guilty one.... Our vices and our degradation are ever arrayed against us, but our virtues are passed unnoticed ....

The timeliness of this editorial, written over a hundred years ago, and the dynamics of its intellectual content, are far ahead of most editorials that appear in present-day African-American newspapers.

During the later years of his life, John B. Russwurm moved to a position that today would be called black nationalism. After receiving his master's degree from Bowdoin College in 1829, Russwurm went to Liberia in West Africa, where he established another newspaper, *The Liberia Herald*, and served as a superintendent of schools. After further distinguishing himself as Governor of Maryland Colony of Cape Palmas, this pioneer editor and freedom fighter died in Liberia in 1851.

The Back-to-Africa idea has long been a recurring theme in African-American life and thought. This Africa consciousness began during the closing years of the eighteenth century and was articulated by the first African-American writers, thinkers, and abolitionists. This agitation was found mainly among groups of "freed blacks" because of the uncertainty of their position as freed men in a slave-holding society. "One can see it late into the eighteenth century," Dr. DuBois explains in his book, *Dusk of Dawn,* "when the Negro Union of Newport, Rhode Island, in 1788, proposed to the Free African Society of Philadelphia a general exodus to Africa on the part of at least free Negroes."

DuBois addressed himself to the broader aspects of this situation on the occasion of the celebration of the Second Anniversary of the Asian-African (Bandung) Conference and the rebirth of Ghana on April 30, 1957, when he said:

> From the fifteenth through the seventeenth centuries, the Africans imported to America regarded themselves as temporary settlers destined to return eventually to Africa. Their increasing revolts against the slave system, which culminated in the eighteenth century, showed a feeling of close kinship to the motherland and even well into the nineteenth century they called their organizations "African," as witness the "African Unions" of New York and Newport and the African Churches of Philadelphia and New York. In the West Indies and South America there was even closer indication of feelings of kinship with Africa and the East.
>
> The Planters' excuse for slavery was advertised as conversion of Africa to Christianity; but soon American slavery appeared based on the huge profits of the Sugar Empire and Cotton Kingdom. As plans were laid for the expansion of the slave system, the slaves themselves sought freedom by increasing revolts which culminated in the eighteenth century. In Haiti they won autonomy; in the United States they fled from the slave states in the South to the free states in the North and Canada.
>
> Here the Free Negroes helped form the Abolition Movement, and when that seemed to be failing, the Negroes began to plan for migration to Africa, Haiti and South America.
>
> Civil War and emancipation intervened and American Negroes looked forward to becoming free and equal here with no thought of return to Africa or of kinship with the world's

darker peoples. However, the rise of the Negro was hindered by disenfranchisement, lynching and caste legislation. There was some recurrence of the 'Back-to-Africa' idea and increased sympathy for darker folk who suffered the same sort of caste restrictions as American Negroes.

Professor E.U. Essien-Udom of the University of Ibadan, Nigeria, outlined the beginning of this consciousness and how it developed, in three lectures in the CBS Black Heritage television series Summer, 1969. In the first lecture on, "The Antecedents of Marcus Garvey and His Movement." Professor Essien-Udom gives this analysis:

In the United States it may be said that Garvey's ideas or variants of his ideas, are becoming increasingly relevant for the independent African states in their struggles for real political and economic independence as well as relative cultural autonomy.

A history of the freedom movements of Black Americans is the history of the aspirations for nationality and dignity. The reasons for this are not far to seek. Firstly, the Africans who were forcibly removed from their ancestral homelands to the New World were dramatically alienated from any vital human community, except the community of color, common deprivation, and persecution. Because they were drawn from various and distinct African nationality groups and scattered throughout the New World, they lost many vital ingredients as a distinct nationality group, such as a common language, religion, traditions, and more important, the freedom to shape their own destiny.

Secondly, because they were excluded from meaningful participation in the emergent American nationality, they became not only non-citizens, but also, in a sociological sense, non-nationals of the United States throughout most of their history. Early in their history, the Africans were simply an aggregation of persons who were non-citizens and consequently possessed no civic rights in the United States. Such for a long time was their political status.

Similarly, as a group without recognizable nationality, which derives from belonging to a definite and meaningful human community, they could not feel a sense of human dignity. Inevitably, therefore, and from slavery to freedom, the black freedom movements have had two ambivalent objectives. The first being the aspiration for nationality, a term which I shall use interchangeably with collective identity. And secondly, the aspiration for full citizenship in the United States.

In the past, the history of the black freedom movement, especially in the United States, was interpreted principally in terms of integration or in terms of assimilation into the mainstreams, whatever that is, of American society.

If integration is understood as the enjoyment of full rights of citizenship and full participation in the live activities of the United States, then this has been one of the most important objectives of the African-American freedom movement. But to interpret this movement principally in terms of assimilation, is a mispresentation of historical fact and a negotiation of the long and tragic history of the struggle for black identity and dignity. Assimilation necessarily entails the withering away of the distinctly African-American nationality which has been forged by the history of the Africans and their descendants in the United States.

In the United States, in the Caribbean Islands, and in Africa itself, a century-long struggle had unfolded before Marcus Garvey was born. His movement for African redemption and for the enhancement of all African people, everywhere, developed mainly in the United States in the community of Harlem. This community was Marcus Garvey's window on the world.

Marcus Garvey came to the United States at a time when African-Americans were realizing that the American dream was not dreamed for them and the American promise was not made to them. The Marcus Garvey program of African redemption, told African-Americans, both in word and in action:

> I will give you a new dream
> And Make you a new promise—
> And I will lead you back to
> your own land.

MALCOLM X: THE GENESIS OF HIS AFRICAN REVOLUTION

▼

SOON AFTER HIS ASSASSINATION on February 21, 1965, Malcolm X became the subject of a number of articles appraising his career and his effect on the black freedom movement. Most of these articles were too hastily written and showed little understanding of what Malcolm X and his mission meant to his people. The evaluation of Malcolm X is related to the evolution of black America in the great human drama now being called "the Black Revolution in the United States."

After the death of Malcolm X, a number of writers discussed how well they "knew" him. Some of these new "authorities" on Malcolm X would not come near him when he was alive. Black writers, however, with few exceptions, did not rush to print with hurriedly written articles on Malcolm X. They seem to have been recovering from the shock of his death. When their articles did begin to appear, they were generally better than the large number of articles by white writers that were published on Malcolm X soon after his death.

Malcolm X was forced out of the Black Muslim movement and into a dangerous wind current of history. Figuratively speaking, he did not have the time to balance himself in this wind current before he was swept off his feet and into his death. His challenge to mid-twentieth century America is both simple and complicated. He merely asked America to keep its promise of democracy to his people.

After leaving the Black Muslim movement he immediately put himself in danger by attempting to organize the black community for self-defense. He called upon all sections of the black community to formulate a solution to the problems facing Black Americans. Out of this coalition of various elements in the black community came the Organization of Afro-American Unity. His trips to Africa are significant because they took the black Americans' struggle out of the confines of the continental United States and linked it with the non-white world. The civil rights problem, to him at least, became a human rights problem and he attempted to internationalize it.

C. Eric Lincoln's article for this book, "The Meaning of Malcolm X," represents an extension of his interest in this subject. His book, *The Black Muslim Movement in America*, is the first extensive examination of that movement and its effect on black America.

Reverend Albert Cleage takes up some of the myths about Malcolm X that seemed to have grown faster than they could be printed. His article puts some of these myths to rest. When Malcolm X broke with Elijah Muhammad, he changed his direction, his focus, and his emphasis. He did not discard all of the things that he had learned while he was a follower of the Elijah Muhammad teachings. The Black Muslim movement was the political and spiritual incubator for Malcolm X: it was the area of his basic training and his proving ground. He modified what he had learned in this university of the ghetto, but he never repudiated it. This is, in part, what Rev. Cleage is saying in his article.

No matter how much is said about what Malcolm X was, the speculations about what he could have been will go on for a good number of years. The triumph and tragedy of his short-lived leadership have their mystique, which is, on reflection, both intriguing and sad, like the memory of lost love.

The influence of Malcolm X on the political consciousness of black Americans has had its greatest growth since his death. His statement, "Freedom by any means necessary," has been both used and abused by young black militants.

His dream of a world where his people will walk in freedom and dignity was temporarily deferred by his assassination. The assassin killed the dreamer but not the dream. This dream is the legacy he left us.

Malcolm X was easy to meet and difficult to know. He listened to all and learned from many, while being careful not to mistake the trivial for the profound. The article "The Last Days of Malcolm X" by

Earl Grant was extracted from a much larger work that is a book in preparation. Grant is one of the few people who can say that he was a personal friend and associate of Malcolm X. All of the contributors to my book knew Malcolm X personally.

The other contributors to this section—including Betty Shabazz (Mrs. Malcolm X)—present a picture of a Malcolm X not generally known to the public. What comes through in these articles is the profound humanness of the man himself.

Malcolm X and his activities got some of the best and worst press coverage of any personality of our time. Fortunately, Malcolm X was the master of press conferences, and he always got the best out of them. Many writers arrived at sweeping conclusions about Malcolm X without ever confronting him or seriously trying to understand the nature of the movement that his personality, almost solely, brought into being. Those who viewed him at close range got a different picture than others who attempted to view him from a distance with detachment and what some people call objectivity.

The many dimensions in the personality of Malcolm X made him a difficult person to understand and to interpret. He was a person always in the process of growth and change. He had outgrown the Black Muslim movement led by Elijah Muhammad long before he was forced out of it. It was inevitable that Malcolm X would see the major weakness of this movement and try to grapple with it. The major weakness is the escapist method it uses to offer identity to black Americans.

In an attempt to bolster its appeal by identification with Islam, the Black Muslim movement advocates complete withdrawal from American society—either by the concentration of all blacks (apparently to the exclusion of whites) in a part of the territory of the United States or by a mass return to Africa. This approach is not feasible under prevailing circumstances. The main consideration is this: Withdrawal from American society is most decidedly not what most black Americans want. First and foremost they want justice in a country that promises justice and dignity to all of its citizens.

The personal evolution of Malcolm X brought him to an understanding of this fact. The United States, the country that made him, was his special vantage point—his window on the world. From this vantage and from this window he attempted to see how the struggle of the Black man in the United States related to Africa, Asia, and the other parts of the so-called Third World. This was the essence of his evolution and growth.

* * * * *

The four articles on Malcolm X presented here represent four different stages of his development. First, there was Malcolm X. He was a master debater and defender of his ideas and his movement. He was particularly sharp in debating ideas and issues affecting the freedom of black Americans.

In the "Open Mind" program of Sunday, October 15, 1961, he was on a panel consisting of two college professors, a social scientist (Dr. Kenneth Clark), and a woman lawyer who is now a federal judge. He was not less than equal to the best of this lot. The quickness of his mind and the sharpness of his articulation are well demonstrated here, and the academicians of this panel seem to fall somewhat behind him.

At the time of this dialogue, the Black Muslim movement was growing rapidly, and Malcolm X had fully emerged as its public spokesman.

When Dr. Kenneth Clark interviewed Malcolm X two years later, his respect for the sharp mind of Malcolm X had grown considerably. In referring to this interview and the public personality of Malcolm X, Dr. Clark has said: "Although Minister Malcolm X seems proud of the fact that he did not go beyond the eighth grade, he speaks generally with the vocabulary and the tone of a college-educated person. Happy when this is pointed out to him, he explains that he has read extensively since joining the black Muslim movement. His role as the chief spokesman for this movement in the New York-Washington region is, he insists, to raise the level of pride and accomplishment in his followers."

Dr. Clark further said of him: "He shows the effects of these interminable interviews by a professional calm, and what appears to be an ability to turn on the proper amount of emotion, resentment, and indignation, as needed."

A transcript of a visit to Malcolm X by the FBI is included verbatim because it is self-explanatory and once more shows how well Malcolm X could handle himself in relation to ideas and pressures. It also shows that Malcolm X was a prize that the power establishment in the United States wanted to capture. This establishment that has been successfully buying or destroying men and governments the world over could not believe that this man was not for sale, at any price. In or out of the black Muslim movement, his ultimate objective was the freedom of his people, by any means necessary.

During the early part of February 1965, Malcolm X stopped in Paris on his way home from his last visit to Africa. He was shocked to discover that he would not be permitted to enter the city. This event, more than anything else during that last period of life, made him believe that there were forces with international motives and connections moving to destroy him. The telephone conversation between Malcolm X and Carlos Moore was Malcolm's last contact with the black community in Paris, which had built a program of action around his teaching.

Malcolm X had planned to address audiences in London and in Paris during the month of February 1965, and to inform the African and Afro-American residents of these cities about the denial of human rights suffered by Afro-Americans—about the brutal treatment inflicted upon them as they attempted to exercise those rights guaranteed by the American Constitution. He had already elevated the civil rights struggle to a human rights struggle, and he had already internationalized it.

In a few short visits during the last year of his life, Malcolm X did more to enhance the position of the African-Americans abroad than any other personality. He single-handedly convinced a large number of Africans, including some heads of state, that the African independence explosion and what was being referred to as the Black Revolution in the United States were events produced by the same historical experience—the Africans were colonized, the black Americans were enslaved. In his speeches in Africa he emphasized the convincing parallels between these two African peoples and their respective freedom struggles.

The expatriate African-American communities in Paris, London, and Accra, Ghana, thought of Malcolm as the one black American worthy of leadership.

In August 1964, Malcolm X addressed a meeting of the Organization of African Unity and first called attention to the plight of the people of African descent in the United States. He called the then recently passed Civil Rights Bill one of the tricks of this century's leading neocolonial power. Then he said:

> Our freedom struggle for human dignity is no longer confined to the domestic jurisdiction of the United States Government. We beseech the independent African states to help us bring our problem before the United Nations, on the grounds that the United States Government is morally incapable of protecting the lives and property of 22 million African-Americans. And on the grounds that our deteriorating plight is definitely becoming a threat to world peace.
>
> Out of frustration and hopelessness our young people have reached a point of no return, we no longer endorse patience and turning the other cheek. We assert the right of self-defense by any means necessary and reserve the right of maximum retaliation against our racist oppressors, no matter what the odds against us are. From here on in, if we must die anyway, we will die fighting back, and we will not die alone. We intend to see that our racist oppressors also get a taste of death.

Because he wanted his African listeners to know that they shared some of the same dangers as the black Americans, he added:

> No one knows a master better than his servants. We have been servants in the United States for over three hundred years. We have a thorough inside knowledge of this man who calls himself "Uncle Sam." Therefore, you must heed our warning: Don't escape from European colonialism only to become even more enslaved by deceitful, "friendly" American dollarism. Asalaam Alaikum.

Now the issue had been joined on a broad stage for all the world to see. If the American power establishment wanted a sound reason to kill him, he had boldly given it to them.

Upon his arrival in Cairo to attend this second Cairo conference, a number of African leaders and their various delegations asked him to prepare a memorandum on the real status of black Americans. With the guidance of this memorandum, the thirty-three heads of independent African nations, meeting in Cairo, U.A.R., from July 17 to July 21, 1964, passed a resolution condemning the brutal treatment of the African-Americans in the United States.

In the weeks that followed, Malcolm X was invited to visit sixteen African nations and most of these invitations were accepted. In every nation that he visited he made an effort to build a bridge of good will between Africans and African-Americans. Unknown to himself, Malcolm X had succeeded where other black men had tried and failed for over a hundred years. From the middle of the nineteenth century, and afterward, every genuine black nationalist has dreamed of a union with Africa and other people of African descent scattered throughout the world.

In a subsequent visit to African nations, Malcolm X continued to build a bridge of good will between Africans and African-Americans. This was his best and final contribution to the eventual liberation and union of his people.

* * * * *

The best interpreter of Malcolm X is Malcolm X. He was a man in transition. In his short and eventful lifetime, he made many changes because he learned many things. Most important of all, he learned how to correct himself. He was principally a speaker, and his style was as effective as any orator of this century. His language was direct and to the point and could be understood on all educational levels. His speech "Message to the Grass Roots," delivered in November 1963, is a perfect example of his mastery of language and the projection of ideas. It was this kind of creativity in Malcolm X that literally built the Black Muslim movement in the United States. This speech also proves that Malcolm X was an astute revolutionary theoretician.

The speech "God's Judgment of White America" set in motion or brought to the surface the difficulties precipitating the forces and circumstances that caused him to be forced out of the Black Muslim movement.

The speeches of Malcolm X in Africa are bridge building efforts that were partly successful. The fact that these speeches were made at all is remarkable. Even more remarkable is the fact that they were listened to respectfully by most of the heads of state in Africa, who responded quite favorably to the message of Malcolm X.

The African projection of Malcolm X and his brief travels in Africa, on behalf of the plight of black Americans, showed that he had an insight into the worldwide struggle of black people that was over and above that of any other designated leader. His speech to the domestic Peace Corps, made in December 1964, proves again how effective Malcolm X was in getting his message across to young people. To them he was more than a public orator; he was a great teacher and an intellectual father.

The article "Some Reflections on 'Negro History Week' and the Role of the Black People in History" is an excerpt from the pamphlet *Malcolm X on Afro-American History*. Malcolm X clearly understood that history is an instrument of both enslavement and liberation, and he was trying to tell his people, especially the young, how to use history affirmatively.

While the untimely death of Malcolm X is tragic and unfortunate, the positive aspect is that he left behind a philosophy of liberation. When seen in total context, it will effect his emergence as the finest revolutionary theoretician and activist produced by America's black working class in this century.

* * * * *

The man best known as Malcolm X lived three distinct and interrelated lives under the respective names Malcolm Little, Malcolm X, and El-Hajj Malik El-Shabazz. Any honest attempt to understand the total man must begin with some understanding of the significant components that went into his making.

The racist society that produced and assassinated Malcolm X is responsible for what he was and for destroying what he could have been. He had the greatest leadership potential of any person to emerge directly from the black working class in this century. In another time under different circumstances he might have been a king—and a good one. He might have made a nation and he might have destroyed one.

He was a creation of the interplay of powerful and conflicting forces in mid-century America. No other country or combination of forces could have shaped him the way he was and ultimately destroyed him with such unique ruthlessness.

Malcolm X knew, before he could explain it to himself and others, that he was living in a society that was engaged in the systematic destruction of his people's self-respect. His first memories are of conflict. In this respect his early life was no different from that of most black Americans, where conflict comes early and stays late. In his own words:

> When my mother was pregnant with me, she told me later, a party of hooded Ku Klux Klan raiders galloped up to our home in Omaha, Nebraska, one night. Surrounding the house, brandishing their shotguns and rifles, they shouted for my father to come out. My mother went to the front door and opened it. Standing where they could see her pregnant condition, she told them that she was alone with her three small children and that my father was away, preaching, in Milwaukee. The Klansmen shouted threats and warnings at her that we had better get out of town because "The good Christian white people" were not going to stand for my father's spreading trouble among the "good" Negroes of Omaha with the "Back to Africa" preachings of Marcus Garvey.

This was how he remembered his father, an ambitious dreamer attempting to maintain himself and his family while bigoted white policemen, Ku Klux Klansmen, and Black Legionnaires were determined to teach him to stay in "his place." The father of Malcolm X was killed while fighting against the restricted place that was assigned to his people in this country. Much later, and in many different ways, Malcolm X continued the same fight and was subsequently killed for the same reason.

Every major event in Malcolm's life brought him into conflict with the society that still thrives on the oppression of his people.

His mother was born as a result of her mother being raped by a white man in the West Indies. When he was four, the house where he and his family lived was burned down by members of the Ku Klux Klan. When he was six, his father met a violent death that his family always believed was a lynching.

After the death of his father, who was a follower of the black nationalist Marcus Garvey, his family was broken up and for a number of years he lived in state institutions and boarding homes. When he finally went to school he made good marks, but lost interest and was a dropout at the age of fifteen. He went to live with his sister in Boston and went to work at the kinds of jobs available to Negro youth—mainly the jobs not wanted by white people, such as shoeshine boy, soda jerk, hotel busboy, member of a dining car crew on trains traveling to New York, and a waiter in a Harlem nightclub.

From these jobs, he found his way into the underworld and thought, at the time, that his position in life was advancing. In the jungle of the underworld, where the fiercest survive by fleecing the weak and defenseless, he became a master manipulator, skilled in gambling, selling drugs, burglary, and hustling. A friend who had helped him get his first job gave him the rationale for his actions. "The main thing you have to remember," he was told, "is that everything in the world is a hustle."

Malcolm returned to Boston, where he was later arrested for burglary and sentenced to ten years in prison. The year was 1946 and he was not quite twenty-one years old. Prison was another school for Malcolm. He now had time to think and plan. Out of this thinking he underwent a conversion that literally transformed his whole life. By letters and visits from his family he was introduced to the Black Muslim movement (which calls itself officially The Lost-Found Nation of Islam). He tested himself in the discipline of his newly chosen religion by refusing to eat pork. The event startled his fellow inmates, who had nicknamed him Satan.[2] He describes the occasion in this manner:

> It was the funniest thing—the reaction, and the way that it spread. In prison where so little breaks the monotonous routine, the smallest thing causes a commotion of talk. It was being mentioned all over the cell block by night that Satan didn't eat pork. It made me very proud, in some odd way. One of the universal images of the Negro—in prison and out—was that he

[2] Malcolm X was called Satan because of the reddish tint in his light skinned complexion.

couldn't do without pork. It made me feel good to see that my not eating it had specially startled the white convicts. Later I would learn, when I had read and studied Islam a good deal, that unconsciously my first pre-Islamic submission had been manifested. I had experienced, for the first time, the Muslim teaching, "If you take one step toward Allah—Allah will take two steps toward you." My brothers and sisters in Detroit and Chicago had all become converted to what they were being taught was the "natural religion for the black man."

His description of his process of self-education in prison is an indictment of the American educational system and a tribute to his own perseverance in obtaining an education after being poorly prepared in the public schools. While in prison he devised his own method of self education and learned how to speak and debate effectively so that he could participate and defend the movement after his release from prison. He started by copying words from the dictionary that might be helpful to him, beginning with "A." He went through to "Z" and then, he writes, "for the first time, I could pick up a book and actually understand what the book was saying."

This aspect of his story calls attention to the tremendous reservoirs of talent, and even genius, locked up among the masses in the black ghettos. It also indicates what can be accomplished when the talent of this oppressed group is respected and given hope and purpose.

Within a few years he was to become a debater with a national reputation. He took on politicians, college professors, journalists, and anyone—black or white—who had the audacity to meet him. He was respected by some and feared by others.

Malcolm was released from prison in 1952, when he was twenty-seven years old. For a few weeks he took a job with his eldest brother, Wilfred, as a furniture salesman in Detroit. He went to Chicago before the end of that year to hear and meet the leader of the Nation of Islam—Elijah Muhammad. He was accepted into the movement and given the name Malcolm X. He went back to Detroit and was made assistant minister of a Detroit Mosque. From this point on, his rise in the movement and in the eyes of the public was rapid.

At the end of 1953, he went to Chicago to live with the leader of the Nation of Islam and was trained by him personally. After organizing a mosque in Philadelphia, he was sent to head the movement in Harlem in 1954 before he was thirty years old.

In a few years he was able to transform the Black Muslim movement into a national organization and himself into one of the country's best-known personalities. As the public spokesman and defender of the movement, he literally put it on the map. This was the beginning of his trouble with his leader, Elijah Muhammad. When the public thought of the Black Muslim movement, they thought first of Malcolm X.

Malcolm X had appeal far beyond the movement. He was one of the most frequent speakers on the nation's campuses and the object of admiration by thousands of militant youth.

In his pamphlet "Malcolm X—The Man and His Ideas," George Breitman gives the following description of Malcolm's appeal as a speaker:

> His speaking style was unique—plain, direct like an arrow, devoid of flowery trimming. He used metaphors and figures of speech that were lean and simple, rooted in the ordinary, daily experience of his audiences. He knew what the masses thought and how they felt, their strengths and their weaknesses. He reached right into their minds and hearts without wasting a word; and he never tried to flatter them. Despite an extraordinary ability to move and arouse his listeners, his main appeal was to reason, not emotion.... I want only to convey the idea that rarely has there been a man in America better able to communicate ideas to the most oppressed people; and that was not just a matter technique, which can be learned and applied in any situation by almost anybody, but that it was a rare case of a man in closest communion with the oppressed, able to speak to them, because he identified himself with them, an authentic expression of their yearning for freedom, a true product of their growth in the same way that Lenin was a product of the Russian people.

From 1954, when he was made responsible for the Black Muslim movement in Harlem, the history of that movement is essentially the history of the rise of Malcolm X.

In public speeches, where he nearly always prefaced his remarks with the statement, "The Honorable Elijah Muhammad teaches us," Malcolm X was teaching lessons about the black American's fight for basic dignity that were more meaningfully logical than anything that Elijah Muhammad had ever conceived. He was the public figure most identified with the movement and most sought after as its spokesman. Louis E. Lomax referred to him as the St. Paul of the Black Muslim movement and added, "Not only was he knocked to the ground by the bright light of truth while on an evil journey, but he also rose from the dust stunned, with a new name and a burning zeal to travel in the opposite direction and carry America's 20 million Negroes with him."

In these years, Malcolm X was preaching separation and frightening more white people than the social protest organizations that were demanding integration. The bold act of refusing integration was a challenge to a society that never intended to integrate the black Americans in the first place. With this act, Malcolm X put American society on the defensive by questioning its intentions toward his people and proving that those intentions were false. Also he made black America question itself and face reality. He identified the enemy of their promise, indicted that enemy, and still did not relieve the victim, his own people, of the responsibility for being the instrument of their own liberation.

To place Malcolm X and his roughhewn grandeur in proper perspective, one must first understand the nature of the society that produced him and ultimately destroyed him. To a large extent, the shadow of slavery still hangs over this land, and affects the daily life of every American. Slavery was the black gold that produced America's first wealth and power. Slavery was the breeding ground for the most contagious and contaminating monster of all time—racism.

It was this racism and oppression by white America that convinced Malcolm X of the necessity of black nationalism as the vehicle for black liberation, as opposed to "integration," while he was in the Black Muslim movement. Although his black nationalism, while he was in the Muslim organization, was narrow and sectarian, this did not prevent him from playing a tremendously important role in the evolution of the black freedom struggle.

Prior to the arrival of Malcolm X on the scene, most of white America looked upon the established civil rights organizations as "extremists," although most of them were creatures and creations of the white controllers of power. But Malcolm came along and said, "Not only do I refuse to integrate with you, white man, but I demand that I be completely separated from you in some states of our own or back home in Africa; not only is your Christianity a fraud but your 'democracy' a brittle lie." Neither the white man nor his black apologist could answer the latter argument.

Because they could not answer Malcolm in this area, they attacked him where he was most vulnerable—the concept of separatism and that all white folks were "blue-eyed devils"—labeling him a "hatemonger," "racist," "dangerous fanatic," "black supremacist," etc. In reality, he was none of these things. Certainly he didn't preach "black supremacy." Malcolm X preached black pride, black redemption, black reaffirmation, and he gave the black woman the image of a black man that she could respect.

The fact that Malcolm X, while in the Black Muslim movement, could reject a white person on any terms caused most of white America psychological turmoil. And instilled admiration and pride in most black Americans. For the egos of most white Americans are so bloated that they cannot conceive of a black man rejecting them.

It can be stated categorically that Malcolm X, while in the Black Muslim movement and out of it, created the present stage of the civil rights struggle—to the effect that he was a catalytic agent—offstage, sarcastically criticizing the "civil rights leaders," popping a whip that activated them into more radical action and programs. He was the alternative that the power holders of America had to deal with, if they didn't deal with the established "civil rights leaders."

On December 1, 1963, shortly after President Kennedy's assassination, Malcolm X addressed a public rally at Manhattan Center in New York City. He was speaking as a replacement for Elijah Muhammad as he had done many times before. After the speech, during a question and answer period, Malcolm X made the remark that led to his suspension as a Muslim minister. In answer to a question, "What do you think about President Kennedy's assassination?" Malcolm X answered that he saw the case as "The chickens coming home to roost." Soon after the remark, Malcolm X was suspended by Elijah Muhammad and directed to stop speaking for ninety days. After some weeks, when Malcolm X realized that there were a number of highly placed persons in the Black Muslim movement conspiring against him, seemingly with Elijah Muhammad's consent, he left the movement.

He devotes a chapter in his book (*The Autobiography of Malcolm X*) to the growth of his disenchantment and his eventual suspension from the Black Muslim movement. He says:

> I had helped Mr. Muhammad and his ministers to revolutionize the American black man's thinking, opening his eyes until he would never again look in the same fearful way at the white man.... If I harbored any personal disappointment whatsoever, it was that privately I was convinced that our Nation of Islam could be an even greater force in the American black man's overall struggle—if we engaged in more action. By that I mean I thought privately that we should have amended, or relaxed, our general non-engagement policy. I felt that, wherever black people committed themselves, in the Little Rocks and the Birminghams and other places, militantly disciplined Muslims should also be there—for all the world to see, and respect and discuss.

On March 8, 1964, he publicly announced that he was starting a new organization. In fact two new organizations were started, the Muslim Mosque, Inc., and the Organization of Afro-American Unity.

Malcolm X was still somewhat beholden to Elijah Muhammad in the weeks immediately following his break with the movement. At his press conference on March 12, he said, in part:

> I am and always will be a Muslim. My religion is Islam. I still believe that Mr. Muhammad's analysis of the problem is the most realistic, and that his solution is the best one. This means that I too believe the best solution is the complete separation, with our people going back home, to our own African home-land. But separation back to Africa is still a long-range program, and while it is yet to materialize, 22 million of our people who are still here in America need better food, clothing, housing, education, and jobs right now. Mr Muhammad's program does point us back homeward, but it also contains within it what we could and should be doing to help solve many of our problems

while we are still here."

Internal differences within the Nation of Islam forced me out of it. I did not leave of my own free will. But now that it has happened I intend to make the most of it. Now that I have more independence of action, I intend to use a more flexible approach toward working with others to get a solution to this problem. I do not pretend to be a divine man, but I do believe in divine guidance, divine power, and in the fulfillment of divine prophecy. I am not educated, nor am I an expert in any particular field ... but I am sincere and my sincerity is my credential.

The problem facing our people here in America is bigger than other personal or organizational differences. Therefore, as leaders, we must stop worrying about the threat that we seem to think we pose to each other's personal prestige, and concentrate our united efforts toward solving the unending hurt that is being done daily to our people here in America.

I am going to organize and head a new mosque in New York City, known as the Muslim Mosque, Inc. This gives us a religious base, and the spiritual force necessary to rid our people of the vices that destroy the moral fiber of our community.

Our political philosophy will be black nationalism. Our economic and social philosophy will be black nationalism. Our cultural emphasis will be black nationalism.

Many of our people aren't religiously inclined, so the Muslim Mosque, Inc., will be organized in such a manner as to provide for the active participation of all Negroes in our political, economic, and social programs, despite their religious or non-religious beliefs.

The political philosophy of black nationalism means: We must control the politics and the politicians of our community. They must no longer take orders from outside forces. We will organize and sweep out of office all Negro politicians who are puppets for the outside forces.

Malcolm X had now thrust himself into a new area of conflict that would take him, briefly, to a high point of international attention and partial acceptance.

During the last phase of his life Malcolm X established this Muslim Mosque, Inc., and the non-religious Organization of Afro-American Unity, patterned after the Organization of African Unity. He attempted to internationalize the civil rights struggle by taking it to the United Nations.

In several trips to Africa and one to Mecca, he sought the counsel and support of African and Asian heads of state. His trip to Mecca and Africa had a revolutionary effect upon his thinking. His perennial call had always been for *black unity and self-defense* in opposition to the "integrationist's" program of nonviolence, passive resistance, and "Negro-white unity." When he returned home from his trip he was no longer opposed to progressive whites uniting with revolutionary blacks, as his enemies would suggest. But to Malcolm, and correctly so, the role of the white progressive was not in black organizations but in white organizations in white communities, convincing and converting the unconverted to the black cause. Further, and perhaps more important, Malcolm had observed the perfidy of the white liberal and the American Left whenever Afro-Americans sought to be instruments of their liberation. He was convinced that there could be no black-white unity until there was black unity; that there could be no workers' solidarity until there was racial solidarity.

The overwhelming majority of white America demonstrates daily that they cannot and will not accept the black man as an equal in all the ramifications of this acceptance—after having three hundred and forty-five years of racism preached to them from the pulpit, taught in the primer and textbook, practiced by the government, apotheosized on editorial pages, lauded on the airways and television screens. It would be tantamount to self-castration, a gutting of the ego. It would be asking white America to purge itself completely of everything it has been taught, fed and believed for three hundred and forty-five years.

It was this recognition of what racism had done to the white man and to the mind of the black man that the following paragraph was and is a keystone of the Organization of Afro-American Unity's program:

> We must revamp our entire thinking and redirect our learning trends so that we can put forth a confident identity and wipe out the false image built up by an oppressive society.

We can build a foundation for liberating our minds by studying the different philosophies and psychologies of others. Provisions are being made for the study of languages of Eastern origin such as Swahili, Hausa, and Arabic. Such studies will give us, as Afro-Americans, a direct access to ideas and history of our ancestors, as well as histories of mankind at large.

More so than any other Afro-American leader, Malcolm X realized that there must be a concomitant cultural and educational revolution if the physical revolution is to be successful. No revolution has ever sustained itself on emotion.

When Malcolm X returned from his trip to Mecca and Africa, he completely repudiated the Black Muslims' program of separation, their acquisitive thirst for money and property and machine idolatry. He felt that they were merely imitating the racist enemy. He still believed in separation from his racist enemy, but his was an ideological separation.

To Malcolm X, the Afro-American must transcend his enemy, not imitate him. For he foresaw that both the Black Muslims and the "integrationists" were aping the oppressor; that neither recognized that the struggle for black freedom was neither social nor moral. It was and is a power struggle; a struggle between the white haves and the black have-nots. A struggle of the oppressor and the oppressed. And if the oppressed is to breach the power of the oppressor, he must either acquire power or align himself with power.

Therefore, it is not accidental that Malcolm's political arm, the Organization of Afro-American Unity, was patterned to the letter and spirit after the Organization of African Unity. Nor should it be surprising that he officially linked up the problems of Afro-Americans with the problems of his black brothers and sisters on the mother continent. Malcolm X's vision was broad enough to see that the Afro-Americans were not a "minority" as the enemy and his lackeys would have us believe. Afro-Americans are not an isolated 25 million. There are over 100 million black people in the Western Hemisphere—Cuba, Brazil, Latin America, the West Indies, North America, etc. Malcolm knew that when we unite these millions with the 300 million on the African continent the black man becomes a mighty force. The second largest people on earth. And so Malcolm's perennial theme was unity, unity, unity.

The formation of the Organization of Afro-American Unity and the establishment of an official connection with Africa was one of the most important acts of the twentieth century. For this act gave the Afro-Americans an official link with the new emerging power emanating from both Africa and Asia. Malcolm X succeeded where Marcus Garvey and others had failed. Thus, doing this, Malcolm projected the cause of Afro-American freedom into the international arena of power.

When he internationalized the problem, by raising it from the level of civil rights to that of *human rights*, and by linking up with Africa, Malcolm X threw himself into the cross fire of that invisible, international cartel of power and finance which deposes presidents and prime ministers, dissolves parliaments, if they refuse to do their bidding. It was this force, I believe, that killed Malcolm X, that killed Lumumba and that killed Hammarskjold.[3]

There is another and more potent reason why the American oppressors feared Malcolm X and wished him dead. And that is the publicized fact that he was going to bring the oppression of African-Americans before the United Nations, charging the United States Government with genocide. Many of the oppressors had conniptions when confronted with the prospect of a world body discussing the problems of African-Americans.

In the introduction to Malcolm X's autobiography, M.S. Handler has said: "No man in our time aroused fear and hatred in the white man as did Malcolm, because in him the white man sensed an implacable foe who could not be had for any price—a man unreservedly committed to the cause of liberating the black man in American society rather than integrating the black man into that society."

He was, more precisely, a man in search of a definition of himself and his relationship to his people, his country, and the world. That a man who had inhabited the "lower depths" of life could rise in triumph as a reproach to its ills, and become an uncompromising champion of his people, is in itself a remarkable feat. Malcolm X went beyond this feat. Though he came from the American ghetto and directed his message to the people in the American ghetto first of all, he also

---

[3] Dag Hammarskjold, United Nations secretary-general from 1953 to 1961, was investigating the Congo situation when he was killed in an airplane crash.

became, in his brief lifetime, a figure of world importance. But he was assassinated on February 21, 1965, while on the threshold of his potential.

About the men of his breed, the writer John Oliver Killens has said: "He was a dedicated patriot: DIGNITY was his country, MANHOOD was his government and FREEDOM was his land."

TOM MBOYA AND THE ABORTED POLITICAL DREAM[1]

▼

TOM MBOYA WAS ONE of the three great African personalities who may have determined the future of that emergent continent and its people. Gamal Abdel Nasser, President of the United Arab Republic, and Kwame Nkrumah, Prime Minister of Ghana were two other stalwarts engaged in bringing light to the once-labeled "Dark Continent."

Tom Mboya, member of the Kenya Legislative Council, was the general secretary of the Kenya Federation of Labor and chairman of the International Confederation of Free Trade Unions' East Central and Southern African Subregional Organization. He was also president of the Nairobi Peoples' Convention Party. In December 1958, he was elected chairman of the first All African Peoples Conference in Accra, Ghana.

Judging by his impressive record of achievement, one could conclude that Tom Mboya had already lived a long lifetime; quite the contrary. At the time, he had not yet reached his thirtieth birthday. He was born fifty-nine years ago on a sisal estate in Kenya's "White Highlands," the area then preserved for European settlers. Both his father and mother were illiterates who had been converted to the Catholic faith. Though he was baptized Thomas, his mother, according to the traditional custom of her people gave him the name Obhiambo,

[1] Reprinted from *Journal of Human Relations* (Central State College, Wilberforce, Ohio) Autumn Issue, 1960.

signifying that he was born in the evening. Tom Mboya was the first of his parent's six children. As the oldest child, the tradition of his people decrees that he become the head of the family when his father dies.

Mboya's father worked as a laborer for fifteen years at an average salary of $3.00 per month before he was promoted to an overseer with average salary of $11.00 per month. In spite of illiteracy, his father believed in education for his children. From his meager earnings he saved the fees to send Tom to elementary and high schools. At first Tom attended the Catholic Mission School at Kabaa, in the Ukamba District of Kenya. Often he had to learn his lessons under a tree. Since the students had no books or slates on which to learn writing, they used sand. The teacher, a Catholic priest and a few Africans, shared a few blackboards between the classes. Some of Tom's classmates walked 15 to 20 miles to school. In 1942, Tom went to a boarding school—a Catholic Secondary School—in his home province of Nyanza. In 1943, he passed the Secondary School three-year examination and was awarded the Kenya African Primary School Certificate. Then, in 1946, he went to Holy Ghost School, a few miles from Nairobi. At the end of 1947, he passed the examination for the African Secondary School Certificate again with enough points to go for the Cambridge Certificate. By this time he had to leave school and help supplement his father's efforts at home.

In the meantime the activities of the Kenya African Union disturbed the Europeans who had long been too complacent about the lot of Africans. A number of new African leaders had emerged. Among them Eliud Mathu, Apolo Ohanga, James Jeremiah, and Chomallan, the four African members of the Kenya Legislative Council. The young men, together with some of the old guard, had succeeded in reorganizing the masses under the banner of the Kenya African Union. This organization called for the unity of all Africans regardless of tribal affiliation.

On June 1, 1947, the Kenya African Union held a conference in Nairobi. The delegates representing branches throughout the country adopted the following declaration of aims:

1. That the political objective of the Africans in Kenya must be self-government by Africans for Africans; and in

that African State, the rights of all racial minorities should be safeguarded.

2. That more African seats should be provided immediately in Kenya Legislative Council, and the inequality of racial representation in the Interterritorial East African Central Assembly should be eliminated.

3. That more land must be made available both in the Crown Lands and in the Highlands for settlement by Africans.

4. That compulsory and free education for Africans, as given to the children of other races, is overdue and must be provided.

5. That the Kipandi with all its humiliating rules and regulations should be abolished immediately.

6. That the deplorable wages, housing, and other conditions of African laborers should be substantially improved, and the principle of "equal pay for equal work" be recognized.

In 1948, Tom Mboya joined the Royal Sanitary Institute's Medical Training School for Sanitary Inspector in Nairobi and later moved to the Jeanes School, a few miles out of Nairobi. By this time, seeds of discontentment were spreading throughout Kenya. Mboya knew, now more than ever, that it was not the preordained lot of the Africans to live in poverty and squalor. He was determined to work to improve the conditions of African workers and to work for the education of African children. At the school he was elected president of the student council. There he learned something of administrative techniques. He qualified as a sanitary inspector in 1950 and was appointed to the staff of the Nairobi City Council the following year. However, his salary was less than one-fifth of that of the European inspectors. In Nairobi he joined the African Staff Association and was later elected president. By 1952, the Association was powerful enough to command the attention of the British authorities.

In the meantime, the sound of the Mau Mau was heard in the land. The tribes of Kenya, mainly the Kikuyu, had lost patience. Their pleas for improvement in their status for too long had gone unheeded. Across a triangle of mountains, jungle, bush, and farmland—16,000 square miles lying across the equator—a battlefield was extended representing a desperate form of African nationalism challenging British rule. Within this triangle, less than twenty miles from the capital city, a bitter guerrilla war raged for nine months. The once secret society of the Mau Mau was no longer a secret. Although 20,000 troops, police auxiliaries, and home guards were sent to put down the uprising, it continued to spread. The campaign against the Mau Maus was costing the British $700 thousand a month in cash money, to say nothing of the vast drain on business and economic life disrupted by the emergency. The British finally put down the Mau Mau rebellion by bringing in one of their toughest and most experienced military commanders, General Sir George Erskine. Jomo Kenyatta, dynamic and intelligent African nationalist, was arrested and tried as the leader of the Mau Mau terrorists. The court that convicted him never really proved this charge. After fours years of bloody struggle between blacks and whites, the Mau Mau rebellion in Kenya was showing signs of drawing to a close. The Africans, especially the Kikuyu people, had paid a terrible price. Over 15,000 had been killed. At one time over 70,000 were behind the barbed wire of detention camps.

The crux of the matter was the land question. In dispute was the system of allocating land according to race, irrespective of any other conditions. The system was in conflict with that of a free and democratic society. It was particularly offensive to the Africans. Land hunger was the underlying cause of the Mau Mau uprising. There are over eighty different tribes in Kenya; the Kikuyu, numbering 1,200,000 is the largest.

In the midst of this emergency, Tom Mboya continued to grow until his life's mission was clearly formulated. Resenting the arrest and detention without trial of African leaders, he became an active member of the Kenya African Union. This meant he was risking the loss of his job, possible arrest, or both. The Medical Officer of Health fired him from his job with the City Council after he had founded and registered the Kenya Local Government Workers Union as a functioning trade union. He became treasurer of the Kenya African Union after the arrest of the acting president, the Hon. Walter Odede. He was also by now a full-time trade union official but without pay. By April 1954, his union was one of the best administered in all of Africa. Then came anther crisis; 35,000 workers were arrested in Nairobi in one day, and the Kenya African Union had been affiliated with the Kenya Federation of Labor. Mboya was general secretary of the Federation.

The Asian community in Kenya was for a while uncertain about the part they would play in the future of Kenya. For a while they were split among themselves and reluctant to give the Europeans any support in putting down the Mau Mau uprising. They made it clear on numerous occasions that they thought the Africans had been mistreated. As for themselves, they continued to demand equality of status with the Europeans. The leader of the Asian community joined the members of the Kenya African Union in demanding that an outside commission be appointed to propose changes in the Kenya Constitution.

By now Mboya was probably having a difficult time remembering all of his titles and appointments. To improve his education, he had enrolled for a Matriculation Exemption Certificate with the Efficiency Correspondence College of South Africa, taking six subjects, though he was mainly interested in economics. After visits to Geneva and Brussels in 1954, he presented a memorandum on the Kenya Emergency to the International Confederation of Free Trade Unions and the British Trade Union Congress. He later attended a seminar on workers education in Calcutta, India. Back home in 1955, he played a leading part in the settlement of the Mombasa Dock strike, obtaining a 33 1/2 percent increase for the dock workers. In August of the same year he represented Kenya, with two other delegates, at an Inter-Africa Labor Conference held in Beira, Portuguese East Africa. Among his own people he was secretary for one year of the Luo Union. From May to September 1955, he was acting representative for the International Confederation of Free Trade Unions in East Africa. In 1956, he took a one-year course at Ruskin College, at Oxford, specializing in industrial relations and political institutions, on a scholarship from Workers Travel Association.

African political parties were permitted only on a regional level. An attempt to form an African National Congress with African barrister, Mr. Argwings Kodheck as chairman, was banned earlier in the year. The European settlers went out to destroy the fledgling African Trade Union movement, which was growing in political power. Mboya, the chairman of the Kenya Federation of Labor, a protégé of the ICFTU, had announced his intentions to be a candidate for the Legislature, in the coming elections.

In the fall of 1956, Mboya toured the United States and Canada under the auspices of the American Committee on Africa. He returned to Kenya as Africans were preparing to participate in the elections for the first time. The Kenya Federation of Labor had asked him to contest the seat for the Nairobi Area Constituency. Early in March 1957, the Africans of Kenya went to the polls for the first time. Tom Mboya fought off three opponents to become the first African to be elected to the Kenya Legislature. Winning of election marked the beginning of a fight for increased African representation. Tom Mboya and the seven other African representatives refused to join the multiracial government by accepting ministries. They stated their reason in unison: "We are firmly and unequivocally opposed to any system which serves as a device to secure for certain people permanent political and economic domination of other sections of our community which in the Lyttleton plan (constitution) is promoting to the advantage of the European community in Kenya. . . . " Together they demanded that African representation be increased from eight to twenty-three. The groundwork for the political future of Tom Mboya had been laid. "Look at him", said one worried Englishman, "and I ask myself how would I like to face him twenty years from now, when he has twenty more years of legislative experience behind him."

Before Mboya had time to warm his seat in the Legislative Council, he was once more in trouble in court. He did not like the terms of the Colonial Office's 1957 Constitution. He insisted on complete parliamentary democracy for the African masses. When a group of moderate Africans agreed to run for the special seats held by Tom Mboya and his supporters, they were denounced as "stooges and traitors." With this, the British authorities hauled Mboya and his supporters into court for conspiracy and criminal libel. After a short and colorful trial, Mboya paid a token fine and went back to continue the fight for the complete freedom of Kenya.

In July 1957, Tom Mboya was one of the two delegates sent to London to plead for a new constitution. In March 1958, he was in Ghana participating in the First Anniversary Celebrations of that nation's independence as a guest of Prime Minister Nkrumah. Honors, appointments, and increasing responsibilities continued to pour upon Tom Mboya. In July 1958, he was elected chairman of the International Confederation of Free Trade Unions, Eastern Central and Southern Africa. In October he visited Ethiopia as the guest of Haile Selassie.

After attending a union meeting in Brussels he went to London again for a conference with the colonial secretary. Here he presented a public affidavit in which Rawson Macharia declared that he had been bribed to give false evidence in the Jomo Kenyatta trial in 1953.

The greatest moment in the life of Tom Mboya was reached on December 1, 1958 when he was elected chairman of the First All African Peoples Conference at Accra. The Conference, held in Accra from December 13, 1958, drew world attention. The All African Peoples Conference brought together the most representative gathering of African leaders ever assembled. In Tom Mboya's words:

> The Conference of Independent African States marked the birth of the African *Personality*. The representatives of the African States at Accra unanimously agreed on the need for Africa to rise and be heard at all the councils of world affairs; and to effectuate this objective they created the Organization of African States, which now consults on all questions affecting Africa before the United Nations and which represents the united will of all Africans on such issues. Equally important was their decision that Africa's total liberation was the task for all Africans.

Speaking earlier in the Conference he said: "Today in Accra we announce to the world that these same Powers which meet to decide on the partitioning of Africa, will from here, from this Conference, be told in a firm, clear, and definite voice: 'Scram from Africa.'" With this said, the Conference took on a new lease of life. Solidarity had been achieved.

At the invitation of the American Committee on Africa, Tom Mboya—of whom *Life Magazine* stated: "He is not only the outstanding political personality in Kenya, but among the most important in all Africa"—traveled 9000 miles to the United States to be the guest of honor and keynote speaker at the first Africa Freedom Day Celebration held in the United States. The contagious charm of his personality immediately found a large American audience. At his first press conference, April 9, 1958, after he arrived from London, he summarized his position on a number of matters relating to Africa's future:

1. On Kenya, he complained that he was often misinterpreted and said that he continued to believe that there was room in Kenya for those whites who wanted to make Kenya their home. However, he declared that the country must be run on a democratic basis of "one man, one vote" and not as at present, with 62,000 whites maintaining control over 6,000,000 Africans.
2. In London he sought to get a judicial inquiry into the 1953 trial of Jomo Kenyatta, convicted in 1953 of organizing the antiwhite Mau Mau terrorists in Kenya.
3. He believed that the political situation in Kenya was changing and that the former unanimity of the European white settlers showed evidence of breaking down, although restrictions on Africans persisted.
4. The Communist Party was nonexistent, legal or otherwise, in Kenya.
5. The dual struggle of the Africans was a fight for political freedom for over a hundred million people still under colonial rule and a fight against poverty, disease, and ignorance.

At other times and places during his visit to the United States, Mboya uttered other significant statements:

1. On Sunday, April 12, 1959, he "met the press" on a nationwide television program. Here he showed his skill in answering the sharp questions of the most astute news gatherers in the United States. He said emphatically that he opposed colonialism of any kind, whether British, French, Belgian, Portuguese, Dutch, or Russian. He stated further that the long-term objective of the All African Peoples Conference in Accra, Ghana, the previous December was "the possibility of a United States of Africa."
2. On April 15, at the Africa Freedom Day Celebration, three thousand New Yorkers rose from their seats in the cultured atmosphere of Carnegie Hall, to roar the African cry of "uhuru" the African word for freedom. Later, during his one-hour speech, Mboya said: "Our only quarrel is with colonialism and European domination. With those we shall never

compromise.... We have a right to self-determination. It is a birthright which we need not either justify or explain."

3. Three days later, Tom Mboya had joined the pilgrimage to Washington, sponsored by the "Youth March for Integrated Schools." Addressing the thirty thousand marchers Tom Mboya declared: "We Africans seek the same peace, stability, security, and well-being that all decent people seek the world over, and we are unwilling to be used as pawns in a great power struggle."

4. In an article written for the North American Newspaper Alliance, Mboya said in essence: Today Africa is a giant awakening. Slowly, but surely, she is moving forward, determined to catch up with the rest of the world.

5. When he spoke at the World Affairs Conference, on the campus of the University of Colorado, he drew the largest audience of any speaker. While referring to the European and American criticism of such troubles as the riots in Brazzaville, in the newly independent Congo Republic, he said: "I am flattered that the older nations expect us to be perfect in our first years of independence, even though they have been unable to attain perfection themselves."

6. He later addressed more large audiences at Harvard University and other places of high repute.

7. In his last public appearance in New York City, on May 11, 1959, Mboya addressed an overflow audience at the Church of the Master in Harlem.

All of these cogent ideas, emphatically and courageously uttered, bore testimony that Tom Mboya, the "world's youngest statesman," was a leading exponent of the new "African Personality."

Three

DIFFERENT ROADS TO FREEDOM

▼

COMMENTARY

▼

AMONG AFRICAN PEOPLE of the world, after the event of slavery and colonization beginning in the fifteenth century, there have been two main roads to freedom. There have been other roads leading in the same direction using different methods and slightly different ideologies. There have been millions of people of African descent living in Asia and other parts of the world who did not begin to recognize this fact until the middle of the twentieth century. African people are the most widely-dispersed of all the ethnic groups in the world. This was recently called to our attention in the publications, "African Presence in Early Asia" and "African Presence in Early Europe," both published in two special issues of the *Journal of African Civilization* in 1985.

In the United States, which is a nation composed of immigrants, the Africans have a special and tragic uniqueness. We are the only immigrants who came to America against our will. We are the immigrants who came with an invitation. The nature of this invitation, the chains, the filthy ships, the guns, and the vile sailors who had no respect for our humanity, will not be discussed here. But the invitation was special just the same. When we arrived in America we had no housing problem, no employment problem. There were plenty of jobs waiting for us, with no pay for nearly 300 years. Our contribution to the economy of the United States, the Caribbean Islands, and the world in general laid the basis for global capitalism in the modern scientific and technical world.

As slaves, we did not forget Africa. We longed for the continent of our birth. Some of us returned in mind, if we could not return in body. The American Colonization Society was the first formal movement committed to this idea. As a result of this society, the country of Liberia was settled, and the country of Sierra Leone and some other English possessions. During the first half of the nineteenth century, there were massive slave revolts in large parts of the United States. In his book, *American Negro Slave Revolts*, Herbert Aptheker documents 250 of these slave revolts. This was also the period when "free" blacks in the North and in the New England states began to publish newspapers, magazines and pamphlets indicting slavery. A lot of this activity unfolded in and around the newly-formed independent black church that called itself the African Methodist Episcopal Church. David Walker's *Appeal* (1829), recharged the energy of the antislavery movement, coming practically on the eve of the Nat Turner Revolt in 1831. By mid-nineteenth century, African-Americans and some Caribbean-Americans living in the United States had planned visits to Africa in search of a place for settlement. Two of the most notable of these searchers for a place in their ancestral home, Africa, were Martin Delany and Robert Campbell.

Slavery was the principal emotional issue on the eve of the Civil War, though the Civil War was not principally about slavery. The objective of the Civil War from a federal point of view was the reunification and the continuation of the United States as one nation. When emancipation of the African-Americans did come, it was a strategic move to weaken the South and end its resistance to reunification. The aftermath of the Civil War began a period called Reconstruction. For a brief eleven years, black Americans enjoyed a mild form of political independence until that independence was betrayed during the Tilden-Hayes presidential election in 1884–1885. This period is best portrayed in Professor Rayford Logan's book, *The Betrayal of the Negro* and Dr. DuBois' historical classic, *Black Reconstruction*. During this period African Americans had two senators, at least two dozen congressmen, mayors of some major cities in the South, and they controlled both the upper and lower houses in one state, South Carolina. Professor Rayford Logan referred to as the Nadir, the period of our darkest hour. The aftermath of this period in turn led to the Booker T. Washington era with both positive and negative results. We entered the twentieth century facing new troubles and new challenges.

The entire African world had been in revolt during the whole of the nineteenth century. Some men (and movements) were trying to bring African people together to work toward their common interest. Early in the twentieth century a Trinidadian lawyer, H. Sylvester Williams, put a name to this effort. He called it Pan-Africanism. The struggle in the West Indies, in Africa, and in the United States was basically the same, the struggle for direction and definition. We were asking and trying to answer the questions: Whom do we need, and who needs us? We were trying to regain what slavery and colonialism had taken away. In many ways this was a preface to the future fights for civil rights in the United States, for a federation of islands in the Caribbean and for the end of colonialism and for the independence and unification of all Africa.

TWO ROADS TO FREEDOM: THE AFRICANS' AND THE AFRICAN-AMERICANS' LONG FIGHT

▼

THE AFRICANS WHO CAME to the United States as slaves attempted to reclaim their lost African heritage soon after they arrived in this country. They were searching for the lost identity that the slave system had destroyed. Concurrent with this search for an identity in America has been the search for an identity in the world, that is, in essence, an identity as a human being with a history, before and after slavery, that commands respect.

Some African-Americans gave up the search and accepted the distorted image of themselves that had been created by their oppressors. As early as 1881, Dr. Edward Wilmot Blyden, the great West Indian scholar and benefactor of West Africa, addressed himself to this situation when he said:

> In all English-speaking countries the mind of the intelligent Negro child revolts against the descriptions of the Negro given in elementary school books, geographies, travels, histories ... having embraced or at least assented to those falsehoods about himself, he concludes that his only hope of rising in the scale of respectable manhood is to strive for what is most unlike himself and most alien to his peculiar tastes.

In spite of the alienation spoken of here by Dr. Blyden, the Afri-

175

can-Americans' spiritual trek back to Africa continued.

During the eighteenth century there was strong agitation among certain groups of black people in America for a return to Africa. This agitation was found mainly among groups of "free Negroes" because of the uncertainty of their position as freedmen in a slave-holding society. "One can see it late into the eighteenth century," Dr. W.E.B. DuBois explains in his book, *Dust of Dawn*, "when the Negro Union of Newport, Rhode Island, in 1788, proposed to the Free African Society of Philadelphia a general exodus to Africa on the part of at least free Negroes."

The "Back to Africa" idea has been a reoccurring theme in African-American life and thought for more than a hundred years. This thought was strong during the formative years of the Colonization Society and succeeded in convincing some of the most outstanding black men of the eighteenth and nineteenth centuries such as: John Russwurm, the first African college graduate; and Lot Care, the powerful Virginia preacher. Later the Society fell into severe disrepute after an argument with the Abolitionists.

Two freedom struggles emerged early in the nineteenth century— one African, one African-American. While Africans were engaged in their wars against colonialism, American blacks were engaged in slave revolts.

In 1839 Joseph Cinque, the son of a Mandi king in Sierra Leone, West Africa, was sold into slavery and shipped to Cuba. Cinque and his fellow Africans revolted on board the ship and ordered the ship's owners to sail to Africa. The Spanish ship owners steered northward when they were not being watched and eventually landed off the coast of Long Island. The Africans were arrested and sent to New Haven, Connecticut, where they were put on trial.

When the trial began, there was great excitement in the country. People talked about the case and took sides. Southern politicians wanted to give the Africans back to the Spaniards, who had bought them. The trial lasted all winter.

In court, Cinque made a wonderful speech in his own language, telling the story of how he and his men had fought to be free. After that speech, the court ordered the Africans to be set free.

Cinque and his men were sent to school to be educated and were found to be very intelligent and quick to learn.

Meanwhile, the two Spaniards and the Spanish government appealed to the United States Supreme Court to have the Africans returned to them as slaves. The friends of Cinque and his men asked John Quincy Adams, the former President of the United States and a great lawyer, to speak for the Africans. On March 9, 1841, after Adams had spoken, Chief Justice Taney of the Supreme Court ruled that Cinque and the others were to be freed.

After that, Cinque continued his schooling, and in 1842, he and his men returned to Africa.

All America had been stirred by this case. The slave owners feared that the news about the freedom and return to Africa of Cinque and his fellow Africans would cause their slaves to revolt and also demand to be returned to their homeland.

In the years before the Civil War plans for the migration of the "free" Africans back to Africa were revived and agents were sent to South America, Haiti and Africa. Paul Cuffee, a free black ship owner from New Bedford, Massachusetts, had founded the Friendly Society for the Emigration of Free Negroes from America and had taken a large number back to Africa at his own expense.

In the middle of the nineteenth century, while the issue of slavery was being debated in most of the country, the feeling for Africa among American blacks was growing stronger. Publications like *Freedom's Journal* and *Douglass' Monthly* edited by Frederick Douglass, called attention to the plight of the people of Africa as well as the black Americans.

"I thank God for making me a man simply; but Delany always thanks him for making him a black man." Thus spoke Frederick Douglass of his old friend, Martin R. Delany, spokesman, physician, explorer and scientist.

Martin R. Delany was proud of his African background and the Mandingo (Manding) blood that flowed in his veins. He was one of the leaders of the great debate following the passage of the Fugitive Slave Act in 1850. He was the spokesman for the black people who felt that the bitter racial climate in America had made life for them, in this country, unbearable. Delany was the strongest voice in several conventions of free Africans to discuss plans for emigrating to Africa. In 1859, he led the first and only exploratory party of American-born Africans to the land of their forefathers. In the region of the Niger River, in the area that became Nigeria, Delany's party carried out scientific studies and made agreements with several African kings for the settlement of emigrants from America. This interest in Africa was continued under the leadership of men like Reverend Alexander Crummell and Bishop Turner. Turner was the best-known of the radical black ministers during the latter half of the nineteenth century; Crummell was a missionary who functioned mainly in Liberia, raising considerable amounts of money for missionary schools in West Africa.

During the latter part of the nineteenth century Edward Wilmot Blyden, who was from what was then the Danish West Indies, called attention to the important role that Africa could play in emerging world affairs. He was convinced that the only easy way to bring respect and dignity to his people was by building progressive new "empires" in Africa. He was of the opinion that the "New World Negro" has a great future in Africa. He saw Liberia, in West Africa, as the ideal place where African-Americans could build a new and great civilization by making use of the things that they had learned in the West and preserving the best of the African way of life. Because of his work and that of many others, the African consciousness was translated into useful programs of service to Africa. African-American institutions of higher learning joined in this service through their training of the personnel of the churches as well as their support of Africans studying in their institutions.

The idea of uniting all Africa had its greatest development early in this century. In 1900, the Trinidadian lawyer, H. Sylvester Williams called together the first Pan-African Conference in London. This meeting attracted attention and put the word "Pan-African" in the dictionaries for the first time. The thirty delegates to the conference came mainly from England, the West Indies and the United States. The small delegation from the United States was led by W.E.B. DuBois.

This meeting had no deep roots in Africa itself, and the movement and the idea died for almost a generation. Then came the First World War. At the close of this war, W.E.B. DuBois led the determined agitation for the rights of African people throughout the world, particularly in Africa. Meetings were held and a petition was sent to President Wilson, who was meeting with other leaders of the Western world at the Peace Congress at Versailles.

Dr. DuBois went to Paris with the idea of calling a Pan-African Congress with the purpose of impressing upon the members of the Peace Congress sitting in Versailles the importance of Africa in the future world. In spite of being without credentials and influence some attention was paid to the idea. President Wilson's assistant, Colonel House, was sympathetic but non-committal. The *Chicago Tribune* reported, January 19, 1919, in dispatch from Paris dated December 30, 1918:

An Ethiopian Utopia, to be fashioned out of the German colonies, is the latest dream of leaders of the Negro race who are here at the invitation of the United States Government as part of the extensive entourage of the American peace delegation. Robert R. Moton, successor of the late Booker Washington as head of Tuskegee Institute, and Dr. William E.B. DuBois, Editor of the *Crisis*, are promoting a Pan-African Conference to be held here during the winter while the Peace Conference is in full blast. It is to embrace Negro leaders from America, Abyssinia, Liberia, Haiti and the French and British colonies and other parts of the black world. Its object is to get out of the Peace Conference an effort to modernize the dark continent, and in the world reconstruction to provide international machinery looking toward the civilization of the African natives.

The Negro leaders are not agreed upon any definite plan, but Dr. DuBois has mapped out a scheme which he has presented in the form of memorandum to President Wilson. It is quite Utopian, and it has less than a Chinaman's chance of getting anywhere in the Peace Conference, but it is nevertheless interesting. As "self-determination" is one of the words to conjure with in Paris nowadays, the Negro leaders are seeking to have it applied, if possible, in a measure to their race in Africa.

Dr. DuBois' dream is that the Peace Conference could form an internationalized Africa, to have as its basis the former German colonies, with their 1,000,000 square miles and 12,500,000 population.

"To this," his plan reads, "could be added by negotiation the 800,000 square miles and 9,000,000 inhabitants of Portuguese

Africa. It is not impossible that Belgium could be persuaded to
add to such a State the 900,000 square miles and 9,000,000
natives of the Congo, making an international Africa with over
2,500,000 square miles of land and over 20,000,000 people.

"This Africa for the Africans could be under the guidance of
international organization. The governing international commission should represent not simply Governments, but modern
culture, science, commerce, social reform, and religious philanthropy. It must represent not simply the white world, but the
civilised Negro world.

"With these two principles the practical policies to be followed out in the government of the new States should involve
a thorough and complete system of modern education, built
upon the present government, religion, and customary law of
the churches. Within ten years 20,000,000 black children ought
to be in school. Within a generation young Africa should know
the essential outlines of modern culture. From the beginning the
actual general government should use both coloured and white
officials."

W.E.B. DuBois wrote extensively about the idea of Pan-Africanism
and world unity of People of African descent. This is the essence of his
statement on the intent of the Pan-African Congress of 1919:

This Congress represented Africa partially. Of the fifty-seven
delegates from fifteen countries, nine were African countries
with twelve delegates. The other delegates came from the
United States, which sent sixteen, and the West Indies, with
twenty-one. Most of these delegates did not come to France for
this meeting, but happened to be residing there, mainly for
reasons connected with the war. America and all the colonial
powers refused to issue special visas.

The Congress influenced the Peace Conference. *The New
York Evening Globe*, February 22, 1919, described it as "the first
assembly of the kind in history, and has for its object the
drafting of an appeal to the Peace Conference to give the Negro
race of Africa a chance to develop unhindered by other races.
Seated at long green tables in the council room today were

Negroes in the trim uniform of American Army officers, other American coloured men in frock coats or business suits, polished French Negroes who hold public office, Senegalese who sit in the French Chamber of Deputies .... "

The Congress specifically asked that the German colonies be turned over to an international organization instead of being handled by the various colonial powers. Out of this idea came the Mandates Commission. The resolutions of the Congress said in part:

(a)   That the Allied and Associated Powers establish a code of law for the international protection of the natives of Africa, similar to the proposed international code for labour.

(b)   That the League of Nations establish a permanent Bureau charged with the special duty of over-seeing the application of these laws to the political, social, and economic welfare of the natives.

(c)   The Negroes of the world demand that hereafter the natives of Africa and the peoples of African descent be governed according to the following principles:

1.   The land and its natural resources shall be held in trust for the natives and at all times they shall have effective ownership of as much land as they can profitably develop.

2.   Capital: The investment of capital and granting of concessions shall be so regulated as to prevent the exploitation of the natives and the exhaustion of the natural wealth of the country. Concessions shall always be limited in time and subject to state control. The growing social needs of the natives must be regarded and the profits taxed for social and material benefit of the natives.

3.   Labour: Slavery and corporal punishment shall be abolished and forced labour except in punishment for crime; and the general conditions of labour shall be prescribed and regulated by the State.

4.   Education: It shall be the right of every native child

to learn to read and write his own language, and the language of the trustee nation, at public expense, and to be given technical instruction in some branch of industry. The State shall also educate as large a number of natives as possible in higher technical and cultural training and maintain a corps of native teachers ....

5. The State: The natives of Africa must have the right to participate in the Government as far as their development permits in conformity with the principle that the Government exists for the natives, and not the natives for the Government. They shall at once be allowed to participate in local and tribal government according to ancient usage, and this participation shall gradually extend, as education and experience proceeds to the higher offices of State, to the end that, in time, Africa be ruled by consent of the Africans.... Whenever it is proven that African natives are not receiving just treatment at the hands of any State or that any State deliberately excludes its civilised citizens or subjects of Negro descent from its body politic and cultural, it shall be the duty of the League of Nations to bring the matter to the civilized World.

The New York Herald, Paris, February 24, 1919, reported:

There is nothing unreasonable in the programme, drafted at the Pan-African Congress which was held in Paris last week. It calls upon the Allied and Associated Powers to draw up an international code of law for the protection of the nations of Africa, and to create, as a section of the League of Nations, a permanent bureau to ensure observance of such laws and thus further the racial, political, and economic interests of the natives.

The idea of Pan-Africa having thus been established, Dr. DuBois now attempted to build a real organization. The Pan-Africa movement began to represent growth and development. Soon, the DuBois approach to Pan-Africanism was challenged by the approach of Marcus Garvey.

The National Association for the Advancement of Colored People began their interest in Africa with their support of the various Pan-African Congresses called by Dr. DuBois. The African and African-American freedom struggle that had met and joined forces, briefly, in the nineteenth century was now meeting again in the twentieth century.

Two great personalities were bringing the message of Africa's awakening to the world's attention. Both of them were saying in different ways that Africa was great once and will be great again. Both of them told African-Americans they had a part to play in Africa's redemption. The two personalities were W.E.B. DuBois and Marcus Garvey.

The Italian-Ethiopian war renewed interest in Africa. This interest sustained and was increased when, in 1957, the Gold Coast gained its independence and took back its ancient name—Ghana.

Black American grassroots identification with African problems burst upon the international scene during the first Congo crisis when a group of black nationalists created a disturbance in the galleries of the United Nations in protest against alleged U.N. connivance in the murder of Patrice Lumumba. This identification with African political affairs amongst the black masses reached its zenith with the visit to Africa of the late Malcolm X and his effort to enlist the support of the Organization of African Unity.

This growing interest in Africa and a rediscovery of the lost African heritage initiated the spread of black consciousness among young civil rights militants. Out of this feeling the concept of Black Power was born.

THE BERLIN CONFERENCE

▼

THE 100TH ANNIVERSARY OF THE Berlin Conference was celebrated in 1984 and 1985. The significance of this conference is that it put an end to the remaining free territories in Africa and gave the European powers entry and eventual control over Africa's hinterlands. With the exception of Ethiopia, with its pseudo-independence, and Liberia, which was then as now an economic colony, all Africa was under one European power or the other after this conference. United States involvement in the conference was through the back door with the pretense that this nation had no interest in colonies. But, as a result of the Berlin Conference, Germany acquired four large pieces of Africa: The Cameroons; part of what is now Togo or Togoland; Tanzania that they called Tanganyika; and Southwest Africa now called Namibia. The Belgians acquired all of the Congo, which for a number of years was ruled as the private property of King Leopold of Belgium. Belgian rule and misrule in the Congo was a disaster transcending the status of a holocaust. The wholesale murder and mutilization of Africans in the Congo caused an international investigation when colonialists expressed their condemnation and shame for the crimes of another colonialist. The American writer, Mark Twain, wrote a small but well-circulated book called *King Leopold's Soliloquy*. The best-detailed accounts of this atrocity came from E.D. Morel in his books, *Black Man's Burden* and *King Leopold's Congo*. The Congo section of *The Diaries of Roger Caseman* is also informative on this subject. In this African Holocaust the indigenous people of the Congo were killed in large numbers, far in excess of six million.

African-American newspapers of the day were strong in editorial

185

condemnation of these atrocities. The outstanding African-American figure investigating conditions in the Congo was George Washington Williams. The details of his investigation and further information about his life can be found in John Hope Franklin's book, *George Washington Williams, A Biography*.

The Berlin Conference and the subsequent partitioning of Africa is often referred to as the scramble for Africa. To some extent this is a historical error. The real scramble for Africa started in the fifteenth and sixteenth centuries. The Berlin Conference and the distribution of large portions of Africa to European colonial powers was the end of the scramble. As a result of this event in history, anticolonial wars began that lasted well into the twentieth century. Though it is not thought of as being so, this event is the preface to the anticolonial wars in Africa that would ultimately lead to the African Independence Explosion early in the second half of the twentieth century.

The Berlin Conference (1884-1885) and its influence on African-Americans cannot be understood by a focus on the conference alone. This was an event that occurred during the last years of the nineteenth century when Africans all over the world were fighting to regain the nationhood that had been lost in slavery and colonialism. In Africa itself, anticolonial wars were sporadic throughout the continent. In the Caribbean Islands and in South America, Africans were still the backbone of the plantation. Their freedom from slavery that was proclaimed during the first half of the nineteenth century, was still less than complete. The organized concern for Africa that had started early in the nineteenth century in the United States had already developed the African Colonization Movement (1816–1865). The Republic of Liberia was founded with the help of this movement.

At the time of the Berlin Conference, two decades had passed since the Emancipation Proclamation had freed the black Americans from slavery. The black family in the United States, outlawed in most of the country, prior to 1863, was near completing the first generation of its existence. The African Methodist Episcopal Church had already been established by Reverend Richard Allen, who became its first Bishop.

Politically, black Americans were building new institutions and trying to make their presence in the United States constructive, along with other larger immigrant groups, in a nation of immigrants. In order to end a terrible Civil War, the United States had made promises to black Americans that could not be easily kept. The Africans in the United States were in the dilemma of being a nation within a nation, searching for a nationality.

The black American press was making itself heard among the blacks looking for new directions and leadership. The Berlin Conference, and Africa, in general, was the subject of many of the articles and editorials that appeared in black newspapers and magazines.

There is a background to black Americans' concern for Africa, as reflected in their reaction to the Berlin Conference of 1884–1885. The concept of "Return to Africa," had been a recurring idea in the life of a large number of African-Americans for a hundred years before the Berlin Conference.

Professor Sterling Stuckey alludes to this fact in his book *The Ideological Origins of Black Nationalism*:

> The precise details of certain experiences that bear directly on Black Nationalism will remain forever enshrouded in obscurity—the degree to which Africans during the 17th and 18th centuries continued to think positively of their ancestral home; the extent to which they preferred living apart from white people; the length of time the majority of them remained essentially African in America.

Professor Elliot P. Skinner of Columbia University speaks of a "continuing dialectic between Africans and African-America." He further states that:

> Since Paul Cuffee's time (1759–1817), concerted efforts by African-Americans to achieve equality in America have been accompanied by an increased dialogue about Africa. . . .

Paul Cuffee, among black Americans, is considered to be the father of the African Consciousness Movement. The African Consciousness Movement was developed, partly, from his ideas. He was responsible for the resettlement of a large number of black Americans in Sierra Leone and in Liberia. He founded the Friendly Society for the Emigration of Free Blacks from America. He was a sea captain who used his personal funds to return Africans to their motherland.

The black American had been expressing a concern for Africa for nearly a century before the Berlin Conference. They were concerned about the history and condition of African people before and after slavery. Large numbers of so-called "free" blacks did not feel secure in the English colony that became the United States. The revolutionary talk that they had heard from white people did not improve their condition nor free a single slave. In the first half of the nineteenth century they were making themselves heard through their newspapers, magazines, books and pamphlets. In 1812, Paul Cuffee published his pamphlet, *Brief Account of the Settlement and Present Situation of the Colony of Sierra Leone in Africa*. This work was followed by other black American writers looking at Africa from different vantage points. The whole African world was awakening to the cruelty of slavery and colonialism. The anti-colonial wars had already started in Africa. In the Caribbean Islands the slave revolts had led to the establishment of Haiti as the first independent African state in the New World. In the midst of this atmosphere of change, challenge, and conflict a "free" black man, named David Walker published an antislavery pamphlet, "Appeal to the Coloured Citizens of the World." This document was a call for a world revolt against slavery. Throughout the United States, including parts of the North, slavery was opposed. In principle, the pamphlet was denounced as inappropriate and incendiary by some of the Abolitionists who thought David Walker had gone too far and overstated the case against slavery.

From the introduction to the book, *David Walker's Appeal*, the writer, Charles M. Wiltse presents the following brief account of David Walker:

> David Walker was born in North Carolina in 1785. His father was a slave, who, according to some accounts, died before David's birth. His mother was a "free" Negro who passed on to her son both her own freedom and a burning indignation toward the enslavers of her people. We know nothing of the boy's early life, except that somehow he acquired an education. We have his own testimony that he traveled widely throughout the United States, and particularly the South, where he saw slavery in all its aspects, and found those who lived under it to be "degraded, wretched, abject." Nor was the lot of the free Negro

much better in a society dedicated to the doctrine of racial inequality. "It is a notorious fact," he wrote, "that the major part of the white Americans have, ever since we have been among them, tried to keep us ignorant, and make us believe that God made us and our children to be slaves to them and theirs."

In many ways the intellectual antecedent of David Walker was the black New England sea captain, Paul Cuffee and the African-consciousness personalities who emerged in the United States early in the nineteenth century, mainly, Prince Hall, founder of the African lodge that became the first black American masonic lodge.

In his book, *Pioneer in Protest*, Lerone Bennet, Jr. gives us the following background on Prince Hall and his achievements:

His major contribution was the organization of the first black Masonic lodge. He attempted first to enter a lodge of the white American Masons. Rebuffed, he applied to a lodge attached to a British regiment stationed near Boston. On March 6, 1775, Prince Hall and fourteen other black men were initiated into Masonry in the British Army lodge. When the British regiment withdrew, the black Masons formed, under a limited permit, African Lodge No. I, one of the first black organizations in America. After the war, Hall was granted a charter from the Grand Lodge of England. On May 6, 1787, African Lodge No. 459 was formally organized in Boston with Hall as master. This event, coming less than a month after the founding of the Free African Society in Philadelphia, was an epochal leap forward in black consciousness. In 1797, Hall helped organize African lodges in Philadelphia and Providence, Rhode Island, thereby becoming a pioneer in the development of a black interstate organization.

This is only part of the eighteenth century origins of the nineteenth century revolt against slavery. After the first massive slave revolt during the first half of the nineteenth century, the American Colonization Society was an organized fact.

Martin Delany and a new breed of black radical thinker had

emerged. They were intellectually prepared to question the entire American society—especially slavery. In Delany's own time he was a lecturer on many subjects, a talented writer and an associate of men such as Frederick Douglass, William Lloyd Garrison, and John Brown. He was co-editor of the magazine *North Star* with Frederick Douglass. At one point in his life he had some misgivings about American blacks migrating to Africa. At first he favored Central and South America. After his first visit to Africa he advocated the establishment of a separate nation for African-Americans in the Niger Valley in West Africa.

> The back-to-Africa idea has been a recurring theme in the lives of Black Americans for more than a hundred years. The thought was strong during the formative years of the Colonization Society and some of the most outstanding black men of the eighteenth and nineteenth centuries came under its persuasion. In the middle of the nineteenth century, while the issue of slavery was being debated in most of the country, the feeling for Africa among American Blacks was growing stronger. Publications like *Freedom's Journal* and *Douglass' Monthly*, edited by Frederick Douglass called attention to the plight of the people of Africa as well as the black Americans.
>
> As far back as 1881, the renowned scholar and benefactor of West Africa, Dr. Edward Wilmot Blyden, speaking on the occasion of his inauguration as president of Liberia College, sounded the note for the organized teaching of the culture and civilization of Africa and decried the fact that the world's image of Africa was not in keeping with Africa's true status in world history. I quote from his address on this occasion:
>
> > The people generally are not yet prepared to understand their own interests in the great work to be done for themselves and their children. We shall be obliged to work for some time to come not only without the popular sympathy we ought to have but with utterly inadequate resources.
> >
> > In all English-speaking countries the mind of the intelligent Negro child revolts against the descriptions of the Negro given in elementary books, geographies, travel, histo-

ries....

Having embraced or at least assented to these falsehoods about himself, he concludes that his only hope of rising in the scale of respectable manhood is to strive for what is most unlike himself and most alien to his peculiar tastes. And whatever his literary attainments or acquired ability, he fancies that he must grind at the mill which is provided for him, putting in material furnished by his hands, bringing no contribution from his own field; and of course nothing comes out but what is put in.

Dr. W.E.B. DuBois, the elder scholar among African-Americans looked at the same situation and was more hopeful. In a speech entitled "The American Negro and the Darker World," delivered in New York City, April 30, 1957, DuBois referred to the aftermath of the crisis that developed in the African family of nations early in the fifteenth century. This division between Africans and Africans came at a time when the Europeans, having emerged from the political lethargy of the Middle Ages, were looking for new energy, new raw materials, and new lands to conquer. The slave trade and subsequently colonialism had saved Europe from economic collapse. Throughout the world some of the surviving victims of European expansion and influence were still longing to return to their African motherland on the eve of the Berlin conference of 1884.

Among individual personalities of this time the concept of African reclamation and redemption is best reflected in the life of Edward Wilmot Blyden and in the books written and compiled about him by Professor Hollis R. Lynch of Columbia University. Dr. Blyden lived in the past and prophesied the future of African people. A serious study of his life is as relevant today as it would have been when he lived and was active during the last half of the nineteenth century.

Edward Wilmot Blyden, who was born in what is now the Virgin Islands, was the intellectual bridge between Africa, the Caribbean Islands and the United States during the second half of the nineteenth century. The study of his life by Hollis R. Lynch throws new light on his life and work for a world union of African people. His dream fell far short of being realized. However, in the pursuit of this dream he became the intellectual focus of the English-speaking African of his time; the African personality, Pan-Africanism, and negritude are all concepts that developed, partly, from the stimulus of this thinking and activity. Some of his nineteenth century plans and programs for the redemption of Africa were realized in the twentieth century. Many of our present-day African-American youth who are mouthing the phrase "black is beautiful" do not know that Edward Wilmot Blyden said the same thing earlier.

Blyden went back to Africa, physically and spiritually and began to reclaim his heritage in the 1850s. He became, in many ways, more African than some Africans, and he became the defender of the history and culture of that continent and its people.

The dilemma of the nineteenth-century black American continued in the twentieth century. Dr. Elliot P. Skinner calls attention to this dilemma and refers to a statement in the book *Souls of Black Folks* by W.E.B. DuBois, in this manner:

> But the Blacks of America never accepted the basic premises of the whites, and over and above the physical impossibility of suddenly becoming white, they never completely accepted the idea that they could not be black, free and American. Consequently, whenever African-Americans have fought hardest to achieve all the rights of Americans, they have invariably found themselves defending their Africanness. DuBois recognized this dialectical process when he declared that:
>
> > The history of the American Negro is the history of this strife—this longing to attain self-conscious manhood, to merge his double self into a better and truer self. In this merging he wishes neither of the older selves to be lost. He would not Africanize America, for America has too much to teach the world and Africa. He would not bleach his Negro soul in a flood of white Americanism, for he knows that Negro blood has a message for the world. He simply wishes to make it possible for a man to be both Negro and American, without having the doors of opportunity closed roughly in his face.

The expressions of both Elliot P. Skinner and W.E.B. DuBois were prevalent among African-Americans before the Berlin Conference of 1884. Their reaction to this conference and the partitioning of Africa in general has been a motivating factor in their African consciousness from the latter part of the nineteenth century to the present.

The editors of the *A.M.E. Church Review* and other black American owned publications were quick to inform the Africans in the United States about the Berlin Conference and its consequences for African people everywhere. They noted that: "There is a remarkable unanimity of feeling between the powers of Europe when a slice of Africa is the question."

In a major work on the subject of black American reaction to the partitioning of Africa, Professor Sylvia M. Jacobs refers to the historical background of the event when she says:

Early nineteenth century expansion and colonialism were the antecedents of the "new imperialism" that evolved in the late nineteenth century. In the last two decades of the nineteenth century this resurgent expansionist spirit resulted in the scramble for colonies by the major powers. By the end of the century, the idea that the world was divided between "civilized" and "uncivilized" peoples and that it was the responsibility of the "advanced" nations of the world to carry "civilization" to alien areas had been universally accepted. In his poem, *The White Man's Burden*, first published in 1899, Rudyard Kipling fictionalized the philosophy of this period. European nations, motivated by nationalistic ambitions, commercial advantages, racism, and destiny, began their "assault on barbarism." The period from about 1880 to 1920 has been labeled the age of the "white man's burden." These years closed with the partitioning of the world among the great powers.

By 1880, European imperialism in Africa had come to be identified with the concept of mission and trusteeship as "a sacred duty which a superior civilization contracts toward less advanced peoples." Africa was seen as new field for missionary work, in need of the "humanizing influences of Christian civilization," as well as an area ripe for economic exploitation. The scramble for and partitioning of Africa were inevitable consequences of the European powers' desire for overseas empires.

This period should be more correctly called the last of the scramble for Africa. The actual scramble for Africa began in the fifteenth and the sixteenth centuries with the start of the slave trade and subsequently colonialism. During this period Europeans not only colonized most of the world, they colonized information about the world. The rationale for European world dominance was now an evolving theme in Western social thought. The pretence of "freeing the slaves" had created a new form of slavery called colonialism. In the Western world it was supported, in part, by the church and a new dimension of racism. Basically this was the condition that the black Americans and the African world had to deal with on the eve of the Berlin Conference.

The following statement is extracted from the European rationale for the conference:

> The General Act was drawn-up in Berlin on February 26, 1885, between France, Germany, Austria-Hungary, Belgium, Denmark, Spain, the United States, Great Britain, Italy, The Netherlands, Portugal, Russia, Sweden, Norway and Turkey to regulate freedom of commerce in the basins of the Congo and Niger Rivers, as well as the new occupation of the territories on the West African coast.
>
> ... Desiring to regulate, in the spirit of mutual good understanding. The most favourable conditions to the development of commerce and of civilization in certain regions of Africa, and to guarantee to all the people the benefits of free navigation on the two principal rivers which emptied in the Atlantic. Desiring also to prevent misunderstandings and disputes which could arise in the taking of new possessions on the African coast, and at the same time attempting to increase the oral and material well being of the indigenous population, the Chiefs of State resolved on the invitation extended by the Imperial Government of Germany and in accordance with the government of the Republic of France, to convene a Conference in Berlin towards this goal.

The documents relating to this conference were widely published and debated in Europe. The last of Africa's independent territory was now passing into European hands without any Africans being a part of the decision.

Elliot P. Skinner calls attention to black American reaction to the Belgium take-over of the Congo.

> Blacks from America were among the first persons to report and to protest the cruelty to Africans in the congo (Zaire), and thereby contributed to the termination of King Leopold's private rule there. In 1890, Colonel George Washington Williams, a black historian, minister, politician and lawyer, denounced Leopold's administration of the Congo. Levelling twelve specific charges against the king of the Belgians, Colonel Williams concluded:
>
> > Against the deceit, fraud, robberies, arson, murder, slave-raiding, and general policy of cruelty of your Majesty's Government to the natives, stands their record of unexampled patience, long-suffering and forgiving spirit, which put the boasted civilization and professed religion of your Majesty's Government to the blush. . . .
>
> All the crimes perpetrated in the Congo have been done in your name and you must answer at the bar of public sentiment for the misgovernment of a people whose lives and fortunes were entrusted to you by the August Conference of Berlin, 1884–1885.

Black American reaction to the Congo crisis was part of the motivation for their relationship to the early Pan-African Movement. Skinner describes their reaction in this manner:

> These first Pan-Africanists saw the plight of the Black man in world perspective. DuBois proposed that the Congo Free State should become "a great central Negro state of the world," and that the integrity and independence of the still free states of Haiti and Ethiopia be maintained. The assembled delegates also expressed their chagrin that the blacks in America had the "misfortune to live among a people whose laws, traditions and prejudices had been against them for centuries." Finally, the

conferees asked for simple "justice for Black men, and for their right to achieve as much as they were capable of." They had the satisfaction of obtaining a promise from Queen Victoria, through Joseph Chamberlain, not to "overlook the interests and welfare of the native races," and planned to meet every two years, with the next meeting planned for New York in 1902.

DuBois was quite impressed with the work of this conference, and from this time onward he divided his efforts between fighting for the rights of blacks in the United States and struggling to help those in Africa.

The influence of this movement was far-reaching. The late Kwame Nkrumah wrote his first book, *Toward Colonial Freedom* under this influence when he was a student in the United States.

We believe in the rights of all peoples to govern themselves. We affirm the right of all colonial peoples to control their own destiny. All colonies must be free from foreign imperialist control, whether political or economic. The peoples of the colonies must have the right to elect their own government, a government without restrictions from a foreign power. We say to the peoples of the colonies that they must strive for these ends by all means at their disposal.

The object of imperialist powers is to exploit. By granting the right to the colonial peoples to govern themselves, they are defeating that objective. Therefore, the struggle for political power by colonial and subject peoples is the first step towards, and the necessary prerequisite to complete social, economic and political emancipation.

The Fifth Pan-African Congress, therefore, calls on the workers and farmers of the colonies to organize effectively. Colonial workers must be in front lines of the battle against imperialism.

The ground work for the African Independence Explosion had already been started. This was the preface to the Africa of today.

MARCUS GARVEY AND THE CONCEPT OF AFRICAN NATION-FORMATION IN THE TWENTIETH CENTURY

▼

Part I

SINCE THE REDISCOVERY of Marcus Garvey during the early part of the second half of the twentieth century when his ideas were again influencing Africans throughout the world, who were trying to reclaim their history and the definition of their being on the earth, writing about Marcus Garvey has become an academic industry. It can be said that Marcus Garvey is one of the most written about and still the least understood of the great black personalities of our time. While great attention is paid to his Back-to-Africa concept and his concept of total African redemption, not enough attention has been paid to his idea of the re-establishment of nation-states in Africa ruled by the Africans themselves. Marcus Garvey was well aware of the artificial borders in Africa established by Europeans that cut across cultural and political lines within Africa with no consideration being given to the prior formation of territories before the coming of the European. The modern nation-state with its tight borders and security check points is a European invention, that did not exist in precolonial Africa. What did exist in Africa was the territorial state based on cultural (sometimes mistakenly referred to as tribal) formations and affiliations.

Marcus Garvey's aim was for a self-sustained African state that could relate without conflict with neighboring African states. Another important aim not often emphasized was Garvey's intent to restore the self-confidence of African people so that they could believe in themselves as the future rulers of their own states in Africa.

His thinking in this matter is fully emphasized in the book, *Life and Philosophy of Marcus Garvey*, edited by his wife, Amy Jacques Garvey, and in the recent book, *Marcus Garvey: Life and Lessons*, edited by Robert A. Hill. Garvey's essay, "African Fundamentalism," is a blueprint for the re-establishment of an African state beginning with the reactivation of African confidence based on an understanding they have played in human history. His explanation, in part, is as follows:

> The time has come for the Negro to forget and cast behind him his hero worship and adoration of other races, and to start out immediately, to create and emulate heroes of his own.
>
> We must canonize our own saints, create our own martyrs, and elevate to positions of fame and honor black men and women who have made their distinct contributions to our racial history. Sojourner Truth is worthy of the place of sainthood alongside of Joan of Arc; Crispus Attucks and George William Gordon are entitled to the halo of martyrdom with no less glory than that of the martyrs of any other race. Toussaint L'Ouverture's brilliancy as a soldier and statesman outshone that of a Cromwell, Napoleon and Washington; hence, he is entitled to the highest numbers of men and women, in war and in peace, whose lustre and bravery outshine that of any other people. Then why not see good and perfection in ourselves?

On the point of the restoration of self-confidence and the building of independent African institutions, Marcus Garvey was consistent throughout his entire career. His Liberia scheme is further proof of this intention. In 1921 Marcus Garvey had made connection with the African state, Liberia, then ruled, in the main, by African Americans and Caribbeans who had migrated from the United States and the West Indies. Because this state was originally sponsored by the United States from its beginning to the present time, it was and is an unofficial American colony. The United States had control over the economic and political direction of this state. The flunkies and weaklings who were in control of Liberia in 1921 gave Marcus Garvey the illusion that settlement of American and Caribbean blacks would be permitted in Liberia. By 1924, their masters had given them a new message. They were now telling Marcus Garvey that there would be no settlement.

Marcus Garvey had sent basic technical personnel to Liberia and was in a position to send more basic building skills and other elements of the technical maintenance of a nation. Had this scheme succeeded, the African independence explosion experience would have come a generation ahead of its appearance in the 1950s.

There is a tendency in appraising this situation to hurriedly cast blame on W.E.B. DuBois and other black Americans. This is a hurried reading of history that ignores the basic facts involved in the Liberia scheme. The people who are accused of stopping and betraying the Liberia scheme did not have the power to start it or stop it. This scheme failed because of an internal conflict within Liberia itself: Mainly its failure to be a purely African state with global African interest and connection. This is a tragically neglected aspect of the trials and troubles of the Garvey movement. It is of vital importance nonetheless.

There is a need to look at Marcus Garvey as in institution builder. He attempted to build institutions among blacks similar to those whites had directly under their control that showed no visible interest in blacks. He established the Black Cross Nurses as substitute for Red Cross Nurses. His organization was paramilitary with a respected officer corps. The Black Star Line was an illusion to some people. He made it real to a large number of Africans the world over. He was the first international personality of African descent who lived in the twentieth century. Through his newspaper *Negro World* that was smuggled into parts of Africa and South America, his opinions penetrated the then colonial world, bypassing security barriers that today would be considered formidable. The Black Star Line, like so many of his other projects, was built too fast and with poor personnel. Millions of dollars were lost by Caribbeans and African-Americans that they could ill afford. When it was all over, there was no crying and no condemnation.

Marcus Garvey and the terrible insecure years after the First World War had rescued the spirit of a depressed people. He told them that no people had an exclusive monopoly on greatness, and they, too, could aspire to greatness and be inspired by the great men and women they had already produced. In essence, for a brief moment in history, he took a people for their spiritual walk in the sun.

Today, his teaching is, figuratively, like a mountain that is so high you can't go over it; so wide you can't go around it. Marcus Garvey and his dream of the formation of African states are matters that African people must face frontally. Some of his work can be edited and modified, but none of it can be ignored. In the light of the new documentations on Marcus Garvey coming from the research and writing of Professor Robert A. Hill, University of Los Angeles, and of Professor Tony Martin, Wellesley College, Massachusetts, the reappraisal of Marcus Garvey and the long-range value of his thinking can now be set in motion.

Part II[1]

The present reassessment of Marcus Garvey and the impact of his movement on the African world is being made during the 100th anniversary of his birth, the 200th anniversary of the American Constitution, and the twenty years after the publication of the controversial book, *The Crisis of the Negro Intellectual*. These three events either related to Garveyism or indicated what Garveyism was going to be about. In essence, Garveyism is about the "Nation" concept, something that we had lost during slavery and colonialism.

New writings about Marcus Garvey and some newly discovered and reappraised documents have emphasized this point. I am referring mainly to the planned ten volumes of documents on Marcus Garvey and the Universal Negro Improvement Association papers, edited by Professor Robert A. Hill and the writings of Professor Tony Martin. Both professors approach the life and movement of Marcus Garvey using some new and previously neglected documents and a new analysis showing insight about the man and the impact of his movement, the Universal Negro Improvement Association (UNIA).

[1] Prepared for the conference, "Garvey: His Work and Impact," November 5–7, 1987, The University of the West Indies, Kingston, Jamaica.

While the roots of the UNIA and Garveyism are deep in the twentieth century, events that influenced the movement started early in the nineteenth century. In a paper called, "Three Black Giants of the Twentieth Century: W.E.B. DuBois, Paul Robeson and Marcus Garvey," I wrote:

The best way to look at the three personalities presented here is to look at the radical tradition of African people, in general, and the African and Caribbean Americans, in particular. We must consider the fact that the African people who were brought to the Americas and the Caribbean Islands against their will did not come here culturally empty-handed. In the whole of the 19th century, all over the African world, there was a search for definition and direction. The Western educated Africans, mainly, became aware of the fact that their people had been many things in the world other than slaves. They began to ask questions about themselves and their slave masters. These questions led to an attempt to understand the place of African people in world history, before and after slavery. Some of them realized that African people had a rich and colorful history before slavery. The three men mentioned here looked back at the historical and cultural past of African people in order to look forward politically. They and others of their generation were trying to restore what slavery and the colonial system had taken away.

They realized that African people have in their ancestry memories of rulers who expanded kingdoms into empires and advanced military science and produced scholars whose vision of life showed foresight and wisdom.

Garveyism eventually, became a global movement not only awakening in African people a concept of what they were, but a vision of what they still could be.

In a paper, "Marcus Garvey and Southern Africa," written for the United Nations Center Against Apartheid, Martin has called attention to the impact of Garvey, the UNIA and Garveyism on the struggle against white domination in South Africa.

The following article appeared in the newspaper *The Cape Town*

Argus in 1923:

> One of the many absurd stories that are being circulated among the natives is that the notorious Marcus Garvey of the Black Star Line fame will soon arrive in South Africa with a large force of black soldiers to drive the white man out of the country.

To further illustrate his point, Professor Martin quotes Marcus Garvey on the importance of the UNIA and the African connection:

> It can be readily seen that the propaganda of the Universal Negro Improvement Association is bearing fruit in Africa. If we have accomplished nothing else but the bringing to the natives of Africa a consciousness of themselves and a desire on their part to free themselves from the thralldom of alien races and nations, we would have justified the existence of this great organization, because the primary object of this movement is to redeem Africa; to make Africa the land of the black peoples of the world, even as Europe has become the land of the whites and Asia the land of the brown and yellow peoples.
>
> ... it will mean not so much fighting from without as the rising of the people from within with a new consciousness of their power which is gradually being realized, even by the admission of General Smuts and his white compatriots. Let us, therefore, redouble our energies in putting over the program for the liberation of Africa.

Both professors, Robert A. Hill and Tony Martin, have made good use of the South African files of the UNIA. The following information is taken from Professor Martin's paper:

> The UNIA spread rapidly in Africa, in general, and South Africa, in particular. Cape Town especially, as a major seaport, became an important focus for the spread of Garveyite activities to the surrounding areas. The 1921 Report of the South African Department of Native Affairs noted the presence of Garveyite propaganda in Cape Town and Johannesburg and reported four

UNIA branches operating in the Cape Peninsula.

Early in 1922, Garvey's Harlem-based organ, *The Negro World*, reported the organization of UNIA division in Claremont, Cape Town, by T.L. Robertson of New York. The Woodstock, Cape Town, division was founded the same year. In July 1923 five new South African divisions were reported, followed by the formation of divisions in West London and Pretoria in 1924. The Pretoria branch, in 1929, had about one-hundred members and was under the leadership of Mr. P.A. Mokharia, president and Mr. L.B. Sabata, acting executive secretary. Meetings took place in the Marabastad location.

Surviving UNIA files list seven branches for South Africa (more than for any other African country) ca. 1926, their locations, together with the names of their chief officers.

Over the years, the view of Marcus Garvey and his movement has been all too narrow. The many dimensions of this man and his talent is generally missed by most of the people who write about him. There is now a new renaissance of interest in the life of Marcus Garvey. The African Independence Explosion that started in 1957 when the former West African colony called the Gold Coast became an independent country, now called Ghana, helped to set this renaissance in motion. Some of Marcus Garvey's dreams about African redemption were being realized. In his lifetime, he was a man who had a stubborn belief in the impossible, and came close to achieving it. During the uncertain years that followed the First World War, he built the largest black mass movement that this country has ever seen. There was never a leader like him, before or since. His popularity was universal, his program for the redemption of Africa and the return of African people to their motherland, shook the foundations of three empires.

In nearly all matters relating to the resurgence of African people, in this country and abroad, there is reconsideration of this man and his program which seemed impossible in his lifetime. His prophecy has been fulfilled in the independence explosion that brought more than fifty African nations into being. The concept of Black Power that he advocated, using other terms, is now a reality in large areas of the world where the people of African origin are predominant.

Marcus Garvey's main headquarters was among the African-Americans in the United States, in the community of Harlem. This was his window on the world. From this vantage point he became one of the best known black personalities of the twentieth century.

In the book *The New World A-Coming*, Roi Ottley has observed that Marcus Garvey leaped into the ocean of black unhappiness in the United States at a most timely moment for a savior. He further observes that:

> He had witnessed the Negro's disillusionment mount with the progress of the World War. Negro soldiers had suffered all forms of Jim Crow, humiliation, discrimination, slander and even violence at the hands of the white civilian population. After the war, there was a resurgence of Ku Klux Klan influence: another decade of racial hatred and open lawlessness had set in, and Negroes again were prominent among the victims. Meantime, administration leaders were quite pointed in trying to persuade Negroes that in spite of their full participation in the war effort they could expect no change in their traditional status in America. Newton D. Baker was particularly vocal on this issue. The liberal white citizens were disturbed by events, but took little action beyond viewing with alarm.
>
> Blacks were more than ready for a Moses—and only a black man could express the depth of their feelings. Intellectuals of the race tried to rationalize the situation, but not so the broad masses: Their acknowledged leader, DuBois, had gone overboard with the war effort and now found himself estranged from his people. Blacks were faced with a choice between racialism and radicalism. Marcus Garvey settled the question for thousands by forming the Universal Negro Improvement Association, called UNIA for brevity, and preaching with great zeal for a pilgrimage of black men, "Back to Africa." He rallied men to the slogan, "Africa for the Africans." For talk was then current about self-determination for subject peoples.

Marcus Garvey's plans for the self-determination of his people was outlined in the following excerpts from, "Aims and Objects of Movement for Solution of Negro Problem," issued by Marcus Garvey as President-General of the UNIA in 1924.

The Universal Negro Improvement Association, as an organization among the Blacks, sought to improve the condition of the race, with the view of establishing a nation in Africa where American blacks would be given the opportunity to develop by themselves, without creating the hatred and animosity that now exists in countries of the white race through blacks rivaling them for the highest and best positions in government, politics, society and industry. This organization believes in the rights of all men, yellow, white and black. To us, the white race has a right to the peaceful possession and occupation of countries of its own and in like manner the yellow and black races have their rights ... only by an honest and liberal consideration of such rights can the world be blessed with the peace that is sought by Christian teachers and leaders.

Of the spiritual brotherhood of man, the following preamble of the constitution of the organization speaks for itself:

The Universal Negro Improvement Association an African communities' league is a social, friendly, humanitarian, charitable, educational, institutional, constructive, and expansive society and is founded by persons, desiring to the utmost, to work for the general uplift of the black peoples of the world. And the members pledge themselves to do all in their power to conserve the rights of their noble race and to respect the rights of all mankind, believing always in the brotherhood of man and the fatherhood of God. The motto of the organization is: One God, One Aim, One Destiny. Therefore, let justice be done to all mankind, realizing that if the strong oppresses the weak, confusion and discontent will ever mark the path of man, but with love, faith and charity toward all, the reign of peace and plenty will be heralded into the world and the generations of men shall be called blessed. ...

The declared objects of the Association are: To establish a universal confraternity among the race; to promote the spirit of pride and love; to reclaim the fallen; to administer to and assist the needy; to assist in civilizing the backward tribes of Africa; to assist in the development of independent Negro nations and communities; to establish a central nation for the race; to establish commissionaries or agencies in the principal countries and cities of the world for the representation of all blacks.

The early twenties were times of change and accomplishment in the Harlem community. It was the period when Harlem was, literally, put on the map. Two events made this possible: the literary movement known as the Harlem Renaissance and the emergence in Harlem of the magnetic and compelling personality of Marcus Garvey. He was the most seriously considered and the most colorful of the numerous black Messiahs who presented themselves and their grandiose programs to the people of Harlem.

Marcus Garvey's reaction to color prejudice and his search for a way to rise above it and lead his people back to Africa, spiritually, if not physically, was the all consuming passion of his existence. His glorious and romantic movement exhorted the black people of the world and fixed their eyes on the bright star of a future in which they could reclaim and rebuild their African homeland and heritage.

Garvey succeeded in building a mass movement among American blacks while other leaders were attempting it and doubting that it could be done. He advocated the return to Africa to the Africans and people of African descent. He organized, very boldly, the Black Star Line, a steamship company for transporting cargoes of African produce to the United States. A little known, though very important aspect of the founding of this black steamship company was the urgent pleas of West African farmers and producers to Marcus Garvey for a shipping service that would relieve them of being victimized by white shipping agencies and produce dealers who offered them very low prices for their produce, delivered at the wharf. African passengers paid for first-class service and were given second-class treatment on too many white-owned shipping lines and the founding of the Black Star Line was an attempt to end this and part of a program to restore the nationhood concept of the African world.

Marcus Garvey's principal areas of agitation were the African-American struggle in the United States, in his native Caribbean Islands, and in the universe of black humanity everywhere. From the year of his arrival in the United States, in 1916, until his deportation in 1927, the ethnic community called Harlem was his base of operation. From this vantage point he became one of the great figures of the twentieth century.

In the years following the end of the First World War, when America's promise to black America had been betrayed, again we looked once more toward Africa and dreamed of a time and place where our essential manhood was not questioned.

To some black Americans the idea of returning to Africa was over 100 years old before Marcus Garvey arrived. In a speech entitled, "The American Negro and the Darker World," delivered in New York City on April 30, 1957, the scholar W.E.B. DuBois said:

> From the 15th through the 17th centuries, the Africans import-
> ed to America regarded themselves as temporary settlers des-
> tined to return eventually to Africa. Their increasing revolts
> against the slave system, which culminated in the 18th century,
> showed a feeling of close kinship to the motherland and even
> well into the 19th century they called their organizations
> "African," as witness the "African Unions" of New York and
> Newport, and the African churches of Philadelphia and New
> York. In the West Indies and South America there was even
> closer indication of feelings of kinship with Africa and the East.

The Garvey movement had a profound effect on the political development of Harlem and on the lives of the Adam Clayton Powell father and son. The fight to make Harlem a Congressional district began during the Garvey period. The attitudes held during this period had helped to create the atmosphere into which a Marcus Garvey could emerge. In many ways the scene was being prepared for the emergence of Marcus Garvey one-hundred years before he was born.

The Garvey movement began to take effective roots in America when millions of blacks had begun to feel that they would never know full citizenship with dignity in this country where their ancestors had been brought albeit against their will, and where they had contributed to the wealth and development of the country in spite of conditions of previous servitude. Against this background of broken promises and fading hopes, Marcus Garvey began to build a worldwide black move-ment. This, the first black mass protest crusade in the history of the United States began to pose serious problems for white America. This movement also posed serious problems for the then existing black leadership, especially for Dr. W.E.B. DuBois.

In the article, "DuBois Versus Garvey: Race Propagandists at War," the writer Elliott M. Rudnick outlines the origins of the conflict between these two black giants who looked at the world from different vantage points. Both of them were Pan-Africanists and both of them had as their objectives the freedom and redemption of African people everywhere. Yet, there was no meeting of the minds on the methods of reaching these desirable goals. In the article Rudnick says: "Unlike DuBois, Marcus Garvey was able to gain mass support and his propaganda had a tremendous emotional appeal." Adam Clayton Powell, Sr., wrote of Garvey, "He is the only man that made Negroes not feel ashamed of their color." In his book, *Marching Blacks*, Adam Clayton Powell, Jr., wrote: "Marcus Garvey was one of the greatest mass leaders of all time. He was misunderstood and maligned, but he brought to the Negro people for the first time a sense of pride in being black."

He spoke no African language, but Garvey managed to convey to African people everywhere (and to the other peoples of the world) his passionate belief that Africa was the home of a civilization which had once been great and would be great again. When one takes into consideration the slenderness of Garvey's resources and the vast material forces, social conceptions, and imperial interests that automatically sought to destroy him, his achievement remains one of the great propaganda miracles of this century.

Garvey's voice reverberated inside Africa itself. The king of Swaziland later told Mrs. Marcus Garvey that he knew the names of only two black men in the Western world: Jack Johnson, the boxer who defeated a white man, Jim Jeffries, and Marcus Garvey. From his narrow vantage point in Harlem, Marcus Garvey became a world figure.

Now that we are living through the last years of the twentieth century we African people, the world over, need to ask ourselves: How did we lose the concept of nation and the talent for nation-management? Marcus Garvey and his movement may have been ahead of his time considering the political atmosphere in the African world, he may also have been ahead of this time. Garveyism goes far beyond Pan-Africanism, it is the basis of world union of African people.

Part III

In the Appendix to the second edition of his book, *The Black Jacobins*, the Caribbean scholar C.L.R. James observes that two West Indians "using the ink of Negritude wrote their names imperishably on the front pages of the history of our times." Professor James is referring to Aimé Cesaire and Marcus Garvey. He places Marcus Garvey at the forefront of the group of twentieth-century black radicals whose ideas and programs still reverberate within present-day liberation movements. Marcus Garvey was a man who, in retrospect, was far ahead of his time. This is proved by the fact that his ideas have resurfaced and are being seriously reconsidered as a major factor in the liberation of African people the world over.

To call the movement he brought into being a "Back-to-Africa movement" is to narrow its meaning. This was only one aspect of his movement. Marcus Garvey's plan was for total African redemption. The crucial legacy of slavery and colonialism helped to produce a Marcus Garvey. When he was born in 1887, in Jamaica, West Indies, the so-called "scramble for Africa" was over. All over Africa the warrior nationalists, who had opposed European colonialism throughout the nineteenth century, were being killed or sent into exile. The Europeans with territorial aspirations in Africa had sat at the Berlin Conference of 1884 and 1885 and decided how to split up the continent among them. In the United States, black Americans were still suffering from the betrayal of the Reconstruction in 1876. The trouble within the world black community that Marcus Garvey was later to grapple with had already begun when he was born. In the years when he was growing to early manhood, his people entered the twentieth century and a new phase of their struggle for freedom and national identity.

In 1907 Marcus Garvey was involved in the Printers' Union strike in Jamaica. After this unsuccessful strike ended in defeat for the printers, he went to work for the Government Printing Office and soon after edited his first publication, *The Watchman*.

In 1900 Garvey made his first trip outside of Jamaica to Costa Rica. In this poor and exploited country he observed the condition of Black workers and started an effort to improve their lot. His protest to the British consul was answered with bureaucratic indifference. He was learning his first lesson about the arrogant stubbornness of a European colonial power.

Garvey made several attempts to start a newspaper, hoping that it could expose the bad working conditions of the blacks. These workers had no funds to support such a venture. He then went to Bocas-del-Toro, Panama, where he met a large number of Jamaicans who had originally come into the country to work on the Canal. With their help he was able to start a newspaper, *La Prensa*. The paper and Garvey's stay in Bocas-del-Toro lasted only a few months. He left Panama and went to Ecuador, Nicaragua, Honduras, Colombia and Venezuela. Again he observed that black workers were being taken advantage of in the mines and in the tobacco fields; the black man totally lacked power to improve his lot.

In 1912, Garvey was in London working, learning, growing and seeing new dimensions of the black man's struggle. The ideas that would go into the making of his life's work were being formulated. His close association with Duse Mohammed Ali, Egyptian scholar and nationalist of Sudanese descent, helped to sharpen his ideas about African redemption. He worked for a while on the monthly *The African Times and Orient Review*, edited by Ali, an association that was a continuation of Marcus Garvey's political education. It was not by accident that he came to London, the administrative headquarters of the British Empire, to continue his education, an education more practical than formal. He set out to acquaint himself with the realities of dealing with massive power and London was a storehouse of information about the colonial world.

A year before Marcus Garvey arrived in London the city had been host to a World Congress on Race (July 1911), more often referred to as the Races Congress. The Congress had been planned by Gustave Spiller working under the auspices of the English Ethical Culture Movement. Felix Adler was among the distinguished persons who took part.

The literature, the attitudes and the debates about the Congress were very influential when Marcus Garvey began his London years. Also important was the new anticolonial literature coming out of West Africa, such as the writings of the Great Gold Coast (now Ghana) nationalist E. Casely Hayford and the Caribbean scholar Edward W. Blyden.

Dr. W.E.B. DuBois, a future adversary of Marcus Garvey, attended and gives this account of the Races Congress in his book *Dusk of Dawn*: "The Congress would have marked an epoch in the cultural history of the world if it had not been followed so quickly by the World War. As it was, it turned out to be a great and inspiring occasion, bringing together representatives of numerous ethnic and cultural groups, and new and frank conceptions of the scientific bases of racial and social relations of people."

Dr. DuBois further states that he not only had his regular assign-ment, but, due to the sudden illness of Sir Harry Johnson, represented him at one of the main sessions and made a speech on race and colonialism that was widely quoted in the London press. "Thus," he said, "I had a chance twice to address the Congress."

Dr. DuBois wrote one of the poems that greeted the assembly. The interesting thing about the poem is that in tone and content it is similar to some of the poems that Marcus Garvey would later write:

> Save us, World Spirit, from our lesser selves,
> Grant us that war and hatred cease,
> Reveal our souls in every race and hue,
> Help us, O Human God, in this Thy truce,
> To make Humanity divine.

"Even while the Races Congress was meeting," Dr. DuBois reported, "came the forewarning of coming doom: in a characteristic way a German war vessel sailed into an African port, notifying the world that Germany was determined to have larger ownership and control of cheap black labor: a demand camouflaged as a need of 'a place in the sun.'" And thus, the issue was joined.

Some of the questions about the future of colonial peoples had been put forward by the Races Congress. While trying to understand these questions, Garvey was seeing the British at close range and learning more about the difficult job still ahead of him. He obtained a copy of the book *Up from Slavery* by Booker T. Washington. This book and its ideas had a strong influence on his concept of leadership and its responsibility and helped form the theoretical basis of what would later become Garveyism.

Black Americans had entered the twentieth century searching for new directions politically, culturally and institutionally: Booker T. Washington's Atlanta Cotton Exposition address (1895) had set in motion a great debate among black people about their direction and their place in the developing American social order. New men and movements were emerging. Some, principally Bishop Henry McNeal Turner, the best known of the Back-to-Africa advocates before the emergence of Marcus Garvey, were questioning whether black people had any future in America. Bishop Turner, now with failing health, continued to direct the last phase of his Back-to-Africa program which had been started in the closing years of the nineteenth century. In an outlined history of his movement, *Bishop Henry McNeal Turner: A Political Biography*, Anne Kelley made the following assessment of his career:

> When considering the historical period between 1890 and 1915, when Bishop Turner's political thought was at its most mature level, two powerful black figures come to mind, namely Booker T. Washington and W.E.B. DuBois. Most blacks are familiar with Washington's major theme of accommodation and DuBois' major theme of integration; but, few are equally as aware of Turner's presence and nationalist theme with emphasis on emigration of blacks back-to-Africa.... During this particular period both Washington and DuBois advanced plans that were basically aimed at "liberation" of the black middle class. Washington's plan sought the creation of a class of black entrepreneurs; DuBois sought to create a black intelligentsia. But Turner's Back-to-Africa brand of black nationalism was rooted in a concern for the masses of black people, i.e., that most oppressed segment of black society represented by the southern rural population.

Other black Americans answered the question of direction in a more affirmative way, by pouring massive energy into the building of new institutions, mainly schools. The institutional building aspects of the Booker T. Washington Program were an attraction for Marcus Garvey.

Marcus Garvey returned to Jamaica in 1914 and founded the Universal Negro Improvement and Conservation Association and African Communities League (UNIA and ACL). These organizations were not an instantaneous success. For nearly two years he struggled to bring a semblance of unity to Jamaicans and to make some of the educated classes conscious of the needs of poor people. He was up against the plutocracy—the land barons and the white shipping and fruit companies who made millions exploiting the cheap labor of the islands. The newspapers and all public media were against him. Also against him was an English institution, "prejudice based on class," that was compounded in Jamaica by color. He continued to struggle to bring a people's organization into being though at times it seemed like a stillborn child.

In the pamphlet "Marcus Garvey," Adolph Edwards gives the following capsule history of the early days of the Universal Negro Improvement Association:

> Garvey landed in Jamaica on 15th July, 1914. The Caribbean isle had not changed. Kingston remained hot, depressing, inactive; above all, the social atmosphere was just as stultifying as before. Garvey's brain was afire and his existence was a world of thoughts. Within five days of his arrival he organized and founded the movement whose name was destined to be on the lips of millions—The Universal Negro Improvement Association. Briefly, the purpose of the Association was to unite all the Negro peoples of the world into one great body to establish a country and government absolutely their own. The Association's motto was short and stirring: "One God! One Aim! One destiny!"

Garvey was designated President and Travelling Commissioner.

The UNIA not only had plans for the universal improvement of the Negro, but it also had plans for the immediate uplift of the Negro in Jamaica. The most important of these was the proposed establishment of educational and industrial colleges for Jamaican Negroes on the pattern of the Tuskegee Institute in Alabama, which had been founded by Booker T. Washington. This plan received the support of a few prominent citizens, including the Mayor of Kingston and the Roman Catholic bishop, but on the whole, it came in for sharp criticism within the more articulate circles. Garvey said about his persecutors and the decision he made:

Men and women as black as I and even more so, had believed
themselves white under the West Indian order of society. I was
simply an impossible man to use openly the term "negro"; yet
every one beneath his breath was calling the black man a
"nigger." I had to decide whether to please my friends and be
one of the "black-whites" of Jamaica, and be reasonably prosper-
ous, or come out openly, and help improve and protect the
integrity of the black millions, and suffer. I decided to do the
latter.

In *Philosophy and Opinions* Marcus Garvey would later ask himself:
"where is the black man's government? Where is his king and his
kingdom? Where is his president, his country and his ambassador, his
army, his navy, his men of big affairs?" He could not answer the
question affirmatively, so he decided to make the black man's government, king and kingdom, president and men of big affairs. He taught
his people to dream big again; he reminded them that they had once
been kings and rulers of great nations and would be again. The cry "Up
you mighty race, you can accomplish what you will" was a call to the
black man to reclaim his best self and re-enter the mainstream of world
history.

When Marcus Garvey came to the United States in 1916, Booker
T. Washington was dead and World War I had already started. The
migration of black workers from the South to the new war industries
in the northern and eastern parts of the United States was in full
swing. Dissatisfaction, discontent and frustration among millions of
black Americans were accelerating this migration.

The appearance of the Garvey Movement was perfectly timed. The
broken promises of the post-war period had produced widespread
cynicism in the black population which had lost some of its belief in
itself as a people.

The Garvey Movement had a profound effect on the political
development of the Harlem community. The migrations from the
South during the First World War had, by the time Marcus Garvey
arrived, made this an almost solidly black community. In the freer
atmosphere of the North, many blacks who could not vote in local
elections before were now demanding the right to run for public office.
In these formative years of the Movement, Marcus Garvey had awak-

ened in black people a desire to be the masters of their own destiny.

One year after he entered the United States, he made a speaking tour (1917) of the principal cities, building up a national following. By 1919, a banner year for the growth of the UNIA, he had branches established all over the world. These branches were already preparing to send delegates and representatives of fraternal organizations to "The First International Convention of the Negro People of the World" that was planned for the following year.

Reaction to this growth and to the grievances of black Americans in general came hard and fast. Race riots flared in nearly every part of the United States. Most of them occurred in the summer, and are collectively referred to as "the red summer of 1919."

These riots convinced Marcus Garvey more than ever that the black man had no secure place in America. His newspaper, the *Negro World*, became the most widely read weekly in America. The Black Star Line Steamship Company had been founded. The UNIA as an organization had been transformed from a wild dream to a reality that now commanded worldwide attention. Great masses of black Americans began to relate to Garvey and his Movement. Harlem was his window on the world; from this ethnic ghetto he inspired millions of black people to hope again and dream again.

Also, in 1919, under the leadership of Dr. W.E.B.Dubois, then editor of the NAACP magazine *The Crisis*, another drama claiming African redemption as its objective was displayed in the capitals of Europe. It was the 1919 Pan-African Congress called by W.E.B. Dubois.

Dr. DuBois had mapped out a scheme that he would attempt to present to President Woodrow Wilson and other heads of state or their representatives, who were meeting at the Peace Conference at Versailles. Dr. DuBois' dream was that the Peace Conference could form an internationalized Africa, its basis the former German colonies with their 1,000,000 square miles of territory and population of 12,500,000. "To this," his plan reads,

> could be added by negotiation the 800,000 square miles and 9,000,000 inhabitants of Portuguese Africa. It is not impossible that Belgium could be persuaded to add to such a state the 900,000 square miles and 9,000,000 natives of the Congo, making an international Africa with over 2,500,000 square miles

of land and over 20,000,000 people.

This Africa for the Africans could be under the guidance of international organizations. The governing international Commission should represent not simply Governments, but modern culture, science, commerce, social reform and religious philanthropy.

This was a plea by the Western-educated elite for a place in the African sun. Sure, they had the interest of what they called "the natives" at heart. But there was no question about who would rule if the plan materialized. The plan brought nothing but scorn from Marcus Garvey.

An excerpt from Dr. DuBois' report on the Congress:

Members of the American delegation and associated experts assured me that no congress on this matter could be held in Paris because France was still under martial law; but the ace that I had up my sleeve was Blaise Diagne, the black deputy from Senegal and Commissaire-General in charge of recruiting native African troops. I went to Diagne and sold him the idea of a Pan-African Congress. He consulted Clemenceau, and the matter was held up two wet, discouraging months. But finally we got permission to hold the Congress in Paris. "Don't advertise it," said Clemenceau, "but go ahead." Walter Lippmann wrote me in his crabbed hand, February 20th 1919: "I am very much interested in your organization of the Pan-African Conference, and glad that Clemenceau has made it possible. Will you send me whatever reports you might have on the work?"

The *Dispatch*, Pittsburgh, Pennsylvania, February 16, 1919, said:

Officials here are puzzled by the news from Paris that plans are going forward there for a Pan-African Conference to be held February 19th. Acting Secretary Polk said today the State Department had been officially advised by the French Government that no such Conference would be held. It was announced recently that no passports would be issued for American delegates desiring to attend the meeting. But at the very time that

Polk was assuring American Negroes that no congress would be held, the Congress actually assembled in Paris.

The international Garvey Movement continued its preparation for its great convention of 1920. This convention ended the formative years of the Garvey Movement and projected it into a new era of "Triumph and Tragedy." The following description of the convention was taken from the book, *Garvey and Garveyism*, by Amy Jacques Garvey:

The first International Convention of the Negro Peoples of the World held its opening meeting at night at Madison Square Garden—the largest completely covered auditorium in New York. The first half of the program was musical, and the best talent in the race took part. The second half was devoted to speeches. White newspapers estimated the crowd inside and outside as between 20,000 to 25,000 persons; it was like an invasion of the white section. The thousands who could not get in the auditorium just stayed around the adjacent streets and discussed the day's happenings as something they never thought possible.

The other sessions were held at Liberty hall for thirty days, strenuous days for the Speaker-in-Convention. The first item on the agenda was reports from delegates on conditions in their localities and territories. For the first time in history all peoples of African descent sat together in brotherly understanding and sympathy to listen to accounts of the awful conditions and handicaps under which they were born, lived and worked. Even this privilege and the results were worth the enormous costs involved.

Spanish and French interpreters helped those who could not speak English fluently. Africans were helped by others to write their speeches in basic English. Committees were appointed to deal with various matters; their terms of reference were investigatory, planning and advisory. This saved time, and the best informed and trained persons were given opportunities to serve in their particular line. The committee on Africa had to hear certain delegates privately. These had to register under assumed names, for their freedom and lives might be endangered if they openly exposed conditions in their home territories.

The culmination of this work was the Declaration of Rights of the Negro Peoples of the World, which commenced with a preamble, then twelve causes for grievous complaints of injustices, and fifty-four demands for future fair treatment of our people everywhere. The UNIA held sessions for members only, at which the association's business was discussed, constitutional amendments made, and officers elected.

After the historic first UNIA International Convention of the Negro Peoples of the World at Madison Square Garden in 1920, the cry "Africa for Africans, those at home and those abroad" became part of the folklore of the black Americans. The most important document that came out of this convention was the *Declaration of the Rights of the Negro Peoples of the World.* Marcus Garvey had started negotiations with the President of Liberia for colonization and development of Africa by Western-world blacks. This was the beginning of the hope and heartbreak of Marcus Garvey's colonization scheme.

Between 1920 and 1925, the Garvey movement rose to great heights and, in spite of its troubles, continued to grow. This is the period in which the movement had its greatest success and was under the severest criticism. The Convention of 1920 was a monumental achievement in black organizations. This convention came in the years after the First World War, when the promises to black Americans had been broken, lynching was rampant, and when blacks were still recovering from "the red summer of 1919" in which there were race riots in most of the major cities and the white unemployed took out their grievances on the blacks, who many times were competing with them for the few available jobs. During this time, Marcus Garvey brought the Black Star Line into being and into a multiplicity of troubles. He divorced his wife and married another and made his name and his organization household words in nearly every part of the world where black people lived.

The trials and tribulations of the Black Star Line would read like the libretto of a comic opera, except that the events were both hectic and tragic, and there were more villains than heroes involved in this attempt to restore to black people a sense of worth and nationness.

Marcus Garvey's trouble with the courts started soon after the formation of the Black Star Line. The charges and countercharges relating to the Black Star Line were the basis of most of his troubles and the cause of his conviction and sentencing to Atlanta prison. This was the beginning of the end of the greatest years of the Garvey Movement.

The years of triumph and tragedy were building years, searching years and years of magnificent dreaming. Marcus Garvey's vision of Africa had lifted the spirit of black Americans out of the Depression that followed the First World War. The UNIA's African Legions and Black Cross Nurses became familiar sights on the streets of Harlem. The UNIA grew in membership and in support of all kinds. Garvey was the beating heart of the Movement. His persuasive voice and prolific writings and his effective use of pageantry struck a responsive chord throughout the black communities of America and abroad. Branches of the Movement were established in Latin America, wherever there were large Caribbean communities. An African Orthodox Church was founded in America. Now the Black man was searching for a new God as well as a new land.

DuBois and Garvey were not strangers to each other before Garvey came to the United States in 1916. DuBois had heard of Garvey when he vacationed in Jamaica in 1915; he had been very well received by both white and colored people, and Garvey and his associates had joined in the welcome.

After this brief first meeting, Garvey and DuBois went their separate ways, organizationally and ideologically. Garvey had been accused of "introducing" the Jamaican-black-Mulatto schism to the United States, where DuBois claimed it had no relevance and only bred disunity. While the color situation in the United States differed appreciably from that in Jamaica, both situations were serious and tragic. In my opinion, both DuBois and Garvey erred in the way they handled this matter and in the way they handled each other. DuBois often addressed advice to Marcus Garvey as if the President of the UNIA were a misguided child, and Garvey spoke of DuBois as if he were a fraud and a traitor to his people. At a critical period this kind of conduct was a negation of the cause that had been the life work of both men.

Garvey's reaction to the Pan-African Congress of 1919 had not been positive. He accused DuBois of sabotaging his work abroad, especially in Liberia. DuBois was pictured as a fallen old warrior who had already seen his best days. The editorial writers on Garvey's newspaper, *Negro World*, joined A. Philip Randolph's *Messenger* Magazine in saying that W.E.B. DuBois was "controlled" by the white capitalists on the NAACP's Board of Directors. Besides, Garvey thought that DuBois was being given too much credit as founder of Pan-Africanism.

Criticism notwithstanding, DuBois began the preparation for the second Pan-African Congress during the early part of 1921. He stated that his intention was to invite not only "Negro Governments," but "all Negro organizations interested in the people of African descent." DuBois was careful in pointing out the difference between the Pan-African Congress and the Garvey Movement. The NAACP printed a letter from the President of Liberia to the effect that his country would not be used as a base from which the Garvey Movement could harass other governments in Africa.

Now the issue was joined and the lines were drawn. After this date peace between Marcus Garvey and W.E.B. DuBois seems to have been an impossibility. The second Pan-African Congress was held while crosscurrents of accusations were still passing between DuBois and Garvey. In the booklet *History of the Pan-African Congress* DuBois describes how the Congress started:

> The idea of Pan-Africa having been ... established, we attempted to build a real organization. We went to work first to assemble a more authentic Pan-African Congress and movement. We corresponded with Negroes in all parts of Africa and in other parts of the world, and finally arranged for a Congress to meet in London, Brussels, and Paris in August and September, 1921. Of the 113 delegates to this Congress, forty-one were from Africa, thirty-five from the United States, twenty-four represented Negroes living in Europe, and seven were from the West Indies. Thus, the African element showed growth. They came for the most part, but not in all cases, as individuals, and more seldom as the representatives of organizations or of groups.
>
> The Pan-African movement thus began to represent a growth and development; but it immediately ran into difficulties. First of all, there was the natural reaction of war and the

determination on the part of certain elements in England, Belgium, and elsewhere to recoup their war losses by intensified exploitation of colonies. They were suspicious of native movements of any sort. Then, too, there came simultaneously another movement, stemming from the West Indies, which accounted for our small West Indian representation. This was in its way a people's movement rather than a movement of the intellectuals. It was led by Marcus Garvey, and it represented a poorly conceived but intensely earnest determination to unite the Negroes of the world, more especially in commercial enterprise. It used all the nationalist and racial paraphernalia of popular agitation, and its strength lay in its backing by the masses of West Indians and by increasing numbers of American Negroes. Its weaknesses lay in its demagogic leadership, its intemperate propaganda, and the natural fear which it threw into the colonial powers.

Speaking even more bluntly, DuBois says in his book, *Dusk of Dawn*:

... the Pan-African movement ran into two fatal difficulties: first of all, it was much too early to assume, as I had assumed, that in 1921 the war was over. In fact, the whole tremendous drama which followed the war, political and social revolution, economic upheaval and expression, national and racial hatred, all these things made a setting in which any such movement as I envisaged [probably] at the time impossible. I sensed this in the bitter and deep opposition which our resolutions invoked in Belgium. Both the Belgian and French governments were aroused and disturbed and the English opposition hovered in the background.

There came, too, a second difficulty which had elements of comedy and curious social frustration, but nevertheless was real and in a sense tragic. Marcus Garvey walked into the scene.

In 1921, Marcus Garvey made a tour of Central America, Cuba and Jamaica. He was encouraged by the growth of the Garvey Movement and the acceptance of his teachings throughout the Caribbean islands. His main objective was to boost the sales of Black Star Line stock. He achieved this while trouble was developing with the ships of the Black Star Line and the crews.

After his tour Marcus Garvey was prevented from re-entering the United States for a while.

In the face of other troubles brewing, in Jamaica in June 1921, Marcus Garvey sent a letter to the *Daily Gleaner* that antagonized the ruling elite on the island, black and white. The letter read, in part:

> Jamaica as I see it is controlled by a few inexperienced "imported strangers" whose position in Jamaica as officials and heads of departments has come to them as "godsends." These fellows know well that they could find no place in the body politic of their own native lands because of their inferiority and their inability to perform technical work, yet through the system of any white man being better than a native, these "imported gentlemen" are continuously being sent out to the colonies ("dumping grounds") to administer the affairs of our governments. It is time that a halt be called. If Jamaica is to be saved, if Jamaica is to take her place among the progressive nations of the world, then we must have a change of policy. Jamaica is void of that National spirit that should characterize every country. Everybody in Jamaica seems to be looking to the Mother Country for everything.... I feel that Jamaica wants a political awakening and it should come from within and not from without.... We feel that we are quite competent to handle the affairs of our country and now all that we ask is a chance.... Jamaicans as I can see, worship too much that which comes from abroad and from anywhere. If a thing, a man or an animal is imported it is supposed to be better than the native product. How silly! As for individuals, I have seen some of the greatest idiots abroad.... I would recommend that the poorer classes of Jamaica, the working classes, get together and form themselves into unions and organizations and elect their members for the Legislative Council. With few exceptions the men in the Council represent themselves and their class ....

When Garvey was eventually given permission to return to the United States he began immediately to prepare for the second UNIA

Convention in 1921. This second Convention was not as impressive as the first one held the previous year. Rumors about the mismanagement of the Black Star Line were rampant, and no one was putting these rumors to rest. It was discovered that some of the funds of the Black Star Line had been deposited in the personal bank accounts of some of the officials.

In January 1922, Garvey and three of the main officials of the Line were arrested and indicted for using the mails to defraud. They were released on bail as the investigation of the Black Star Line continued.

The third Convention of the UNIA was held in August 1922, but was not as well attended as the previous ones. Some of Garvey's enemies organized anti-Garvey rallies, and literally started a "Garvey Must Go" movement.

There was some indication of the worldwide influence of the Garvey movement while the third Convention was being held: For a number of years the British secret service had been keeping a record of Garvey's activities and making efforts to halt the spread of Garvey's ideas in the colonies. There is some indication that the French were engaged in similar surveillance.

Also in 1922, Marcus Garvey had a talk with the members of the Ku Klux Klan that was seriously misinterpreted. The Imperial Wizard had expressed a desire to see and talk to Marcus Garvey. He was head of the largest organization of whites then existing in the country. Marcus Garvey was his black counterpart. The meeting did not result in an alliance and was probably ill-advised, mainly because of the misinterpretation that has been put upon it through the years.

In September 1923, the reported failure of the Black Star Line and allegations of financial fraud in the UNIA led DuBois to write Marcus Garvey off as a failure. Exactly one year later, while Garvey was awaiting bail in The Tombs, the government of Liberia honored W.E.B. DuBois by inviting him to the inauguration of President Charles D. King. In the meantime, Marcus Garvey and the officials of the Black Star Line were being brought to trial in New York City. The following account of the trial was prepared by Mrs. Amy Jacques Garvey:

> After the indictment of the officers of the Black Star Line, the Federal District Attorney sent two trucks up to the offices of the Black Star Line, the local branch [of the UNIA] and the *Negro*

World which were housed in three different buildings and which functioned independently. They took away files, books, records, etc. Garvey tried to stop them, as only the Black Star Line books, etc., should have been taken in order to get evidence in the case, but he was told that he would be cited for contempt if he dared to prevent them from "getting everything connected with Garvey." This was intended to halt the work of the organization; but the members, and even outsiders, realized that Garvey was being persecuted, not prosecuted, so the membership increased.

The Black Star Line was incorporated under the laws of the State of Delaware. The four indicted officers were Marcus Garvey, President, Orlando Thompson, Vice-President, George Tobias, Treasurer, and Elie Garcia, Secretary. They were released on bail of $2,500 each, until the day of trial, which started May 21, 1923, in Federal Court, New York City. Each defendant had an attorney. Judge Julian Mack presided with a white jury. At the start of the trial, Garvey, through his attorney, made application that the trial judge declare himself disqualified to try the case on the ground that he was a member or contributor to the NAACP, an association whose officers were actively opposed to Garvey and his Movement. Judge Mack admitted his connection with the NAACP, but denied bias. The motion was denied, and the same judge proceeded to try the case.

At the end of the second day of the trial, Garvey's attorney came to our flat and said he was acting on advice and in Garvey's interest. As his lawyer he was advising him to plead guilty to the technical charge. He had reasons to believe that he would be fined and admonished of future activities. Garvey was surprised at his suggestion and told him that he did not seem to understand what was behind the prosecution. After a lengthy argument on the matter, which brought out other facts, Garvey felt that his attorney was being used innocently to trap him, and asked him to withdraw from his court defense. In leaving, the attorney warned him, "It will go hard with you," Garvey retorted, "I will prove to the jury that I am not guilty of any fraud."

Party politics plays an important part in the judiciary, as

judges are elected on their selection by politicians. Garvey tried to get another attorney, whose politics were Republican, as the judge and District Attorney were Republicans, but failed, as some were warned not to handle the Garvey defense. The trial lasted about four weeks, during which time the District Attorney's henchmen circulated rumors that Garveyites were armed so as to justify the indignity of searching them daily. The climax came when it was alleged that an anonymous letter was received at the District Attorney's office, stating that one of Garvey's men was "going to get the judge." The letter was released to the press, with the consequent exaggerated headlines. Bomb-squad men and Secret Service Police cordoned off the courtroom.

The attitude of the Prosecutor is summed up in his final plea to the jury: "Gentlemen, will you let the Tiger loose?" It was clear he was not prosecuting the officers of the Black Star Line, only Garvey. So the other three officers were acquitted, and Garvey found guilty on one count, to with "that on or about December 13, 1920, for the purpose of executing said scheme and artifice Garvey placed in a post office of the Southern District of New York a certain letter or circular enclosed in a postpaid envelope, addressed to Benny Dancy, 34 West 131st Street, New York City." An empty envelope was put in evidence, and the Prosecutor assumed that either a letter or circular was enclosed in it inducing Dancy to buy shares. Any one could have rubber-stamped the return address of the Black Star Line on that envelope, and Garvey never took letters to the post office. Nor was there any evidence that this envelope came from the president's office.

W.A. Domingo sent a telegram to Prosecutor Mattocks: "Congratulations on bagging the Tiger." When Garvey read about it, he commented, "There are millions of cubs loose all over the world who are determined to fight their way out of any corral." The judge said he would not pass sentence for a few days. The Prosecutor immediately asked that Garvey be held in custody without bail. He made the startling statement that Garvey had arms and ammunitions in Liberty Hall and that he was a menace to society. Garvey, in protest said, "I am disappointed that your Honor has taken into consideration the remarks made by the Prosecutor, for whom I have nothing but contempt. His statements are utterly false, and this trial has been a conspiracy to ruin Marcus Garvey.... I am satisfied to let the world judge me innocent or guilty. History will decide." Several bomb-squad men and policemen closed in on him, and he was pushed toward a freight elevator. He was conveyed in armored car to The Tombs. Government raids were made on Liberty Hall, also the offices of the organization, but they did not find even a pistol or a cartridge. But the press did not publish the results of the raids.

On June 21, 1923, Garvey was escorted to the courtroom heavily guarded, and Judge Mack pronounced sentence of five years' imprisonment, $1,000 fine, and the costs of the case. Garvey's attorney gave notice of appeal. Bail was denied, and Garvey was hustled back to prison. He was kept in The Tombs for three months, during which time his attorney made several applications for bail. Each time the trial judge and the District Attorney refused to recommend same. When the judge left for Europe on vacation we were successful, but the bond was set for $15,000.

The lawyer contacted the leading bonding companies, but all refused when they heard the name Garvey. Some said, "Sorry, just can't touch it." One said, "Frankly, if we carried this man's bond, we would be blacklisted." The officers of UNIA and I had to arrange speaking tours in all the states and borrowed the bond money from the members. When the cash bond was posted, he was released.

In 1924, Marcus Garvey had completed plans for a large settlement of American Blacks to Africa. He intended to make Liberia the African headquarters of the UNIA. The European powers who were occupying Africa brought pressure on Liberia to deny Garvey the right to start a settlement in that country. They feared that the spirit of nationalism would spread throughout Africa and put an end to colonial rule. The President of Liberia eventually reversed the decision to permit the settlement, and Garvey suffered another defeat.

The party of UNIA engineers assigned to construct housing was arrested and deported the moment their ship reached

Monrovia, and the police seized $50,000 worth of construction material that was to be used by the black settlers.

Marcus Garvey never cried over defeats or wasted any time between them. While waiting for a hearing on the request for appeal in his case, he started another maritime venture—Black Cross Navigation and Trading Company to replace the defunct Black Star Line.

Early in 1925, Garvey's appeal came for a hearing and was dismissed. He was sent to federal prison in Atlanta. What can be called "The Golden Age of the Garvey Movement" was over, but the Movement itself was not over.

The conviction of Marcus Garvey and the fragmenting of his great movement during his imprisonment at Atlanta, Georgia, were events of great sadness to black Americans. It was the end of a brief era in which Marcus Garvey would instill in a people the gift of dreaming that would make them visualize again being a whole people ruling nations. Many critics of Marcus Garvey, including W.E.B. DuBois, began to have second and somewhat more reasonable thoughts about him after he was behind prison bars. They began to deplore the internal strife that was pulling apart what so recently had been the largest black movement in America. Factions within the UNIA began to bid for power, and this power struggle destroyed the effectiveness of this organization. The greatest losers were the ordinary black people who had found a home within the movement, who had been a part of something that had hope and possibly a future for them, and for their children.

Garvey's impact was still felt from behind prison bars. The period referred to as the Harlem Renaissance was midway in its ten-year existence. Garvey had brought about a political awareness that was influencing this literary awareness. His imprisonment and deportation did not break his spirit; he proceeded to Jamaica, through Panama, where he was hailed as a hero who had not failed his people but who had been betrayed by the people he trusted. Garvey's conduct on this occasion was characteristic. He rarely ever had a defeatist attitude. In Jamaica he attempted to pick up the pieces of his organization and continue his work.

There is serious doubt as to whether Dr. W.E.B. DuBois had enough influence alone to persuade the Liberian Government to reverse its decision on permitting the members of the UNIA to establish a settlement. The important point here is that the settlement dream and the steamship line were being lost before Marcus Garvey was sent to jail. While in jail, his enemies made every effort to wreck the rest of these plans. It should be remembered that in spite of the charge that can be made against Dr. DuBois for not understanding the objective of the UNIA and its leader, Marcus Garvey, and who functioned within the framework of the UNIA. During the time Marcus Garvey was in jail and in the years immediately following his release, this motley crew of self-seeking pretenders destroyed the national and international structure of the UNIA.

In Garvey's absence, Mrs. Amy Jacques Garvey and a few loyal followers of the Movement held the organization. At a UNIA Convention that was held in 1927, a petition was sent to President Calvin Coolidge requesting clemency for Marcus Garvey. He was released later that year but was not permitted to return to UNIA headquarters in Harlem. He was put on a ship at New Orleans and deported to his home country—Jamaica.

Marcus Garvey's manner of dealing with those who had disagreed with him seemed to have been designed to create adversaries, of which there were many. While the best known of these adversaries were W.E.B. DuBois and W.A. Domingo, he had several lesser known opponents. Richard B. Moore, who lived through the rise and fall of the Garvey era, was a former member of the Communist Party and was in opposition to Marcus Garvey because at that time a lot of the black radicals were either Communists or Socialist-inclined, and they thought of Marcus Garvey's Movement as a negation of this ideology. Some of Marcus Garvey's critics had formerly been his supporters.

In the United States Marcus Garvey moved into an atmosphere that in some ways was being prepared for him before he was born. He managed to strike the right chords in the temperament of black Americans and achieved what other leaders had not achieved; he managed to build a black mass movement where others had failed. Some of his critics were those who had failed. In the rapid rise of the Garvey Movement some of the observers acted as though they were witnessing the impossible and had to deny it.

It is generally assumed that the greatest opposition to Marcus

Garvey came from the NAACP and Dr. W.E. B. DuBois: This is not true. Opposition to his program and his teachings came from many quarters, including the Caribbean community in the United States and abroad. Opposition to Marcus Garvey by the black working class was practically nonexistent. Now that we know what class of people opposed Marcus Garvey, the next question is, why?

Dr. DuBois and the NAACP did not at first oppose Marcus Garvey. *The Crisis* published fine articles on Marcus Garvey. The first appeared in March 1920 and January 1921 and ended with: "To sum up: Garvey is a sincere, hardworking idealist; he is also a stubborn, domineering leader of the mass; he has worthy industrial and commercial schemes but he is an inexperienced businessman . . . . "

The third and fourth articles dealt with the Black Star Line and the Universal Negro Improvement Association and were based on published documents with little comment. It was not until September 1922 that *The Crisis* had a sharp word of criticism. This was based on Garvey's threats against his critics, his connection with the Ku Klux Klan and his distribution of pamphlet propaganda against American Negroes. Quoted, among other things, was: "The white race can best help the Negro by telling him the truth, and not by flattering him into believing that he is as good as any white man."

The Crisis commented:

> Not even Tom Dixon or Ben Tillman or the hatefullest enemies of the Negro have ever stooped to a more vicious campaign than Marcus Garvey, sane or insane, is carrying on. He is not attacking white prejudice, he is grovelling before it and applauding it; his only attack is on men of his own race who are striving for freedom; his only contempt is for Negroes; his only threats are for black blood.

On the other hand, Garvey's attacks on the NAACP in the pages of the *Negro World* were continuous, and according to the NAACP, preposterous. Some of the charges he made against them were:

1. That they kept his representative from activity in Paris in 1919.
2. That Moorfield Storey came from Boston to secure his conviction in 1924.

3. That the collapse of the Black Star Line came about "because men were paid to make this trouble by certain organizations calling themselves Negro Advancement Associations. They paid men to dismantle our machinery and otherwise damage it so as to bring about the downfall of the movement."

4. That the NAACP was responsible for his incarcerations and deportation.

The NAACP denied all of the charges.

All black intellectuals did not oppose Marcus Garvey; some of the most able in America supported him, to name a few: William H. Farris, author of *The African Abroad*; T. Thomas Fortune, Editor of the *Negro World* from 1923 until his death in 1927; and Hubert Harrison, one of the foremost African-American intellects of his time. Some black intellectuals were sufficiently interested in the Garvey Movement to ally themselves with it at one time or another. Emmett J. Scott, for example, became "Duke of the Nile" in Garvey's visualized African Empire.

Another cause for opposition was Garvey's repatriation schemes. Black Americans have been divided on this issue since the early days of the nineteenth century. This was the period when the African Colonization Movement began.

In his article "The Negro Intellectuals' Criticism of Garveyism" Charles Willis Simmons describes Garvey's early days in Harlem and the introduction of his program:

Garvey brought his program of Negro Zionism to New York on March 23, 1916. There among the transplanted, poorly educated, superstitious and disillusioned southern Negroes, he found fanatical supporters for his schemes. He made use of each opportunity to present his beliefs. On one occasion he was invited to speak for the organization of a Liberty League at Bethel A.M.E. Church. His speech when it came was not for such a league, but for the Universal Negro Improvement Association and its programs.

On this occasion, Marcus Garvey was introduced by Hubert Harrison, founder of the Liberty League. This Black Socialist, who was also a nationalist, had a profound influence on the thinking of Marcus Garvey during the formative years of his movement in America.

George S. Schuyler, then a young man, but later a severe journalistic critic of the foibles of the American Negro, in a letter to the editor of *The Messenger*, wrote of Garvey:

> An ass was created to be ridden. Keep on riding Garvey by all means. Remember the much quoted maxim of Mr. P.T. Barnum and don't let up brother Marcus as long as he continues his mess, lest more foolish Negroes be taking in by this sable Ponzi.

When William Pickens, field organizer for the NAACP, was offered a position in the UNIA, he refused, saying, "I cannot feel myself quite bad enough to accept any honor or alliance with such organizations as the Ku Klux Klan or the Black Hand Society.... You compare the aim of the KKK in America with your aim in Africa—and if that be true, no civilized man can endorse either of you."

Later Pickens gave additional expression to his contempt of the alliance between Garveyism and the Ku Klux Klan. [Here Pickens is distorting the facts. There was never any alliance between Marcus Garvey and the Ku Klux Klan.]

> Dr. DuBois in later years described the movement as a "grandiose and bombastic scheme, utterly impractical as a whole ..." but DuBois considered the movement sincere and said of Garvey that he "proved not only an astonishingly popular leader but a master of propaganda." Displaying even greater admiration for the leader of the UNIA and seemingly refusing to acknowledge that the profound impact of that organization had fallen upon United States Negroes, DuBois wrote that Garvey had "made vocal the great and long suffering grievances and spirit of protest among the West Indian peasantry." He describes the UNIA as "one of the most interesting spiritual movements of the modern world."

Other black intellectuals, who at first had been overtly critical of Marcus Garvey, began to look at him with more respect.

E. Franklin Frazier, in 1926, commenting upon Garvey and his movement, wrote: "As a leader of a mass movement among Negroes, Garvey has no equal." Later, in 1949, Frazier described Garvey as being the "leader of the most important, though ephemeral, nationalistic movement among Negroes."

Alain Locke, in *The New Negro*, saw in Garveyism "the sense of a mission of rehabilitating the race in world esteem from the loss of prestige for which the fate and conditions of slavery have so largely been responsible. Garveyism may be a transient, if spectacular, phenomenon, but the possible role of the American Negro in the future development of Africa is one of the most constructive and universally helpful missions that any modern people can lay claim to."

A. Philip Randolph, one of Garvey's persistent opponents, pointed out that the UNIA "had stirred Negroes to the realization of a need for organization and had demonstrated the ability of Negroes to organize under Negro leadership." Randolph credited Garvey and his organization with having aided in the destruction of the "slave psychology which throttles and strangles Negro initiative."

One Negro intellectual, observing the impression which Garvey was making upon the American Negro said that "whatever may happen to his grandiose schemes of finance and politics, he is the best point at which to study what is going on inside the hearts of ten million colored people in the United States."

James Weldon Johnson believed that if Garvey had possessed a more tactful personality and had used more moderation he would have been successful in his Back-to-Africa Movement. "He had," wrote Johnson, "energy and daring and the Napoleonic personality, the personality that draws masses of followers ... he had great power and possibilities within his grasp, but his deficiencies as a leader outweighed his abilities. To this man came an opportunity such as comes to few men, and he clutched greedily at the glitter and let the substance slip from his fingers."

The reappraisal of Marcus Garvey went on for years—until some of his original critics and opponents became defenders of this movement.

After Marcus Garvey returned to Jamaica he attempted to rebuild the UNIA. He was now dealing with an organization, once massive, that had been divided against itself. Many of the units in the United States did not cooperate with the main unit, now in Jamaica under Garvey's leadership. In addition to attempting to rebuild the movement, he began an active political career, being elected to public office in Jamaica and serving out one term before the opposition to him had destroyed his effectiveness as a public official. He immediately began to organize conventions in Jamaica and subsequently, would bring that island blacks from large areas of the world who still held on to the dream of African redemption.

Back in Jamaica, as in the United States, maybe Marcus Garvey tried to build too many things and could not have possibly done justice to all of them. Many times, on tours of Jamaica, he would speak as often as five times a day. In addition to building the UNIA, he attempted to build business enterprises reflecting his more successful years in the United States. By 1932, his efforts in Jamaica had begun to fail and the movement was once more divided against itself. This would lead to the calling of the last massive UNIA convention in 1934 before Marcus Garvey went to London to set up new headquarters.

The last Jamaican years started as his eleven years in the United States ended. He did not leave the country a broken man, though he had every reason to be. Mrs. Garvey gives this account of his deportation:

> On November 18, 1927, President Coolidge signed a pardon for Garvey. When the order reached Atlanta, the deportation order was served simultaneously. Secrecy prevailed, but we were able to rush Attorney Armin Kohn to New Orleans, as this was the nearest seaport to Atlanta. He tried to get a stay of the deportation order, but his application was denied. On his return to New York City, he gave the following statement to reporters: "In my twenty-three years of practice at the New York Bar, I have never handled a case in which the Defendant has been treated with such manifest unfairness and with such a palpable attempt at persecution as this one."
>
> Under heavy guard Garvey was put on board the S.S. *Saramacca*. He spoke from the deck of the ship to hundreds of Garveyites who had rushed to the docks to see him off. He thanked the millions who had helped and supported the cause, and for their confidence in him despite the machinations of his enemies. His desire to serve was greater than ever, as the work had to be completed. Said he, "The UNIA is not something I

have joined, it is something I have founded. I have set everything aside to do this work. It is a part of me, I dream about it,
I sacrifice and suffer for it, I live for it, and I would gladly die
for it. Go forward come what may. We must win by God's help
and guidance."

[When] the ship docked at Cristobal, Panama, he was not
allowed ashore, but Garveyites secured permission to send a
delegation on board. They presented him with a purse and
discussed the future of the organization. He was transferred to
the S.S. *Santa Marta*. He got a hero's welcome in Jamaica. The
people pushed his car from the wharf to Liberty Hall.

Marcus Garvey arrived back in Kingston with Mrs. Garvey on December 10, 1927, and was indeed given a welcome befitting a popular head
of state. The humble Jamaicans who came to see him were welcoming
home a man who, in spite of setbacks, had given them status in the
eyes of the world. They were not thinking about the loss of the ships
and those who opposed him both in America and Jamaica; they were
reacting to the hope that he had awakened in them. A meeting
followed in the Ward Theater later that night. In fact, the first week
of his return to Jamaica was a week of welcoming ceremonies. There
was at least one negating factor to his arrival back in Jamaica. The
ruling elite on the island, black and white, were none too happy and
were not a part of the thousands who came to welcome him home. The
Daily Gleaner published the following lament upon his arrival:

It is with profound regret that we view the arrival of Marcus
Garvey back in Jamaica. And it is with more than profound
regret that we picture any leader of thought and culture in this
island associating himself with a welcome given to him. But
Kingston has reached such a level of degeneracy that there is no
knowing what she will do.... A new spirit has passed over the
lower classes which has nothing to commend it except its
ignorance ... is to receive another impetus through the dumping
upon us of a man who indeed is a Jamaican but for whom the
island as a whole or the more intelligent section of it has no use.

He immediately began to put his organizational house in order, and planned a trip to Central America and Europe. Mrs. Garvey gives this account of the trip:

> He had planned a trip to Central America but none of the consuls for these countries would give him a visa, so in April 1928 he left for England and Europe after setting up Headquarters. He brought down from America the Vice-President, Miss Davis, and left her in charge of the office. An American secretary also came, who traveled with him.
>
> During his stay in England he busied himself contacting African and West Indian seamen and students and organized and financed an underground movement. He formed a branch of the organization among the colored people and spoke in Hyde Park on Sunday afternoons. He sent circular letters to members of Parliament, leading ministers of the Gospel and liberal-minded persons, explaining his program, and pointing out to them the grave unrest in the Colonies and Protectorates because of bad living conditions, urging them to become interested before it was too late. So as to crystallize interest he planned a big meeting at the Royal Albert Hall, London. For weeks before the meeting he had a typist address envelopes from telephone subscribers' names and addresses, in which he put invitations and handbills.
>
> To Garvey's amazement and disappointment [only] about two hundred persons attended the meeting, but he went through just the same with a concert and speaking program. Garvey did not fully realize the lack of concern on the part of the British people.

Marcus Garvey's Albert Hall speech, in addition to being one of his best thought out explanations of his program for black people, holds its own as a piece of living literature.

In the brief few months he and Mrs. Garvey were in England, he organized a chapter of the UNIA and set up committees for the support of the organization. He and Mrs. Garvey left England at the end of September 1928. They landed in Montreal, Canada, where Marcus Garvey was arrested on a technicality—illegal entry. After some embarrassment and humiliation that seemed to have been intended, he was released. He was not allowed to land in Bermuda. The British authorities were sensitive about the conditions on the island which created a Jim-Crow paradise for white people. He was allowed to speak in Nassau, Bahamas, where a former supporter used this occasion to get a judgment against the UNIA for $30,000. These financial squabbles were now threatening to tear the organization apart while he was trying to put it back together.

In August of 1929, the sixth International UNIA Conference was held in Jamaica. This was the first conference that had been held outside the United States. It was well attended, and representatives came from most of the black world, including a surprising representation from Africa. These representatives who came to this conference risked their lives and personal safety to defy their colonial governments in journeying across the world to a conference which was dedicated to the liberation of all colonies.

The number of legal difficulties which tied up Garvey's time that year did not deter his desire to build a political party in Jamaica that would represent working people.

In the tenth plank of his manifesto he stated that judges should be tried for dealing unjustly and as a result was sent to prison for three months and fined $200.00 (Jamaican) for contempt of court. Charged with seditious libel, arising from an editorial written by T.A. Aikman, literary editor of the *Blackman*, Garvey won the appeal. In October, he was elected Councilor of the Kingston and St. Andrew Corporation. He had to forfeit his seat since being in prison he could not attend the meetings.

During 1930-1931, Edelweiss Park became headquarters for the UNIA and a major culture center for the Black population in Jamaica. In 1932, he started a new publication, the *New Jamaican*. The UNIA was having problems of growth and finance, and Marcus Garvey was approaching the end of his stay in Jamaica.

Mrs. Garvey gives this account of his last years in Jamaica, before going to London:

> Because of the underhand methods used to keep him out of the City council, an article was written in the *Blackman* newspaper, which stated in part: "The Corporation is entirely opposed to the welfare of the country . . . . [T]he Government is also bereft

of common decency, not to say dignity and common sense."
Counsel was retained for Garvey, T. Aikman, Editor, and
Coleman Beecher as Circulating Manager who were charged for
seditious libel. Beecher was acquitted, Aikman (who wrote the
article) was sentenced to three months in prison, and Garvey to
six months. Notice of appeal was given. The Appellate Court
upheld the appeal. Garvey was justified in that later on a
Commission was set up to probe into the affairs of the City
Council, and the body was dissolved. Garvey was opposed in the
City Council in getting his resolutions passed and put into
practical use. As these would have set in motion works of
reproduction financed by loans from the Imperial Government
at a low interest rate of three percent, so in June 1930 he
formed the Workers and Laborers Association. He headed a
deputation to the Governor, asking him to investigate the
appalling conditions of the masses, and to use his influence
towards remedial measures. The Governor nonchalantly replied
that in his opinion, there was "no unusual suffering."

Garvey's next effort was to draw up a petition to the King,
through the Colonial Office, copies of which he sent to members
of Parliament and liberal-minded editors in England. The
result was the appointment of a Royal Commission to investigate the political and economic condition in the West Indies.
At the end of September 1930 he held a mass meeting at Coke
Chapel steps (the outdoor forum) to celebrate the good news.

Our first son was born September 17, 1930, and was named
Marcus. Julius was born August 16, 1933. Garvey was proud of
being a father, but the work of the organization and financing
of it came first in his planning.

Early in 1934 he felt the full effects of the two-year depression in America, as Negroes suffered more than whites and were
unable to support the work of the organization. Garvey called
the seventh Convention in Jamaica, and the decision was made
to remove the headquarters to England, where he would not be
subjected to such colonial pressures and would have easier
contacts with Africa. Before this could be done all our household furniture was sold, as he could not meet the payments on
the bill of sale. I had mortgaged the home and furniture when

he was in Spanish Town prison and paid the overdue install-
ments on Edelweiss Park, the organization's property. This was
also sold. After he left for England I was served with summonses
for doctors' bills and overdue acceptance on printing machinery.

He would now go to the seat of the British Empire and petition
directly for the redemption of Africa. He did not succeed. In fact, his
presence in London caused the British fear. The Empire was spread
around the world and the sun was not setting on the British flag. It was
the last of England's age of splendor, domination and arrogance. They
were not inclined to listen to this subject of the Crown who was acting
like a citizen and demanding the basic rights that go with being a
citizen. During the early part of Marcus Garvey's London years the
Italian-Ethiopian War had broken out and had destroyed his dream of
a place in Africa where Africans could go and start nation-building. He
cautioned Haile Selassie, but to no avail, against leaving Ethiopia
during its hour of trial.

The last five years of Garvey's life were years in which he struggled
to hold on to a semblance of the once-great mass organization. Funds
and supporters of the organization had dwindled almost to nothing and
while the Great Depression was over for a lot of white people due to
the beginning of the war in Europe accentuating employment, this was
not true in the black community, where depressions come early and
stay late; and so the last years of Marcus Garvey were years in which
he lived in poverty without losing one iota of the Jamaican-Maroon
pride that had projected him out into the world thirty years before. His
death came at a time when many of his predictions were coming to
pass. European powers were engaged again in a massive world struggle,
and the colonized people were once more beginning to defy European
rule. The legacy that he left behind would be part of the stimulus for
the African freedom explosion that came twenty years later.

In a long article in the magazine *RACE*, published in London in
1967, the writer Richard Hart has said that "The last five years of
Marcus Garvey's life marked the decline in influence and popularity,
almost to the point of oblivion, of a man who had once inspired
millions." The statement is only partly true. The Italian-European War
started soon after Marcus Garvey re-established residence in London.
This attack on Ethiopia, the last remaining independent African

nation, awakened black people around the world. It also gave rebirth to Garveyism. In the midst of this war and in the Depression years many conservative blacks became radical and nationalists, and a new political consciousness was born. A young Ghanaian student, Kwame Nkrumah, came to the United States and began his studies in this atmosphere. During those years he came under the influence of Garveyism.

Black Americans were becoming more Africa-conscious. The Italian-Ethiopian War was responsible for this new interest and anger about Africa. A number of study groups showed interest in African history. The best known of these groups was the Blyden Society, named after the great nationalist and benefactor of West Africa, Edward Wilmot Blyden.[2] I personally remember Kwame Nkrumah attending several meetings of this society.

The American black press improved its coverage of news about Africa. In the reporting on the Italian-Ethiopian War this press was fortunate in having in its service at least two reporters who had been well schooled in African history in general, J.A. Rogers,[3] an historian and journalist, and Dr. Willis N. Huggins, historian, teacher and community activist. In his dispatches from Ethiopia, J.A. Rogers gave an astute analysis of the war to the Pittsburgh *Courier*. He was the only reporter on the scene who was looking at the Italian-Ethiopian conflict from a Black point of view. Rogers also commented on the political intrigues in Europe that led to this conflict. Later, in a small book, *The Real Facts About Ethiopia*, he digested his reports and produced the most revealing document about the Italian-Ethiopian War that has so far appeared in print.

[2] Edward Wilmot Blyden, a Presbyterian minister, went to Africa from the Virgin Islands in the 1850s. He became Liberian ambassador to England on two occasions. His Inauguration Address as President of Liberia College, in 1881, on liberal education for African people, is considered a pioneer statement about the significance of higher education in Africa. His best-known writings are included in his book, *Christianity, Islam and the Negro Race*.

[3] J. A. Rogers, a Jamaican, who came to the United States in the 1920s, was a self-trained historian, researcher, and biographer. Most of his life was devoted to gathering information about the role of the African personality in world history.

Dr. Willis N. Huggins, a high school history teacher and founder of the Blyden Society for the Study of African History, went to Geneva and reported on the League of Nations meetings concerning the Italian-Ethiopian War for the Chicago *Defender*. Dr. Huggins had already written two books on Africa: *A Guide to Studies in African History*, and *Introduction to African Civilizations*.

The "Back-to-Africa" teaching of Marcus Garvey was now being reconsidered. The Harlem literary renaissance had died. The black urban communities, especially in the North, were entering a renaissance of African consciousness and nationalism. The first nationwide black student unions, which included African students from all over the continent, were formed. The attack on Ethiopians and the re-emergence of Garveyism and the hardships of the Depression years had created a semblance of unity among black Americans.

Kwame Nkrumah's plans for the eventual independence of his country were formulated during his student years in the United States. In the book *Kwame Nkrumah* by Bankole Timothy, we are told that Nkrumah dreamed of organizing all Africans in the United States so that they might return and perform useful services for Africa. He was the moving force behind the organizing of the first General Conference of Africans in America, in September 1942. At the same time, he dreamed of a West African Federation and together with Nuamdi Arikiwe of Nigeria and Durosimi Johnson of Sierra Leone, planned on returning to their respective countries to start political agitation toward this objective.

While Nkrumah was finishing college in America and writing his important booklet, *Toward Colonial Freedom*, Marcus Garvey was in London trying to hold together the structure of the UNIA while war clouds were gathering Europe.

Mrs Amy Jacques Garvey written this account of her husband's last London years:

> While in England he published *The Blackman* as a monthly magazine. He had pneumonia in the winter of 1936. As all of the finances had to be used for the work of the organization, he did not send for his family until June 1937.
>
> Every summer he was allowed to go to Canada and conduct meetings and conferences, which American Garveyites attended.

In 1937 he left from Halifax and visited and spoke at all port cities of the Leeward and Windward Islands down to Guyana. He had enthusiastic crowds and appreciative listeners.

In June 1938 Junior contracted rheumatic fever because the bedroom was not adequately carpeted. He was in hospital with a drawn knee after the fever subsided. At the end of the summer the specialist and the school doctor decided that as the knee could not keep straight without a plaster cast, he would have to be sent to an orthopedic home in the south of England, or I could take him back to the West Indies, as he needed sunshine on his limbs. This I did, and we stayed at my mother's home. Julius, who had bronchitis in the winter, was glad to be able to play outdoors all year round. Garvey was in Canada convening the eighth International Convention. He sent us $20.00 some months, but not regularly as money was coming in slowly, agents did not pay promptly for the magazine, and rent and staff had to be paid.

In January 1940 he had the first paralytic stroke; his condition improved, but in May a black reporter in England maliciously gave out the news that Garvey had died in poverty in England. Cables and letters poured into the office, and although his secretary did not let him see them, he suspected that something was wrong, by the constant ringing of the door bell. He demanded that he see the correspondence. When he saw the black streamer headlines of the Negro newspapers, he motioned to her that he wanted to dictate a statement; but he cried out aloud in anguish, and fell back on his pillow. He was unable to speak again, and the brave soul returned to his Creator on the tenth of June 1940. But his message to the world had been delivered.

> O Africa awaken
> The morning is at hand
> No more art thou forsaken
> O bounteous Motherland.
>
> From far they sons and daughters
> Are hast'ning back to thee
> Their cries ring o'er the waters

That Africa shall be free.

In his lifetime, Marcus Garvey managed to convey to African people that Africa was their homeland, and it had to be reclaimed.

The black nationalists and freedom fighters before and after Marcus Garvey were saying no more or less than what Garvey had said in word and in deed: "Up, up you mighty race. You can accomplish what you will."

A revival in thinking about Marcus Garvey and his movement started about five years before his death, with the Italian invasion of Ethiopia and the destruction of the last sovereign nation in Africa. I am mindful of the existence of Liberia in West Africa and its pseudo-independence since 1847. But most black Americans think of Liberia as an American colony, and this thinking is not too far wrong. Garvey's attempt to establish settlements in Liberia failed, and it failed precisely because American influence in Liberia prevented it.

With the loss of Ethiopia, black people began to revive their relation to Marcus Garvey's dream of nationhood. This revival in thinking was to continue through the Second World War and in part to stimulate the convening of the Fifth Pan-African Congress in Manchester, England, in 1945. This Congress was the political incubator for a large number of African future heads of state, especially, Kwame Nkrumah.

With the publication of the books *Black Moses: The Story of Marcus Garvey and the Universal Negro Improvement Association* in 1962, by Edmund D. Cronon, and *Garvey and Garveyism*, by Amy Jacques Garvey, in 1963 (reprinted 1970), the new interest in Marcus Garvey went beyond the papers written by students, many of whom considered Marcus Garvey an academic curio piece. He has now become part of a new literature. Both Professor and Mrs. Garvey have called attention to a lot of material on the rise and fall of the Garvey Movement and the Garvey revival is now something of an epidemic. (Mrs. Garvey maintains that her husband was the forerunner of the "Black Power" and "Black is Beautiful" concepts of this century.)

Certainly Garveyism was one of the main ingredients that helped to set the African independence explosion in motion. Mrs. Garvey says:

Let us trace the source and course of Black Power to determine its effectiveness as a weapon of defense of a black minority. I propose to do so by submitting questions sent me by a student of research on the work of Marcus Garvey. I added other questions, and the answers, so as to round out my subject. Here they are.

Is there any connection between Marcus Garvey's teachings and the philosophy of Elijah Muhammad and Malcolm X? Have Garvey's teachings been corrupted?

This question can partially be answered by my quoting from a letter written by Mr. Thomas Harvey, President-General of the Universal Negro Improvement Association to the Jamaica *Gleaner*, November 17, 1964, in which he states: "Please allow me space to express my thanks to your government for inviting us down from America to attend the ceremonies in connection with the reinterment of Marcus Garvey in George VI Park. I think I am in a position to speak on behalf of Negroes in America and Canada, and to affirm our belief in the sincerity and courage of Marcus Garvey as the only international Negro leader at the close of this century. He paved the way for all local leaders who have emerged since his death. Most of them were his understudies or followers who were inspired by his dynamic leadership and the universality of his appeal for justice, equality and independence for the Negro peoples throughout the world. For instance, Elijah Muhammad was formerly a corporal in the uniformed ranks of the Chicago division. Malcolm X's father was a vice-president of the Detroit division, so Malcolm X grew up under the influence of Garveyism. Mrs. M.L. Gordon of the Peace Movement of Ethiopia was formerly an active member of the organization in Chicago. The Ethiopian Federation is also an offshoot of Garveyism."

Here are some of the events that tend to support Mrs. Garvey's assumption:

1957: Dr. Nkrumah as Prime Minister of Ghana in their independence year launched the Black Star Line Steamship service in memory of Marcus Garvey.
1963: Mrs. Garvey wrote and published *Garvey and Garveyism*, the

world distribution of which brought about the renaissance of Garveyism.

1964: Garvey's remains returned to Jamaica and reburied at George VI Park. Proclaimed Jamaica's First National Hero.

1965: Marcus Garvey Scholarship for Boys established by the government of Jamaica.

1968: Mrs. Garvey wrote and published a collection of essays updating Garveyism.

1969: Human Rights Year. The government offered a prize of $10,000 in the name of Marcus Garvey to a person who contributed most to world peace. The award was made posthumously to Dr. Martin Luther King. His widow, Mrs. Coretta King, received the award at a public ceremony at the National Stadium.

The Federal Republic of Cameroon, West Africa, issued a fifty-franc commemorative stamp bearing the likeness of Marcus Garvey.

1971: The government of Jamaica issued a ten-cent-stamp and fifty-cent note in honor of Marcus Garvey.

1972: A plaque unveiled in London to mark the office where Garvey worked. Ground-breaking ceremony for Marcus Garvey East Village in Brooklyn, New York. (This is part of a state urban renewal project which is being built at a cost of $11,950,000.)

In Jamaica, Marcus Garvey's home, the subject of repatriation is once more being discussed. In February 1972 a number of African organizations in Jamaica, West Indies, came together and formed the Joint Committee on Repatriation. The Joint Committee has since that time been working steadily to effect the return of Africans in Jamaica to their motherland, Africa.

In pursuit of this aim, the Committee has started a drive to collect 100,000 signatures to support a petition to the United Nations to take up the matter of the repatriation of the descendants of the Africans formerly held as slaves. The campaign has been well received initially. There have been good attendances at outdoor meetings and the majority of the people giving their names for repatriation have been under thirty years of age. This shows the awakened interest of Black youth in Jamaica in their ancestral motherland of Africa.

WHITE NATIONALISM

▼

WHITE NATIONALISM IS A SUBJECT that has been with us in some form for well over 1000 years. White racism coupled with white nationalism began in the fifteenth and sixteenth centuries with the Atlantic slave trade and subsequently the colonial system. There is a small library on this subject that most people have consistently ignored, and this includes most scholars. The book, *The Iceman Inheritance* by Michael Bradley, published in 1973, is about white nationalism working in conjunction with white racism.

The Crusades was in part a form of white nationalism disguised as religious fervor. After the Crusades, when plagues and famine had taken one-third of the population of Europe, and Europeans had lost a lot of sentimental attachment to one another, at the time the feudal system was becoming obsolete, Europe gradually rediscovered itself. For nearly 800 years Europeans had lived in fear of what they called the infidel Arab in North Africa and in the Mediterranean who had ended their domination of this part of the world after the decline of the Roman Empire.

In 1415, after the Portuguese had freed themselves from the domination of the Africans and Arabs, collectively called Moors, the Portuguese attacked a small enclave on the coast of what is now Morocco, called Cuetra. This battle, not considered to be of any great significance in history, had some significance in reawakening the spirit of Europe that had at last drawn the blood of the so-called infidels that had been blocking their passage to the Mediterranean for nearly 800 years. In 1455, Spain, which had been under the domination of the Moors since the year 711, freed part of their country from this domination. This Mediterranean country, not totally free from colonial domination, began to have colonial aspirations of its own.

Spain and Portugal would go to the Pope, then the major arbitrator of disputes between European nations at the time. He would tell Spain and Portugal, in essence, you two Catholic nations should cease fighting among yourselves. Both of you are authorized to reduce to servitude all infidel people. At this time, the Portuguese had already made contact with the coast of West Africa. The slave trade had already begun. In his book, *Capitalism and Slavery*, Eric Williams is very precise on his point in this period in history.

European preference had started along with the rationale of European domination of the land, people and resource of non-European people. Professor Leonard Jeffries of City College, New York, has emphasized that Europe emerged from the Middle Ages land-poor, people-poor and resource-poor. This is the period that I have referred to, from 1400 to 1600, as the turning point in world history. The plan for European dominance of most of the world was brought into being during most of this period. Stripped of its romanticism and its pretense of spreading civilization, this was one of the most tragic periods in human history. The Europeans began to propagate a concept that the world waited in darkness for them to bring the light. The truth is the exact opposite. With the coming of the European, the cultural and commercial light in most of the countries outside of Europe was put out. To accommodate the expansion of Europe into the broader world, cultures and civilizations were mutilated, altered and sometimes destroyed that were old before Europe was born. This was the essence of white nationalism.

The propaganda in defense of this nationalism is still with us in some form to this very day. These concepts will stay with us until we deal with certain myths in history, one being the myth of the invader and conqueror as civilizer. No people takes over the countries and resources of another people in order to civilize them. No people have spread any civilization anywhere at any time. The invader and conqueror spreads his way of life at the expense of conquered people. To be civilized is first to be civil. The very act of invading and conquering a people against their will is uncivil. Therefore, this act has no relationship to civilization.

In the spread of European influence in Africa and Asia, the

Europeans not only colonized history, they colonized information about history. They propagated a concept that is still with us. That concept is that the Europeans are the only people who have made anything worthy of being called history. In the propagation of this concept, there's a glaring fact that the propagators neglected, and that is that nearly half of human history was over before the people of Africa and Asia knew that Europeans were in the world.

The most effective and most tragic of all the Europeans' colonization schemes is the colonization of the image of God. When you destroy a people's self-confidence and their concept and image of God as they conceive Him to be, it is not necessary to build prisons to contain them because psychologically you already have them in a prison.

In both Africa and Asia, white nationalism was the enemy of indigenous nationalism. The European colonizer makes every attempt to deny both the Africans and the Asians the right and the privilege of loving themselves and giving themselves and their way of life preference.

This same pattern would continue throughout the colonial wars encompassing the whole of the nineteenth century and the massive slave revolts in South America, in the Caribbean Islands, and in the United States during the same period and the emergence of various forms of African and Asian nationalism late in the nineteenth and twentieth centuries. The suppression of these revolts was a form of white nationalism. The Europeans knew if Africans and Asians reclaimed their lands, they would also claim their resources and deny Europeans the privilege of taking them cheaply or for nothing. They wanted to continue the privilege of domination over African people and access to their labor and resources. Various organizations in the Caribbean Islands and the United States and to a large extent in Africa fought for regional consolidation and some called for the total unity of African people all over the world. Collectively, this effort was eventually called Pan-Africanism.

Pan-African Congresses were held between 1900 and 1945. The 1945 Pan-African Congress in Manchester England, was, in my opinion, the most significant because it called for the reformation of African states under African rule and the end of colonialism which meant the end of an external form of white nationalism that had threatened the existence of Black Nationalism. The African Freedom Explosion, beginning with the independence of Ghana, March, 1957, would set in motion other challenges to European rule. To some extent, more than we have been willing to admit, Marcus Garvey influenced the Pan-African Conference in Manchester, England, 1945, though he had been dead five years at the time. His influence would also be felt in the emergence of independent states in Africa, where some of the leaders of these states had been influenced by his thinking.

My subject, White Nationalism, Enemy of Black Nationalism, has been a subject that most of our thinkers have deliberately avoided talking about. It is a delicate, under-the-rug subject. In fact, they have not talked about white nationalism at all. And they have not dealt with the fact that principally for the last 500 years the world has been ruled by white nationalists and white nationalism. And that in the fifteenth and sixteenth centuries what brought about the second rise of Europe and the European takeover of most of the world was the rebirth of white nationalism and a decision among Europeans that whosoever controls the world, it would be a European.

That decision, that Europeans made, has not been broken. They have broken all kinds of decisions among themselves. They have fought two world wars and have killed over 100 million people of their own. They have killed 100 million of their own people and three times more other people. But the decision that *whosoever controls the world, it will be one of them* has not been broken. They have changed political cults but that decision holds. And it holds for Europeans irrespective of political label. And our confusion is that once the European changed from one political label to the other the assumption is that he is about to make another agreement to the world. He is not, and he never will. And the difficulty, especially among blacks who are Socialists politically, and I number myself among them. My only difference of opinion with blacks who are socialists is that I have always defined my position. I have seen no difficulty in being socialist, Pan-Africanist and black Nationalist all at the same time. So in my socialist package comes a firm commitment to the preservation of African people wherever they are on the face of the earth. And when I say I am a Socialist, I am not necessarily talking about what Karl Marx was talking about. Because the socialism that I am talking about existed before Karl Marx was born and before Europe was born. I am talking about the socialism that came out of communal societies in Africa and parts of Asia that dictated that man should have, in each society, goods and services according to his own needs. And this was not a European creation, because the European has never been humane enough to create any system that gives to each according to his needs.

If you look at the climates of the world, social systems generally developed based on what is available in those climates. Nature was stingy in Europe. When that icebox thawed out there wasn't enough fruit, there wasn't enough bread, there wasn't enough meat to give each according to his need. They couldn't even afford to propagate anything as humane and as decent as this. So, the strong took the most and enslaved the weak to serve them. This is the basis of European feudalism. Now they call it feudalism in Europe, but in other places they don't play around with fancy words, they just go ahead and call it slavery.

So when Europeans enslaved other Europeans they called it feudalism. But once you study feudalism and study slavery, many of the aspects of feudalism were worse than chattel slavery. And if you understand the nature and administration of feudalism and if you understand the Crusades, especially the Children's Crusades, 1212 A.D., when the Europeans marched more than 100 thousand children across Europe, half of them froze to death during the preceding winter, and when they got to the warm waters of the Mediterranean, in the spring, they sold the other half to the infidel Arab they were supposed to have been fighting. If you understand that, there is something logical about the slave trade in Africa; logical that any man who would do that to his children would do even worse to yours. So, when Europeans were first seen along the coast of Africa, they did not know him and they do not know him now, which is the heart of white nationalism. But, if you knew him, knew his history, you would know that this is a gangster, and you had better kill him before he kills you.

Because you did not know him, because you thought he was humane, because you thought he was just another human being, a long way from home, instead of killing him, you invited him for dinner. Invited him for dinner. In many ways, figuratively speaking, you became the dinner. Never in your life had you encountered a people who would come in your home, eat your food, rape your wife, and enslave the host. You could not deal with that mentality then and cannot deal with it now. You came from a society where if somebody is going to fight you, they let you know days ahead of time so you can get ready for the fight. And when they come to fight you, they approach you and then step back six feet and wait for you to get ready. They don't come and hit you in the back. Even fighting in your culture had a code of honor. And sometimes fighting starts at dusk, at the end of the day, where after, if you want to change your mind and go on home, so be it.

So, if you came out of a society as humane as that you couldn't deal with a thug from an icebox called Europe. Can't deal with it now. And sometime, because the movies have spoiled you, you think in every human drama there's a good guy and a bad guy. So, when the Russians and the United States are meeting, because the United States has treated you so badly, you think the United States must be the bad guy, and the Russians must be the good guys. And you don't know that there are dramas in the world without a hero. And you can't deal with the fact that two white nationalists, very clearly, two white nationalists, and the one thing that they are sure about is that they are going to preserve themselves by any means necessary. And if all of you have to be washed down the drain of history, they are going to preserve themselves.

Now, we, collectively, have been in this country about 500 years. And there are boat people who came over a few years ago who are getting better positions than we are. And even taking over our communities. This is being done because someone is facilitating their doing this. There are people in Miami, Cubans, whom the United States government provided with a home. Their apartments were ready when they arrived. And you were looking for an apartment, and you've been here before the Mayflower people.

So they didn't bring you here to give you justice. And now they are bringing people here to protect them from you—as buffers. And because you are naive enough to use the words called "third world," and talk about "our allies," you think if you don't have any friends among whites, you must have some friends among the newly arrived nonwhites.

You're joking again. They will sell you for a white person's smile or without it. Now what am I saying? I'm saying that white nationalists will manipulate anybody to protect themselves against us. Because they see in us a creativity and an energy far more dangerous than the atomic and hydrogen bombs. And they fear another thing in us that they dare not even whisper about which is genetic annihilation. We have a thousand and one thoughts, but the one thing that they know scientifically, their sperm bank is going bankrupt. Their birth rate is going down, but we've got a plentiful supply in that department.

Now, we're not doing the right thing with it. We're not handling it scientifically. We're not taking care of our productions, but it's there. In the twenty-first century there will be a billion African people in the world. We haven't planned well how to take care of them, how to feed them. We haven't planned the sea captains that will take the ships across the sea to deliver the goods we're going to have to have. We haven't planned the airports to land the airplanes we're going to have to have. We haven't realized that there's a whole continent called Africa that belongs solely to us. We haven't recognized the fact that we're the only ethnic group on the face of the earth with an entire continent all to ourselves. All ethnic groups on the face of the earth must share a continent with somebody else. We own Africa lock, stock and barrel. Every grain of sand, every leaf of grass. And that everybody there who cannot be called an African is either an invader or a descendent of an invader. And that the destabilization of Africa is not accidental. Look what's at the front door and look what's at the back door.

It is no accident that Egypt and Israel got together. Partly politically. It's no accident that South Africa is at the back. It's no accident that the United States is supporting it. It's no accident that America can't afford to permit stability anywhere in Africa. It is no accident that there is not a single African head of State who is a Pan-Africanist. Not one. It is no accident that with the killing of Nkrumah, driving him out, every African head of state who advocated even regional unity was driven from office.

We have not understood the international implications of white nationalism. It's all white nationalism.

And the white Left is no less a part of white nationalism than the white Right, but they have given us the option of changing from one white slave master to another one. And we assume that the Left one is a liberator, because we have not studied the machinations of the party in different parts of the world. What did that Party do for the

Algerians when they were fighting against French colonialism? Nothing. And what did they do for the Vietnamese when the French were engaged in a struggle to hold onto Southwest Asia? Nothing. Because their whiteness took precedence over their politics. Everyone in the world seemed to know this except us. In a case of nationalism and people's survival, blood calls blood and blood answers.

Now, what I'm trying to say, because the subject is so big and so old, is that nationalism in itself is not bad. And it is a part of the life of every people—and should be. But what makes the nationalism of Europeans, of white people, so different and so dangerous? Racism. The addition of racism added to nationalism. Love of nation is nothing that one needs to look down on. It is something that can be respected in every man, in every nation. It is universal. But what we need to recognize, in dealing with white nationalism is that the ingredient of racism was added to nationalism, and this made it dangerous because it assumed that one people had preference over another people to the point where their gods told them to take away from another people anything they needed from that other people. Where they demeaned the concept of their religion and altered it to justify their thievery of the lands and the resources of other people. And that's what I'm attempting to deal with because we, as a people, have been universally naive in this regard and have not been able to practice what I have referred to as the essential selfishness of survival. We have not recognized that we as a people have been under siege for 3000 years. And that we have been under more pressure than any people on the face of the earth. And we have been under pressure because we are a very rich people who have not protected our great riches.

We have always had and still have things that other people want, think they can't do without, and don't want to pay for. So, for most of our existence the enemy has either been at the door, in the house, or in our beds.

The third factor is a form of white racism, which they have used to capture us and to confuse us, that we have not even dealt with and dare not even whisper about. And I have studied it down through the ages, and I have always threatened to write a massive book about it and never wrote a line. In my mind I visualize the title of the book, and I talk out chapters in the book, but I never write the book. It is so delicate and dangerous, so painful that a person like me, who has opened many doors and talked about many things, even at the risk of being killed, hasn't even put it down. The book is called *The Role of the Bastard as a Factor in History*. How people have bastardized other people through their women and used the bastard to control them. Then having used the bastard, refuse to accept the bastard in the home of the father that created him and send him back to his mother's people to start confusion.

When and if I dare, and somebody is going to have to give me a twenty-four-hour-a-day bodyguard if I ever did, I would have to write about how the mulatto factor destroyed the Haitian Revolution. How the mulatto generals, sons and daughters of African mothers and French fathers betrayed the Haitian Revolution and went over to the French against Toussaint L'Overture. And a French general, who hated both blacks and mulattoes, called Rochambeau, decided to teach the mulatto generals a lesson: That I hate you just as much as I hate the blackest of the black. So he gave a gala party for the wives of the mulatto generals. At the end of the party he said, "I have some presents for you ladies in some boxes. Go in the room and open the boxes." It was the heads of their husbands. He had cut their heads off to show you: I have just as much contempt for you yellow niggers as I have for the blackest of the black.

The Rochambeau incident in Haitian history was so embarrassing and so painful most Haitian historians have written the history of Haiti and left it out. Couldn't face it. It is too embarrassing. And Christophe, one of the last of the powerful of the three generals mentioned in passing and one of the last of the mulatto governors, Petion, had a conflict about democracy versus dictatorship, but the real conflict was really about mulatto rule in opposition to black rule. Christophe had a dictatorship but everybody was fed and going to school and doing well. And Petion had another part of the island that was called a democracy, modeled after Europe but everybody was starving over there.

Now, after the death of Christophe, supposedly engineered by the mulattos, they came to power begging for French acceptance and got it. The mulattos adopted a French constitution that crippled Haiti and killed the revolutionary spirit of Haiti to this very day. French white nationalism and French bastardization killed that nation before it could be born.

I'm too old, and I've had one stroke already. I can't afford another one. In the first place, we should be clear about what a nation is and what a culture is within a nation. A nation is more than one culture, generally. It is a combination of cultures but it cannot be a nation unless it can function with some degree of harmony and some degree of respect, one to the other.

Then, the question is, "What is a race?" Scientifically, there is no such thing. Race is an invention. Nature created no race. What you call race is nothing but an ethnic, a cultural entity. People created races to put one group over the other; to create a rationale for taking from one things that they wanted; and to justify it. And they also use race and religion, sometimes together. And because of nationalism all of the three major world religions have been used by nationalists, and nearly always used against blacks. Islam has been used for blacks for a while but mostly against them.

It is a pity, maybe, that if a person like Jesse Jackson knew Christianity, he probably wouldn't be a Christian. If he knew Judaism and the relationship of Jews to blacks, he wouldn't have apologized at all. Least of all for "Hymie." If Farrakhan really knew Islam, he would either be a better Muslim or none at all. He's sharper on the Bible than Jesse. He uses it much better and he still doesn't know it as well as he could. But if he knew ... along with true history, he would be devastating. Because he cannot quote the Bible all the way as truth, because there is a point where the Bible departs from history and becomes fable and folklore. If you know pure history, then you know the points of departure. Some parts of the Bible can be proven true. And some parts of the Bible can't be sustained at all, because it is nothing but Jewish fairy tale. The Bible in general is a Jewish survival book and a very good one. And the Jewish people in general are people who invented themselves and did a very good job of it. But you have to understand, this is an invented people. When you invent yourself you invent a whole lot of nice things about yourself. You've got privileges. You give yourself victories in wars that didn't even occur. What's there to prevent you from doing so? You let the sea open up and let you go across. And why not? You've got nothing but your imagination. There's nothing to prevent you from it. And yet there is no man alive, this might break your heart now, there is no man alive who can give me one iota of positive proof that the Exodus actually occurred.

I told my students that if you prove to me that Exodus actually occurred, I'd give them one month of my salary. Nobody proved it. But you see, they were studying the Bible. They went to the Bible again and again and again. I knew where they were going to go. They are never going to find it there. But then when it was all over I said, this is where I trapped you. I studied the period on this side of the river. I studied the pure history on this side of the river, and the pure history has no record of anybody departing in that number at that time. The purest.

Then I go on the other side of the river, and I see if there is any record of anybody arriving at this time. No record. Then I searched the military history of Egypt. Is there any record of any Pharaoh's army being drowned? No record. Then I searched the records and found that was one of the finest record-keeping periods in Egyptian history because this was the Ramses Period, and if Ramses had a pimple on his behind, they made a record of it. And if he made a record of one pimple on his behind, 600,000 people can't leave a country without them also making a record of that.

If he stumped his toe on his way through the garden to see his wife *Nefetari*, then there is a record of it. "He was delayed in meeting his wife because he stumped his toe and fell against a tree. And his guards picked him up and braced him, you, know, in sitting down. He rested a while, you know, and they brought him cool water to drink and he was on his way to see his beloved *Nefetari*." If he made a record of that, which might have taken ten to fifteen minutes, don't you think if 600,000 people left his country, there would also be a record of that. Or somebody. And besides there was a sixteen mile land bridge connecting Egypt with Western Asia. The Hebrews did walk into Africa, and they could walk out. Nobody needed to go by sea.

Now, I'll admit that the story of the Exodus is a beautiful one. It's wonderful. Cecil B. DeMille made so much money his grandchildren won't even finish spending it. Charleston Heston did nicely, too. He probably got money playing Moses, wrongly. And the true story of Moses won't be told until black people start making movies. The modern movie industry and the images that it projects is another form of white nationalism. The true story is that an African prince got in trouble with the Pharaoh, consorting with one of the Pharaoh's messengers, and he wanted to put some space between himself and Egypt. He took up with the Hebrews late in his life. He decided to lead them out of Egypt, the alleged house of bondage, and he converted them to a religion that was 2000 years old before he was born. But, they thought they were getting some new laws. All of what you refer to as the Ten Commandments were in the *Book of the Dead*, referred to by the Africans as *The Book of the Coming Forth by Day and Night*. The components that went into the making of this book were made 1000 years before the Hebrew entry into Egypt. Judaism, Christianity and, to some extent Islam, are forms of white nationalism.

If you want to be brutal and somewhat honest at the same time, you can refer to Moses as an ancient con man. He got away with it. He told them, "I'll be your leader if you obey my god." They adopted *monotheism*, the concept of oneness of god which they said they invented. That he got from *Akhenaten*.

But, white nationalism let them get away with telling us that. And if we knew our history well, we wouldn't let white people get away with half of the nonsense that they get away with. Now, when we deal with white nationalism, we have to deal with it in the classroom with our children. When our children go into a history lesson, and they would be taught that the Code of *Hamarabi* was the first civilized law known to man. And the children would come home and tell you that: Studied the *Laws of the Code of Hamarabi*, the first law of a civilized society. It was civilized law 300 years before, in Africa.

See, if you had a countering black nationalism, they would point that out. Now if they learn that Moses was the law giver, there is an assumption that there was no law before him. When he led the Hebrews out running from the law. He was wanted for murder, that was the law.

You see, white nationalism makes you think there was no law before them. And no order before them. And no humanity before them. And this what we have to deal with because we haven't dealt with it today. We haven't dealt with it as it manifested itself in the ancient world. Let's deal with it now in relationship to racism. Because racism is older in its manifestation than the concept of nationalism. And yet, nationalism and the love of nation existed before they added racism to it. And the blatant form of racism did not exist and really came into full existence in the fifteenth and sixteenth centuries. But the beginning of the concept that developed into racism in a formal intellectual sense might have started with the philosopher Aristotle. For Aristotle was the first to put down on paper the concept that some people were born to serve other people. Now what Aristotle intended was to justify Greek slavery. While we are talking about Greek and Roman civilizations, please remember at the height of Greek and Roman civilizations 85 percent of the population were slaves, and I am talking about Europeans being slaves to other Europeans.

Africans weren't even a part of the picture. And when Europeans entered history and founded their first societies, mostly Mediterranean societies, those societies didn't get off the ground until they made contact with African societies, which were mainly the Greeks. And that slavery, from the beginning, was a part of white nationalism.

Chattel slavery was not a part of African nationalism, and we have to distinguish between slavery and servitude. I am not trying to justify servitude, because in wars, in Africa, certain groups who lost wars did serve periods of servitude to other groups. But that servitude did not last forever. After a period they went out of servitude. Then the people in servitude had certain basic and guaranteed rights. And sometimes the royal family of the conquered group married into the group that had conquered them and became heads of the very house that had conquered them. So there was some basic consideration between the conquered and the vanquished, and basic consideration between the people, one and the other. And sometimes there was a merger between one culture and the other and they became one people.

There was one people, the Mossi people, in what is called the Upper Volta, now called Burkina Fasso, which makes far more sense than Upper Volta. If you can't understand either one of them don't worry about it. Burkina Fasso, even though you do not understand it, makes more sense. But Upper Volta don't mean anything. That's a word that the French gave it because they couldn't understand that this was the home of the Mossi people. The home of the Wagadugu people. And they couldn't understand, the Wagadugu didn't run smooth off the French tongue. So, they said, "Upper Volta." And they called the country Upper Volta. I'm glad when the nationalists came to power they gave the country a name that was local. And whether the people can understand it or pronounce it is another matter. It's of no significance. It's Africa, whatever it means.

Now, the Mossi people, now here's a case of black nationalism at its finest, in ancient times were called the *Cultural Chastity Belt of Africa.* When they conquered people they extracted labor. They never permitted the people they conquered to marry into their group. And if you lived among them and wanted a wife, they gave you time to go back to your group and get a wife. They did not want their bloodstream to be polluted by anybody, not even another African. And they did not want their religion to be polluted. They didn't accept Islam. They didn't accept Christianity either. And they were very careful about what other African religions they accepted. Because of this aspect of their approach to outside religion, this is black nationalism, this is cultural nationalism too. Here you see it practiced without racism. Here you see it practiced with cultural preference, and practiced well. And it stayed that way straight up to the end of the nineteenth century. Now there were a few Catholics there and a few Moslems, but generally they were still a homogeneous people.

Go among the Mossi, you'll find them uniform in size for they generally marry among themselves. They respect themselves. And they only let so many of their children go to European schools. Local education and fairly good, too. And their greatest intellects, the intellects that go to European schools, must come back and help to preserve the local culture. The heart, the soul, the kernel of white nationalism in the world has been Christianity and still is. Before that, or after that, really after that, they had a conference at a place called Nicaea. Now the Bishop and the priests who called the meeting of the council were so ignorant about the religion they didn't know whether Christ was a man or a woman. And they rejected the books in the Bible that they didn't want to deal with. They rejected the *Book of Mary* because they wanted to invent something called the Immaculate Conception. I'm using my words advisedly. I said, invent something called the Immaculate Conception. Because they had to reject the *Book of Mary* because this told you what Joseph said when he discovered that Mary was with child and knew it was not his child.

And this is in one of the so-called *Lost Books of the Bible*, that's not even lost anyway. You can find them easily in almost any good book store. The so-called *Lost Books of the Bible* are easy to find. I've got three different editions in my house. I've got all kind of oddball things in my house. So, they put the books that they want to accept on top of the table, put *all* the books on top of the table, and they say, the books the Lord doesn't want them to use will be gone by morning. So during the night somebody came and took out the books that the Lord didn't want them to use. And those books became the *Lost Books of the Bible*. They weren't lost at all! They deliberately misplaced them. Because they didn't want to confront the truth. But really, now the basis of white nationalism is really Christianity. And they use it.

All three major religions, where we are concerned, became murder cults. I'm not saying that you should not believe in any of them. Hear me clearly. I'm saying, inasmuch as all people make religions into what they want them to be and need them to be, based on the nationalist needs of that people, why don't we do the same? They painted, after Nicaea, the saints that were black because black was once considered a royal, fortunate, and lucky color. They painted them white. They began to Europeanize the faith, change the symbols. In some parts of Europe they let the symbols remain. Throughout Germany, even after the rise of Martin Luther, they let the saints remain black. It was only after Hitler rose to power that he ordered many of the black saints to be taken out of the churches and destroyed. A lot of people didn't destroy them but took them and hid them.

In Poland, the Patron Saint Chasakovich, is still there. They just hid it when the Germans came. And that's the saint that the Pope in Rome worships every time he goes to Poland, a black saint.

Question from the Audience: He kisses a black woman?

JHC: Yep, to this day. Of course, I think he must kiss a real one, too, but that's a little beyond the lecture here. I'm going to stick to what I can prove and leave that one alone.

Now, the Europeans continued to use and misuse this religion but the internal fight between the Europeans over this religion wrecked and disgraced the religion until a camel boy, who later became the prophet Mohammed, delivering goods to the masters and other places, began to talk to other camel boys about the dissatisfaction and disgrace of the religion. And he began to ask for reform. Failing to get reform, he sent a message from Mecca asking and demanding a new religion. And the new religion was Islam. The latest and the largest of the world's new religions. A religion that came into being so fast it is the least original of the world's religions. It borrowed a saint from here, a saint from there, some psalms from there. It has no great psalm literature. And there is no great vocal literature in Islam.

Have you ever heard them sing? Alright. Didn't even have time to create any great songs. Wouldn't do in a Baptist church anywhere.

When we hear the brothers say this is the black man's true religion, the black man existed for thousands of years before this religion came into being. What did he do for a religion before it came there? This religion rose in the seventh century A.D. The black man has had religion 10,000 years before that: From those great Nile Valley religions came Judaism, Christianity, and the elements that went into Islam. Islam came out of the Nile Valley. All these great religions are derivative religions. I mean religions that came out of that were drafted from the great river of the original religions that came out of the Nile Valley.

This is dangerous now. I'm saying that all these religions were transplants. If I wanted a great religion I would bypass all of them and go to the original. Go right straight to the original. I'd go to where they started. Go where they got theirs from. So what's wrong with *Amon-Ra?* These other religions came from there and the great female goddess Maat and these other sun worshiper gods.

Now you can change anyway you want to or not change if you don't, you know, that's your personal business. But all of these religions, Christianity, Judaism, and Islam have been turned into nationalist religions, white nationalist religions. The Arabs turned Islam into Arab nationalism. And all of it has been turned on you. All of it has been turned into a murder cult and turned on you. This is why I don't worship any of them. And hear me clearly, I'm a very religious person. I refer to myself as a spiritual person. There are sources of being spiritual other than going to them.

Now, because the Arabs use Islam as their personal property and use it for nationalism; the whites use Christianity as a form of their nationalism; the Jews use Judaism as a form of nationalism to take what doesn't belong to them: Everybody in the world uses religion to take what doesn't belong to them. Now what are we going to use to take back what belongs to us? And everybody worships a god. Everybody worships a god that physically resembles them but us. Because everybody uses religion based on their national need and their cultural understanding of themselves. We need an internal culture revolution, and it's going to have to start inside of our minds. We might have to step back in order to move forward.

When we talk about the great tragedy, the clash in the black family, I think everybody is talking about the wrong thing. If we are going to restore the black man as a symbol of authority in the black family, that restoration might start when we have the nerve to change the symbol of God in our church. And you know most of us don't have that kind of nerve. Then you're making Him second rate.

As Europe continued to develop, Islam pushed Europe out of North Africa and Europe went into the Middle Ages, their terminology. They awakened a little bit during the Crusades. The Crusades was not a religious movement. It was a form of white nationalism. Are you prepared to look at the Crusades as a form of European awakening and a form of white nationalism ... warring on the rest of the world? What they learned they never forgot: That the rest of the world had moved, to some extent, ahead of them. They brought back fabrics they had never heard about and even dishes they never heard about. And one of the reasons they were barred from the Holy Land in the first place, by *Saladin*, was that every time those flea-bitten, unwashed Europeans went to the Holy Land they spread fleas and ticks and lice. *Saladin*, a puritan Iranian, a lot of people say he was a Persian, and of course Arabs say he was an Arab, and it doesn't matter who he was, but he was a man who bathed three times a day. Oiled himself down. Had a great sense of sanitation. Those stinking Europeans kept coming over lousing up the place, so he started barring them.

Maybe if he had minded his business there would not have been any Crusades. He should have let them in—stupid and ignorant and in their dirt. Maybe the world would have been different. But he didn't. Peter the Hermit went across Europe waking them up, and at the time the Pope needed an issue. The church had been selling *dispensations*. The church had been hustling on the people to the point where the people were about to explode against the Catholic church. The church had been building great edifices, living in luxury off of the people. They had invented something called purgatory. And they were hustling on that to the limit.

Your grandmother, dearly beloved, dead and gone, didn't get to heaven, stopped in purgatory. Give me so much money I will pray her out of purgatory into heaven. So the purgatory racket was being run. So the people got tired of all this. Then phoney priests came selling dispensations. You buy one; the more you buy, the closer you get to God. They discovered some of them weren't even priests, hustlers. And, they would split that with the church. So, the people were getting angry. So, when Peter the Hermit came across Europe saying that the infidel Arab had barred them from the holy places, the Pope was glad for people to go on marches. He was glad for people to direct their attention from the hucksterism of the church, because otherwise they would have turned on the church.

Now he endorsed the Crusades. "Let's rescue the Holy Grail!" It wasn't lost anyway. So, the Crusades gave the European a drain-off, an emotional issue. But it was nothing but an act of white nationalism. They went across Europe raping everything in sight: Not only taking the farmer's daughter, taking the farmer's corn and everything, in the name of God.

Then came the tragic Children's Crusade, when they marched more than 100,000 children across Europe. Half of them died and they sold the rest to the infidel Arabs when they reached the warm waters of the Mediterranean. No heart.

Now the Africans and the Arabs (the Berbers), had been ruling Spain for hundreds of years, successfully. They controlled trade in the Mediterranean. In the 1400s (watch this because it's happening right now), Africans and Arabs began to argue among themselves, and the Arabs began to argue among themselves. And this weakness signaled the European they had been ruling that it was time to strike. And the Europeans took advantage of the weakness and they struck and came back into the Mediterranean. White nationalism again made them re-occupy the Mediterranean. And they went to the schools, erected by the Africans, the University of Salamanca, where they got information coming form China, on maritime skills. China's maritime skills were 150 years ahead of Europe's. The Europeans had forgotten longitude and latitude. They didn't even know how to sail a ship East or West.

Then some maps fell into the hands of a Portuguese prince named Henry the Navigator, who to the best of my knowledge never went to sea. Why they called him a navigator I'll never know. And, some of these maps had been collected by Jewish gold dealers who had been in the Western Sudan. And Henry the Navigator opened up a school of chart-making, map-making and navigation. Now, Europe is back at sea, and Africa is doomed. It's a certainty. Because Africans do not understand, then nor now, the evil intentions of the Europeans. And when the Portuguese came down that west coast, the Africans began to trade with them. Then the Europeans, especially the Portuguese, began to arbitrate differences of opinion between one African and another. He would ultimately see this weakness and enslave both of them.

Don't ever let an outsider settle a family dispute. Even the Mafia knows that. So, if you haven't seen *Godfather I* and *II*, the main lesson to learn, never let an outsider settle a family dispute. Sober up old drunken Uncle Willie. Let him come and do it. Don't bring no outsider into your family conflicts.

If a guy brings an outsider to settle a family dispute, knock him off; married to a wife who was an outsider, keep her out of it. Your wife is your own business, but she doesn't get into this family dispute. She came into the family, by marriage. When it becomes a family dispute, she's out. She's not in the family that deeply. We haven't learned that. We invite white people into our business. We go on the job and talk about our business. We haven't learned anything. We're really telling about our weakness.

Now, Europe is back at sea. By 1455, they've driven the Africans and the Berbers and the Moors out of half of Spain. They're ambitious. They're going to Rome to ask the Pope, "What're we going to do now that we are coming to power?" They have ambition to divide up the world among themselves. We want to do our thing! And what does the Pope tell them? "You are both authorized to reduce to servitude all infidel people." The Catholic Church became the heart, the soul, the planner, and the architect of white nationalism still to come and the rationale for the slave trade. The Pope would issue another Papal Order where he would have lines of demarcation. He would tell the Spanish and the Portuguese, "You take the East, and you take the West. You two Catholic nations stop fighting among yourselves." He would divide the world between these two little states. And when the hustler, Christopher Columbus, comes along, bad navigator, liar, he couldn't get the slave trade off the ground. It actually started in 1438. But, there was no place to sell any slaves. There was nothing for a slave to do. You can't start a slave trade unless you've got labor for them to do. They had to open up the so-called "New World." Now they've got something for them to do.

At this point in history, white nationalism is also becoming white racism. This 500-year-old disease, which constantly multiplies itself in volume and in effect, was then the main political motive for European expansion and for the beginning of the establishment of European settler-states outside of Europe.

The noted child psychiatrist and public speaker, Dr. Frances Welsing has defined the origin and growth of racism through the control of image, especially, the image of God:

> The overwhelming majority of the peoples on the planet Earth have a conceptualization of—the existence of God (no matter how named or defined) as the supreme force or the supreme being responsible for the creation of the universe. This conceptualization constitutes the highest and ultimate focus of a people's worship, devotion and obedience.
>
> ... the orientation of the person to the concept of God in a given culture begins at the earliest possible age of comprehension. Thus, long before there is true cognitive understanding, there is for even the very, very young child a participation in the practice of God recognition. This participation and practice becomes a part, then, of the child's—and ultimately the adult's—concept and image of self. It is from this self image and self concept that evolve all patterns of behavior, that the determination of mental health or mental illness is made.

Dr. Welsing's inquiry continues as follows:

> The *critical* question that now arises is what does the "concept of color of God" have to do with "self and group respect, and respect for harmony in the universe?"
>
> Let us begin with the recognition of the fact that black people in the United States of America are an oppressed people. Indeed, all black, brown, red, and yellow peoples on the planet Earth are oppressed.
>
> The existence of oppression means that there is no self-determination on the part of the oppressed. The existence of black and other non-white oppression also means most fundamentally that there can be no functional self respect, or the existing levels of self respect are extremely low, and for the most

part, negative. All nine areas of people activity are used in the system of non-white oppression. Religion is no exception. The global system of white supremacy, oppression, and domination developed a religion called "Christianity."

Most fundamental and absolutely critical to the white supremacy system of religious thought was the formation of the image of a *white man* as the "son" of God. This white male image was then referred to as "Christ"; it doesn't matter that the prophet Jesus was a black man.

Because of the nature of the human brain that functions on logic circuits, once a white male image is established in the brain computer logic as the son of God, then the brain computer at deep unconscious levels automatically concludes that God the Father is also a white male, since black or other non-white males would have produced a non-white son.

Thus, any person accepting the Christian religion—whether conscious of it or not—*has* the image and concept of God as a *white man*.

(From: *"The Concept and the Color of God and Black Mental Health,"*
an article by Dr. Frances Welsing.

The world is still gathering the harvest of racism set in motion by Christopher Columbus, the alleged discoverer of America and the slave trade.

But after Christopher Columbus came, on his way back he was shipwrecked off the coast of Portugal. And the Portuguese asked him, "What were you doing over there?" The Portuguese had no question about the so-called "New World." They didn't have to go and discover anything. They knew where it was. And the Pope had assigned them to that side of the world anyway. The Pope had said, "You take the East, and you take the West. What are you doing over there? That's the side the Pope has given to us."

Can you imagine one man sitting in Rome dividing up the world and telling one state, you take that part and you take the other part? That was not only nationalism, it was white gangsterism. The godfather of the gangsters of the world was in Rome. And he was assigning territory to the other white gangsters. "You take the world and you two good Catholic nations stop fighting among yourselves." It is hard to imagine but it happened. And I plead to you to read, if you're only going to read but one book on this subject, let it be *Capitalism and Slavery* by Eric Williams. The first three chapters will give you the essence of what I'm saying. How Eric Williams wrote this when he was a young scholar at Howard, and he did his research in London in the Public Records Office before they closed it to the public. The British were letting those records out; they closed it. They don't let them out now. Eric Williams was a brilliant scholar and a fine teacher. He was a lousy Prime Minister of Trinidad, but that is neither here nor there.

A whole lot of people should have been college presidents, instead of country presidents, but that's another discussion. Because of the intellectual shortage in the last 20 years, a lot of people had to be something they probably would not have been otherwise. Had there been more able men in Trinidad I think Eric Williams might have preferred heading a university instead of becoming the head of state. I never thought he was comfortable being Prime Minister. But that's another lecture. But he was a fine writer, and he's a fine historian, too. A fine human being in off-seasons, too. It just happened that I happen to have known him personally, before he became a recluse and a person who is so hard to contact. And being also a historian and a teacher, I got to know him as an intellect. And he's a fine political scientist. I still think his last books were written hurriedly. His book, *The Caribbean: From Columbus to Castro*, is a commendable history of the Caribbean. There is very little good history of the Caribbean Islands, but that's one of the better ones. And he admits that he had to write in a hurry. His *History of Trinidad and Tobago*, which he told me personally he wrote in two months (he dictated it), is still worth reading. And he was just that brilliant. He could do something like that.

Now, back to the subject, in the conclusion, if I can. I'm skipping half of what I came to say. Now, after the discovery of a New World, and the world wasn't new, Christopher Columbus says in his diary, "As man and boy, I sailed up and down the Guinea Coast for twenty-three years." The Guinea Coast of West Africa. What was he doing in West Africa for twenty-three years? Hanging out with African sailors who had already gone to the New World. And I can prove that too. They told him about the currents in the ocean that would take him there.

They also told him something that he didn't seem to believe. If you pick up a current in the ocean that will take you to that part of the world, you have to wait six months for the current to reverse itself to bring you back. And he came back in less than six months, and that's why the ships were wrecked off the coast of Portugal. Hard-headed, stupid Italian. He wouldn't listen. But white nationalism. You can see it's manifestation in this so-called New World discovery. I say so-called because it wasn't new at all.

Now, Professor Ivan Van Sertima of Rutgers University has done an incredible job in his work, *They Came Before Columbus*. There were other people in the field long before Van Sertima. J.A. Rogers was doing work in this area. A young man named LeGrand Clegg was doing credible work in the field only he never published his in book form. Another man, Ronald Davis, who published a book as scholarly as Van Sertima, and different articles but never in book form. But Van Sertima is not the pioneer in the field, but the person who did the best in putting it between the covers of books and getting out there and selling it. That's to his credit. But black scholars in New World scholarship, and pre-Colombian scholarship, were old in the nineteenth century. Delany mentions that.

Now, after "discovery," white nationalism would show itself in its cruelest form in the destruction of the indigenous population of the Caribbean Islands. On his third voyage, Chrisopher Columbus brought over Father Bartholomé de Las Casas, who noticed the rapid disappearance of the people referred to as Indians. Christopher Columbus suggested the capture of Africans. The Africans who had befriended him. Remember, nearly everybody we ever befriended has turned on us. People never return our favors. He suggested the enslavement of the Africans to save the Indians. Father Bartholomé de Las Casas agreed. That's a form of white nationalism again. And he went to Rome to sanction the increase in the African slave trade in order to save Indians. And Rome sent commissions throughout the West Indies to look at the life, look into the conditions of the Indians only to find on many islands, all of the Indians were dead: disease, smallpox, rape and ruin. Some islands didn't even have one left.

Father Bartholomé de Las Casas made the best record at the end of his life, called *History of the Indies*. The book was so devastating an indictment of the European destruction of the Indians Father de Las

Casas said, "From 12 to 25 million people have died, unnecessarily." He was talking about the destruction of the Indians. Africans were brought to replace them, and the replacement is the black population of the Caribbean Islands today.

Near the end of his life, again, de Las Casas said, "Maybe all slavery is wrong. Maybe it's wrong for the Africans, too." But, it was too late then. It was all over. Africans died in large numbers too. But the Africans finally adjusted and survived. To adjust to a condition does not necessarily mean to accept a condition. We have to understand that. White nationalism was the basis of slavery, and eventually, when slavery reached a saturation point, white nationalism invented another form of slavery called colonialism. And after colonialism they computerized colonialism with a form of racism. Early in the nineteenth century they began a form of pseudoscientific justification for white world dominance. They began to measure hands and heads. They began a pseudoscience called "craniology." Who had the biggest head or the biggest brain or forehead? You know, it didn't mean a damn thing. Long before these others, Shockley and all those fools of today, there was another group. There's a whole literature on it. The leopard spots. Literature called *The White Man's Burden*. A concept called "divine white right" propagated to a great extent by the British writer Rudyard Kipling. Then when Admiral Perry went to Japan, a nice people minding their own business, wearing their beautiful little kimonos, raising their crops. An agrarian people who had no intention of ever being industrial. Kicked open the door: "Trade with the West whether you like it or not."

The Japanese said, "Well, we didn't want to trade with them. We didn't want to trade with anybody." They didn't particularly want any machinery. They had a leader, the like of which I wish the hell we had. He put all the young people together, mostly men, "Go to the West. Get the education. Bring it home." He said, "Accept their humiliation, but bring their education home and teach your people. If they smear their body waste in your face, apologize for your face being in their way." So for two generations, Japanese students came to this country. If they bumped into you, they said, "So sorry." Humble as they could be. Accepted the humiliation. Studied engineering. Studied everything. You always saw them with little cameras. Nobody would date them. "Girl, who would be found with a dirty Jap?" Taking their little pictures. And when they left they knew how to make every building, every train in this country. Went to the Virginia Military Academy, at a time when they wouldn't even let an American black person in to sweep the floor. But even before that, they had studied militarism. In 1905, when the Russians started harassing them they jumped on those Russians in the Sino-Japanese War and beat the living hell out of them. That was the first time a non-white nation had beaten, militarily, a white nation. And that created something in the world called the "yellow peril," the "yellow danger." Now the threat to white nationalism was coming from the East as well as from Africa. And Teddy Roosevelt directed their attention to the "threat from the East." The little Japanese had kicked their behinds and kicked them good. And they weren't about to do anything about it. But the Japanese, what did the Japanese have? That nerve. They got their nerve back. That wasn't god. And the Japanese went throughout Asia trying to tell the Asian, you don't need this man here to rule over you. You can do it. Come on now, get yourself together. And they would tell old sleeping China, come on, wake up now. You're bigger than we are. You've thirty times more people than we've got. These people are coming into your country, building hotels for Europeans only, and with signs on hotels in your country, saying, "Chinese and dogs not allowed." In your country! This is true. The pictures still exist of the hotels in Shanghai. "Chinese and dogs not allowed."

And the only Chinese woman allowed was the cleaning woman.... The humiliation of a country like China, under some corrupt Chinese. So the Chinese, in 1931, kept begging "Come on, don't accept this humiliation." And because they let the Europeans kick their behinds and wouldn't accept the Japanese telling them to do so, then the Japanese said, to hell with it. If you can't get with me to kick them, I'm going to come and kick you. And so they invaded Manchuria and subsequently went down into China. So, systematically, Japan began to take over territory in Asia. And European white nationalism felt threatened by yellow nationalism.

Now the Japanese continued to come to this country and continued to study. And most of the Japanese staff officers at Pearl Harbor were trained at Virginia Military Academy. And a lot of the Japanese who built Japanese industry, which built the ammunition that struck America at Pearl Harbor, was trained at MIT, Massachusetts Institute of Technology, at a time they wouldn't let a black student in from America, the Caribbean or South Africa. And most of the scrap that went into the bomb was bought from the Sixth Avenue El and the Third Avenue El stations. They accepted that humiliation. They kept quiet and they studied. Japanese students of that day always strategically pretended to lose their textbooks. As a matter of fact, they were sending them home and bought another copy. "So sorry, lost my textbooks." And they sent that home so that another group back in Japan would be studying the same textbook.

So they discovered that once a Japanese student came to an American school he would sometimes finish a course in two years, because his brother, who was here before him, had sent him back the textbooks he was using before. That's cooperation. We haven't developed that kind of a network, because we're too selfish. We won't do it because somebody's socks don't match, you know. Or somebody failed to return a telephone call. "I ain't gon' do that." We haven't developed that kind of *camaraderie*, a kind of brotherhoodness, sisterhoodness. We're going to have to have it if we're going to survive. We have got to rebuild it. We must regain it. It was once a part of our way of life. Helping each other was once a part of our very way of life. Helping each other without asking a whole lot of stupid questions, what's in it for me? What have you done for me? We didn't even ask these questions. Brother needs. Here!

Now their success came from national cohesion. but reaction to Pearl Harbor was a white nationalist reaction. World War II was white nationalism. And when I was drafted, and I *was* drafted (damn sure wasn't silly enough to volunteer), and I was trying to figure—since I couldn't fight or anything—how I was going to get out of it; I didn't figure how to get out of it. But I knew it wasn't our war. And when they lynched two black men in my hometown, Columbus, Georgia, in their uniforms, near Fort Benning (I grew up near Fort Benning), where I among other things, was a caddie, I used to carry the golf clubs of a major named Eisenhower long before he became a general. And one named Bradley long before he became a general. Has nothing to do with the lecture, but I never did like Eisenhower. But I've got my personal reasons. Poor tipper. He didn't tip very well. That's good enough reason in those poor times. There are other reasons too, but that's good enough. But, I knew that World War II was mainly a war of white nationalists fighting among themselves. I was still angry about the Italian-Ethiopian War, which wasn't anything but a form of white nationalism. Because they let Italy get away with it. And from Harlem we sent Willis Huggins to the League of Nations in Geneva to protest and the late J.A. Rogers to Ethiopia to report back from the battlefield.

But, there was a rebirth of Garveyism after the war when we began to give black nationalism some form of cohesion that it needed. March 7, 1957, after many years of struggle, Ghana became an independent state, and Nkrumah announced, "At last, Ghana our beloved country," called the Gold coast then, "is free forever." An African-Independence Explosion was in motion. We should have known at that moment that white nationalism would turn that movement back. After the death of Lumumba ... after the death and exile of Nkrumah, white nationalism, the CIA and British and French intelligence, along with the cooperation of minor colonial powers like the Portuguese would wreck and fragment all Africa. After the heroic Civil Rights Movement, white nationalism literally fragmented black organizations to the point where it is difficult to mount any successful campaign in black America. The Caribbean Islands are literally an American colony. After the invasion of Grenada, because we never rise in righteous indignation when things happen to us, they continue to happen. We never deal with the brothers and their misconception of Marxism, which caused Maurice Bishop to be killed. Arguing over somebody else's ideology. He was one of the finest young leaders to emerge in the Caribbean in the past fifty years. And his life, even with error, meant more to the Caribbeans than anybody's down there today.

He had an international outreach that meant something to the whole of the African world. And we are never going to prosper as a people until we collectively save lives like his. When we can turn back white nationalism and its effect, with strong black nationalism, and our nationalism does not have to be racist, but it has to be nationalist to the point of realizing who we are in the world. And where we have to go in the world.

All too long we have been following people who don't know where they are going. We have to decide where *we* are going. We have to reject terminology. We have to reject the concept that we are a minority. We have to realize that we are a world people. If we are world people, between the Caribbeans, between South America and the

United States, there must be over 150 million people in the Western Hemisphere, not to count the millions in the Pacific and in other parts of Asia. Now with over 500 million Africans in Africa and with the new prophecy that in the twenty-first century there will be a billion African people on the face of this Earth, we might be the first if not the second largest ethnic group in the world. We have to rethink black nationalism. Where are we going with black nationalism? Where are we going in the world? We must establish some kind of a leadership over ourselves and some kind of discipline among ourselves and some kind of responsibility to ourselves. And I suggest that you start seeking out an ally by finding a mirror. And you look in that mirror and look at what's staring back at you until you find your leader, your theoretician, your sage,and your philosopher. Then you start the revolution that will change and put African people on a new road and give them a new destiny. And you say that in order to change, we are a people that need a revolution. But say first to yourself, our revolution starts right now. Our revolution starts with me.

Four

AFRICA, ZIONISM, AND FRIENDS WITHOUT FRIENDSHIP

▼

COMMENTARY

▼

THE SUBJECT OF THE RELATIONSHIP of the Jewish people to the African world is both delicate and dangerous: Delicate because very few people want to talk about it; dangerous because if you dare to speak honestly on this subject, people will hear what you did not say and stubbornly refuse to hear or understand what you actually said. Many Zionist Jews will label you an anti-Semite without explaining the meaning of the word "Semitic,"[1] which has been mistakenly applied to a cultural group.

The relationship of African people to people of the Hebrew faith is long and complicated. Africans have never been the declared enemies of the Jewish people. In fact, they have a sentimental attachment to the Jewish people that goes back to 1700 B.C. It requires no difficulty to admit that what happened to the Jews in Germany at the hands of the Nazis was one of the great crimes in human history. No sane person with his humanity intact endorses this crime. But there is one thing we must make explicitly clear: This was a crime of the Europeans against Europeans. European racism, which had spent itself outside of Europe, turned inward on itself within Europe and created what is referred to as the Holocaust.

Africans, the people of mainland Asia, and the Arabs of Western Asia were not participants in this European tragedy, which must forever be laid at Europe's door. In the United States, African-Americans have

---

[1] The word "Semitic" was originally a linguistic term and pertained to certain people in Africa and in Western Asia who spoke what is referred to as a Semitic language. Originally, it did not refer to race at all.

275

always had a sentimental attachment to the Jews because of their reading (and sometimes misunderstanding) of the Bible. During the slavery era in the United States, the story of the Exodus became real to black people because they wanted to attach themselves to an historic event in which people escaped their oppressor. It was not clear, then as now, whether they were reading fact or folklore. Because black ministers, scholars, and teachers are shy about examining the Bible, misconceptions about it continue to prevail. There is a small library of books concerning the Bible and how it came to be written. But it is still difficult to get scholars or laymen to read Sir James G. Frazer's monumental three volume work *Folklore in the Old Testament* or T.W. Doane's *Bible Myths and Their Parallels in Other Religions*.

Most African people have not read the best works written by their own writers on the subject of the role of the Jews in history and the rise of Christianity as a factor in history. Some of John G. Jackson's neglected works are very informative, e.g.: *Was Jesus Christ a Negro?*; *The African Origin of the Myths and Legends of the Garden of Eden* (1987); *Pagan Origins of the Christ Myth*; *Ethiopia and the Origins of Civilization* (1976); and his latest works, *Christianity Before Christ* (1986) and *The Ages of Gold and Silver* (1990).

The most extensive work on Africans of the Jewish faith is *We, the Black Jews* by Josef ben-Jochannan. Another work, *The Hebrew Heritage of Black Africa* by Steven Jacobs, is an extension of the same subject. *Hebrewism of West Africa*, by Father Joseph Williams gives details about Hebrew elements among African people in the Caribbean and in West Africa. The books cited thus far are some of the neglected writings on this subject.

There is a need, now, to study the migration of the Jews after 70 A.D., when the Romans destroyed their temples and started the dispersal of the Jews of that day. Where, indeed, did they go? There is some evidence that some of them migrated south into the body of Africa. Some lived in the ancient kingdom of Ghana from the first century to the year 770 A.D., when they were expelled for collaborating with Arabs in an attempt to take over that kingdom politically. Incidents of that nature pertaining to African and Jewish relationships are not known because both European and African scholars are reluctant to study the African component within Judaism.

In an unpublished article written over ten years ago on black

Americans and the Jewish mystique, I discussed what is being called black anti-Semitism as an exaggeration of black American discontent with all white people, including Jews of European extraction. Recently I have been compelled to call attention to the fact that there are more than 250 Jewish organizations within the United States with paramilitary units. I know of no unified Jewish attack or criticism of a single one of these organizations. This raises the questions: Why all the Jewish furor directed against Jesse Jackson or Louis Farrakhan, neither of whom has an army or the economic power to harm the Jews in any way?

In the same article "Black Americans and the Jewish Mystique: Some Barriers to Understanding the Arab-Israeli Conflict." I have made the following observation:

The people now referred to as Jews have met Africans and Arabs many times on the crossroads of history and most of the time they have complimented each other. As a matter of fact, the longest periods of peace, prosperity, and security that Jews have had in their history were those periods when they lived in and around countries ruled over, or mainly populated, by Africans and Arabs. While the relationship between the Africans, the Arabs and the Jews have long historical roots, the present conflict does not. This conflict is a Zionist creation that belies all of the known truths about the past relations between these three different peoples.

The mystique[2] referred to in this paper had its beginning during slavery in the English colony that later became the United States. When these African slaves read the Bible, or when it was read to them, they began to identify their plight with the biblical account of the Jews in bondage in Ancient Egypt and saw hope in the story of the Exodus—when the Jews escaped, led by an Egyptian prince named Moses, with the help of the Lord who parted the sea and let them walk across to safety on dry land. The part of the story when the Lord released

[2] The "mystique" consists of Africans' misinterpretation of the Bible: their mistaken assumption that the Jews are a sacred people.

the water and drowned the army of the "wicked" Pharaoh reinforced the slaves' belief that escape from their cruel masters was possible. In my opinion, this and other stories from the Bible saved the slaves' sanity because they showed that slavery was not perpetual and somewhere there was a God who would help them out of it. They did not, at this time, question whether the story of the Exodus, the escape from Egypt, was true. They could not distinguish between truth and allegory. They had no knowledge about how the Bible was written and who wrote it. They did not know then that a large part of the Bible is folklore and fable. Many of the stories in the Bible were told to illustrate a point or teach a moral lesson. If the lesson gets across, the story need not, necessarily, be the truth. This is an elementary fact that still eludes most black people who call themselves Christians. They accept everything in the Bible as the truth, including the story of Noah, the biblical flood, and the "Curse of Ham," which is still the basis of most of the antiblack prejudice among white "Christians."

And thus, black Americans' association with the Jewish mystique began. This association lasted until the decade following the decline of the Civil Rights Movement, when blacks in the United States and in Africa began to ask some questions about their relationship to the Jews, and the Jews' relationship to other white people whom we consider to be our oppressors. Black Americans in slavery did not and could not ask these questions. They did not know that concurrent with their fascination for the Jews in the Bible, the Jews of their day were willing participants in the slave trade. They also did not know that the Jews of their day, and the present day Jews who came from Europe, may not have any provable ethnic connection with the Jews of the ancient world.

We can understand and even excuse the past: That the Africans who were slaves in the United States had not done their homework—research—and could not tell the story of the Jews in the Bible and outside of it. They did not have the rationale or the intellectual curiosity that was needed to explain the history of the people called Jews and their relationship to other people in the world, especially to African people. When myth gave them hope in their struggle against slavery, myth became their reality. We can excuse the black slaves for their misconceptions and confusion about the Jews, but we cannot, and will not, excuse present day "scholars," blacks, whites, and otherwise, for not dealing honestly with the myths of history and how they were created and institutionalized as truth.

Israel's previous relations with the colonial world and her present relation with South Africa is a contradiction for the Jews of the world. The white South African racial policy against Africans is not appreciably different from Hitler's anti-Jewish policy. Jewish participation through Israel in the South African policy is one of the tragic ironies of history. The Europeans Jews who survived what is referred to as the Holocaust inherited one of the great moral incentives they could have used to call for a new humanity for all people. Israeli-Jewish participation with the apartheid government of South Africa betrays that moral incentive. The following reference works present this situation with a high degree of clarity: Alfred T. Moleah, *Israel and South Africa Ideology and Practice* and *Zionism and Apartheid: The Negation of Human Rights*; Roselle Tekiner, *Jewish Nationality Status as the Basis for Institutionalized Racism in Israel*; Benjamin M. Joseph, *Besieged Bedfellows and Israel and the Land of Apartheid*; Richard P. Stevens and Abdelwahab M. Elmessiri, *Israel and South Africa*; Walter Lehn, *The Jewish National Fund: An Instrument of Discrimination*; and Christopher Mansour and Richard P. Stevens, *Internal Control in Israel and South Africa, the Mechanism of Colonial Settler Regimes*.

It is difficult for African people to realize that Jews of European extraction are no different from other Europeans in their relationship to Africans. They, too, profited from both slavery and colonialism. The raid at Entebbe (in Uganda) is a neglected event in history, which is nonetheless of vital importance in spite of being misunderstood by most of the African people of the world. This was an act of aggression against an African state, and on several television shows and in one motion picture this event has been presented to the world as a great, heroic rescue and a symbol of Israeli bravery. It required no act of bravery to invade a defenseless African state. Israel had the assistance of another African airport to make the strike. This raid and the pro-Israeli propaganda that followed is a good example of how myths are made. The Organization of African Unity proved to be weak in their understanding of this issue. African journalists and scholars also proved to be weak in their interpretation of the situation.

Among contemporary thinkers of African descent, Malcolm X was the only one to deal with the land basis of nationhood. Without the land, of course, there is no nationhood. The Israeli confiscation of Arab land and the destruction of their home by bulldozers is identical with the same act being perpetrated against Africans in South Africa. No rationale about the Jewish need for a homeland can destroy this fact. In many ways, Israel is an extension of European colonialism both in attitude and in policy.

The resignation of Andrew Young as American Ambassador to the United Nations in 1979 brought the black-Jewish relationship to a tragic climax in which both groups seemed to have been misinterpreting each other's intentions; both blacks and Jews felt betrayed.

Jesse Jackson and other black ministers argued that the Arabs had a right to be heard in the United Nations and other councils around the world. Jackson's trip to the Middle East and his meeting with Yassar Arafat and the PLO was a kind of Black Declaration of Independence. The black ministers had decided to investigate for themselves the conditions of the Palestinians and saw some parallels between their plight and that of the Palestinians and Africans still living under colonialism.

In their interpretation of the disenchantment of African-Americans with the role of the Jews in the power structure of the United States and in making the false charge of anti-Semitism against nearly every black person who disagreed with the Jews on any issue, Jewish editors and some heads of major Jewish organizations have made a political error that will come back to haunt them. The loss of sentimental attachment to the Jewish mystique extends beyond African-Americans to the whole of the African world. Blacks are not unaware of Israel's relationship to the racist regime in South Africa. Many of us see this state as an extension of European colonialism and a betrayal of the friendship that some Africans extended to the burgeoning state of Israel. There is a similarity between present time and the first African-Jewish meeting, when the friendship was broken, and, as the Bible said, "A king arose who knew not Joseph."

The most tragic aspect of the alliance between Israel and South

Africa is that it is a perfectly logical alliance. By the rationale and intent of Western racism and colonialism, the alliance makes sense.

Both Israel and white South Africa are artificial settler states created by the political backwash of Europe. They are parts of Europe mentally and culturally, while being removed from it geographically. This is the basis of the political schizophrenia that prevails in Israel and in South Africa. These European settlers are involved in a perpetual contradiction. They are stubbornly trying to establish a nationality in nations that never belonged to them. They are doing this at the expense of the indigenous populations in the countries they have settled. In making an assessment of the relationship of Israel to white South Africa, this dilemma must be taken into consideration.

In order to understand the present dilemma and its forecasts for the future, there is a need to consider the interplay of forces in South Africa and in the world at large that created the state of Israel and the apartheid-dominated state of South Africa.

This dilemma has long historical roots that predate the European settlement of South Africa and parts of Palestine now called Israel. It was in or near Africa that the people now referred to as Jews entered the pages of history for the first time. Like all people who came to Africa from other lands, they took more than they gave. The following is a description of their first entry into Africa from the A.H. Sayce book, *The Egypt of the Hebrews and Herodotus*:

> Abram went down into Egypt to sojourn there. When he entered the country the civilization and monarchy of Egypt were already very old. The pyramids had been built hundreds of years before, and the origin of the Sphinx was already a mystery. Even the great obelisk of Helipolis, which is still the object of an afternoon drive to the tourist at Cairo, had long been standing in front of the temple of the Sun-god.

The early and present relationship of Jews to African people is beclouded by the often-told but exaggerated stories of four hundred years of Jewish persecution in Egypt and the eventual Exodus, both of which is probably the creation of a brilliant and highly imaginative Jewish fiction writer.

The people who would later be called Jews entered Africa around

1680 B.C. at a time when Egypt had grown weak and had been invaded by an army of nomads from Western Asia called Hyksos, but often referred to as Shepherd Kings. The first Hyksos king was Salatis, who directed his special attention to the security of Egypt's eastern frontier. The Hyksos adopted many of the customs of the Egyptians and assumed the Egyptian royal titles. According to an account by the Egyptian writer and priest Manetho, the Hyksos treated the Egyptians, who had once been their colonial masters, with great cruelty.

According to the Scriptures the Jews lived many years in Egypt before a king arose "who knew not Joseph." They lived in this African land with African people, and they prospered and grew. They held many high positions in Egypt. They were in fact clerks and administrators for the foreign rulers of Egypt.

The Jews actually became a people during their stay in Egypt, whose civilization was old when Israel was born. These Jews left Egypt, according to the traditional account, four hundred years later, 600,000 strong, after acquiring from African people all elements of their future religion, tradition, and culture, including monotheism. Whatever the Jews were before they entered Africa, they left, four hundred years later, ethnically, culturally, and religiously an African people.

This, in essence, were the minutes of the first meeting between the Jews and African people. At this juncture in world history, Europe did not exist. In their book, *A History of the Modern World*, R.R. Palmer and Joel Colton noted "There was really no Europe in ancient times. . . . To the Romans 'Africa' meant Tunisia-Algeria, Asia meant the Asia Minor peninsula; and the word Europe, since it meant little, was scarcely used by them at all."

For most of their existence the Jews have lived in the nations of Western Asia, called the Middle East, and in North Africa. Jewish people did not live in Europe in any appreciable numbers until the first century. The Jews of Europe are, in the main, creations of Europe. Sephardic Jews developed into a community in Spain, where their achievements in the arts, government and letters made them the most influential Jewish community of the diaspora until their expulsion in 1492. The so-called Oriental Jews are scattered from North Africa to Afghanistan. Beyond the basic groups of Jews, such as the Ashkenazim (European Jews) and the Sephardim (Mediterranean and Middle Eastern Jews), there are several smaller Jewish communities with long histories of their own, such as the Jews of the Caucasus, the Cachin Jews of India, and the Black Falasha Jews of Ethiopia.

In Israel there are Jews of almost every kind, color, and Judaic language. This diversity of color and culture—adhering to the same religion—has not been the basis for an attempt to develop a concept of Jewish world unity. The Jews in Israel who came from Europe have all of the power there that matters. The European Jews are, in the main, Zionists. Zionism, which led to the creation of the state of Israel, was animated in nineteenth-century Europe after an upsurge of anti-semitism following the rise of modern imperialism.

The settlement of Israel by European Jews is an extension of European imperialism and internal racism. The relationship of Israel to South Africa extends from these two factors. Another factor is the rise of political Zionism. In a recent book on the subject, Abdelwahab M. Elmessiri wrote:

> It is difficult to think of a political phenomenon that generates more controversy and elicits more violent reaction than Zion-ism.... Some Zionists and Zionist sympathizers even view the establishment of a state in the land of Palestine by a 1948 United Nations resolution as being a fulfillment of biblical prophecy.... Zionism is a political movement, and not a religious doctrine....

The relationship of Israel to South Africa must be seen in purely political terms. This relationship is explained in detail in two recent books: *Weismann and Smuts: A Study in Zionist-South African Cooperation* by Richard P. Stevens; and *Israel and South Africa: The Progression of a Relationship* by Richard P. Stevens and Abdelwahab W. Elmessiri.

This dilemma has long historical roots, that predate the European settlement of South Africa and parts of Palestine now called Israel. The contents of these books can be understood much better after a review of the antecedents of the present situation.

When the European age of exploration started in the fifteenth century, the Portuguese were searching for a sea route to India by way of the Cape of Good Hope (now Capetown, South Africa). During one of their early expeditions they attempted to establish a refueling station along the coast of South Africa. This expedition was undertaken with the advice of Abraham ben Samuel Zacuto, a Jew who was then the Royal Astronomer for the King of Portugal, Manuel II. Before the edict of expulsion was issued against Spanish Jews in 1492, Abraham ben Samuel Zacuto had been a renowned teacher of astronomy and mathematics at the University of Salamanca in Spain, then widely considered the greatest institution of learning in the world.

One of the first Jews to land in South Africa was a seaman, Ferado Martins or Fernam Martinz. He was a mariner on Vasco da Gama's ship, San Gabriel. He was with the Portuguese fleet that landed at St. Helena Bay in November 1497. Between 1492 and the end of the sixteenth century, nearly one half a million Jews left Spain and Portugal. The status of the Jews varied from one European country to another. In Holland, Jews participated in the formation of Dutch East India Company. When the company's undertaking included the occupation of the Cape of Good Hope in 1652, the Amsterdam Jewish community was part of this settlement. Holland had absorbed a large number of Jewish refugees who had spread throughout the provinces. When Jan van Riebeek and his company of servants were preparing to sail for the Cape of Good Hope, the Dutch Jews were petitioning Cromwell for readmission into England. By the end of the seventeenth century, the Dutch Jews were the principal stockholder in the Dutch East India Company.

Small Jewish settlements in what is now Capetown and in other parts of South Africa developed in the seventeenth and eighteenth centuries. On September 17, 1828, the Zulu King Shaka granted Nathaniel Isaacs the use of a large tract of land for himself and the Jewish people. This was a gesture of friendship from the powerful king who would be assassinated by two of his half brothers before the end of the year 1828.

The discovery of diamonds and gold in South Africa profoundly affected the economic status of the Jews. They had a tradition of dealing in precious minerals. From the eighteen hundreds to the present time the Jews of South Africa have been closely related to the marketing of gold and diamonds.

The politics of Zionism in South Africa is mainly a vintage of the twentieth century. This is where Professors Stevens and Elmessiri began their examination of the background of the relationship between Israel and South Africa. This was for many years a quiet relationship with no appreciable international attention. The so-called Six Day War in 1967 changed this picture and made a larger number of people examine Zionism in general as a world-wide political force.

In the ten years after the Independence Explosion which began in Ghana in 1957, the new state of Israel had more goodwill in Africa than any other white-controlled nation. By November 1973, most of that goodwill was lost, and African nations like the Ivory Coast, Ethiopia, Zaire, and Liberia—otherwise considered conservative on many other issues—broke off diplomatic relations with the state of Israel. There are many factors involved and the assumption of Arab influence is the principal one. This is not true, however. The main reason for the break, and the change of minds and hearts among African states, is Israel's long relationship with the apartheid regime of South Africa. There are, of course, many other factors. The Africans were slow to realize that the Israelis in Africa were no different from other whites who wanted to control the resources of this vast continent—by any means necessary.

When the thirtieth session of the U.N. General Assembly adopted, with a large majority, the resolution equating Zionism as "a form of racism and racial discrimination," African nations continued to examine their relationship with Israel with a sharper political focus. The relationship of Israel with white ruled South Africa was the most sensitive area of their examination.

In the book, *Israel and South Africa: The Progression of a Relationship*, the authors deal in depth with many of the neglected dimensions of Israel's relationship with South Africa and the role of the Jews in South Africa as well as their non-Jewish allies such as General Jan Christian Smuts in the development of Zionism in the twentieth century.

The collaboration between the apartheid and Zionist systems is a subject that most "scholars" have been reluctant to examine. The opening of this door also opens other doors, where the rooms, figuratively speaking, are overflowing with political embarrassments.

The Pretoria-Tel Aviv axis shows its inherent dependency on one another and on world imperialism. Both systems are proven enemies of the people of Africa.

South Africa was one of the first states to recognize Israel in 1948, and in 1953, the then premier of the Pretoria regime, Dr. D.F. Malan, visited Israel (the same Malan had supported Hitler during the Second World War, in opposition to the pro-British regime of General Smuts.) The mentality that went into the making of the South Africa-Israeli alliance was developing in the European and in the colonial worlds long before the creation of the state of Israel. The seeds of the future alliance were first planted in late nineteenth-century Europe.

The fight for a Jewish homeland continued into the twentieth century, when the mantle of leadership was taken by Chaim Weizman. The formation of a Jewish state was not seriously considered until the imperialists of Europe found a way to benefit from its creation. Chaim Weizman promised: "We should there [in Palestine] form an outpost of civilization as opposed to barbarism." In a letter in the *Manchester Guardian*, written in November 1914, he stated:

> We can reasonably say that should Palestine fall within the British sphere of influence, and should Britain encourage Jewish settlement there, as a British dependency, we could have in twenty to thirty years a million Jews out there, perhaps more; they would develop the country, bring back civilization to it and form a very effective guard for the Suez Canal.

Both Theodore Herzl and Chaim Weizman promised to use the state of Israel to protect European colonial interest in this part of the world. The promise was repeatedly projected until it culminated in the Balfour Declaration in 1917; both Herzl and Weizman accepted allies wherever they could find them, and had no compunctions about linking the Zionist quest for Palestine with British imperial interests. The Balfour Declaration was the reward for this linkage of interest. The Declaration reads, in part:

> His Majesty's Government view with favor the establishment in Palestine of a national home for the Jewish people.... It being clearly understood that nothing should be done which may prejudice the civil and religious rights of existing non-Jewish communities in Palestine, or the rights and political status enjoyed by the Jews in other countries.

The Declaration was written, debated, and announced without consulting a single Arab person. In fact the word "Arab" does not appear in any part of the Declaration. This high-minded arrogance was the basis of trouble still to come. In the meantime, Chaim Weizman searched for additional support and built on the Zionist foundation that had been started by Theodore Herzl. He found a friend and ally in the person of Jan Christian Smuts, South Africa's first celebrated prime minister. In a recent book by Richard Stevens, *Weizman and Smuts—A Study in Zionist South African Cooperation*, the significance of this friendship is explained. Professor Stevens maintains that "without Smuts there may have been no Balfour Declaration, which committed Britain to supporting a Zionist-Jewish state in Palestine."

While both Herzel and Weizman preferred Palestine as a homeland for the Jews, they were willing to consider other areas of the world where Jews could live under their own government. In 1902, Herzl had approached Joseph Chamberlain, the British Colonial Secretary for support of his idea for large-scale settlement of Jews within the British dominions. He preferred Cyprus or the Egyptian Sinai Peninsula. Herzl recorded his meeting with the Colonial Secretary in this manner:

> As to Cyprus ... the island was inhabited by Greeks and Muslims whom he [Chamberlain] could not evict for the sake of newcomers.... He was willing, however, to help if he could. He liked the Zionist idea. If I [Herzl] could show him a spot among the British possessions which was not yet inhabited by white settlers.

On April 23, 1903, Chamberlain proposed Uganda for a potential Jewish settlement. He thought the Jews might make use of the new Ugandan railway and turn it into a profitable enterprise.

At the Sixth Zionist Congress in 1903, Herzl accepted the British proposal for the settlement of Jews in Uganda. He did not give up the claim for Palestine. His goal was to win over world leaders to the general idea of planned Jewish settlement. Though the Ugandan scheme was dropped without fanfare, it was seriously considered. It is noteworthy that the most overt offers of support for the Zionist Commission established to visit East Africa came from South African Zionists.

This is part of the "Background" to the book, *Israel and South*

Africa: The Progression of a Relationship. This book is essential to the understanding of the crisis in South Africa today and of the relationship of Israel, another European settler state, to that crisis. Both Israel and South Africa are at the crossroads, on a collision course, in opposition to the full citizenship status of the indigenous people in their respective countries. Geographically, the position of Israel and South Africa epitomizes this point. South Africa is located at the back door of Africa; Israel the side door of Asia and the front door of Africa. Figuratively speaking, one of the most tragic power struggles in the history of the world is waiting to explode behind one or all of these doors.

All of Southern Africa is shaping up for a final battle against the forces of racism and Western colonialism. This is not a battle to be fought by the Africans who live in Africa alone. This is a fight that involves the entire African world.

THE RAID AT ENTEBBE[1]

▼

THERE IS NO WAY TO REVIEW this book about the sensationalized Israeli raid at the Entebbe Airport, in Kampala, Uganda on July 4, 1976, by focusing on the contents of this book alone. There are other more complex issues involved both topical and historical, that stem from the important, and often avoided question, "Why was the state of Israel created in the first place?" While the raid was at an airport in Uganda, the repercussions were felt around the world, especially the world of African people. The timing of the raid compounded the disaster for Uganda and exposed the fact that the continent of Africa is, in the main, unprotected. The raid at Entebbe could have occurred at almost any airport in Africa with the same success. While the raid was being planned and subsequently executed, the members of the Organization of African Unity were having a summit meeting on the island of Mauritius. Among other subjects, the members of the OAU talked about the establishment of an African High Command that would be responsible for the protection of the entire continent of Africa. This talk has been going on among African heads of state for over ten years, and a unified defense force for Africa still has not been created. While the OAU was in session at Mauritius,Israeli paratroopers raided Entebbe airport, rescued their hijacked nationals, killed the pro-Palestinians hijackers and twenty Ugandan soldiers, escaped, almost intact, and used another African nation as a refueling station on their way home.

---

[1] Reprinted from the publication, *Twenty Minutes Over Entebbe*.

In the newspaper, *Bilalian News*, Chicago Ill., August 13, 1976, the writer, Ali Baghdadi, calls attention to another dimension of this African tragedy. The Israelis managed to fly three C-130 Hercules transports that carried the Israeli raiders, two Boeing 707's, eight jet fighters as an escort and three tankers to refuel the fighters in the long trip from Tel Aviv to Entebbe, Uganda. Mr. Baghdadi raises this question:

> What happened to the radar system installed by the United States in the aftermath of the Sinai agreement and operated by the Egyptians and their American "friends" .... Where were the Egyptian and Saudi fighters whose duties were to keep a close eye on Israeli aggressive activities? How could the Israeli planes cross the Red Sea's narrow waters and travel thousands of miles without being confronted or detected?

It is tragically clear that Arab as well as African states are preoccupied with the conflicts among themselves and are hampered in dealing with plots and aggressive intentions of their common enemies. This weakness opened the door for the Israeli raid at Entebbe.

The press of the Western world hailed the successful raid as a victory over terrorism and ignored the indignation of the press in Africa. The Western press also ignored the African side of the debate in the United Nations and the forty-eight member Organization of African Unity's condemnation of Israel for the invasion of a sovereign African state. The raid made most of the world forget (if indeed they knew) that the terrorism of the racist government in South Africa now being inflicted on the blacks who are in the majority, is presently the greatest threat to world peace. South Africa and Israel are allies. This fact has a dangerous implication for all Africa.

Israel is located at the back door of Europe, the side door of Asia and the front door of Africa. From this strategic location and vantage point, the Israelis can move through a door that swings three ways, at the power crossroads of the world. This is no accident. Israel is now, and for some time, has been an ally of the apartheid regime of South Africa, a racist colonial settler state that is located at the back door of Africa. The apartheid regime, like Israel, was established at the expense of both countries' indigenous population. These facts can not be ignored while looking at the raid at Entebbe, before and far beyond.

The Europeans have always been geniuses in their ability to drain the diseased pus of their political sores on the soil of other people and nations. The Jewish problem, in all of its complicated dimensions is neither Arab or African created. This is a problem that was created in Europe by Europeans and should have been resolved in Europe by Europeans. Both the Africans and the Arabs are victims of this problem. The road that led the Israeli army and air force to Entebbe is long and torturous, and it started in Europe during the closing years of the nineteenth century.

Political Zionism, that led to the creation of the state of Israel, was animated in nineteenth century Europe after an upsurge of anti semitism following the rise of modern imperialism. A chief exponent of this concept was Moses Hess, who had been associated with Karl Marx before he became a Jewish nationalist. In his book, *Rome and Jerusalem*, published in 1863, he expounded his ideas in this manner:

> We Jews shall always remain strangers among the nations ... he said. Each and every Jew, whether he wishes it or not, is auto-matically, by virtue of his birth, bound in solidarity with his entire nation.... Each has the solidarity and responsibility for the rebirth of Israel.

These ideas were premature at the time. They were restated and expanded later in Leo Pinsker's book, *Auto-Emancipation* (1882) and in *The Jewish State*, by Theodore Herzl, who is considered by a large number of people to be the father of Zionism. This concept was closely connected with ideas of innate distinctness of the Jews as a "chosen people" destined to play a unique role in history and thereby set apart from other people.

Political Zionism developed beyond ideology and became an organized world movement. Theodore Herzl spoke of the settlement of Palestine in terms of "a people without a land to land without a people." For him the indigenous people of the country, the Arabs, did not exist; this is an arrogant European racist attitude. This attitude has prevailed because most of the so called Western scholars have failed to deal honestly with the Jews as a people in world history. They have not asked and answered the question: "Are we dealing with a religion or an ethnic group?" The modern white Jew is a European creation; and so is the nation of Israel. There is no proof that the Jews of the ancient world were what we now call "white people."

At this point I imagine you, the reader, are asking the question: "What has all of this got to do with the raid at Entebbe and the book that was hurriedly written about the raid?" I maintain that unless you can understand the interplay of powerful forces and events in Europe and in the rest of the world that led to the creation of the state of Israel, you will not understand the raid at Entebbe, that is deeply rooted in the attitude of Europeans toward non-European people.

There is a need to locate the Jews, as a people, on the map of human geography, and to see how they relate to African people. We first hear about the Jews in history around 1675 B.C., at the time Egypt was being invaded by a people from Western Asia called Hyksos, or Shepherd Kings. This invasion turned Egypt's first age of greatness into a nightmare. According to tradition, and the Bible, during this time seventy Jews, grouped in twelve patriarchal families, nomads without industry or culture, entered Egypt. These Jews left Egypt four hundred years later 600,000 strong, after acquiring from African people all of the elements of their future religion, tradition, and culture, including monotheism. The people called Jews did not enter Europe in any appreciable numbers until after 70 A.D.

According to an explanation in *Time* magazine, April 10, 1972, "the ethnic and religious variations among the world's fourteen million Jews are bewildering. Scientifically speaking, there is no Jewish race." The Hebrew religion is followed by a wide range of distinct ethnic groups. The Oriental Jews are scattered from North Africa to Afghanistan. There are Falasha Jews in Ethiopia and Cachin Jews in India. These Jews do not claim Palestine as their homeland.

The *Time* magazine reports state further that, by far the most numerous today are the Ashkenazic Jews, who became an important group in the Rhineland about the tenth century. They take their name from the medieval Hebrew name for Germany, Ashenaz. The Ashenazim, who spread across Europe, and North and South America, suffered most of the casualties in the Holocaust of the Hitler years.

These whites or European Jews are now the spokespersons and main power brokers of the Jewish world. The Sephardic and Oriental Jews, who make up at least half of the population of Israel, have no appreciable power.

It is open to question whether the European Jews have any traceable ethnic and cultural ties to the Jews of the ancient world, who were the first Jews to claim Palestine as their homeland. This first claim by the Jews of Western Asia was based on evidence that is shrouded in myth, and a question that still begs for an answer. Who said that Palestine was theirs to be taken without the consent of the people who were already living there. For over a thousand years the country that the Jews would later call Palestine was populated by a people called the Canaanites. According to the traditional account of the Jewish flight from Egypt, around the year 1200 B.C., the Hebrews led by the prophet Moses, fled from Egypt, and crossing the Sinai Peninsula, settled in the area east of the Dead Sea. Under the leadership of Joshua, the Hebrews invaded the state of Canaan. Crimes of the most heinous nature were perpetrated against the inhabitants. These crimes are recorded in the Old Testament. This was an imperialist invasion, no different from many others in history. The inhabitants who were not killed, were reduced to servitude; and thus the Jews took over Palestine for the first time.

They were only able to occupy parts of Palestine and the area east of the Jordan River. Int the year 1020 B.C., King Saul established their first state. He was followed by King David and King Solomon who ruled until 923 B.C. Here the Jews gained their first experience in agriculture, urbanization, and statecraft.

The second Jewish claim to Palestine started in the closing years of the nineteenth century and climaxed in 1948. On November 29, 1947, the United Nations General Assembly passed a resolution for the partition of Palestine into Arab and Jewish states. This resolution was a violation of the Palestinian people's right to self-determination. It was also the beginning of a protracted tragedy called the Arab-Jewish conflict. The Arabs of Palestine were caught in a crossfire of conflicting forces, before and after the United Nations resolution. Nearly a million Palestinian Arabs were uprooted from their homes. They took refuge in hastily built camps in the Gaza Strip, Jordan, Syria and Lebanon.

At first Africa was only indirectly affected by this conflict. When the Africans finally studied the role of the Israelis in Africa, they found much to their chagrin, that many of them were agents, working against African liberation. Israeli instructors and advisors have been involved in antiguerilla fighting in the Portuguese colony of Angola. Servicemen from Portugal and its colonies have gone to Israel for training. In Nigeria the Israeli government identified itself with the oil imperialism-inspired secession in Biafra.

In the book *Zionism: Its Role in World Politics*, (1973) by Hyman Lumber the statement is made that:

> Up to July 1969, Israel had sent about $500,000 of official aid for Biafran relief and dispatched several medical teams. Foreign Minister Abba Eban, speaking in the Israeli Parliament, stated on July 9, that the Israeli Government had "the duty" to send maximum aid to Biafra. A broadcast on Radio Kaduna (Northern Nigeria) later that month accused Israel of sending tanks, artillery, and rockets to Biafra in the guise of relief supplies and of training Biafrans in Guerilla warfare techniques.... *The Daily Time* (Lagos) denounced Israel's stand as a "clear case of double-dealing" which violated Nigerian friendship and good will.

From the foregoing pattern it can be clearly seen that the ruling circles in Israel can be found on the side of colonialism and neocolonialism. In February 1972, General Idi Amin of Uganda set in motion a process of severing all ties with Israel, by charging that Israeli contractors were "milking Uganda dry." In the following month he made the break complete. The entire corps of Israeli diplomats, military advisers and technicians, numbering 470, together with their dependents were expelled. This was Israel's greatest humiliation in Africa. A humiliation that was neither forgiven or forgotten. This was the basis of the uncompromising fierceness of the Israeli army and airforce during the raid at Entebbe. The Israelis knew Uganda well because as technicians and agricultural advisers they had traveled all over it. They knew the Ugandan Army because they had trained it. They knew the airport at Entebbe because they had built it. Therefore the raid at Entebbe had been prepared for, a number of years before the actual raid occurred.

There are many roads in the different continents, that figuratively, led to the raid at Entebbe. One of these roads starts in South Africa. Israel's relationship with South Africa is as old as its existence. The relationship between Zionism and South Africa is much older. This connection is called the Apartheid Axis.

There are few governments in the world that are willing to invite South African Prime Minister John Vorster for an official visit. On April 9, ,the regime of Prime Minister Yitzhak Perelman of Israel, achieved the distinction as being one of those few. In a report on Vorster's visit to Israel, the writer David Frankel (ACTION Newspaper, May 10, 1976) gives these details:

> The South African flag flew from the King David Hotel during Vorster's four-day visit, which was hailed as "unforgettable" by the grateful Vorster. He also declared that his official talks had been "fruitful, constructive, and informative." ... According to a report in the American magazine *Flight International,* Israel and South Africa have already concluded an arms agreement under which the South Africans will build several Reshef naval patrol boats in the Durban shipyards .... [D]espite Israeli denials, Eric Marsden said in April 11, *London Sunday Times*—"There are reports from Johannesburg that South Africa wants to buy the Israeli-made Kfir [Lion Club] delta-wing warplane and other military equipment from Israel." In addition, Marsden suggested that "South Africa may also hope to benefit from Israel's hard-won experience of guerilla war.... [T]he Israelis are the world's experts at sealing hostile borders, flushing out guerrillas and mounting retaliatory raid."

In the August 7, 1976 issue of the *New York Amsterdam News* writer Jewell Handy Gresham reconstructs the events that led to the raid, the raid itself, and the debate over the raid at the United Nations.

The direct events setting this incident in motion began on June 27th with the hi-jacking of an Air France airbus over Greece. The plane was carrying 256 passengers and en route to Paris from Tel Aviv. The plane landed in Kampala, after refueling in Libya. The French Government had notified Idi Amin, President of Uganda, that the plane had only enough fuel to stay in the air fifteen minutes. Permission was requested to land at Kampala. Let me make one thing clear: there is no proof that President Idi Amin was directly or indirectly involved in the hijacking of this plane or had any advance knowledge of the intent of the hijackers.

The rest of the story is current history and white propaganda. The book *90 Minutes at Entebbe* is the best example of this propaganda and white ego-washing at the expense of African people.

The African side of this story has yet to be told. Jewell Handy Gresham makes a serious attempt to look at the Entebbe Raid, as a person, in her August 8 article in the *New York Amsterdam News*. An excerpt from her article reveals these facts:

> The incident ended in the early morning hours on Sunday, July 4th, when Israeli planes under the pretext of coming in to exchange the prisoners requested landed a military force and in a surprise attack killed Ugandan soldiers securing the airport and the Palestinians involved in the hijacking, and rescued the hostages in an operation lasting under an hour.... In between the two Sundays was a week which saw about half the hostages notably not including Israeli citizens—released and in which Idi Amin secured an extension of the deadline for completion of the negotiations from July 1st to Sunday July 4th. It was a fateful act for Amin because the added time provided the opportunity for the Israelis to plan the military strategy which resulted in the death of the Ugandans and the loss of the few fighter planes possessed by the little country.
>
> Uganda, incidently, does not even possess a bomber, let alone a combat airforce. But the incident probably represents the heart of a grave moral conflict for Israel. For if Amin was not an accomplice in the hijacking—and despite the Israelis' claim, no definite evidence was presented to substantiate such charge then the Ugandan Head of State was in fact betrayed.

This is the heart of the matter, and it stems from a prevailing political naïveté that can be tragically identified in most African leaders. They do not seem to understand the kind of world in which we are living. In historical background, in temperament, and intent, they do not seem to know the Europeans as a people. In the book *90 Minutes at Entebbe*, you should very carefully read the transcript of three telephone conversations between Colonel Baruch Barlev and President Idi Amin, pages 209–216. The essence of the point that I am trying to make is in these conversations the Israelis used the "friendship" confidence game to get information from President Idi Amin that they needed for the raid at Entebbe.

In the following statement of insight into the situation, the writer Jewell Handy Gresham, again reminds us of what most Western newspapermen, writing about the Entebbe Raid, chose to ignore:

> The ultimate confrontation at the UN therefore was not alone, or even primarily between Israel and Uganda. It was between Israel and black Africa, between the Western powers and the newly emerging states which were their former colonies, and between the have and the have not countries in the world. The Israeli representative before the Security Council spoke as a westerner for the west and what he advocated was the establishment of a western force to contain and control those which threaten the prevailing powers.

The debate in the United Nations, which the Africans lost, should have been a lesson for all African heads of state, and African people everywhere. Historically, Africa has always been an undefended continent, and an attraction for invaders for most if its existence. This period in African history must now come to an end, and the talk about an African High Command and a unified defense of all Africa must become a reality. The Israeli raid at Entebbe, and the boastful celebration of that raid throughout most of the western world, taught African people a lesson that they should never forget.

No nation is really independent and free until its people can defend themselves and become the instruments of their own liberation. Nationhood and freedom are not gifts that are handed down from one generation to anther. Each generation, is its own way, must secure its nationhood and freedom with its own hands.

THE LAND QUESTION IN PALESTINE AND IN EASTERN AND SOUTHERN AFRICA[1]

▼

T
HE LAND QUESTION, IN GENERAL, is as old as people and nations. It is part of a world problem and must be seen in this context in order to understand the specific land question that is the subject of this chapter. The striving for land and the attempt to recover it once it is lost is a recurring theme in the drama of human endurance and survival. Stability on a piece of land that a people can call their own is the basis for their nationhood, their culture and religion, in essence, their humanity.

In my assessment of "the fundamental rights of the Palestinian people," I will be, figuratively, looking through several historical windows. My main focus will be the land question. I will emphasize the importance of the land question in Palestine by comparing it with the land question in east and southern Africa. My intent is to show that the method and rationale that was used by the Europeans to take the land from the Africans in the so-called White Highlands of Kenya, in Zimbabwe, then called Rhodesia and in South Africa, where the Dutch or Boers encountered the Khoisan people that they called Bushmen and Hottentots, was basically the same.

The beginning of European settler states outside of Europe in the fifteenth and sixteenth centuries ran concurrently with the establish-

---

[1] Prepared for the Seminar on The Fundamental Rights of the Palestinian People, held at Arusha, United Republic of Ranzania, July 14-18, 1980.

ment of the slave trade and the colonial system that followed. Historically, the settler states had many forms. In fact, both South America and Central America today are European settler continents.

The creation of the plantation system in the Caribbean Islands was followed by European settler island states ruled mainly by the British, French, Dutch, and Portuguese. In most of these settler states, where the European was not the majority in population, they were the rulers. In North America, (the United States, Canada, as well as Central America) the European settlers have been present so long that they no longer consider themselves settlers. Many of them look upon the indigenous population as intruders. The multinational and the immigrant status of most of the people in the United States did not make this nation any less a European settler state that did what most European settlers did: They brought the indigenous population under control or literally destroyed them, such as the almost total destruction of the aborigine population of Australia and the total destruction of the black population on the island of Tasmania.

My focal point is on two European settler states: one with its origin in the twentieth century, Israel; the other with its origin in the seventeenth century, South Africa.

There is a need to raise the disturbing question: Can a settler state ever be a legitimate state in international law? Most of the settler states of the world were established based on the need and the greed of people of European extraction.

Further, I intend to show that the pattern of land encroachment by the Europeans was part of a war against the cultures and customs of non-European people and it differed, only by degree, at different times and in different places. In her Ph.D. thesis, "The Dominant Modes of Western Thought and Behavior: An Ethnological Critique" (1975), Professor Dona Richards has referred to this behavior of Europeans as "the concept of the cultural other," she writes:

> It is in the nature of the Western ethos that one of the most accurate indices of Western man's self-image is his image of others.... The essential characteristics associated with this concept, within the Western world view, are control and consequently power—the theme which reverberates endlessly in the ethnological unfolding of Western culture, echoed in every

Western statement of value.

In another thesis, "The Ideology of European Dominance," Professor Richards continues her examination of the European world view.

> It is possible to isolate certain seminal ideas which have served as organizing principles in Western scientific thought.... These themes are intimately related to the Western European attitude toward other peoples and imply a particular relationship to them, which will subsequently be referred to as "ethos." The western European ethos appears to thrive on the perception that those who are culturally and radically different are inferior. It relates to other cultures as superior or inferior, as powerful or weak, as "civilized" or "primitive." The European world view reflects these relationships. It was the western European ethos that created "the savage."

If we understand what Professor Richards has said, we will also understand, at least in part, the temperament and attitude of the Ashkenazi Jews who control that part of Palestine that is called Israel. They are more European than Jewish. They are, in fact, a European creation. Their problem, however tragic it is, was started in Europe by Europeans and should have been resolved in Europe by Europeans. In the book *Democracy in Israel,* Norman F. Dacey calls our attention to the main aspect of this dilemma, when he says:

> Jews in Israel don't persecute just Arabs—they persecute each other. The discrimination which is the hallmark of the life in the Zionist state is responsible for a widening gap between western Ashkenazi Jews and the Oriental or Sephardic Jews.

Discrimination against the Oriental Jews continues in housing, in jobs, and in education. Their plight in Israel is the plight of a subject people. These Oriental Jews once lived all over Western Asia, called the Middle East. Zionist propaganda enticed them to come to Israel, when the state was created. The European Jews never accepted them as equals, though they belonged to the same religion. Oriental Jews had established communities in Iraq and in other Middle Eastern countries twelve centuries before the inception of Islam. These Jews have not related to Zionism because Zionism was not created by them or for them.

Zionism has a direct relationship to European colonialism and the two developed simultaneously in the same political incubator. In its racist attitudes and treatment of Arabs, Oriental Jews, and the small number of American blacks who have settled in Israel, Zionism relates more to Calvinist Christianity of the Boers in South Africa. The Arab communities in Israel and on the West Bank are surrounded by Jewish settlements that are armed camps, established to contain the Arabs and control the land. These Arab communities are similar to the black communities in South Africa that the Boers call Bantustans. In both cases the intent is the same—to deny the Arabs and the Africans any kind of sovereign rights in their own land. Whether the system is practiced in Israel or in South Africa, it is what the Boers call "apartheid."

The word "apartheid" was coined by the Boer intellectuals for the general election of 1948, that brought the Boers to political power. The condition of apartheid existed long before the word, and the British are more responsible for creating the condition than the Boers. The word, with the promise to keep the Africans "in their place," caught on immediately among the white racialists who saw apartheid as a means to advance themselves at the expense of the Africans. The condition of apartheid also meant that the Africans, like the Arabs in Palestine, could be made to feel alien in their own land.

The Palestinian writer and scholar Dr. Fayez A. Sayegh emphasizes this point in his pamphlet, "Twenty Basic Facts about the Palestine Problem":

> That Israel has additionally imposed a system of *apartheid* upon the Arabs who stayed in their homeland? ... More than 90 percent of these Arabs live in "security zones"; they alone live under martial law, restricting their freedom to travel from village to village or from town to town; their children are denied equal opportunities for education; and they are denied decent opportunities for work, and the right to receive "equal pay for equal work"?

Dr. Sayegh reminds us that, in spite of this fact, Israel is generally portrayed, in the Western press, as the "bastion of democracy," and the champion of peace in the Middle East. The propaganda in Israel's favor could not turn the facts around. This nation was established, at the expense of the Arabs, at the intersection of three continents. Geographically, Israel is located at the back door of Europe, the side door of Asia, and the front door of Africa. Since its inception as a state, the rulers of Israel have behaved as though they were the colonial masters in this part of the world. The Arabs in Israel are treated like colonial subjects.

Dr. Fayez A. Sayegh explains this dilemma more precisely in his pamphlet, "Palestine, Israel and Peace":

The crux of the Palestine problem is the fate of a people and its homeland. It is the piecemeal conquest and continued seizure of the entire country by military force. It is the forcible dispossession and displacement of the bulk of the indigenous population, and the subjugation of the rest. It is also the massive importation of alien colonists—to replace the evicted, and to lord it over the conquered. And it is the colonization, by foreign settlers, of both the expropriated private land and the seized national resources of the overpowered people. It is, indeed, the destruction of the native Palestinian society of Christian and Muslim Arabs, and its replacement by a society of transplanted Jews and a foreign body politic—which views itself as the vanguard of the "Jewish nation," currently spread throughout the world but declared destined sometime to assemble in the seized land.

The refusal of the Arab world to acquiesce in this fate of Palestine and its people explains both the bitterness and the persistence of the Arab-Israeli Conflict. It also underscores the essential difference in character between this conflict and ordinary international disputes. And it explains why the Arab-Israeli Conflict cannot be resolved until the Palestinian Problem is settled through restoration of the rights of the Palestinian people.

There is no intent on the part of the Israelis, not even the Liberals or the Communists, to totally restore the rights of the Palestinian people. The Liberals and the Communists want an improvement in the living condition of the Palestinians. They do not want the Palestinians to come to power, nor are they willing to share power with them. What is called Israel and the West Bank is European-controlled territory. This means Ashkenazi control. The slight improvement in the living and political conditions of the Oriental Jews in Israel in recent years does no mean that they will ever come to power. In an article contributed to the book, *Zionism and Racism*, Naseer H. Aruri explains the plight of the Oriental Jews of Israel in this manner:

> That Israel's Oriental Jews have been subjected to social, economic, and racial discrimination is no longer considered controversial. Although constituting about sixty percent of the population, they are less than first class citizens. Their representation in the state's social, economic, and political institutions is strikingly incompatible with numerical majority, while the European–American (Ashkenazi) communities are represented far out of proportion to their numbers. Disabilities imposed on the Oriental sector are rampant in employment, education, housing, income, social welfare, and political participation. Disparities between the two Jewish communities have grown worse in all these areas since the establishment of the Zionist state in Palestine; and there are no indications that the social gaps are narrowing. On the contrary, the available statistical data reveal a widening of the gaps.
>
> The largest share of the national income in Israel goes to the highest strata of capitalists and managers, predominantly Ashkenazis. The middle state of the highly paid professional workers and government bureaucrats are strategically situated to push for higher incomes. Jews of the Oriental communities have no professional skills to speak of and, consequently, are unable to compete in their category. Their presence is most prominently observed in the lowest strata of the socio-economic pyramid, that of the manual workers in industry and agriculture, "the only groups whose share of the national income has increasingly diminished." Poverty in Israel is closely linked with ethnic origin.

There is no need at this point to argue whether Zionism is a form of racism. In the face of so much persuasive evidence, proving that it is, an argument against this evidence is redundant and a waste. The Arabs in Israel, and to a lesser extent, that is slight, the Oriental Jews, live in a condition that does not differ appreciably from the system of apartheid in South Africa. The Ashkenazi Jews of Israel have almost complete control over their lives—their land, their jobs, their housing and their education.

The chairman of the Israel League for Human and Civil Rights, Israel Shahak, states that "Israel is about as apartheid as South Africa." He referred first to the difficulty Arabs and Oriental Jews have in obtaining decent housing:

> If you go any place where there are so-called twin cities, like Nazareth and New Nazareth, you will see that the old Nazareth is an open city. Anyone can come, and by buying or selling or by agreement can dwell there. But in New Nazareth, the so-called Upper Nazareth, to obtain a flat you have to bring proof that you are a Jew.
>
> A society in which such a thing is required for more than ninety percent of its inhabited areas has no other name than apartheid society. Exactly the same proof is required in Johannesburg. The only difference is that people know about Johannesburg, but not about Nazareth.
>
> This goes for many other areas too. For example, you have now an official plan in Israel for what is called the "Judaization" of Galilee. This means that the government thinks there are too many Arabs in Galilee, so it has decided officially and openly to confiscate some of their land, convert it into pure Jewish land, and settle only Jews there.

What we need to consider here is that the treatment of the Arabs and the Oriental Jews in Israel has no justification in Judaism or Christianity. This treatment violates the moral codes of both of these religions.

Again referring to the treatment of the Arab and Oriental Jews in Israel, Israel Shahak says:

We are on a much lower level than blacks in the United States because there is no recourse. No one can even do the same sort of job that the NAACP does in the United States. There is no possibility of bringing any case about discrimination, even the most blatant, to any court, because in Israel there is no law forbidding discrimination against non-Jews. On the contrary, all discrimination against non-Jews is completely legal.

What we have here is the lack of recognition of the Arab people as human beings. This attitude toward the Arabs is as racist as any attitude the Nazis ever held toward the Jews. In a booklet on the subject, *Looking Beyond Co-Existence—Prospects of a Bi-national Palestine*, Alan R. Taylor recalls the official nature of this attitude.

In 1967, just after the June War, a delegation from England, representing the House of Commons, visited Jerusalem and was told by the Chairman of the Knesset's Foreign Affairs Committee that the Palestinians "are not human beings, they are not people, they are Arab." The same sentiment was expressed by Golda Meir two years later in a *Sunday Times* interview: "There was no such thing as Palestinians. . . . [I]t was not as though there was a Palestinian people in Palestine considering itself as a Palestinian people and we came and threw them out and took their country away. They did not exist."

This inclination to dehumanize an entire people, to deny their very existence, comes out of Western racism. Israel's main difficulty in the Middle East stems from the failure to recognize the Arabs as a people with the right to live in peace, in all or part of Palestine. Before the introduction of Zionism this was no problem. Jews and Arabs had met many times on the crossroads of history and most of the time they complimented each other. Zionism introduced a conflict between the Arabs and the Jews that did not previously exist. The pogroms and persecutions that the Jews suffered in Europe had no counterpart in the Arab world. The early settlements of European Jews in Palestine, in the late nineteenth and in the early part of the twentieth centuries, had the goodwill and co-operation of the Arabs. The early settlers presented themselves as a simple humane people escaping from the religious and political persecutions of Europe. Behind this idealistic guise the real and previously unannounced intention of Zionism was introduced. The leaders of the movement did not want a part of Palestine. They wanted all of it. Humane Zionists who respected the rights of the Arabs and advocated a binational state were ignored or expelled from the Zionist movement.

It became known that the leaders of the Zionist movement intended, from the outset, to colonize and take over Palestine and to establish there a Jewish state "as Jewish as England is English." To this end the Zionists propagated the myth that Palestine was an empty land crying out for settlers. The existence of a large population of Arabs was ignored or brushed aside.

The European Jews who carved a country called Israel out of Palestine created a country with double standards, one for the Israeli Jews and another for the Palestinian Arabs. The conflict between the Arabs and the Jews was built into the fabric of the government. The main intention of the Zionists was to destroy every element of stable life among the Arabs and control the land.

The conveners of the twenty-third World Zionist Congress held in Jerusalem in 1951 were very clear about what they expected of Zionism. This was the first such congress after the establishment of the state of Israel. The program that was adopted began with the statement: "The task of Zionism is the consolidation of the state of Israel."

In summary, the nature and extent of racial discrimination which is built into the administrative and social framework of the Zionist state of Israel are these:

1. An Arab living under Israeli rule in Israel may be arbitrarily excluded from land which he and his forbears have owned for generations. He may have his land confiscated and handed over to Jewish settlers. He may then be prohibited from even working on that land. His whole village may be razed to the ground. (385 Arab villagers in Israel have been wiped out this way.) He and his whole community may suffer gross discrimination in housing, municipal services, education and social welfare. He may be refused nationality and citizenship even though he was born in the territory of Israel and has lived there all his life and even though any Jewish newcomer from anywhere in the world automatically receives Israeli nationality. (Thousands of Palestinian Arabs are in this stateless condition in Israel.)

2. An Arab living under Israeli rule in the occupied territories may be arrested arbitrarily and detained without trial. He may be deported from his native land without judicial process or appeal. His home may be blown up or bulldozed on a simple order from the local military commander. His land may be confiscated for ostensible military purposes, but in fact for the purpose of Israeli Jewish colonization. His freedom of movement may be restricted. He cannot express political opinions or engage in political activities without risk of arrest and detention or deportation.

3. An Arab refugee living in exile whose home is in Israel or the occupied territories and who was uprooted from it in the wars of 1948 and 1967 is prevented from returning home because he is an Arab and not a Jew—and this in spite of repeated U.N. resolutions on Israel to allow him to return. Meanwhile any Jew is free to enter and settle in Israel, even though he has never seen the country before in his life.

The land question was at the base of the Arab-Israeli conflict from the beginning and it still is. The Camp David Agreement, I will come back to later, only accentuated the conflict and further alienated the Arabs.

This conflict has long historical roots, and it was fully developed before the representatives of the Zionist Movement signed Israel's Declaration of Independence on 14 May 1948. They declared that the new state would be "open to Jewish immigration and the ingathering of Jewish exiles." In the meantime nearly a million Arabs were forced into exile. The leaders of the Zionist Movement, now the new rulers of Israel, had stood before the world and promised to "Maintain complete equality of social and political rights for all its citizens, without distinction of creed, race or sex." Further, they had called on "the sons of the Arab people dwelling in Israel to keep the peace and play their part in building the state on the basis of full and equal citizenship." This was a hollow promise that was never meant and never kept. In his report of September 1948, United Nations Chief Mediator General Folke Bernadotte issued this warning:

It would be an offense against the principles of elemental justice if these victims of the conflict were denied the right to return to their homes while Jewish immigrants flow into Palestine, and indeed offer at least the threat of permanent replacement of the Arab refugees who have been rooted in the land for centuries.

The report laid bare the crucial essence of the Palestinian conflict. It did not move the Zionists from their position or help the Arabs at all. Israel's new Prime Minister, David Ben-Gurion had said, "We must do everything to ensure that they [the Arabs] never return." No influential Israelis raised their voice in defiance of Count Bernadotte's call for "elemental justice" for the Arabs now being driven from their homes. The day after completing his report Count Bernadotte was murdered by Jewish terrorists. The Arab refugee problem became an international problem, and as the Jewish-American journalist I.F. Stone would later remark, "the moral mill-stone about the neck of world Jewry."

The Defense Laws that the new state of Israel had inherited from the British Mandatory Government, which had ruled Palestine between 1922 and 1948, were rewritten and made more stringent against the Arabs. Now, at last, some influential Israelis found their voices and spoke out against these laws. At a conference of the Jewish Lawyers' Association, held in Tel Aviv in February 1946, a future Justice of the Supreme Court in Israel made the following statement about these laws:

> These laws ... contradict the most fundamental principles of law, justice and jurisprudence. They give the administrative and military authorities the power to impose penalties which, even had they been ratified by a legislative body, could only be regarded as anarchical and irregular. The Defense Laws abolish the rights of the individual and grant unlimited power to the adminstration.

The representative of the Jewish Agency, Dr. Bernard Joseph, who was later to become Israel's Minister of Justice, went even further:

> With regard to the Defense Laws themselves, the question is: Are we all to become the victims of officially licensed terrorism,

or will the freedom of the individual prevail? Is the administration to be allowed to interfere in the life of each individual without any safeguard for us? There is nothing to prevent a citizen from being imprisoned all his life without trial. There is no safeguard for the rights of the individual. There is no possibility of resort to the Supreme Court and the adminstration has unrestricted freedom to banish any citizen at any moment.

Even more emphatic was a future Attorney-General of Israel, Mr. Ya'acov Shimshon Shapiro, who later succeeded Dr. Joseph as Minister of Justice:

The system established in Palestine since the issue of the Defense Laws is unparalleled in any civilized country; there were no such laws even in Nazi Germany.... They try to pacify us by saying that these laws are only directed against malefactors, not against honest citizens. But the Nazi Governor of occupied Oslo also announced that no harm would come to citizens who minded their own business. It is our duty to tell the whole world that the Defense Laws passed by the British Mandatory Government of Palestine destroy the very foundations of justice in this land.

The Israeli legal system is based, mainly on the Defense Laws, and they have used them more ruthlessly than the British who originally created them. The purpose of these laws is to control the movements of the Arabs and control the land, by any means necessary. This hunger for the land had manifested itself among European Jewish settlers in Palestine long before the creation of the state of Israel. Unfortunately, the Arabs were not aware of the intention of the Zionist. Palestinian writer, Dr. Fayez A. Sayegh, raises the question about the progression of the land problem in Palestine:

Do You Know:

1. That, when the Palestinian Problem was created by Britain in 1917, more than ninety percent of the population of Palestine were Arabs? ... And that there were at that time

no more than 56,000 Jews in Palestine?

2. That more than half of the Jews living in Palestine at that time were *recent immigrants*, who had come to Palestine in the preceding decades in order to escape persecution in Europe? And that less than five percent of the population were *native Palestinian Jews*?

3. That the Arabs of Palestine at that time owned 97½ percent of the land, while Jews (native Palestinians and recent immigrants together) owned only 2½ percent of the land?

4. That, during thirty years of British occupation and rule, the Zionists were able to purchase only 3½ percent of the land of Palestine, in spite of the encouragement of the British government? . . . And that much of this land was transferred to Zionist bodies by the British government directly, and was not sold by Arab owners?

5. That, therefore, when Britain passed the Palestine Problem to the United Nations in 1947, Zionists owned no more than six percent of the total land area of Palestine?

6. That, notwithstanding these facts, the General Assembly of the United Nations recommended that a "Jewish State" be established in Palestine? . . . And that the Assembly granted that proposed "State" about fifty-four percent of the total area of the country?

7. That Israel immediately occupied (and still occupies) 80.48 percent of the total land area of Palestine?

8. That this territorial expansion took place, for the most part, before 15 May 1948: i.e., before the formal end of the British mandate and the withdrawal of British forces from Palestine, before the entry of Arab armies to protect Palestinian Arabs, and before the Arab-Israeli war?

From its inception the state of Israel and the Ashkenazi Jews, who are its rulers, was an extension of Europe. This reflected in their temperament, in their intentions, and in the arrogant, racist attitude they have toward the Arabs and the Oriental Jews. Israel is the most Westernized country in the Middle East. It is only geographically a part of Western Asia. The socio-culture of Israel is completely alien to the Middle East. The Oriental Jews are more a part of the history and culture of the Middle East. They are an Arabized people who have lived in peace in North Africa and in Western Asia for more than a thousand years. If there are any descendents of the Jews of biblical times, the Oriental Jews are most likely those descendents. I repeat, the Ashkenazi Jews are European creations.

There is a need now to look at the history of the Arabs and the Jews, at least briefly, in order to see that the conflict over Palestine and who is entitled to it as a homeland, was not completely settled in ancient times and it is not settled now. Palestine is at the crossroads of the world, a meeting place for the people of three continents. Since 3500 B.C. the main population in this part of the world has been a people called Semites. They were then, as they are now, a people of many colors and cultures. In 2500 B.C. a branch of Semite people settled in what is now Palestine. They were called Canaanites after the first name of the country—Canaan. About 2000 B.C. the migrants from the Arabian Peninsula stabilized themselves into new state formations.

When we meet the people then called Jews for the first time in history, they are migrants from that crossroads of the world in Western Asia, now called the Middle East. Their leader was Abraham. At the time he led his people into Egypt, the civilization and the monarchy of Egypt was already old. The pyramids had been built years before, and the origin of the sphinx was even then a mystery.

Egypt was invaded for the first time in 1675 B.C. by a people from Western Asia called the Hyksos or Shepherd Kings. This invasion turned Egypt's first age of greatness into chaos. According to tradition, and the Bible, during this time seventy Jews, grouped in twelve patriarchal families, nomads without industry or culture, entered Egypt. These Jews left Egypt four hundred years later 600,00 strong, after acquiring from African people all of the elements of their future traditions, culture and religion, which included monotheism. Whoever the Jews were when they entered Africa, when they left, four hundred years later, they were ethnically, culturally, and religiously an African people. The people called Jews did not enter Europe in any appreciable numbers until after 70 A.D.

It is open to question whether the European Jews have any traceable ethnic and cultural ties to the Jews of the ancient world, who were the first Jews to claim Palestine as their homeland. This first claim by the Jews of Western Asia was based on evidence that is shrouded in myth, and a question that still begs for answers. Who said that Palestine was theirs to be taken without the consent of the people who were already there. For over a thousand years the country that the Jews would later call Palestine was theirs to be taken without the consent of the people who were already living there. For over a thousand years the country that the Jews would later call Palestine was populated by a people called the Canaanites. According to the traditional account of the Jewish flight from Egypt, around the year 1200 B.C., the Hebrews led by the Prophet Moses, fled from Egypt, and crossing the Sinai Peninsula, settled in the area east of the Dead Sea. Under the leadership of Joshua, the Hebrews invaded the state of Canaan. The most heinous crimes were perpetrated against the inhabitants, and they are recorded in the Old Testament. This was an imperialist invasion no different from many others in history. The inhabitants who were not killed, were reduced to servitude. Thus, the Jews conquered Palestine for the first time.

The Hebrews were only able to occupy parts of Palestine and the area east of the Jordan River. In 1020 B.C. King Saul established their first state. He was followed by King David and then King Solomon, who ruled until 923 B.C. Here the Jews gained their first experience in agriculture, urbanization and statecraft.

In 586 B.C. the Babylonians brought an end to the reign of the Hebrews in Palestine. During the years of their reign the original inhabitants of Palestine remained in continuous residence. For the next four hundred years one invader after another laid claim to Palestine: the Persians in 538 B.C., the Greeks under the leadership of Alexander the Great in 331 B.C., and the Romans in 64 B.C.

A great wave of Arabs from the Arabian Peninsula settled Palestine in the year 636 A.D. This massive migration was not the first Arab population in Palestine. The Arab identity with Palestine was reaffirmed and that identity with Palestine has not been broken to this day.

From 1517 to 1917, Palestine was under the rule of the Ottoman Empire. For Arab support of the Allies in the First World War, they were promised independence. This promise was not kept. Colonialism and subsequently Zionism followed. This was part of a broader picture of European expansion that had begun in the fifteenth century and would climax in the closing years of the nineteenth century. The

Europeans were looking for new land, labor and raw materials. Jews are a part of this search, more as Europeans than as Jews.

When the European age of exploration started in the fifteenth century, the Portuguese were searching for a sea route to India by way of the Cape (now Capetown, South Africa). During one of their early expeditions they attempted to establish a refueling station along the coast of South Africa. This expedition, undertaken upon the advice of Abraham ben Samuel Zacuto, a Jew who was then the Royal Astronomer for King Manuel II of Portugal was issued before the edict of expulsion against Spanish Jews in Spain.

The Dutch East India Company was the forerunner of the South Africa of today. The Dutch were welcomed to South Africa by the Khoisan that they later betrayed and enslaved. This small people (small only in stature and in numbers) fought the Dutch, in order to hold on to their land and cattle, in a series of well planned wars that the Boers or Dutch call Kaffir Wars. The Khoisan finally lost both their land and their cattle. After the great Zulu warrior Shaka was killed in 1828, the British began to push the Boers, and the Boers tried to move inland and establish a new republic away from British influence. This ignited a land war between the Zulus and the Boers. The British came to the rescue of the Boers when they were about to be defeated by the Zulus. These wars did not end until 1906. By now, because of the superior European weapons, most of the land was lost. The continued loss of the land and the plan to make Africans strangers in their own land led to the establishment of artificial African communities called Bantustans.

In 1970, Dr. P. Koornhof, the Deputy Minister of Bantu Administration and Development admitted that the Bantustans made Africans foreigners: "I am afraid to say that the African males from the homelands have no rights whatsoever in South Africa. Their rights are in their own homelands, and they are in South Africa only to sell their labor."

The best known of the Bantustans is Transkei, one of the first established. When it was declared "independent" in 1976 by the apartheid regime, three million Africans were stripped of their citizenship and they lost thirteen percent of their land area. The whites own or control eighty-seven percent of the land, though they are only seventeen percent of the population.

Most Africans do not live in Bantustans but work in mines, in factories, and on farms owned by whites. Under the Bantustan program, these Africans were turned into foreign migrants, and stripped of all rights in the country where they have lived and worked for centuries. The Bantustans are completely dependent economically on the South African government. The Bantustans have been imposed on the African people against their will. They are white controlled black communities. The ways that the Africans are treated in the Bantustans can be easily compared to the way the Arabs in Israel and on the West Bank are treated in their own land. This explains, in part, the unholy alliance between Israel and South Africa.

The most tragic aspect of the alliance between Israel and South Africa is that it is a perfectly logical alliance. By the rationale and intent of Western racism and colonialism the alliance makes sense. Both Israel and white South Africa are artificial settler states.

In order to understand the present dilemma and what it forecasts for the future, there is a need to consider the interplay of forces in South Africa, and in the world at large, that created the state of Israel and the apartheid dominated state of South Africa.

The land question in Zimbawe did not disappear with the "peace" accord between the British Government Patriotic Front. The roots of the conflict over the land are deep. What is now Zimbabwe was a once well-run independent country. In 1870 when Lobengula became King, the Zulu wars against the British were not over, and the British settlers design on African land was intensified after the discovery of gold and diamonds in South Africa. The British used a missionary, Rev. Moffatt to get Lobengula to sign a treaty that gave the British the right to exploit the land and establish farms and settlements. Lobengula did not know that the treaty went that far. In 1870 parts of Mashonaland, later to be called Rhodesia, were occupied by an expeditionary force of mercenaries funded by the British Africa Company. It did not take long for white settlers to evict the Shona people from their land. In this case they did not buy the land, they took it. The Africans in large numbers were forced off the land. Others were brought in to work the land. Many Africans were forced to sea and worked to pay the heavy British taxes. White political power was consolidated by the unequal tenure and the allocation of land, by white control over the labor power of the blacks. White workers had a monopoly on skilled jobs and the trade unions. In her article, "From Rhodesia to Zimbabwe," Marion

O'Callaghan states the following:

> Land became more important for the settlers as the hopes
> entertained by Cecil Rhodes of vast mineral wealth receded.
> The result was the continuing appropriation of African land
> from the nineteenth century on. Indeed, between 1936 and
> 1959, according to a Rhodesian Select Parliamentary Committee
> on Resettlement (1960), over 113,000 Africans were compulso-
> rily removed from white farming areas.
>
> By 1969, 250,000 whites had legal rights enshrined in the
> Constitution to 44.95 million acres, while five million Africans
> had the right to 44.94 million acres.

The areas in Rhodesia where the Africans lived, which the Europeans called reserves, were the same as those the Boers in South Africa
called Bantustans. Taxes and the need for basic items of food and
clothing forced the Africans to leave the reserves and work on Europe-
an-owned plantations or in the cities. The pay was poor in both places.
The pattern for education followed along the same lines as the division
of the land. Two hundred seventy-five whites got the same appropria-
tion as six million Africans. These are the conditions that led to the
war for independence.

In Kenya, land hunger among the Kikuyu people led to the Mau
Mau uprising and stimulated the fight for independence.

My point in digressing from the land question in Palestine is that
this question cannot be seen or answered in isolation. What is called
Israel, and the rest of Palestine, is a part of an international problem,
created by colonialism and its handmaiden—capitalism. This is a
European problem imposed on the Arabs in Palestine. The accompany-
ing propaganda and mythology regarding who now has a right to the
land in Palestine, and who had the right in ancient times goes on in
spite of a large body of scholarly writing that set the record straight
years ago, There are many people sympathetic towards Israel who do
not agree with their treatment of the Arabs and their settlements on
land formerly considered Arab land.

Dov Ronen, a research associate of the Center of International
Affairs at Harvard University made the following comment on this
subject in the April 5, 1980, issue of the *New York Times*:

I am an Israeli who does not support Jewish settlements in the West Bank, nor the opening of a yeshiva in Hebron. I personally do not claim sovereignty over Judea and Samaria on the basis of a biblical right, nor do I consider Israel's sovereignty there essential to our national security in all circumstances. Furthermore, although I would oppose any plan to redivide Jerusalem, I can envision a new administrative arrangement in the city that would address and seek to satisfy Moslem and Palestinian aspirations.

Having studied the issue of self-determination in world politics, I recognize this as a right that the Palestinians must be accorded. The Palestinians should have the right, both in principle and in practice, to control their lives and not be ruled by Israelis or any one else. If independent statehood rather than "mere" autonomy is what they want, I for one support their quest for statehood.

In spite of strong Jewish voices such as Mise Menuhin, Ahad Ha'am, Martin Buber, Albert Einstein, Alfred Lilienthal, Israel Shahak, and I.F. Stone speaking out against the Zionist treatment of the Arabs and the settlements on Arab land, the expansion of Israel at the expense of the Arabs continues. Also continued is the attempt to justify this expansion on the basis of biblical texts.

On this point the Jewish-American writer, I.F. Stone has this to say:

These contradictions now play their part in the efforts at peace in the Middle East. At one end of the spectrum the Bible preaches justice and universal brotherhood. At the other end it contains some of the most primitive and blood-thirsty ethnocentric teachings in human literature. Menachem Begin, Israel's fundamentalist prime minister and the religious parties on which he depends for a thin and precarious parliamentary majority, claim that they cannot give up the West Bank because God gave it to the Jews.

This can, of course, be supported from Bible texts. Indeed, if we are to go back to a literal reading of Holy Writ for guidance in the Middle East conflict, the religious ultras of the

Israeli community can find much else along the same line, and in the same direction, though carried to lengths that would make even the most fanatical among them quail. It is, of course, true that in the final chapter of Numbers God gave the whole of Canaan west of the Jordan to Israel. But if the Word of God is to be taken literally, those who now dwell on the West Bank may tremble. For only three short chapters earlier, the Lord says, "ye shall drive out all the inhabitants of the land from before you, destroy their holy places and 'dispossess' them."

Nor is that all. Numbers 33 ends with the fiercest warning of all if the children of Israel do not dispossess the inhabitants, "I shall do unto you, as I thought to do unto them." If the Jews do not drive out the Canaanites, God will drive out the Jews. This is the harsh theology of depopulating a land to make room for one's own.

Palestinian leaders add organizations in the United States say Israel is trying to remove all vocal opposition to the Camp David "autonomy plan" by expelling Palestinian mayors in the occupied territories or forcing them to resign.

I will conclude with I.F. Stone's warning, relative to this situation:

Some people have been cooking up a brew that could poison the peace not only of the Middle East but of the world. It is the duty of the American Government and American Jewish leadership to use their leverage, financial and political, to put a stop to this criminal concoction before it is too late. Begin, characteristically, chose this moment to announce ten more settlements on the West Bank. As usual, he promises these will be the last; Israel and Palestine, says his opponents on the right would prefer a military takeover of the Israeli Government. Only recognition of the Palestinian right to self-determination can revitalize the peace talks and avert the slide to catastrophe.

*F*ive

COLONIALISM AND THE
CONQUEST OF THE MIND

▼

COMMENTARY

▼

PROPER ACADEMIC ATTENTION, and serious attention in general, has not been paid to the impact of the rise of Europe in the fifteenth and sixteenth centuries on the mind of the non-European world. Europe's greatest achievement during this period was not enslavement and the military conquest of most of the world. The greatest achievement was the conquest of the minds of most of the people of the world.

By the end of the nineteenth century, Europe effectively controlled or influenced most of the geography and people of the earth. In spite of the military advantage, the Europeans mainly having guns and their victims mainly without guns, there still were not enough Europeans to have effectively taken over most of the world. What they did not achieve militarily, they achieved through propaganda. I have called this achievement the manifestation of the evil genius of Europe.

There is a body of literature on this subject that is still sadly neglected. In the W.E.B. DuBois essay, "The Propaganda of History," included in his classic work, *Black Reconstruction in America*, he gives the reader some revealing insights by making an assessment of the following themes:

> ... the facts of American history have in the last half century been falsified because the nation was ashamed. The South was ashamed because it fought to perpetuate human slavery. The North was ashamed because it had to call in the black men to save the Union, abolish slavery and establish democracy.

Dr. Dubois' conclusion is as follows:

321

Immediately in Africa, a black back runs red with the blood of the lash; in India, a brown girl is raped; in China, a coolie starves; in Alabama, seven darkies are more than lynched; while in London, the white limbs of a prostitute are hung with jewels and silk. Flames of jealous murder sweep the earth, while brains of little children smear the hills.

This is education in the Nineteen Hundred and Thirty-fifth year of the Christ; this is modern and exact social science; this is the university course in "History 12" set down by the Senatus academicus; ad quos hae literae pervenerint: Salutem in Domino, sempeternam!

* * * * *

> In Babylon, dark Babylon
>   Who take the wage of Shame?
> The scribe and singer, one by one,
>   That toil for gold and fame.
> They grovel to their masters' mood;
>   The blood upon the pen
> Assigns their souls to servitude—
>   Yea! and the souls of men.

—George Sterling

"In the Market Place" from Selected Poems.
Used by permission of Harry Robertson, Redwood City, California

* * * * *

When Europe stood up and shook off the lethargy of the Middle Ages, after the disaster of the Crusades, they began to propagate certain concepts that reverberate to this day and which are basically untrue. The most damaging of these concepts are:

1. That the world was waiting in darkness for the Europeans to bring the light of culture and civilization. As a matter of fact, in most cases, the truth was the contrary. The Europeans put out more light and destroyed more civilizations and cultures

than they ever built.

2. Another European concept that is still with us, doing its maximum damage is that the European concept of God is the only concept worthy of serious religious attention. In most of the world where the Europeans expanded, especially in Africa, they deprived the people of the right to call on God in a language of their creation and to look at God through their own imagination. They inferred or said outright that no figure that did not resemble a European could be God or the representative of God. In the book, *The Role of Missionary in Conquest*, Nasipho Majeke gives a good evaluation of this European concept.

3. That the European invader and conqueror is a civilizer. Conquerors are never benevolent. In nearly all cases they spread their way of life at the expense of the conquered people.

4. That the European is the discoverer. This myth is still with us on the eve of the 500-year anniversary of Christopher Columbus' alleged discovery of America. This is one of the most prevailing myths in history, because Christopher Columbus discovered absolutely nothing. Conversely, he did help to set in motion a pattern of European expansion, slavery and exploitation that left its scar on most of mankind. I believe, in essence, this is what Dr. DuBois meant by his essay, "The Propaganda of History."

Image and Mind Control as a Factor in the African World

The role of image and mind control in the African world goes beyond the visual. In many ways it tells the colonized what to wear, what to like, what to hate, and what to consume. The colonials create a market by training the colonized mind to consume what the respective colonial country produces.

The educated African, in most cases, stopped wearing African clothes, stopped eating African food, and, in some cases, stopped reading books and documents created by the African mind. He lost respect for his ability to be creative and stopped using his imagination as a tool of survival. The European man became, in his mind, the image of achievement, and the European woman the image of beauty. As the great scholar, Edward Blyden, said, in effect: "The African so propagandized strives to be those things most unlike himself and most alien to the culture that produced him. He feeds grist into other people's mill and sees nothing of his creative self as a result." If he has lost confidence in himself, he has lost respect for himself. To understand this propaganda achievement by Europeans and to be able to arrest its impact on the African mind, it is necessary to take a serious look at everything that the African has been and is exposed to: the print media, the visual media, popular magazines, the anti-African propaganda that is a result of the misinterpretation of the Bible. On this point, you should read *Hebrew Myths* by Robert Graves and Raphael Patai.

Tarzan and other jungle movies have further distorted the image of African people in the eyes of the world. This distortion is so widespread that when people generally meet an African intellectual (and there are many), they are shocked into disbelief. This means they have not read the work of important Caribbean intellectuals, such as Eric Williams' *Capitalism and Slavery, Documents of West Indian History*, and his last book, *The Caribbean from Columbus to Castro*, to name only a few of his important works. There are many whites who will say boldly that Africa has nothing to offer to solve its own problems without reading one line of the many competently written books by Cheikh Anta Diop, the greatest single African intellect produced in the twentieth century. His work, *African Origins of Civilization: Myth or Reality*, broke new ground in historical writing. Another smaller book, *Africa: The Politics of a Federated State*, is a long essay on how the mineral wealth of Africa was taken over by Europeans and what the Africans will have to do to preserve what is left for the African generations still to be born. His last work, finished before his death, is *Civilization or Barbarism*. This is a long essay on civilization in general and how African people relate to its creation and maintenance.

The Crisis of the African Intellectual

The crisis that Professor Harold Cruse (Black Studies Program, University of Michigan) has referred to is both historical and topical. This crisis is historical because it dates from the 1700s B.C. with the first Hebrew visitation to Africa, and it continued through the period of 1675 B.C., when Africa saw its first invaders from western Asia, now referred to as the Middle East. The historical basis of the crisis of the African intellectual is rooted in the fact that the Africans have never been able to assess successfully the temperament and the intentions of visitors to Africa and invaders. Most of the visitors to Africa and the invaders were first accepted by the Africans as friends because, in most cases, the Africans thought their intentions were good. The invaders stayed on in Africa as conquerors and enslavers, and most of the visitors stayed on as their collaborators. The aftermath of Africans' political naïveté in relationship to visitors and invaders reverberates to this day. This is what I mean when I said the crisis of the African intellectual has both an historical and a topical meaning. At the basis of this crisis is what we lost as a people during slavery and colonization, and what we are still losing under neo-colonialism, that is another form of slavery and colonialism. The world crisis among African intellectuals, and so-called leaders in particular, is that we as a people have been out of power all too long. Nearly all of the methodology we used to obtain and maintain power before the Arab and European disruption of independent states in Africa has been lost from our memory. Therefore, when we gain power and the rule of the state, we become imitators of our former colonial master, whose methodology in power will never be suitable for our case.

African people should never enter into the silly argument between capitalism and communism, because insofar as we are concerned, both of them have failed us. Because the argument is not about us. The hidden agenda between the two European arguers is which one of them will ultimately rule over us and our tremendous resources, mineral and otherwise. Because of our political naivete, we have not learned that all Europeans, irrespective of political label or ideology, think that they are worthy of ruling over African people.

The Europeans are clear on this point, but we African people remain confused. We do not know that everything that has been developed by the European mind was done to facilitate European control over the world, and there are no exceptions.

The concept that the European would later call "communism" or "socialism" was old in Africa before Europe was born. The same is true of the concepts called Christianity and democracy. Therefore, if the African wanted a political ideology, he could find the basis of it at home. The same thing is true of politics, religion and culture.

For anything to benefit the African people in the long range, the African intellectual must remake the concept to suit the African case and discard the "made-in-Europe" label. This is the basic crisis of the African intellectual the world over. We cannot turn back the influence of Europe by imitating Europeans. We must find enduring values among ourselves. We need an operational definition of African unity and Pan-Africanism that can be understood by Africans wherever they live on the face of the earth. The Africans living outside Africa need to go back to Africa, first within their own minds.

Dr. Willis N. Huggins, founder of The Harlem History Club in the 1930s, once said to me, "We as a people will encounter no difficulty getting to the door of the promised land. But we will get to the door and bunch up at the door and start an argument whether we should cross the threshold with our right foot or our left." What I think Dr. Huggins was saying is: when people are out of power a long time, they long desperately for power. And when they get close to power they panic, because they realize they have not prepared themselves to handle power.

A situation of this nature makes a people power-imitators instead of creative power-innovators. Their values become the values of their former colonial masters. Their method of handling power becomes a facsimile of the method of the former colonial masters. This is the essence of the crisis of the African intellectual, both at home and abroad. If we were as creative and innovative in handling governments as we are in music, dance and in all forms of sports, we would not only have changed Africa around to benefit ourselves in the world, we would have made a principled statement to all mankind, and through our action we would have called for the recognition of a new humanity for all people.

Can African People Save Themselves?

The question can be answered in many ways, both negative and positive. I have chosen to answer it positively, because I am an African person and I have hope for a commitment to every African on the face of the earth. My commitment to mankind comes first through my commitment to African people. If African people are to save themselves, they must first know themselves. They must first know where they have been and what they have been, where they are and the significance of what they are.

Knowing this, they will get some idea of what they still must be. African people must stop being the market and the dumping ground for the shoddy consumer goods of other people. We must, on an international basis, begin to produce the things we wear, the food we eat, the cars we drive. We must train our children to follow our footsteps and complete the mission, a self-sustained and contained people. At least a third of the Africans in the world can be employed providing goods and services for other Africans.

Once we create an internal economic system, we can relate to the external economic systems in other parts of the world. No African state can be truly independent when it does not produce every single item essential to its survival. Education must be geared to produce the large number of technically trained Africans essential to this task, and they, in turn, through apprenticeship, must produce other Africans to replace them. No African nation in the world should beg for the skills of another nation or people to sustain itself.

Africans can save themselves by having the will to do so and the commitment to hold on to the will until the job of self-protection and true independence will have been achieved. The salvation of Africa by African people will contribute to the peace and the salvation of the world. This salvation should be the mission of every African on the face of the earth. The completion of the mission and the benefits that will accrue from it will be the legacy that African people can leave for the whole world.

IMAGE AND MIND CONTROL IN THE AFRICAN WORLD: ITS IMPACT ON AFRICAN PEOPLE AT HOME AND ABROAD

▼

> What we do for ourselves
> depends on what we know
> of ourselves and what
> we accept about ourselves.

—Timothy Callender, "The Basis of African Culture"

BECAUSE WHAT WE SEE ABOUT ourselves often influences what we do about ourselves, the role of image and the control of the mind is more important now in a media-saturated society than ever before in history. For the last 500 years, the history of African people has been locked in what Professor Ivan Van Sertima of Rutgers University has referred to as a "500-year-room." Professor Van Sertima is referring to the fact that most of the history of African people throughout the world is told through slavery, a short period in our history, considering that we are the oldest of the world's people.

There is a need now to look behind the slavery curtain in order to see what African people achieved before slavery, as an independent people. Because this independence existed for thousands of years before Europe itself existed, we should now examine the far-reaching power of a European-created media over the minds of most of the world, especially over the minds of our children. There is a need to examine education and miseducation in order to confront the fact that oppressors cannot afford the luxury of educating an oppressed people. If people are truly educated, they will find a way out of their oppression.

The image before the African child of today, both in Africa, the United States, and throughout the world, is a clear indication of what they will be as adults and what they will think as adults. In the "500-year-room" of history, where African people experienced slavery, colonialism, anticolonialism, the African Independence Explosion, and the rise and the decline of civil rights movements in the United States, these images have been both negative and positive. These images, indicating that we do not control the mass media, have influenced African people the world over and could be correctly assessed as the vanguard of a new imperialism and a new slavery. I am referring to the images reflected in the mass media, such as television, radio, newspapers and religious literature, where African people are rarely ever portrayed as playing a heroic role and the most of the time are not portrayed at all.

This subject is both current and historical, and I often say to the young faculty in my department at Hunter College who are forever trying to get a new person on staff, preferably someone who will agree with their interpretation of Marxism, that you have not lived long enough, cried enough, been disappointed enough to know what you are talking about. What I was trying to get over to them is that no matter what the subject is, ultimately the subject is education, image control, and thought control. Because we African people are dreamers and true believers, we live out a lot of our lives in fantasy, especially as it relates to education and reality. The one thing that might save the world (and it is not the oppressor because the oppressor will not save the world) is the oppressed. They will save the world because they are just politically naive enough to believe in the higher ideals that the oppressor announces and violates. They are just naive enough to actually believe in Christianity and actually believe in democracy, not realizing that their oppressor could not live by democracy or Christianity for 24 hours. And if he practiced either for 24 hours, that would be the end of his power.

If the subject is imagery, imagery before the black child in a race and color-conscious society, then why is it that the focus of this part of the paper seems to be away from the subject? As a matter of fact, I am still on the subject. I am exercising the prerogatives of my Baptist upbringing. We take our text, we leave our text, and we come back to our text sometime before the speech is over just to let you know that we know what we are talking about. Because I have never been able to afford a psychiatrist in my years when I probably needed one most, when I finally got to the point where I was earning the kind of salary where I could afford one, I didn't want one, having met enough psychiatrists who were absolutely nuts. I said to myself, if this caliber of person must treat me, then there is no hope for me. So the way that I relax in front of an audience, in other words, give myself some therapy to get into my speech, is to talk away from the subject, but talk about something that is relevant to the subject in an indirect way, and maybe in a direct way.

What I'm talking about is education, a current event, a kind of fantasy that exists throughout the world. I am referring to people who are oppressed reading their oppressor the wrong way. If the oppressed understood how power is maintained they would know that powerful people cannot afford to educate powerless people for fear that they will ultimately take their power away from them. Because if powerless people are properly educated they would become so restless they would tear the nation apart and would make claims on the nation over and above anything the nation could satisfy. What you need to understand is what education is all about. Education has but one honorable purpose. The purpose of proper education is to prepare the student to be a responsible handler of power. Any other type of education is a waste of time.

What am I referring to? When a child learns the word, "stop," the child begins to exercise power over the safety of his self. Every form of learning is supposed to be some way of instructing one better in the exercise of power. I am not ruling out the liberal arts. I am not ruling out philosophy, because once you study the philosophies that guide the mind of man you have power over how to choose an idea that is relevant to you and relevant to your own life. All education must lead to some kind of an exercise of power. If the education is proper, then the education must ultimately improve one's understanding of what power is and how power manifests itself and how one has to have power in order to be a total human being. Once he understands this, he can make an assessment of other things. When you are under the power of others, where other people determine your destiny, your actions are those of a slave. To be a slave is not the fact of being poor. A lot of people are poor and they are not slaves. To be a slave is not to be able to determine your own destiny. It is not to be able to make the correct choices for your own life, where you have been in your life and where you still have to go. That is what power is all about.

By this definition, then, most of the world, including some white people, are slaves. What we need to do in looking at the crisis in America is to look at the crisis in the world, because the crisis in America is the crisis of power, and we need to look at fifteenth and sixteenth century Europe. People keep telling me, you keep hammering on the subject of fifteenth and sixteenth century Europe. I do this because our modern world was designed at that time. After the awakening of Europe, starting with the Crusades, Europe stirred itself and came out of the lethargy of its Middle Ages and began to learn and began to use the information brought back into Europe by the Crusaders. The Crusades were a military failure; however, they were an information success.

Cecil B. deMille, the movie producer, showed the Crusaders winning all the battles; as a matter of fact, they lost militarily, but they won in many other ways. They brought back into Europe information about high cultures that during the European Middle Ages had moved far beyond Europe. They brought back into the mainland of Europe information that the combinations of Africans, Arabs, and Berbers, collectively, preserved at the University of Salamanca in Spain. They unlocked Europe from its lethargy and drew it out into the broader world.

Europeans had partly recovered from the Middle Ages; however, this partial recovery had not fed them. They were looking for many things, among them sweets and spices. Anything to put on that god-awful European food so that they could eat it. They had lost sentimental attachment to themselves and they had lost sentimental attachment to the rest of the world. And now with maritime skills, gained indirectly from China, from the information brought into Europe through the University of Salamanca and its great translators, who had preserved the intellectual heritage of the ancient classical civilizations, Europe had fallen heir to a heritage, a heritage that Europe had forgotten.

China was the leading technical nation in the world of that day, and they were 150 years ahead of Europe in maritime skills. Europe had not made a boat that could take the roar of the ocean. They had not perfected the compass, and it was this ignorance that had pinned them into Europe since the fall of Rome. Now they had to get out of Europe. They had lost one-third of their population through famine and plagues. They had partly put themselves together, thanks to the framework of the Catholic Church, but they were still hungry.

To be locked into conditions that are harsh and unfriendly produces a people with a particular type of temperament. This temperament was about to be projected onto the world, and we still have to deal with it until we understand it and stop transferring our sentiment onto a people who do not share our cultural and historical background. Deal with them with reality. In this redesigning of the world, the Europeans decided that whosoever controls the world, it's going to be one of them. That decision has not changed.

The idealistic Black Marxist thinks that racism stops at the door of socialism and communism. It does not stop there; it changes its coat and becomes paternalism. These paternalistic Marxists explain away other lowly positions in the world. They tell them, you are less than other people because of these circumstances, and because of this you need us, and you need us to lead you. It is almost like the situation in the public schools in Harlem, where the teachers were of one ethnic group, the Irish. This was when the Irish were controlling Tammany Hall, controlling the politics of New York, and controlling the quality of education in New York. The Irish teacher never pretended to like black people, or black students. She said, figuratively, "Lowly though you may be, you too can learn mathematics. And I will teach you." And teach she did.

The Irish lost out and another ethnic group took over. This group said, "I just love you and I understand your position. I understand why so many of you are on welfare. Don't raise your ambitions too high because you cannot make it—you haven't got the mental capacity." This mentality does a great deal of damage to a people. I want those old Irish teachers back who openly did not like me, but who took it upon themselves, as a challenge, to say, "I can teach even you mathematics," and who did just that. The caliber of black students that they turned out, and who showed up later when black students were being appointed as assistant to somebody or other, always carefully acknowledged their indebtedness to her. She never pretended any social equality or anything like that. She had made up her mind that she had succeeded in educating even an inferior being. She had accepted the challenge.

When I returned to my hometown, Columbus, Georgia, a few years ago, for some kind of commemorative as a distinguished writer returning to his home, I remembered a different caliber of teacher who did not think of me or the black students as superior or inferior. These dedicated black teachers who let you know that you have a destiny and who would sit you down and take time with you explaining that your playing days in this school were over would say, "You are going to get an education or walk by me and pay some dues." What she meant was that if she had to punish you, she would walk you to your home and punish you a second time, right in front of your parents. This was understood and appreciated because it was part of our extended family arrangement. They established their authority in the classroom. You saw a teacher as an educational deity standing before you in the classroom, and you respected her for that. It was inconceivable that anybody could go into that classroom to learn and leave without learning how to read. There was no such thing as anybody passing into third grade without learning how to read. She would be professionally insulted, and she would accept no excuses. I will tell you the advantage of this system, and I'm not saying there is an advantage in a Jim-Crow set-up. The advantage of this system is being together so that you can caucus, one to the other. The teacher very often belonged to the same church as the students and their parents. She was still an educational deity outside of the classroom. When you got outside school with your little gang and scattered your dirty little words around, to try to prove your manhood, the minute you saw your teacher, you policed-up yourself. Someone would say, "Hey, hey, watch your mouth. Here comes the teacher." It was a symbol of respect for her, or him, but more often it was her; when she came into our presence certain words were not ever spoken and we acted as though we never spoke them.

Now, in a ragged sort of way, I am coming around to the subject. What I am saying is that there has to be some reassessment of our approach to education. There must also be some reassessment of the good role that the NAACP played, and there has to be a reassessment of the terrible mistakes they made by not designing what integration should be. The 60,00 to 70,000 black teachers in the South that were integrated out of their jobs by integration was not in the bargain. What we did was set ourselves up for that loss by not understanding the nature of power. I am saying that we must understand the nature of power, how it operates, and how powerful people operate.

If the people in Iran understood the nature of power they would never have asked this nation for an apology for the aborted attempt to rescue alleged hostages from their country. The fact that they deserved 10,00 apologies is not the issue here. Powerful people never stand before their victims and say, "We were wrong. We are sorry." The Germans haven't said they were sorry for killing millions of people, and they haven't said they were wrong. They said, "We will pay compensation in order to tone down the ill-will against Germany so she can function commercially and politically in the world's family of nations." They didn't say they were sorry; they paid compensation as a form of public relations so that they could function in the world. A powerful nation killed millions of people and scattered around a few dollars to some of the survivors. There was something they could do very easily; they wouldn't even miss this money from their treasury. For a people to expect a powerful nation like the United States, who has designs on the whole world, to say it is sorry, is to be out of their mind.

The people in power in Iran are young politically, and the young are dreamers. They have forgotten what I am constantly driving at in my going back to the fifteenth and sixteenth centuries in Europe. When Europeans decided they were going to dominate the whole world they also meant that they were going to dominate the other people in this world with white faces, and who were not of European descent. There is obviously some confusion on this point; a lot of those people in Western Asia are confused. They wonder, since their faces are white, why are they doing this to me? What they fail to realize is that they're not of European extraction and that makes them just another part of the overall design—for one or the other of the Europeans to control the world.

Now I am coming directly to the subject. What has the preface been all about? The preface has been about reality as opposed to fantasy. Our new theoreticians, who are not theoreticians at all, in their fascination for Karl Marx have made Marxism applicable to our case. This proves they do not thoroughly understand our case. I have no anger against Karl Marx, but I've got a lot of anger against Marxists who do not understand that for a people to be whole in any kind of political structure, even if they adopt Marxism, they will have to re-adapt it to suit their own special political needs. Any other way, what they will be doing is swallowing Marx whole and regurgitating him undigested.

Marx is obsolete in Europe, and nobody knows it more than the Russians, who are still editing him and changing him around to suit their current needs. There is no point in telling me, "religion is the opiate of the people." I know it is, and I accept that. But I know one thing more: If I go back to the Baptist community where I was raised and say, "religion is the opiate of the people, " they would have my head examined. So in my socialism, that "opiate" is going to have to come over and be integrated. Also, we will have to deal with our ministers in another way. I would certainly never go into a Baptist church and say that "religion is a myth and a fable," which it is, unless I was ready to face the consequences. Those old sisters would have my head for tampering with their pastor. I would barely get out of that church with my life. So no matter what I think about socialism, I must face reality when I am selling it to my people. I am a life-long socialist, I am a Pan-Africanist and an African World Nationalist, too. I have no problem with being all three, but ny socialism has to fit that prevailing reality.

The subject of this paper, *Image and Mind Control In The African World*, is directed to the adults of our community. I will begin with personal references. It is about, as a young writer in my early days in New York City, having the good fortune of becoming a member of the Harlem History Club from almost the second week after my arrival from Georgia; having learned under a great teacher, unfortunately forgotten now, Willis N. Huggins, who gave history classes at the Harlem YMCA; having met Arthur Schomburg, who founded the Schomburg Collection; and having taken advantage of the fact that during the Great Depression there were master teachers of African descent roaming through Harlem who would teach anybody who would listen, free of charge. There were street speakers who taught from a step ladder. Part of my own training in communicating with an audience was either from the pulpit of a Baptist church or in a community center or from a step ladder on the streets of Harlem. It proved to be the best training you could possibly have had as a teacher. In these formats you can only hold your audience by putting one fact in front of another fact and making them interesting and logical. Any other way, they would leave you the minute you cannot support your stand. Not only will they leave you, they will denounce you, and they will take the audience with them. They will show you no mercy. And they will hold no sentiment. You must either deliver or you come down from the ladder and yield to someone else. It was brutal training, but it was the best training I could have possibly had.

As a young boy, I felt not only proud but kind of smug while doing chores in a Rosenwald-sponsored High School, and I wish I had the space here to explain the Rosenwald-Sponsored School in the South. Briefly, Rosenwald gave one-third to the establishment of the school, the community gave another third, and the city gave another third, and the black community got schools they would not otherwise have had. We as a people were suspicious of all gifts coming from white folks. Therefore, we developed a folklore that said that Rosenwald, who owned Sears and Roebuck, wanted black people to read so they could read his catalog and order from his company. If this was not true, we reasoned, why would he be giving us his money to learn to read? But that's enough of folklore; we did learn to read, and we did order from the catalog because there was nothing that we could possibly need, including a new stove, that was not in the Sears and Roebuck catalog, and we were not treated too kindly in the stores. At that time—and the younger generation does not know this—if you would go into a store in the South and try on a hat, if it didn't fit you, you still had to buy the hat because the custom was that it could not be sold to a white person once it touched the head of a black person. All of this might seem utterly insane to you, but I lived through it. And this kind of humiliation in the stores made a whole lot of blacks order their suits, their stoves, and their coffee grinders from Sears and Roebuck.

While I was at this school I had been introduced to an essay called "The Negro Digs Up His Past," written by a Puerto Rican of African descent, with a German-sounding name, Arthur Schomburg. Shortly after I arrived in New York, I located Arthur Schomburg. He began to teach me how to read history and how to look at history in an area broader than my own people's history. I began to study the history of Europe and I can teach any aspect of European history if you give me

20 minutes notice, right now. Why 20 minutes notice? Well, I would need time to sift through my mind and unravel the mountain of knowledge it contains on Europe until I come to the specific piece that I intend to analyze. That is all the time I need. I would need no notes. If you don't know the history of those who stole your history, then you don't know your history, and you will not know why it became important to render you non-historical. No one can oppress a consciously historical people. A consciously historical people know that they are part of the world's humanity. To know you are part of this humanity leads you to understand that you are an extension of every man, and no one can oppress you unless you oppress yourselves, directly or indirectly.

What I learned from Schomburg was how to read history systematically. Willis Huggins taught me the political meaning of history and how African history related to world history. He was the man that the black community of Harlem sent to Geneva to look into the circumstances of the Italian-Ethiopian War. He was a man who managed to survive, somehow, and got a scholarship to study for his Ph.D at Fordham University because someone thought him to be a Catholic. He went along with this and every time the other Catholics prayed, he prayed an extra long time (to make sure he got his scholarship money). Finally, he finished Fordham University, writing a brilliant thesis on the role of the Catholic Church in relationship to the social welfare of blacks.

The mass media, aimed at oppressed people in particular and African people in general, is part of an attempt at controlling the minds of the world. Most Bible interpretation and religious training is part of this attempt at mind control. In the years immediately following the Civil War, when churches were sending missionaries to the South, there were in New England large numbers of white women who represented the first large contingent of educated women in America. The New England man seemed to be afraid of them—he surely wasn't marrying them. Probably he didn't know what to say to these educated women. They made a trek to the South to teach in newly established schools for blacks. They were called New England schoolmarms, although most of them were not marms; however, many of them were spinsterish though young. They taught at places like Hampton Institute, and it was one of these schoolmarms that examined Booker T.

Washington to determine whether he was capable of entering Hampton. These women made a major contribution to black education. They were masters of Latin and Greek and they trained some of the finest teachers we had during that period.

Most of these teachers came from finishing schools, and they taught many of the black farm girls how to set a table for a banquet. In most poor houses there weren't enough forks in the house to set a proper table for the meager crowd who ate the meager meal. They introduced us to something else, something we had been eating all along, the salad. We had been eating "salad" in our very own way. We would take some salt and pepper. We would go to the field, pick some tomatoes, wash them off, dash a little salt, a little pepper, and walk down the road eating them. We'd pick some radishes and do the same thing. We'd peel some cucumbers and we would eat them almost like a fruit. We had not organized it, put it on a plate, or given it a name. That was one of their contributions, and now as I walk far from the fields of home, I thank them for that.

In my early twenties, I was in Harlem. I had begun to write, and my stories were beginning to appear in different magazines. There was an annual anthology called *Best American Short Stories*. I had appeared on their Honor Roll as one of their most distinguished American Writers, because they considered my short stories outstanding. At this point, I became curious. I wondered if anybody in my hometown was reading my work and wrote a story, totally fiction, but using the names of living people as characters. I used the name of the black principal of my elementary school, and I had him do something in the story that he never would have done in real life. I had him defy the white Superintendent of Schools. My story was about a young black student who was brilliant and who wanted to do something for the teacher's birthday. This young student painted a picture of Christ. His picture of Christ looked like his father, and I called my story "The Boy Who Painted Christ Black." It has become the most anthologized and the most reprinted short story ever written by a black writer. Very often, my students read the story and rave about it without knowing that I am the author. It seems inconceivable to them that an old history teacher once had a reputation as a poet and a fiction writer.

This brings me to what I am dealing with, imagery. In the story, the principal defends the right of the child to paint the picture to resemble his father because most people think of the deity and the father image as having a relationship. Having defended the child's right to do this, he loses his job and he takes another job at another school in another part of Georgia. He takes the child with him to continue training him. And that is where my story ends. It ends on what is called "a high note." I have them walking away from the school for the last time and watch them in the first person until their bodies become blurs. I say, ending the story, "They were still walking brisk and proud like two people who had won some kind of victory."

Now, of course, the principal who got in trouble with the white Superintendent of Schools for defying him, even in fiction, sued me. It was a fine compliment during those early years of my writing career. He sued me for $7,500. I was living in a furnished room in Harlem that cost me $3.75 per week, and this was the best I could afford. I lived in a furnished room in a brownstone in Harlem that was so small it didn't even have a table, and I hadn't earned anything near $7,500 during my entire writing career. I grew accustomed to this small room and did most of my writing in the public library or propped up in bed with a clipboard. I now own a brownstone. My wife says it has 18 rooms. I swear 21, but be what may, who argues with wives. But even now I still, with all that space, get into bed and write with a clipboard.

What I'm saying is that we must look at the impact certain images have had on children and on ourselves. We must look at the impact on the child in an educational system where every hero he sees looks like somebody else, and where a lot of heroes don't even look like heroes at all; when he must look at Christopher Columbus as a hero, and he could not possibly be a hero to a black person or to an Indian if the person understood what and who Christopher Columbus was. The child is deceived. History has proven Christopher Columbus to be a fraud, a liar and a welsher on his debts, plus a lousy navigator, and this places a false image before a child. Christopher Columbus pulled off many deceptions besides missing a golden opportunity to develop a partnership between Africans, Indians and Europeans that would have benefitted all three. He blew it by trying and succeeding to enslave the Indian, and it was Christopher Columbus who suggested, after all the Indians were killed off, that the African be enslaved to replace the Indians. This man is then placed before the black child as a hero, as a European who discovered America by starting out for the East Indies and ending up in the West Indies. This was not a navigational error. It was a game. African sailors who had already traveled to the New World had told him about the New World and he went there instead of going where he had conned Queen Isabella into believing he was going. It was a double cross. Then how did he become a hero? He became a hero because they said he was a hero.

In looking at the heroes in the textbooks we must look at the most glaring of all of the heroes that shape the mind of African people, both in Africa and abroad, the heroes of the Bible. When I began to look for a definition of myself in the literature of the world, being a young Baptist Sunday School teacher at the time, I naturally looked in the Bible. There I couldn't find the word "Negro." The word was not invented then. It took some lazy Spaniard or Portuguese to take a descriptive adjective and make a noun out of it and slap it on a people. A people's name is a powerful force. When you answer to a name that is not your name you become the name. The proper name of a people must relate to land, history and culture and not to a condition, but I didn't know any of that at that time.

I read the story of Moses and I was fascinated. I learned that Moses was an African, born in Africa. I see Moses going down to Ethiopia, to quote his first Ethiopian wife, who was really his second. The Bible give him one Ethiopian wife. My research gives him three. But among the other inaccuracies, Moses gets white and Zipporah gets white. I see people going to the land of Punt, which is the present-day Somalia. They are black now, and we could assume that they were blacker still then. They too got white. I see people going to the land of Kush, which is part of present-day Sudan and a part of what is now Somalia; they got white too. I couldn't find black people anywhere in the Bible, and therein lies my confusion.

Still looking, I read the story of Noah to see where and why we got cursed. I began to mull over how a whole people would get cursed for the actions of one man. I wondered why "Mrs. Noah" didn't take charge of her son when he laughed at his father's nakedness. Where was the scolding of her son, where did she say, "Your father has been working hard loading the ark, waiting for the flood. Some of the animals didn't smell so well. He worked many long hours. He has finished his job and now is entitled to a little recreation. Of course he overdid it and disrobed himself, but let's put some clothing on him and put him to bed. But remember now, drunk or sober, he is your father, a good provider and a decent man. While addressing him keep a civil tongue in your head or I will take care of the matter." Those or words to that effect, would have settled the matter and it would not have entered into history at all. But I never found these words, and the story comes down through history. Ham is cursed, the sons of Ham are cursed, and they did not do anything. This is very cruel, kind of overacting. The ancient myth-makers made God a monster. They made God ungodly. I knew even then that no God of love and beauty would ever curse an entire people no matter what crime was committed. But black people are religious puritans, they out-Pope the Pope, out-Muhammad Muhammad. They accept things literally, believe the Bible word for word and have difficulty in understanding that a lot of the stories in the Bible are not only not true, were never meant to be presented as truth, were meant to illustrate a point, and often the scribe did not understand the point and sometimes altered the story so that the message got lost in the telling.

We need, also, to look at the hero in our mass media. We need to look at our heroes in fiction. We need to look at our heroes in society. We need to monitor what our children see on television. And I ashamedly confess, as a father, that I am telling you to do something that I have not succeeded in doing. We need to ask some questions about the black hero who is always the hustler, the pimp, or always doing somebody in. We need to ask questions about the total image of our people in the literature of the world and in the mass media of the world. We need to change some of this around. We need to use history for what history needs to be. I have often said, and it deserves repeating here, that history is a clock that tells a people their historical time of day. It is a compass that people use to locate themselves on the map of human geography. A people's history tells a people where they have been and what they have been, where they are, and what they are. More importantly, a proper understanding of history tells a people what they still must be and where they still must go. This knowledge of our history will elevate us beyond the "Black and Beautiful" stage. We must move beyond that to understand that to be black and beautiful means nothing in this world unless we are black and powerful. What we have to do is to gain the kind of confidence that will help us to understand that beauty is internal and that beauty must come from within. It must be used as a carriage. You do not frighten white people by telling them you are black and beautiful—they will hurry up and make cosmetics and sell them to you so you can be even more so, and laugh all the way to the bank.

This world is not run by beauty. It is run by power. When we become confident that we are black and powerful in the sense of being aware of our mission, we will walk into a room and not have to say we are black and beautiful. Everybody will know we are, because it will radiate from inside of us. Beauty will be in that place because we are in that place—have brought it with us.

I am talking about the impact of image in the influencing of the mind. In an indirect way the image we accept of ourselves determines what we think of ourselves and what we do for ourselves.

In the fifteenth and sixteen centuries, during the rise of the Atlantic slave trade, the Europeans not only began to colonize the minds of the people of the world, they also colonized information about the world. By colonizing the information they began to project a picture of themselves and another picture, a negative picture, of the people they hoped to oppress in their attempt to convince them that they deserved to be oppressed. They had begun to colonize the Bible and its interpretation at the Conference of Nicaea in 332 A.D. The Bible is an effective part of the European-controlled media that is often misused as a form of mind control. The predominantly white image in the Bible infers that the world waited in darkness for the European to bring it to spiritual light. The prevalence of white angels in illustrated Bible texts and in Sunday school lessons infers that no non-white people, of the many millions who have died, had been good enough to reach that celestial place called heaven. Modern Christianity was formalized around the first century A.D., and it originally affected the people of North Africa and part of Western Asia (sometimes referred to as the Middle East). When you consider that most of mankind is non-European and non-white, we should at least assume that some of them lived a life good enough to be rewarded a place in heaven after their death.

These are the questions that started my inquiry into the Bible and religious literature in general as part of the mass media that plays a major role in mind control. Prior to the second rise of Europe, in the fifteenth century, the slave trade, colonialism and the world expansion of the Europeans, most of the people of the world had a concept of God shaped by their own culture and their own understanding of spirituality. They generally saw God or any deity as a figure resembling themselves. The expanding presence of the Europeans made them, in large numbers, not only consider a new God, but a new image of God. Because the Europeans did not have enough manpower to control the vast territories and population they were taking over in Africa and Asia, they used the media of the Bible and religious literature as a form of mind control. Their emphasis was principally the image of God and the image of God as being a European creation.

With the rise of the American movie industry early in this century, black men rarely ever appeared as heroes. They were mostly pictured as clowns and buffoons. This reached a tragic culmination in the historically incorrect depiction of black people in *Birth of A Nation*. In the great epic movies based on biblical stories, mainly those produced and directed by Cecil B. deMille, blacks in Egypt, a country that is very much a part of Africa, were depicted as slaves and servants. The character, Moses, who was born and raised in Africa, was always played by a white actor. In the jungle movies and in the Tarzan movies, Africans were referred to as "natives" fearful of a few powerful white men, especially Tarzan.

The period of the black exploitation movies, the 1970s, further demeaned the image of black people in the eyes of the world, except for one character in the movie, *Lydia Bailey*, when the veteran actor William Marshall played the part of a hero. This was an exception that we would not see again until the rise of the career of Sidney Poitier. Except for the few better than average movies such as *Buck and the Preacher*, about black migration in the West and *Uptight*, a movie about some aspects of the civil rights movement, starring Julian Mayfield, the image of African-American people in the 1970s was exceptionally poor.

In television documentary series that focus on Africa, a lot of the information is not true to historical facts. In these series, Africa generally is interpreted by a European with European colonial interests. It was expected that the television series called *The Triple Heritage*, narrated by Ali Mazrui, would be the exception. Technically, this was a far better than average series, and if looked at too hurriedly, one might assume that it was about African history. Beneath all the pretense, this series was a unique glorification of Islam in Africa, with emphasis on the assumption that Africa was waiting in darkness until Christianity and Islam brought the light. While the title was intriguing, it was basically misleading because Africa has no triple heritage—Africa has a single heritage, with a triple impact.

Professor Mazrui is a brilliant scholar in spite of the misleading information in his series. He knows what he did not tell his audience: that the main elements that went into the making of Judaism, Christianity and Islam came out of the Nile Valley civilization and the country that the Greeks referred to as Egypt. In general, this series was one of the greatest opportunities in television history. It is my belief that this series was surreptitiously turned into a form of pro-Arab and pro-Islamic propaganda.

In the television series, *Eyes on the Prize*, it is my opinion that the thrust and meaning of the civil rights movement was toned down to appease the sensitivity of what they hoped would be a mass audience. This movement still awaits a more honest and a more creative interpretation.

The tragic and gross image of Africa in another series *Shaka Zulu*, is barely worth a comment. This series was paid for by the apartheid government of South Africa. Enough said.

The motion picture, *The Color Purple* made from a novel by Alice Walker, was a brilliant study in media sociology and misconceptions about black people, especially relationships between black men and black women. The time of the movie, the end of the nineteenth and the beginning of the twentieth century, needs to be taken into consideration because this was the beginning of a period of building and rebirth in black America. We had barely been out of chattel slavery fifty years and we were already involved in building new institutions, mainly churches, lodges and community institutions. Black men were fighting to hold onto their disappearing position in the American labor movement. Booker T. Washington was building a great school at Tuskegee. W.E.B. DuBois had finished his Harvard years and his first important major work, *The Suppression of the African Slave Trade to the United States*. In 1903, he had published a small classic, still worth re-reading, called *The Souls of Black Folk*. T. Thomas Fortune, of New York, and Monroe Trotter, of Boston, had begun to produce some of the most creative journalistic literature this country has yet to know. And we were making progress in fighting a new form of slavery at the same time. While the characters in the movie *The Color Purple*, might be true to Alice Walker's mind, memory and research, they were not true to black life in general during this period in our history. Miss Walker is a remarkable writer who I personally admire, but in *The Color Purple*, either she had misinterpreted black life or the producers of the film had misinterpreted her book.

In a current movie, *Mississippi Burning* about the murder of the three civil rights activists, Cheney, Schwerner and Goodman, one black and two white, some of the white characters who were villains in real life become heroes in the movie. As a matter of fact, the law enforcement machinery, both at the governmental and local level, dragged their feet in the search for the real murderers in the case. I know some action was taken in this case, but I do not know that justice was done. This is another case where the media is used to manipulate the mind in order to cover up the truth.

The mass media, in general, consists of every visual object that influences the mind. This includes billboard advertisement, commercials, but especially the movies and television. As a result, school textbooks give school children, both black and white, a misconception of the role their respective people have played in the development of that aspect of history called civilization. By the exaggeration of the life and achievements of the Western hero, especially the exaggeration of the achievements of Christopher Columbus, school children in general are of the opinion that most of the discoveries of the world were made by Europeans. They are also of the opinion that Europeans discovered people in order to spread Christianity and civilization. There are many examples where the contrary is true. In their expansion into Africa, Asia and in the Caribbean Islands and in the Americas, there are many places where Europeans destroyed old and well-functioning civilizations and replaced them with a system that did not work for either race. A true evaluation of history proves that invaders and conquerors never spread civilization. Invaders and conquerors spread their way of life in order to control the people they conquer. The mass media has given us another picture of this phenomenon, and we have forgotten a reoccurring fact of history, i.e., powerful people never have to prove anything, and by extension, powerful people never apologize to powerless people for the actions they take in order to remain in power.

This one-dimensional view of history, generally favoring white people, is also projected by the textbook industry. Black students objected to this projection and throughout the country began to call for black studies programs and new organizations came into being for the purpose of correcting these misconceptions about African people in world history. African people throughout the world today are searching for a definition of themselves in the world and in the broad sweep of world history. All too long they looked at the world from the viewpoint of their oppressor. Their new view of the world is sometimes referred to as "Afrocentricity"—a way of looking at the world from the victim's point of view.

Twenty-one years ago, in 1969, the African Heritage Studies Association was established for the following stated purpose:

> To bring together scholars of African descent, dedicating themselves to the preservation, interpretation and academic presentation of the historical and cultural heritage of African peoples both on the ancestral soil of Africa and in the diaspora, in the Americas and throughout the world.

I have no illusions about the role of the mass media in the controlling of people's minds, and I know that eventually we will have to be more aggressive in calling for change and we must develop the personnel and the funds that will give us some control over at least part of the media. We can start by developing programs, textbooks and newspapers that cater to the African people of the world and that could also be of some interest to other people. We need to seriously question an educational system that fails to give proper direction to our children. We also need to establish an independent educational system, starting in our homes. When we face this reality, we will have taken one giant step forward.

I recently returned from a trip to West Africa, where I go often to get my soul refilled. I was in Ghana, and because I go to Africa more than I go to the Bronx, an outer borough in New York City, it was a meaningful journey to me. It was the thirtieth anniversary of my coming to Ghana. I visited first in 1958 and have been going back constantly there and to other parts of Africa. On this trip, I continued something which I had started years ago and still must complete, that is an investigation of the image of Africa in Africa. My question is,

"How is the African looking at himself in the eyes of the world?" The Barbadian writer, with whose quote I open this article, said it best: "What we do for ourselves depends on what we know about ourselves and what we are willing to accept about ourselves." This is what I base my examination on.

When I went to Ghana the last time, I lectured in the slave forts at night by candlelight in order to show my listeners how cruel and harsh the conditions of slavery were. I was attempting to illustrate that in these darkened dungeons their forefathers were brought, and they were there without light, without beds, without toilets and without sympathy. The people that did this to them are still enslaving their descendants one way or the other through the manipulation of information and the manipulation of image. For what you see about yourself depends to a great extent on how you think about yourself and what you are willing to do for yourself.

My second lecture on this trip to Ghana was delivered on Easter morning at El Mina Castle, where the entire apparatus of massive slave holding started. My subject here was the neglected dimensions of the life of Christopher Columbus, one of the biggest frauds in world history. The distortion of his accomplishments has caused a great dilemma. The image of this man makes people assume that someone went someplace and discovered something and some people. The facts are that he attended the school of navigation in Portugal and that in a 1482 expedition he entered Ghana. Cristobal Colon, who later became known as Christopher Columbus, was a common sailor on that expedition. He said in his diary, and I quote, "As man and boy I sailed up and down the Guinea coast for 23 years ...." Subtract 23 from 1482 and what do you get? You get 1459, the period of the Portuguese slave trade. Now you will have to ask the question, "What was Christopher Columbus doing 'up and down the Guinea coast' for those 23 years?" The only answer could be engaging in the Portuguese slave trade. It appears he was a common sailor on those Portuguese ships who never learned his navigation lessons too well because when he finally succeeded in getting support for his voyage, he got lost several times on his way to the so-called New World.

The image of Christopher Columbus in the eyes of the African is positive. But if the true facts of the situation were learned, this image would quickly turn negative. It was this expedition that forced its way into Ghana (then called the Gold Coast) and built the first permanent slave fortification. What we have missed in our history lessons is a speech made by King Ansa of the Gold Coast to the Portuguese. His main message was:

> Inasmuch as we have engaged in honorable (commodity) trade, let us continue that way and don't visit so frequently. (Maybe we can preserve our friendship)

King Ansa's speech to the commander of the Portuguese expedition is included in every well-written history of Ghana. It reads as follows:

> I am not insensible to the high honour which your great master the Chief of Portugal has this day conferred upon me. His friendship I have always endeavoured to merit by the strictness of my dealings with the Portuguese and by my vessels. But never until this day did I observe such a difference in the appearance of his subjects; they have hitherto been meanly attired; were easily contented with the commodity they received; and so far from wishing to continue in this country, were never happy until they could complete their lading and return.
>
> Now I remark a strange difference. A great number, richly dressed, are anxious to be allowed to build houses, and to continue among us. Men of such eminence, conducted by a commander who from his own account seems to have descended from the God who made day and night, can never bring themselves to endure the hardships of this climate; nor would they here be able to procure any of the luxuries that abound in their own country. The passions that are common to all men will inevitably bring on disputes; and it is far preferable that both our nations should continue on the same footing as they hitherto had done, allowing your ships to come and go as usual; the desire of seeing each other occasionally will preserve peace between us . . . .

He saw what was coming and advised against it. The beautiful last lines of his speech are:

The sea and the land being always neighbours are continually at variance and contending who shall give way; the sea with great violence attempting to subdue the land; and the land with equal obstinacy resolving to oppose the sea.

Nana Kwamena Ansa foresaw clearly that his country was going to be preyed upon by another country and could be left helpless, disorganized, and demoralized. I quote his speech here to show the level of development of the Akan language, and if the richness of a language be an index to the natural eloquence of the Akan people, it is a sure indication of a balanced and highly developed mental status. He knew that a force in the history of the world had been met, and what he wanted to do was to stop that force. He was not successful. They came, they stayed, they conquered. Now, of the forty-two slave forts in West Africa, thirty-six are in Ghana. This clearly shows that this country was the real headquarters of the dirty business of slavery.

In many ways, King Ansa had a much better understanding of what was happening in the Africa of his day than present-day Africans have today. Again, I open the subject with a question, in this case, several questions: What is the image of Africa in Africa more than thirty years after the African Independence Explosion, starting with Ghana in March of 1957? What is the image of Africa in the textbooks used in schools attended by African children? What is the image of Africa in the churches built by the missionaries and, to some extent, still controlled by missionaries? Except for Nigeria, Ghana, and a few schools in Arab-dominated North Africa, I found no textbooks being used in African schools that were written by Africans. Therefore, the image of Africa in Africa is still colonialist, with no emphasis on what happened in Africa before the arrival of the Europeans. J.C. deGraft Johnson's concise but all-too-brief history of Africa, *African Glory*, is read in Ghana, but it is not used in the school system. Another Ghanaian historian, Adu Boahen, has written extensively on Ghana and West Africa. Especially useful is his book, *Topics in West African History*.

The educated Africans worship a God assigned to them by their former colonial masters. The Arabs in North Africa, the Sudan, and in other parts of Africa often act as though there were no gods at all before the emergence of Islam. Rough statistics that are often forgotten are: there are approximately 127 million people in the world. Seventy percent of them live in Africa. There are more Africans in Africa who are Moslems than there are Arabs in the world. My point in calling attention to this fact is that numerically Africans outnumber Arabs as members of the Islamic faith and should be in a position to change both the images and the textbooks in the predominantly Moslem countries of Africa. No people can be spiritually, politically, or psychologically free when they worship an image of God assigned to them by another people. The new revolution in Africa that will usher in real independence will start when Africans begin to look at all aspects of their life based on their spirituality, their culture and their political interests.

Africa is the home of many countries, many cultures and many religions. In this way it is pluralistic. In the work for the unification of Africa and for projection of those images that inspire African people to be better human beings the world over, it is monolithic. Therefore, the spiritual and political future of Africa depends to a real extent on the understanding of a Pan-Africanist approach to Africa's need and self-interest. Africa may need to step back into its history in order to move forward into its future. Africans need to reclaim some of the images of their own creation, and they need to reject the image of Africa projected by missionaries, colonialists, travel writers and adventurers. Africa, in spite of over thirty years of pseudo-independence and partial independence, still has an unfavorable image of itself in relationship to Europe and a favorable image of the European that is undeserved.

At the end of my last trip to Ghana I ran into a good friend, the lady of letters in Ghana. She is one of the finest female writers of our time. Efu Southerland is in charge of the Council For Children and she is trying to fight to change the image of the African inside of Africa. She is fighting against the wide-spread sale of white dolls to black children inside Africa itself. The dolls are manufactured in Ghana by a Syrian. This is ironic. The first changes of the image of Africa came from Western Asia, and these people are still there, doing the same thing.

We need to look at Judaism, Christianity, Islam and all of the remade religions deriving from substantive elements in Africa. The creators of these religions turned on the African people and changed the image of the African people in power in the world. We need to look at Africa since its independence and look at every single textbook in Africa.

Nearly every book is modeled on the European concept of history and nearly every government is modeled on the European concept of handling power. The oppressed can never handle power the way his oppressor handles it and handle it for the benefit of his own people.

We quickly forget that the African concept of social living was the basis of power. We quickly forget that the African had every element that went, ultimately, into the making of a mistaken concept called socialism. They not only had every element of socialism, they practiced it, and they lived by it, before the first European had a shoe or lived in a house that had a window. We need to ask ourselves why, then, do we cater to and take our image from a very young people who came out of the ice-box of Europe and began to make a virtue out of a physical defect, the lack of color. Because they saw their lack of color as a deficiency, they changed this defect into a virtue to make us think it was good. We, all too often, buy this and spend our time trying to be like them instead of seeing them for what they are and understanding the importance of being ourselves.

We need to look at Africa before the Asians entered it, cut her strength and set her up for the European invaders. Africans have no fascination with color, as such, but accepted it as a very normal thing, just like the wind and the rain. When you read the diaries of the early European explorers, especially Mungo Park, they tell of going into an area in Upper Niger where the people had never seen a white man. The people had heard that these were people without skin and they wondered what crime their mother could have committed to be punished by giving birth to a child who had no skin. The African image of a human being was the image of someone blessed with some color, and they pitied Park. One woman heard that they ate the pig. This area was partly Moslem at that time and this woman was curious about how they ate the pig. She brought a pig and tied it near the chair Mungo Park usually sat on and waited for him to notice it. They were surprised to learn that pig-eaters skinned the pig and cooked it. My point in telling this story is to show that the African's attitude toward the first white men they saw was not one of prejudice or hatred, but an attitude that they were seeing an unnatural people cursed by the lack of skin.

The Africans had a broad concept of spirituality. They believed that God was in everything and part of every living thing, and that spirituality was a part of the totality of life. These foreigners began to narrow down their beliefs to religions and twisted them into something called denominations. They kept narrowing them down until another set of foreigners created a religion out of African substance, put a gloss of Europeanism on it and told the world this was the "true" faith. The African lived side by side with many of his religions without changing their images, or saying that theirs was true and everything else was false. He believed that this was his choice. If you made another choice, you had a right to do so. In these societies, before being disrupted by foreigners, families lived close to grandma and grandpa because their home was often the home you were born in. If more space was needed, you just called on as many men as you needed and added more room on to the house; but you built no separate house for them. They had no word for jail, because no one had ever gone to one. They had no word for orphanage, because no one had ever thrown away children. They had no word for nursing home or old peoples' home, because no one threw away their mother or their grandma. They lived in a humane society where the image was that everything belonged to everybody and that grandma and grandpa were closer to the deity—and in part were deities themselves—and that you had to take care of them because they would go before you and say the good word to the deity for you. The foreigners did not see this image of Africa, and their influence changed Africa's concept of humanity and of the deity, and subsequently, the world's concept of the deity.

We need to deal with the Hebrew entry into Africa, because they palmed off the greatest hoax on the world, and they have done the most to colonize the world and to confuse people about the deity. They created gods of wrath, gods of thunder, gods of fire, jealous gods, vengeful gods, and gods who lusted after the women of the earth. They created gods that would burn you in hell if your soul was not in order. They quite forgot that the African had no destructive gods and no image of a god who was not kind and caring. They quite forgot that the god of the African would weigh the soul to see if it were ready to go into the beyond. If it were not, it would be sent back and given time to get ready. No one was sent to hell, because there was no concept of hell. Hell was an invention of the Hebrews who misinterpreted African history then and misinterpret it now. They took old African stories that were told to illustrate a point, personified themselves and put themselves inside the story and said, "This happened to us." We accepted this and never questioned it. In spite of the fact that many modern Jewish scholars have repudiated most of it, we still accept it. We have not yet called Africa our holy land. Somebody else's land becomes holy to us and he is a descendant of an invader and Africa is not his home. We have yet to understand their history; otherwise why are we still singing, "Go down Moses, tell old Pharaoh to let my people go"? Now see how ridiculous that sounds? Have we asked, "Who was Moses?" and "Who was the Pharaoh?"

The Pharaoh was an African nationalist. He chased some Hebrews out of Africa who were threatening to betray it after they were befriended by Africans who saved them from famine, gave them homes, gave them land, and gave them women, too. When Africa was invaded, they didn't join their African benefactors; they joined the invaders against the Africans. We know from religious literature that Joseph was an emissary between the Hebrews and the Pharaoh. The Bible tells us that "Joseph died, his family died and a king arose who knew not Joseph." Why is it, then, that in so many Baptist churches we quote this with such glee, without trying to understand who was "the king who knew not Joseph?" He was an African king, back in power, who now began to ask questions. He decreed that those who were willing to obey African law could stay; those who did not wish to obey would have to go. What was this all about? He was doing a little housecleaning.

Moses was a prince who grew up in the royal palace. There is no proof in existence that he was a Hebrew. There is no proof in existence that he came out of the house of Levi. The Bible tells us that he had committed a crime, the punishment of which was banishment. Moses was in serious trouble and jumped at the opportunity to lead the Hebrews out of Egypt. This was not a religious conversion, but an arrangement of convenience. Did you think that the story as told by the Hebrews was so sacred that it could not be examined? Jewish scholars are now examining it and saying that there was no exodus, and there was no necessity for an exodus to occur. Further, the Bible says that the Hebrews walked into Africa. Why couldn't they walk out? The

Suez Canal was not built then, and there was nothing else stopping them. We never question what comes out of a preacher's mouth, and we have been living with an image of non-sense and untruth that is damaging to the image we hold of ourselves and damaging to our children and the image they hold of themselves.

I am a highly spiritual human being, with suspicions of all forms of organized religion. I do not need a minister to preach the Ten Commandments to me: I have enough humanity and common sense to obey them, or violate them strategically, to give me peace. I believe it shows a lack of common sense and common decency to violate your neighbor's wife. If you have one of your own and have access to others, what is the point to it? When we deal with the bad and negative images of Africa coming out of the Hebrew religion, we will deal with the negativism that we are willing to accept today. No one questions the Queen of Sheba story. She is said to have said, "I am black, but comely, you daughters of Jerusalem." No one would have said that in that period of history when no one boasted or apologized for color. What was done in this instance was to read contemporary prejudice back into an ancient situation. Did they do enough research to understand the nature of the Queen of Sheba's visit?

The Ethiopian commercial czar, Tamerand, went to the Queen and told her that King Solomon owed a lot of money to Ethiopia for the red gold that he had been using to decorate his temples. He complained that every time he went to King Solomon to ask for payment, Solomon would give some wise saying, quote some cliché, some sage advice or some parable. He asked his Queen to see if she could collect the debt for him and said, "Incidentally, while you're there, check out his wisdom." Her visit became part of history; the real reason for her visit was lost from history.

When the Queen of Sheba left Africa her private bodyguards, her train of guards, keepers, and footmen, was three miles long. Ethiopia was thirty times the size of Judea, and her private bodyguards numbered more than the armed forces of Judea. What would Ethiopia be doing bowing to a postage-stamp country like that? Why would she go to Judea and say, "I'm black, but comely," etc., etc., etc? With her magnificent and impressive entry into the country she could very well have said, "Hey, man, give me my money or face my army, and I have an even larger army at home."

Now let's look at Solomon. I don't think he was a gentleman. His royal guest was far more powerful than he. Why would this man, without any rehearsal, without any thorough acquaintance with her, feed her salt and when she got up to get some water assault her? He wasn't much of a gentleman, and this was no way to treat a royal personage. Now that we have an image of Solomon, can we correct the image we have of the Queen of Sheba?

To say that the Hebrew concept of history is negative does not make me anti-semitic. The religion is now controlled by converted Europeans who are not semitic and who have absolutely no relationship to the biblical Jew at all. I doubt if there is anybody on the face of the earth who is a direct descendant of the biblical Jew except African people. These people, now claiming to be part of that faith, are latter-day people who in the thirteenth century, looking at an argument between the Arabs and the Christians, decided they did not want to be part of the argument and chose an alternative, a third religion, one that was neither Islam nor Christianity. They studied the religion and projected themselves onto the world as though they had invented it. There was nothing wrong with their joining the faith, and there are people throughout the world who follow the Hebrew faith and who see no need to claim descendance from the biblical people. In 70 A.D., when the Hebrews were rapidly multiplying in Rome, the Romans expelled them and destroyed their temples. There is no evidence that any of them went to Europe. Very few went to the Middle East. Some of them migrated down into Africa and lived in ancient Ghana for over 400 years. These Middle Eastern and African Jews are left out of the history of the Jewish people because the European Jew wishes to claim all the prerogatives of the faith for himself, so he can interpret the faith as he wishes.

Jewish scholars have said that the so-called Falasha Jews of Ethiopia practice the faith closer to the traditional way than any other Jew on the face of the earth. Yet when the Israeli Jews wanted to take the Ethiopian Jew to Israel and "convert him according to our concept," the Ethiopian Jew could have told them, "You're the one that needs to convert because I'm the authentic and you are the copy." This subject becomes a little sensitive to a whole lot of people because our ministers are not willing to deal with it. You can hear the singers in our church-es singing, "My home is over Jordan. Deep river, my home is over

Jordan." How did our home get to be over Jordan? What's over Jordan that belongs to you? If you study African imperialism, you would have a clear distinction between what is home and what is a colony, and that the area of the Jordan river was once an African colony, but was never our home.

My main point here is that the Roman mismanagement of Christianity, the Romans' tampering with the faith of it, tampering with the images of it, changed the images of the religion in the Holy Roman Empire and throughout the world. In the Holy Roman Empire there were three African Popes, who are nearly left out of the history of the church. There was the African who is considered the "Father of the Church," St. Augustine, who, when he saw the manifestations of this religion, said it made him laugh. He said, "They're trying to give us a religion that we had thousands of years ago."

Once the Romans had disgraced themselves by the mismanagement of Christianity, a young camel boy called for reform. Failing to get reform, he called for a new religion. This religion became Islam. Islam is a sensitive issue with black people. It is an unoriginal religion, the most unoriginal, unimaginative religion of them all. It has no great poetry, very little great literature, and no recognition of the role of Africans in its making. It is a bastard child of Christianity and Judaism, and it came into being so fast that it didn't even have time to choose its own saints. It was perhaps time for a new religion to come into being, because both Judaism and Christianity had been so disgraced that the Africans and the people of Western Asia saw them as the mutilated substance of great religions they once had and were ready to turn against them. When Islam rose, with its simplicity, large numbers of Africans converted to it, but they didn't examine it then, and they don't examine it now.

We have a lot of scholars who are Moslem, but we have no scholars who are scholars about Islam and its manifestations. We have few scholars who can explain how it came to power and who can talk about the good it did along with the bad. The African was the military arm of early Islam. It was the African that took it to Spain, but Arab historians to this day act as though the Africans were not in Spain. When you go to Spain and see the black pictures, the Spanish guide will look at you with a straight face and say they are white.

I am not a Moslem, but I have a great deal of respect for what the honorable Elijah Muhammad did. He dealt with image. He dealt with image, and he tried to restore something which we needed restored and some things which we still need restored: the concept of black people managing a nation, the concept of nation management and nation preservation, and the awareness that they haven't always been dependent on other people. Booker T. Washington, if you understand him and his preparation for self-reliance, said the same thing. DuBois, if you understand him, said the same thing, politically. Marcus Garvey said it more forthrightly, politically, culturally and otherwise. Elijah was a continuation of that same trend.

Judaism, Christianity, and Islam are all carbon copies of African religions. We need to go back and take the original and deal from the original rather than the carbon. Once we did that we would be on the way to restoring the spirituality of the world because spirituality is all-inclusive. Religions and denominations are cultist. They put people in groups, they divide people, they divide families; and this misinterpretation of African spirituality made these religions into something they were never intended to be. They made them into political instruments. With the rise of Christianity in Africa and in Western Asia, the Romans stopped killing Christians and became Christians, strategically. They immediately began to change the images within Christianity: the image of Christ and the image of the deities. They declared war on the African Christians for control of the church. I have said before that if the Europeans had to obey three of the Ten Commandments, they'd go out of business in 24 hours. If they had to obey these Commandments, they would have to give up their power and would have to return the greatest piece of stolen property in the history of the world: the theft of African people out of Africa would all have to be returned, as stolen property.

We, in this country, are a nation within a nation searching for a nationality. A people without a nationality will never be whole. If someone asks you who you are and you say, "I am an American," and don't qualify it, you're in trouble. You ask a German who he is and he makes it very plain, "I am an American who came from Germany." Ask an Italian, and he will say, "I am an American, but my family came from Italy." You have problems if you're not a part of a nation that has accepted you because you have not made the nation either accept you or respect you or the fact of your presence.

We African people have misconceptions about who we are and what we can do. We must realize that potentially the greatest political body of African people on the face of the earth are those in the United States. The fact that we have not developed that potential is partly our fault, and partly because we do not look at the image of ourselves correctly. We have not mended our own fences and built our homes and done our own plumbing and rescued our own communities in the United States, where we have the trained personnel, and we have yet to make an assessment of what we have to offer to Africa and the world.

We have not added up our credits. We are the only branch of African people on the face of the earth trained in combined operational warfare: land, air and sea. If Africa is going to be delivered, it will take more than guerilla fighters to do it. It will take men who know roads and bridges and how to put an air force over a city. It will take people who can land ships and build hospitals. We have been trained to do these things for our oppressor. Why can't we go to Africa and do them for Africa?

One of the main reasons why I continued to study the image of Africa within Africa was because I know that Africa's Independence Explosion brought courage to the whole African world and that the Western world, left or right, never wanted Africa to emerge with stable states. There was one image they had to destroy. They are still fighting to destroy that image: the image of a Pan-African Head of State, the image of Kwame Nkrumah.

Once Ghana became independent, with a Pan-African as head of state, educated in the United States, and who had mingled with us as part of the old Harlem History Club, who was familiar with us, he brought us in droves back to Africa. There were 5,000 black Americans working in Ghana while Nkrumah was President. Here at last, Pan-Africanism, a wandering motherless child, had finally found a home.

One time, in March 1957, he stood at midnight and said, "At last the long night is over; Ghana, our Beloved country is free forever." It was time for every African on the face of the earth to sit down and reappraise Pan-Africanism. The motherless child had found a home. All that Pan-Africanism was before now had to be changed, because now we had the land basis of Pan-Africanism. It had found a home in Africa itself. It had found sympathy with an African head of state.

The Western world did not want this example to exist so they began to knock off the heads of states. Every Pan-Africanist head of state was knocked off. And they are still knocking off heads of state. Thomas Sankara of Burkina Faso was knocked off because he met with African heads of state, he stuck out his feet and said, "I'm the only one here wearing a pair of shoes made by my own people, leather from cows grown by my own people, tanned and processed in my own country. You are wearing shoes from France and shirts from Belgium. You could change the economy of your country if you made your own clothes and ate the foods you grew and developed your economy based on self-reliance."

Nobody in the Western world intends for African people to be free of Western domination, and the left is just as bad as the right. The left no more wants South Africa to be free than the capitalists do. They want it to be free if they can control it and no other way. The Europeans are interested in control and want to control, by any means necessary. The European sold himself to the world as the controller, the governor of things, and we bought this image. Once we gain confidence in ourselves and realize that Europe had a hell of a time getting itself off the ground. Even at the height of the British Empire, there were Englishmen eating out of garbage cans. And we assumed that they had built a perfect society. We assumed that because we have not been able to distinguish between mechanization and civilization. We have not learned that to have a civilization, people must first be civil. This man is not civil; therefore, he could only build mechanics, not a civilization.

Let me give you a gruesome case in point. When Hitler wanted to destroy the Jews, the train arrived on time—that's good mechanics. The gas he needed to murder the people arrived on time, and the people arrived on time. Is this civilization or mechanics? You have to make a clear distinction between the two. I have seen people who have never worn shoes who are more civilized than those who tend elevators. We have to redefine the image of a civilized man. The image of a civilized man is one who is civil. The European, who uses a lot of mechanics, is not civil. Our misunderstanding of this has begun a whole fight among ourselves.

It is a stupid fight. The African is telling the Afro-American that he does not come from a nation so he cannot be much of a man. The

Caribbean tells the Afro-American that he has no culture. Both are talking about slavemaster's values. If you are arguing about African culture, I'd be happy to hear your argument. We are arguing about the slavemaster's culture and we are forgetting some of the basic things in our own history.

In a recent talk in Jamaica, I decided I had been as courteous as I could be, so I told the truth. I asked the question, "If Marcus Garvey were alive today, where in the African world would he be safe?" The answers were slow in coming, but we finally agreed that in Jamaica he might be stoned to death; among the "light brigade" in Washington he might be stoned to death also; in Atlanta, where the middle-class integrationist holds sway, Marcus Garvey wouldn't stand a chance. In Bedford-Stuyvesant, among the Rastas and the few nationalist-conscious Caribbean people, he would stand a chance because he was about nation-building, he was about consciousness; he wasn't about integrating into someone else's house; he was about building his own house.

Now I am going to conclude on a subject that has no conclusion. What we need to look for when we look at ourselves is to look at our failures. We need to look at our failure to see the image of ourselves in power. We need to look at the failure in our own personality, our inability to accept other black people in power as being the authentic holders of power.

We need to look deep into ourselves and what the propaganda of the mass media has done to us and how we have played a role in spreading this propaganda. Anybody who accepts all the propaganda they see about black men and black women proves that they don't understand the dispensers of the propaganda, and they don't understand black men, black women, or themselves. I gave a lecture on black teenage pregnancy to some black professional women who were sorority members. They were so disappointed with my message they didn't even send me the honorarium. As is my custom, I raised some principled questions. I said,

I am not here to get the black man off the hook. I think every black man who sires a child should be responsible for that child. With no apology. But I want to look at the historical origins of this responsibility. There were no teenage pregnancies in Africa.

There were no men in Africa physically assaulting women, calling them outside of their names. There were no men deserting homes in Africa. Where did this deserter come from? Who created him? I am not saying that we did not have to deal with him. I am saying that we have to deal with him if we are going to survive. But who created him? He was created out of a circumstance alien to the culture that produced him, and this is something we have not studied sufficiently. This man is reacting to a cultural incubator that he could not breed in properly, being forced into somebody else's cultural incubator. They not only did not want to hear that they could not integrate into this incubator, they did not want to hear that it was not a desirable or do-able thing.

One summer in Africa, near the end of a trip, I reminded the group, who were all black, "You have been a long time in Africa and you haven't heard anybody calling anyone else any vile names, and you haven't heard children fighting among themselves. The reason for this is that you are seeing a people in the cultural incubator that gave them birth, and they understand it, feel comfortable with it and are not rebelling against it. We, in the Western world, are in an alien cultural incubator, do not feel comfortable with it, and are rebelling against it. We are like a body rejecting an alien organ." When we deal with the whole concept of culture and religion and how one relates to the other, we will no longer be dealing with images, we will be dealing with reality.

My main point is that it is historically our time to assume the responsibility of ruling nations. It is time for us to start making our own shoes, to grow our own cattle, to learn how to tan our own leather. It is time to start trading with our own. It is time to stop using things we do not make. It is time to take care of our own communities, to teach our own children, to support our own families. It is time for us to project this out into the world with the awareness that we won't do any of this until we can see ourselves in this capacity. Until we believe we belong there, we will not get there.

I believe that once we change the image of ourselves we will change the image of humanity, and subsequently we will change the power structure of the whole world and leave for generations still unborn a map and a plan of courage in nation-building that will last and change the world. We are perhaps the only people that can do this because, since we gave the world the first humanity, we can give the world a new humanity at a time when it needs it most.

In restating the central focus of this paper, I repeat: Because what we see about ourselves often influences what we do about ourselves, the role of images and the question of how they control our minds are more important now, in our media-saturated society, than ever before. For the last 500 years, the history of African people throughout the world has been told through the slavery experience—only a short period in our life, considering that we are the oldest of the world's peoples.

There is a need now to look behind the slavery curtain in order to see what African people achieved as an independent people, before slavery. Because this independence existed for thousands of years before Europe itself existed, we should examine the far-reaching power of a European-created media over the minds of most of the world. Prior to the slave trade and European colonialism, which began in the fifteenth century, most of the peoples of the world had a concept of God shaped by their own culture and their own understanding of spirituality. They generally saw God, or any deity, as a figure resembling themselves. The expanding presence of the Europeans made them consider not only a new God but a new image of God as well.

Because the Europeans did not have enough manpower to control the vast territories and populations they were taking over in Africa and Asia, they began to use the media as a form of mind control, colonizing people around the world, just as they also colonized information about the world. Today, the mass media include every visual object that influences the mind—billboard advertisements, commercials and more, but especially movies and television.

Since we don't usually think of school textbooks as an aspect of the mass media, we don't fully understand that both black and white children have a misconception about the role their respective people have played in the development of civilization. Because of the exaggeration of the lives and achievements of Western heroes, especially Christopher Columbus, school children in general are of the opinion that most of the world's explorations and discoveries were made by Europeans. They also believe that Europeans went on discovery missions to other countries in order to spread Christianity and civilization. The contrary is true in many cases. In their expansion into Africa, Asia, the Caribbean Islands and the Americas, the Europeans destroyed many old and well-functioning societies, usually for political or economic gain. The mass media has given us another picture of this phenomenon in history, and we have forgotten a recurring fact of history: Powerful people never have to prove anything to anyone. And by extension, powerful people never apologize to powerless people for the actions they take in order to remain in power.

Because of the prevailing one-dimensional view of history that generally favors white people, who control the textbook industry, African-American students throughout the country began in the 1960s to call for Black Studies Programs to correct some misconceptions about African people in world history.

We will have taken one giant step forward when we face this reality: Powerful people never teach powerless people how to take their power away from them. Education is one of the most sensitive arenas in the life of a people. Its role is to be honest and true, to tell a people where they have been and what they have been, where they are and what they are. Most importantly, the role of education is to tell a people where they still must go and what they still must be.

THE CRISIS OF THE NEGRO INTELLECTUAL BY HAROLD CRUSE: A REAPPRAISAL OF SOME NEGLECTED ASPECTS OF THE CRISIS

▼

WHEN THIS BOOK WAS PUBLISHED, twenty years ago, I observed that the title, though interesting, did not reflect the contents of the book. The crisis of the intellectual of African descent throughout the world and down through the ages is more complex than Professor Cruse's analysis. The crisis that he refers to is deeply rooted in the relationship of African and non-African people. It is also rooted in African people's traditional hospitality to strangers who often came to Africa as guests and stayed as conquerors.

The presently reissued paperback edition of the book refers to the "historical analysis of the failure of black leadership" contained in the book. This statement is misleading. The book is more about Professor Harold Cruse's criticism and disagreement with African world leadership. I do not doubt that this book is still as relevant now as it was when it was first published, nearly a generation ago. This is a book that needed to be written with more insight about African world leadership and the complications African-Americans face in their attempt to lead the one ethnic group that did not come to the United States expecting to be treated as full citizens. In a nation of emigrants, we are the emigrants who came against our will. The black intellectual has not fully understood how we differ radically from the other emigrant groups. This is the basis of some of their misconceptions about the United States and the political world in general.

There is now an urgent need for African intellectuals, the world over, especially those living outside Africa, to approach the subject of African people with a world view. African people are still the most written about and the least known of the human races. There is a need to look at Africans through African eyes, based on an understanding of African history, culture and humanity. We need to understand what mistakes we have made in our relationship with other people and how these relationships are reverberating throughout the African world today and retarding progress.

We need to look at that African nation that the Greeks referred to as Egypt. And we need to challenge those bigoted and misguided scholars who assumed that Egypt is not a part of Africa. There should be more reference to Nile Valley civilization as against Egyptian civilization, because the Nile River stretches 4,000 miles into the body of Africa, and the nation that the world later knew as Egypt was a composite of the cultures of many different people along the banks of this mighty river that was the world's first cultural highway. While Egypt produced the longest and most enduring civilization ever known to man, the achievement cannot be credited to Egypt alone. The civilization of Egypt was a culmination of many civilizations that existed in the Nile Valley.

We need to recognize that Egypt and Africa in general have always been a prize for foreigners, a prize that they insisted on conquering by any means necessary. Africa is and has always been the world's richest continent. It is full of poor and sometimes starving people today because foreigners are in charge of their riches. Africa has always had and still has things other people want, think they can't do without and don't want to pay for. Africans have always been and still are politically naive in their relationship to foreigners. Nile Valley civilization reached its height without any assistance from foreigners, and when the foreigners came, they eventually did more harm than good.

According to the biblical account, in the 1700s B.C., the Hebrews, now referred to as Jews, under the leadership of Abraham entered Africa in search of food, land and employment. The Africans, in their generosity, fulfilled these life-saving needs. In fact, the Hebrews entered world history through the visit to Africa. Very little was known of them as a people before this visit. When Egypt and the Nile Valley were invaded in 1675 B.C. by the Hyksos, sometimes referred to as the shepherd-kings, these Hebrews became permanent as their collaborators, clerks and assistants. During this period, the Hebrews produced the world's first wheeler-dealer politician known as Joseph the Provider. They did very little for the African benefactors who had befriended them. Black historians, intellectuals and teachers have not examined this period in our history. Because of their cultist fascination for a Jewish survival book, best known to the world as the Bible, the African intellect has not examined the literature of the period, or religious literature in general.

The real failure of the African intellect universally is its failure to understand African humanity and its relationship to strangers who never reward Africans for their friendship. Very few African intellectuals are well-schooled in the history of the world. They are too contented with cast-off and hand-me-down religions given to them by missionaries, adventurers and colonialists. There is a respectable body of literature on this subject that very few of the African intellectuals have cared to read, such as Josef ben-Jochannan's *Black Man of the Nile and His Family, Africa: Mother of Western Civilization* and the *African Origins of the Major "Western Religions."*

John G. Jackson was writing about these subjects in the 1930s. Although some of his work has been reprinted, it is still not widely read: *Was Jesus Christ A Negro?* and *The African Origins of the Myths and Legends of the Garden of Eden, Pagan Origins of the Christ Myth,* and *Ethiopia and the Origin of Civilization.* John Jackson's work was extended in his two major works: *Man, God and Civilization* and *Christianity Before Christ.*

I think the African intellectuals and the world's intellectuals, in general, have relied too heavily on the Bible and have neglected major interpretations of the Bible and biblical literature, such as Sir James Frazer's two-volume work *Folklore in the Old Testament* and two books by Alvin Boyd Kuhn, *Who Is This King of Glory?* and *Shadow of the Third Century.*

The American dream was not dreamed for us and the American promise was not made to us. The founding fathers declared us to be three-fifths of a man; therefore, less than a full human being. The legal and legislative literature of this country has not, as yet, repudiated this classification. When the pledge of allegiance to "liberty and justice for all" was made, it was not made to the African-American. And from the very beginning, what was referred to as black leadership was, in some cases, an attempt to integrate into a house where they were not wanted because they were not considered to be full human beings.

At that early point in our history in the United States we were losing our African identity while desperately trying to hold on to it. This dilemma is explained, in great detail in a new book by Professor Sterling Stuckey of Northwestern University entitled, *Slave Culture: Nationalist Theory and The Foundations of Black America*. Much earlier, Carter G. Woodson dealt with other aspects of the subject in his book, *The Miseducation of the Negro*.

Mr. Cruse has opened some new doors with his book and raised some vital issues relative to the survival of African people in the United States in particular and in the world in general. He has not proven to be equal to the kind of historical analysis the situation demanded to give a clearer vision of what the future for Africans can be. In general, his book is full of anger without creative direction and facts without adequate explanation. He raises more questions than he has answers for. The greatest value of his book is that it is the work of an alarmist. Alarmists have a role to play in history; however, very often they put a subject on the agenda that they are not equal to handling. Mr. Cruse has put many subjects on the agenda for black intellectuals to handle that cannot and should not be ignored if we are to survive as a people.

In this paper I intend to focus on aspects of the intellectual crisis that Mr. Cruse neglected. First, we have to look at the book itself, the achievement of Professor Cruse, its shortcomings notwithstanding. In the first section of his book, "Individualism and the 'Open Society'," Professor Cruse, while showing insight into blacks who are in flight from blackness, fails to understand that African people in the United States have been in a white bind, in one way or the other, since they arrived in 1619. They were indoctrinated by an educational system or mass media that told them outright, or specifically implied, that all values were white and the best way to survive was to strive to be most unlike yourself. This is a crime committed against a people. This is one of the many crimes committed against us that we must deal with. We are the only ethnic group in the United States that is somewhat confused about our historical origins. All too often we fail to relate to land, history and culture outside of the United States.

If Professor Cruse were a better student of history, he could have written a much better section on American history. He would have understood the integrationist policy of the NAACP. While volumes have been written on this organization, it must not be overlooked that it was not originally established by blacks for blacks. It was originally established by whites for blacks, and whole groups of blacks came into the organization to follow rules established by whites. Today, to some extent, this is still true of this organization.

The NAACP was a creation of white liberalism. As an organization it has always limited itself in what it could do. A small shelf of books has been written on the founding and development of the NAACP. There are times, especially in the South, when whites consider the NAACP to be a radical organization, and it was radical in comparison to some others that were supposed to be committed to black liberation in the United States. Somewhere along the line, the NAACP failed to keep up with the times and face reality. African-Americans were fighting for justice, not integration. If justice could be obtained, integration was something they could have taken or left.

When you have an eye for the negative, a reoccurring theme in Harold Cruse's book, the negative is not hard to find. I was familiar with the theater group he refers to at the Harlem YMCA. I was active in an earlier theater group at the same YMCA performing in plays with an historical background—in essence, teaching history by depicting great characters and events in our history. What we did was just the opposite of what he saw. I am not in disagreement with what he saw because I know it to be true, but the other side of what he saw was the old Harlem History Club, which also met at the Harlem YMCA. It met under leadership of Willis N. Huggins, with its main emphasis on the recovery and understanding of African values. The currents of African-American social striving moves many ways and Harold Cruse has seemed to see only one way. I have lived through these same times and I have lived another way, a way far more positive than negative.

At the time that Harold Cruse was being introduced to the theatrical activities of the Harlem YMCA, the old Harlem History Club, later called The Blyden Society, was breaking up after the death of its leader, Dr. Willis N. Huggins. The Sunday meetings of the club had attracted a number of outstanding members, people not too well known at this time. One was a young student from the Gold Coast, now called Ghana, who at the time was called Francis K. Nkrumah later known to the world as Kwame Nkrumah. Another occasional visitor to the History Club was Nnamdi Azikiwe, later to become the President of Nigeria.

In a small way, the Harlem History Club was the forerunner of what is now being called, "Black Studies Programs." It was my beginning and proving ground as a historian. Two of the earlier books of Willis N. Huggins and John G. Jackson were developed from lecture notes prepared for the Harlem History Club.

The second section of his book, "Harlem Background—The Rise of Economic Nationalism and Origins of Cultural Revolution," I consider to be one of the better sections in the book. It shows some insight into the formation of New York City. This city is not a city at all, but a combination of cultures that have not crystallized because the political elements that rule it have not wanted it to crystallize. New York City is a city of different ethnic cultures. If these cultures ever came together it would be difficult for the politicians to play one against the other. New York has the potential of being America's richest cultural city. If this ever happens, we would have to discard the "melting pot" theory in favor of a symbolic "salad bowl" approach—the mixing of cultures without the destroying of cultures, a cross-fertilization. The great complication in New York City, when Professor Cruse wrote the book and now, is that the powers that be in a city like New York have not made up their minds about the place of African people and some other people who cannot be classified as either black or white.

With the section entitled, "Mass Media and Cultural Democracy," I have little argument except with the phraseology and the overplaying of the role of the Marxists of that period. The Communist Party was a politically opportunistic organization then, and it is one now. They never really understood the problems of the black American and they approached that problem with assumptions that were alien to the problem. They did not recognize the political dimensions of the Harlem Renaissance. They were opposed to most of the dynamic political and cultural dimensions that came out of the period of the Harlem Renaissance, especially the massive movement organized by Marcus Mosiah Garvey. Marxists preached the class problem in situations relative to blacks where the class problem did not apply and held no significance. A black millionaire, when he is downtown, has as much difficulty getting a taxicab as a black short-order cook. With us the color problem hold precedence over the class problem.

In this section, Professor Cruse's chronology of the political events from the crisis following World War I to the eve of the depression shows some insight that needs serious consideration. What he missed in his appraisal of this period was that this was a period of reclaiming our African history and looking at it from an African point of view. It was the period of great teaching. There was the teaching of William Leo Hansberry at Howard University, who taught a philosophical approach on African people the world over that would go into the making of the Schomburg Collection. This was the period of Charles S. Siefort, Richard B. Moore and Willis N. Huggins and the great activists from the Caribbean Islands calling attention to the missing pages from our history. These men were Hubert Harrison and J.A. Rogers. They were all more positive than negative. There was Claude McKay and his famous poem, "If We Must Die." Of course, we had a crisis, but I think we attempted to clarify the confusion. E. Franklin Frazier wrote his early essay criticizing black intellectuals. Alain Locke had compiled an anthology that is considered to be the best book to come out of the Harlem Renaissance, called *The New Negro*. I am not saying that what Professor Cruse has said is not true: I am saying that some things he neglected to say are also true.

Section four of this chapter entitled, "Cultural Leadership and Cultural Democracy," begins:

> Racial democracy is, at the same time, cultural democracy; and the question of cultural democracy in America is posed in a way never before seen or considered in other societies. This uniqueness results historically from the manner in which American cultural developments have been influenced by the Negro presence. Since a cultural philosophy has been cultivated to deny this truth, it remains for the Negro intellectual to create his own philosophy and to bring the facts of cultural history in focus with the cultural practices of the present. In advanced

societies it is not the race politicians or the 'rights' leaders who create the new ideas and the new images of life and man. That role belongs to the artists and the intellectuals of each generation ....

It is often forgotten that the political impact of the Garvey Movement on the Harlem Renaissance gave this period of black self-awareness a meaning it otherwise would not have had.

While, in the main, I accept Professor Cruse's analysis of the culture of the period, I feel a need to call to his attention the fact that the culture of African people has never been accepted as part of the legitimate culture of the United States, although it is the most original culture in the U.S. It was then and it still is now. In a country where the cultures of most white ethnic groups have neither been accepted nor integrated into the main culture, some questions have to be asked about what the country intends its culture to be. In a country that still feeds on the culture of African people while denying its existence, this continued denial creates a dilemma that needs further analysis, maybe a separate book.

Section One of Chapter II, entitled "1920s—1930s West Indian Influence," is an important section but it contains some misleading information about the Caribbean influence on the United States in relationship to the black American problem. I think this section would have been sharper if it had shown that there was a previous encounter between black Americans and Caribbean people that was not cluttered by white people. This is a problem that needed to be looked at in retrospect. There was another period in African-American and Caribbean relations that was far more positive than the encounter presented here. This was the period when Prince Hall came to the United States, on the eve of the American Revolution, and established the first fraternal African Lodge. This was the period of John B. Russwurm. Russwurm became an editor of *Freedom's Journal*. He later went to Liberia and established a newspaper which is still in existence. While he was in Liberia he became governor of one of the provinces there. During this period Robert Campbell accompanied Martin Delany on a trip to Nigeria to search for a place for a settlement of black Americans and Caribbeans. In general, it was a period when the "free" blacks in New England made contact with the "free" blacks in the Caribbean, and they worked well together. The blacks in the Caribbean did not call themselves New Englanders, and the blacks in New England did not call themselves Caribbeans. They called themselves Africans.

There is a need to look, again, at the Caribbean figures in the Harlem Renaissance. The case for Claude McKay was a little more positive than presented here. He returned to the United States from Europe and was briefly the editor of the magazine called *The African*. He joined the African Students' Union where one of the members was a Ghanaian. At that time, this Ghanaian was named Francis K. Nkrumah. The little known merger between black Americans and Caribbeans at that time followed the rise of the Garvey movement. Of course, some of us did not participate in the marriage between black Americans and Caribbeans; some of us remained estranged, one from the other, while others among us found a way to work out a life together.

Professor Cruse's section on "The Jews and Negroes In The Communist Party," is challenging enough to warrant another entire book. It takes on an issue that black intellectuals are still avoiding. How and why did the American Communist Party capture the minds of so many black intellectuals without rendering any appreciable service to black people, anywhere, anyplace? How did they use black causes for fund raising, as in the Scottsboro Case, and gave very little, if anything, back to the black community?

African people the world over, then and now, were looked upon as a people to be controlled but not as a people who could control themselves. I, personally, related to the Communist Party particularly as a fellow traveler, for over fifty years of my life. I engaged in heated arguments on Black Nationalism, an idea that they feared and preached against with consistency. In my review of Harry Haywood's autobiography, *Black Bolshevik*, I stated that for most of my adult life I was a nationalist, a Pan-Africanist and a socialist and saw no problem being all three, simultaneously. This position never sat well with my colleagues on the political Left. I have often asked my colleagues why we are the only people who are deprived of the right to love ourselves. Why can't we give some preference to ourselves without its seeming that we hate other people? Why, in matters regarding our history, must we look to persons like Herbert Aptheker for the facts when we have so many trained historians with detailed information that Herbert

Aptheker has never heard about? Is there a reason the Communist Party did not see fit to train or sponsor a black historian who would serve as an authority on black history? I do not think that I am less a supporter of socialism because I believe that the Marxist theory, dreamed up in Germany, is not applicable to African people; it may not be applicable to all European people either. Yet, I believe the theory is worth some serious consideration. There is no point in constantly repeating that the Marxist theory is scientific, because nothing is scientific for one people unless it works for all people. This party has earned the attention of some of the finest minds produced in this century, yet it has given us nothing back commensurate with the time and money it has taken from us. A few years ago this was summed up in a paper that came out of Chicago. The paper was *Communist Fund Raising on Black Causes From Angelo to Angela.* It dealt with the funds raised for the defense of the Scottsboro case, the Angelo Herndon case and the Angela Davis case. This paper dared to ask the question: What happened to all the money that was raised after these cases were resolved? In this chapter Mr. Cruse has opened a door where there may be a room of political skeletons. If we examine these skeletons, there will be embarrassment flowing in every direction.

Professor Cruse's section on "The National Negro Congress" needs to be reread for its relevance for today and what we need to learn about soliciting outside support without recognizing the danger of outside control. The National Negro Congress could have been a vital radical black American organization, for it had captured the attention of some of the leading black radical minds of that period. Most of them were radical without being communist. Slowly and surreptitiously the National Negro Congress was infiltrated and slowly came under the control of the Communist Party, which destroyed it. The Communist Party either controls or destroys an organization, and when A. Philip Randolph withdrew from the congress it started on its way to decline. The infusion of the Communist Party into The National Negro Congress did more harm than good. In fact, it was an agent of the Congress' destruction. A. Philip Randolph was right when he warned that you generally get your funds from where you get your control. The National Negro Congress could have been controlled by black Americans because it could have been financed by black Americans. The same was true of the Marcus Garvey movement. The American government was not satisfied with the mass movement of Marcus Garvey because they could not control it, although they had made every effort to do so. Ultimately, it began to decline due to internal differences and FBI harassment. The scenario of the decline of The National Negro Congress was not much different from the scenario for the decline of the Marcus Garvey movement. There were no whites in this country, then or now, that wanted to see a mass movement among blacks that they (the whites) could not control. The black intellectuals did not face this fact then, and they do not face it now. This is a recurring crisis of the black intellectual. Historically, we have a sentimental approach to power. Generally, we are not ruthless in getting power or keeping it, and we are not watchful of the people who come among us seeking power.

Professor Cruse's evaluation of Richard Wright, in the section of his book devoted to this writer, is unique, intriguing and arresting, with some scattered truth, here and there. To me the picture he paints of Richard Wright is less positive than the man himself, and black American writing in this period was richer than in his accounting.

Richard Wright emerged during the period of the pampered black writer. His emergence was a milestone in many literary circles. At last we had a writer who wrote a whole lot better than some of his white contemporaries. His first effort, *Uncle Tom's Children*, was a milestone in the field of African-American literature. His novel, *Native Son*, has the speed of reading that one only finds in a good detective story and the sociological underpinnings of the Russian writer, Dostoevsky. Richard Wright was a craftsman and not an amateur play-acting at being a writer. His emergence was a highwater mark in announcing the maturity of the black writer in America.

Richard Wright's relationship to the American Communist Party was significant and somewhat sad. That party gave him some basic support in getting his career started that should have come from his own people and their respective communities. I cannot say that the influence of the Communist Party on the writings of Richard Wright was all bad. To some extent, Richard Wright gave birth to a generation of writers who have tried to imitate his techniques without acknowledging them. He was then and still is a monumental figure in black American literature.

The section on "Artists For Freedom, Inc.—Dialogue Off-Key" deals with the black confrontation with white liberals. This section is useful, of course, but it needs expansion. While liberals and liberalism are more than an "affliction" on the black movement, it is an obstruction at the fork of the road, confusing us about direction, because the liberal can be a friend one day and confusing to us the next. Liberals are neither permanent friends or enemies. They are opportunists looking on both sides of any situation, ready to take the side of the issue that suits them best. Their convictions are rarely ever strong and their support is rarely ever consistent. I have never really seen any role for them to play in movement. This is why I don't have any argument on this point with Professor Cruse.

In his chapter, "Origins of the Dialogue," Professor Cruse's evaluation of Artists for Freedom is somewhat harsh and misleading. Although this group did not contribute anything outstanding to the cause, each one of the participants contributed to the uplift and achievements of the black artist in his own selected way. This movement was not so negative as Mr. Cruse presents it to be.

In his section, "Freedom Newspaper," the irony is in the bitter truth that during the decade of the rise of the Civil Rights movement that saw the Supreme Court's decision against segregated schools, the Montgomery bus boycott and the sit-ins at lunch counters, the intentions of the Communist Party toward blacks was good. This could have been their most productive decade among blacks. But it was indeed a decade of decline for the Communist Party, while black leadership was again on the rise. I think the error of the black leadership during this period was that it did not develop a political meaning for this decade.

Professor Cruse's section, "From Freedom to Freedomways," describes a transitional period in radical publications focusing on the black situation in the United States. To some extent *Freedomways* was a quarterly magazine and a continuation of some of the same ideas that had been started in the publication *Freedom*, which was edited by Paul Robeson and Lewis Burham.

I was associated with *Freedomways* for twenty-one years of its twenty-five years of existence and was a participant in the most useful years of its development. In my opinion, this publication declined when it became a one-dimensional, political-left-oriented magazine, as against its earlier years, when its approach was much wider and it used a greater variety of writers, the prime requirement being that they wrote well and honestly about their subject matter.

In the section devoted to the writer Richard B. Moore, Mr. Cruse says:

> *Freedomways'* inability to deal concretely with Negro-white realities is characteristic of the peculiar backwardness of the other black publications that have appeared since 1961. Since they cannot deal adequately with the past, they cannot deal perceptively with present social complexities. But what can be expected of the young writers when the old writers, such as Richard B. Moore, writes articles that do not reveal the issues of their own political history?

I can only partly agree with the above statement. To a great extent *Freedomways* did deal realistically with Black and white relationships although they failed miserably in dealing with nationalism and Pan-Africanism and the inability of the American left to understand the issue of African people throughout the world. Principally, they will not admit what is most apparent, the fact that for 500 years the world was ruled by white nationalism, and that Marxism, with all of its potential for the working class of the world is also white-nationalism, because it is the intent of the white nationalist and the Marxist to dominate the world of the new social order that they are advocating. If non-European people are to be Marxist, the European Marxists assume that they will be the ones that tell others the way to become Marxists. This is the essence of political-left white nationalism.

It seems as if Professor Cruse expected Richard Moore to write articles for *Freedomways* revealing the years when he was an active Communist. He was a Communist and was one of the most effective of them around the defense of the young men falsely charged in the Scottsboro case. Mr. Moore never apologized for his activity in the Communist Party nor grieved over the fact that he and a number of other black intellectuals were, literally, expelled from the party for nationalist tendencies. As owner of a bookstore in Harlem, for a number of years and as a lecturer, an historian, and as the effective chairman of the committee "To Present the Truth About the Name 'Negro'," Mr. Moore made a useful contribution, calling attention to the fact that African people are misnamed and this misnaming led them to have serious misconceptions about themselves and their role in world history. His book, expressing these concerns, *The Name Negro: Its Origin and Evil Use*, is still worth serious attention.

There were a number of writers of that day, other than Richard Wright, who did manual labor by day and wrote at night. I know this for a fact because I was one of them, and I think Mr. Cruse knows this, too. A number of the books that I wrote during these difficult days went unpublished because they were challenged by both the left and the right. Both sides, I charged, did not know the condition of African people in this world and neither, through the years, changed my position one iota.

Mr. Cruse's section on Lorraine Hansberry is basically a good accounting, although it is full of truths, half-truths, some confusion, and misconceptions.

I think Professor Cruse is hard on Miss Hansberry who, before the success of her play, *Raisin in the Sun*, was literally getting her feet wet as a writer and was perhaps too reliant on clichés and catch-phrases. Her reliance on these phrases is a true reflection of the political left as an organization of pretenders, people who talk about the proletariat without going near them.

Professor Cruse's section on Paul Robeson is unfortunate because he shows a misunderstanding of the role of Paul Robeson in the African world freedom struggle. In the book *Paul Robeson the Great Forerunner*, I have said in my essay, "Paul Robeson: The Artist as Activist and Social Thinker":

> Paul Robeson was indeed more than an artist, activist and freedom fighter. The dimensions of his talent made him our renaissance man. He was one of the first American artists, black or white, to realize that the role of the artist extends far beyond the stage and the concert hall. Early in his life he became conscious of the plight of his people, stubbornly surviving in a racist society. This was his window on the world. From this vantage point he saw how the plight of his people related to the rest of humanity. He realized that the artist had the power, and the responsibility, to change the society in which he lived. He learned that art and culture are weapons in a people's struggle

to exist with dignity, and in peace. Life offered him many options and he never chose the easiest one.

I maintain that Paul Robeson is still misunderstood in spite of the large number of books written about him. He was a man of commitment and a searcher after the truth. He did not find enough people with similar commitments to work with in his lifetime. The fact that he was used by people who were less than honest is no reflection upon him. The use and misuse of Paul Robeson is a book in itself that needs to be written.

I am very familiar with *Freedomways* and their special issue on Harlem and the issue on Paul Robeson. I was with *Freedomways* during the years these issues were published and was the main editor on both.

In *The Crisis of the Negro Intellectual*, Harold Cruse has challenged us to think about a number of issues that we have, unfortunately, ignored all too long. He has not handled any of these issues as well as they need to be handled. He has, instead, played the role of the alarmist calling attention to issues without promising that he was equal to dealing with them. Yet, in many ways, the real crisis of the Africans throughout the world has been missed because Mr. Cruse has not looked at its historical roots.

I believe this crisis started in the 1700s B.C. when the Nile Valley civilization had reached its height and was in a period of lull. A people from Western Asia (now called the Middle East) assumed that this lull meant weakness and indifference and began to use Africa to solve their own problems. The Hebrew visitors to Africa came in the 1700s B.C. They were given shelter, food and positions in African society. None of them committed themselves to the understanding and protection of African culture. They copied, literally, from African texts, folklore, allegories, and legend and integrated their finds into their own culture. They did not understand Africa then; they do not understand Africa now. They came into Africa seventy in number and when they left they were 600,000 in number. They came to Africa without a clear language, religion or a well-defined culture. When they left they had all three. They had participated in the first disastrous invasion of Africa as collaborators, clerks and supporters of those who entered in 1680 B.C. They were never slaves in Africa because the period in which they said they were slaves was the period when Egypt was dominated by foreign kings, called the Shepherd Kings.

Black intellectuals down through the years have permitted slander-
ous accusations against their people that could have been prevented by
a more intense examination of their history. I maintain that this is the
beginning of the crisis of the black intellectual.

From the first invasion of Africa until the invasion by Alexander
the Great in 332 B.C., which was the first purely European invasion of
Africa, this continent suffered many inroads. After Alexander the
Great came the Romans after many years of their agitation against the
city of Carthage. They finally defeated the African general, Hannibal,
destroyed the city and set up their rule in North Africa, which soon
became the granary of the Roman Empire. Many Africans, despite the
brutality they received at the hands of the Romans, became Roman
citizens and served the Empire. This could well be the beginning of the
integrationist theory that has plagued us through the years. This was
the beginning of our fascination with foreign toys and foreign women.

Our intellectuals have never told us that our role should be the
protection of our language, our culture and our people and the bringing
of dignity to our women. Very few historians in Africa, in the United
States and in the Caribbean Islands have dealt effectively with the
intellectuals' responsibility to their people at a time of crisis and stress.
This is why we did not deal effectively with the slave trade or see the
entire picture of the trade, including the Arab's role which started over
600 years before the Europeans. The Arab slave trade, using Islam as
its rallying cry, drained Africa of its vitality and energy so that it
lacked the ability to withstand the European slave traders.

We have produced few scholars who deal with our traditions,
through the years, including the traditions of our religion, the concepts
of which we created in the first place. Even today, many who claim to
be Moslem cannot distinguish between Islam and Arabism, and many
who know about the Arab slave trade attempt to offer a rationale as to
why it existed.

In the United States and in the Caribbean Islands during the
nineteenth century, which was the century of clear thinking and
radical activity, there was still some confusion as to the definition and
the direction for our people and how to make alliances. It seems that
then, as now, we did not make strong alliances among ourselves or
understand the role that Africa absolutely had to play in our lives to

make it meaningful to our lives. This confusion lasted into the twentieth century and was compounded by misconceptions about the role of Africa in our life as reflected in the writings of E. Franklin Frazier and others. Some students of white sociologist Robert Parks believed that the African in the Western world was a totally new human being, now devoid of anything African. Some of the students of Robert Parks have said, "We lost nothing in Africa ...."

There will continue to be a crisis in black intellectualism until we understand: Pan-Africanism, nationalism and the concept of nation. We have to stop caring what other people think about us. In the words of Malcolm X; "We must liberate ourselves from depending on other people and reestablish ourselves in the world as a sovereign and self-governing people by any means necessary." This, if we achieve it, would be the beginning of the end of the crisis.

While the book by Mr. Cruse offered no lasting solutions to the crisis he at least put the major problems on the agenda and we can no longer ignore the crisis or pretend we do not know what the crisis is. That by itself might be his finest contribution to his people.

CAN AFRICAN PEOPLE SAVE THEMSELVES?

▼

It was the best of times, it was the worst of times, it was the age of wisdom, it was the age of foolishness, it was the epoch of belief, it was the epoch of incredulity, it was the season of Light, it was the season of Darkness, it was the spring of hope, it was the winter of despair, we had everything before us, we had nothing before us, we were all going direct to Heaven, we were all going direct the other way—in short, the period was so far like the present period, that some of its nosiest authorities insisted on being received, for good or for evil, in the superlative degree of comparison only.

—Charles Dickens, *A Tale of Two Cities*

THE ABOVE QUOTE IS APPLICABLE to the African world of today with some slight modifications. African people can have a Golden Age or another Age of Continued Despair, depending on how they view themselves in relationship to the totality of history and its ironies. The cruelest thing slavery and colonialism did to the Africans was to destroy their memory of what they were before foreign contact. Africans have not dealt forthrightly with invaders, slave traders and colonialists, who came among African people as guests and stayed as conquerors. The strongest thing about African people is their respect for the humanity of other people and the hospitality they have shown to strangers. In most cases, Europeans and Western Asians have come into African societies as guests and stayed as conquerors. Africans have never had a strong armed force. They assumed that they did not need one because they had no intention of conquering other people.

Too many times in the past and in the present Africans have had a parochial view of Africa. There is a need now to look not only at the Africans in Africa, but also at how they relate to that vast number of Africans who live outside of Africa. Properly counted, considering the large number of Africans in the Caribbean Islands, North and South America, and the millions of people of African descent in India and in the Pacific, Africans may number at least a billion people on the face of the earth. Africa is the last mineral and geographic reserve in the world. Africa has been and still is the grand prize that non-Africans have always wanted to conquer.

Because Africa is the world's richest continent a great deal of the economic strength of the Western world and parts of Asia is built on what is taken out of Africa. The continent has things that other people want, think they can't do without, and don't want to pay for. Africa is the pawn in a world power game that the Africans have not learned how to play. I emphasized repeatedly that Africa has been under siege for more than 3,000 years, and this condition did not change with the superficial end of colonialism and an independence explosion that had more ceremony than substance. In most African countries the condition of the average African person has not changed one iota with the coming of "flag" independence. All too often Africans fighting for the liberation of Africa pronounced to the world what they were going to do for Africa before they strategically planned how they were going to do it. A case in point is South Africans in the international rhetoric against apartheid. Apartheid is not the main issue in South Africa, bad as it is. If the whites in South Africa eliminated apartheid tomorrow, the Africans would still be in difficulty because they would have no economic power and their land would still be in the hands of foreigners.

Land is the basis of nation. There is no way to build a strong independent nation when most of the land is being controlled by foreigners who also determine the economic status of the nation. Africans need seriously to study their conquerors and their respective temperaments. Neither the Europeans nor the Arabs came to Africa to share power with any African. They both came as guests and stayed as conquerors.

There is a need now to study, at least briefly, the more than 3,000 years when Africa was under siege and under pressure from foreigners who had no understanding or respect for African religions or customs. The Hebrew entry into Africa occurred in the 1700s B.C. They came into Africa escaping famine in western Asia. They were treated as guests by the Africans. In 1675 B.C. Africa was invaded from western Asia by warriors referred to as Hyksos, or Shepherd Kings. The Hebrews were acquainted with these warriors because some of them came from the area of their migration. Therefore many of the Hebrews became collaborators, clerks and administrators for these invaders, working against the interests of the Africans who had befriended them. When after nearly 200 years of this occupation the Africans organized a force large enough to drive out the invaders, they began to ask some questions about the Hebrews who had been their collaborators. The story of Hebrew slavery in Africa is just that, a "story." There is no proof of this matter in Egyptian literature or in western Asian literature.

Outside of the Bible there is no proof of probably the best-known incident in human history, the Exodus. Both the slavery of the Jews in Egypt and the Exodus could be Jewish folklore and nothing more. After this period in history, Nile Valley civilization and Africa in general enjoyed almost a thousand years of peace without antagonism from foreign armies. In 666 B.C. Africa was invaded again by people then referred to as Assyrians. All these wars were assaults on African culture and the different African ways of life. In the year 550 B.C. Africa was invaded again from a country now know as Iran. These invaders were so brutal that some Africans cried out, "Oh God, if you cannot send me a liberator, send me a conqueror who will show some mercy!" The next conqueror was a young Macedonian referred to in history as Alexander the Great. The year was 332 B.C. The Romans invaded North Africa and destroyed the city of Carthage from 264-146 B.C. The greater portion of the Roman Empire rose in Africa and fell in Africa.

If African people are to save themselves, they must first *see* themselves in relationship to the total history of mankind. They must also understand the insecurity of their invaders that caused them to downgrade the importance of African people in history in order to aggrandize themselves at Africa's expense.

This subject is monumental; it is not parochial, not local at all. It breaks out of accustomed mold. We have not asked and answered the question of where we African people are within the context of world history. We see history unfolding around us, and many times we develop a complex, assuming that we are not the makers of history. Something has divided us between the period when we made history and the period when history was made at our expense.

We were once not only the makers of history but we were the makers of the world of our day, and this lasted for thousands of years. One must be reminded that over half of human history was over before anyone else knew that a European was in the world. African people were in the world and had been there for thousands of years. We were not sitting around idly, either. Let me put a timeline on it so you can understand this statement.

As I have noted elsewhere, Africa had existed over 3000 years intact before the first invaders (1675 B.C.); the first European invaders came in 332 B.C. The first trouble came from western Asia. That trouble was persistent and set Africa up for the European invasion under Alexander the Great in 332 B.C. Then he, like all Europeans (although he was more merciful than most and showed more understanding than most), began to misinterpret African people and their place in the history of the world.

We cannot save ourselves and decide where we are going until we understand where we have been and where we are. With history unfolding before us, we've got to become astute in asking and answering the question: Where are we in relationship to what we are seeing right now?

Let's look at some current events and analyze them to see how the Africans living outside of Africa relate to these current events. Where are we in relationship to Panama? How do we relate to it at all? The head of the Joint Chiefs of Staff, the supreme commander of the United States Forces during the invasion was superficially a person of African descent. I mean this both figuratively and literally. He participated with glee in the military encounter. He did not understand nor was it called to his attention that he is a Jamaican and his people died in the thousands while digging that canal. See, when you don't know your own history look at the traps you fall into. You become so "patriotic." It was Jamaicans more than anyone else because they had unemployed people, so they sent more labor. They labored on that canal for years, Jamaicans, Trinidadians, Barbadians, but mainly Jamaicans. When they demanded a raise to ten cents an hour, they were lynched. But we act as though we have no vested interest in the canal, that it's somebody else's show.

Let's play the historical record back 500 years. Let's go back to the opening up of the Americas, back to the 1400s, back to Balboa, the Spanish conquistadors, to the discovery of that area when it was called the Isthmus of Darien. African road builders built a road in what was going to become Panama. They could handle so-called Indian labor, indigenous Americans, without the lash. How could Africans recruit the indigenous population referred to as Indian without the lash, get them to work without mutilating them and humiliating them and whites could not? The African humanity in the recruitment of labor was different. All of this is forgotten history.

The minute we heard about Panama we should have asked, "Well, what role did we play? How do we relate to all of this?" Look at the contradiction of a Jamaican being Chief of Staff. I'm not worrying about whether he's entitled to be it; he's probably more than entitled; that's not the issue. But look at the contradiction. His people dug the ditch and died in the thousands. One of the main reasons his people dug the ditch while whites died of yellow fever in the thousands was because something the Africans believe proved to be true: The mosquito has a taste for white meat.

Let me digress with a relevant personal anecdote. While traveling from Ghana to Togo the bus broke down at the border checkpoint. I didn't know till later that the bus driver gets paid according to the length of time it takes to make the trip; so it conveniently broke down at the border checkpoint. Then we had to spend the night there with no hotels, no resthouses, nothing. So, we slept on the beach. A fellow said, "Mr. Clarke, if you sleep near fresh water with your head lying in the direction of the wind, the mosquito is not going to touch you because the wind will take your scent away. Not only do Europeans lie the wrong way, they smell the wrong way, and attract the mosquitoes."

So, no matter what you think of your smell, it's in your favor in relationship to the mosquito. Therefore, while some blacks did die of yellow fever, most of them survived to dig that ditch. Now you can see how we relate to everything. Nothing happened in Panama that we don't relate to in some way. We can't save ourselves until we become astute at identifying our relationship to everything in the world, because we do relate to everything in the world.

Now let's deal with the so-called dictator, Noriega. He went to American military school. He is a light-skinned one of us. That didn't make it any better for him; they called him a nigger. He didn't associate with the whites for a while. When they found out that they could use him, they let him pass for white. Then they let him engage in skullduggery until he engaged enough to have as much on them as they had on him. They don't want to try him; they want to kill him before he can talk.

Now we can understand that one of us who is a fraction will suffer the same as the blackest of the blacks once we fail to play a power game. My point is that to understand our history (past, present and probably what it will be in the future) we need to know more than our history. We need to look holistically at the world. This is what we have not been doing. Right now we should be getting ready to debunk all of the celebration around the 500 year anniversary of the alleged discovery of America by Christopher Columbus. We should be getting ready now to prove (and we can prove it) that he discovered absolutely nothing. He never set foot on North America or South America. He stumbled up on some islands, and he depopulated every one of them. Everywhere he went he destroyed the people.

We should have conferences, entire conferences, devoted to one item: revelations of Father Bartholomew de Las Casas, the first historian of the New World. We need to read his work and talk about it for three days, and not mix it with a thousand other things. It was Father de Las Casas whom Christopher Columbus went to (when he saw the so-called Indians dying wholesale) in order to get an increase in the African slave trade to save the so-called soul of the Indians. When the Pope sent commissioners to look into the disappearance of the Indians, many islands didn't even have one left. They were dying wholesale of malaria and mutilation, of brooding themselves to death.

Now you have to look at the culture of a one-dimensional people. I'm not dealing with good or bad; I'm dealing with culture and how sometimes such people can get into a culture trap of their own design. We are in such a trap because we believe that the white man was telling the truth when he gave us Christianity. We didn't go beyond what he was saying and look at the spirituality we produced and gave the world before Christianity. We dare not read about it; we dare not think about it. We dare not examine the Conference at Nicaea (325 A.D.) where the fakery that is now Christianity was foisted upon the world, and the reality and spirituality which we gave the world got lost.

I'm not saying anybody should walk the world godless or spiritless. I'm not saying leave any church; stay in them. Make them infuse spirituality in religion. We have a revolutionary dynamic. but without spirituality we are wasting our time. This is why I'm against all the millionaire phonies, imitating black Baptist preachers, like Jimmy Swaggart and others who have the spirit of a dog. They've taken something from us and they are disgracing it. If you understand what is happening before you, you will understand what you've got to do.

Now let's look at what is happening in Europe. It is not an argument between communism and capitalism, it is a difference of opinion on the methodology of European control of the world. Europeans have decided that they would control the world, be it communist, capitalist, socialist or fascist. There are certain Oriental races who have decided that they will help them, but we think that once we deal with our white enemy we have no other enemy. We are dead wrong. People want power by any means necessary, and they will take it from any person on this earth who has not learned how to use it properly. And we African people have not learned to use it properly, not even how to protect our own community.

If we're going to save ourselves, there is something which I have called "the essential selfishness of survival" which we are going to have to start practicing. There are some blacks who will say this is black racism. I say it is not. It is survival. but if someone wants to classify it as black racism, so be it. I think we should own every single house in the famous ethnic community called Harlem, control every single house in this community; control every single store in this community; employ people in the community running these things properly; have our own social agencies; eliminate homelessness and put people to work renovating houses in this community. If we did this and walked upright, began to fix our own shoes, had small factories, independent schools, good day nurseries, good child care, a national theater with its headquarters in this community—if we did all of that, we would be practicing nation building. We will have at last understood what Booker T. Washington was saying, what W.E.B. DuBois was saying, what Marcus Garvey was saying, and what Elijah Muhammad and Malcolm X were saying. I don't separate one from the others.

I am not endorsing Islam. (I think religion without spirituality is a waste of time, anyway. Nor am I looking for a new one.) I would not even name Elijah Muhammad except for the fact that he did make a contribution toward nation-consciousness. In nation-consciousness you can make your own religion. You can go to his or you can make another one or choose another one. The laws of nation-consciousness are the laws of responsibility, and we are not going to save ourselves until we are conscious of nation-responsibility and nation-building. We are not going to save ourselves as individuals; we're going to do it as a collective. To do it as a collective, we're going to have to be bold enough (even if we have to break our own hearts) to find out where we went wrong.

Throughout history we have been politically a naive people. We have trusted the wrong people; we have bought false goods from fake salesmen. We have bought things of a synthetic nature, not knowing that we had real things at home all the time. We have forgotten the facts because we have not studied our history seriously and recognized that before there was a Europe we built enduring civilizations that lasted thousands of years without a jail system. We had family structures that were so tight, and the family was structured in such a way, that crime and punishment were taken care of within the family and jails were not needed.

There was no word in the Africans' languages that meant divorce. Because each party had a support system, the uncles, the fathers, the mothers, all there together. Then foreigners declared war on this support system. Throughout our history we have always been (and still are, in spite of the contradictions) the worlds' richest people: rich in culture, rich in minerals, rich in ideas, rich in imagination. We have not used these great riches to save ourselves.

White musicians can do a good imitation of our music, but they could not do an exact imitation if their life depended on it. Benny Goodman played one imitation of our music over and over and over, but he didn't innovate because he didn't know how. He learned a form and played the form over and over. I remembered Charlie Parker playing "Ain't She Sweet." I listened to him three nights straight, and he played the song a different way each night and yet he still was playing "Ain't She Sweet." He played it according to his mood; he wasn't in the same mood each night, so he didn't play the same way each night. Some nights it sounded better than others, but he didn't kill the tune of the song.

Figuratively speaking we Africans have been put on the world stage without a script, and the audience has said to us, "Act or we'll kill you." And we have acted; that's the nature of our survival. We have learned something about survival that has eluded other people. We have not used what we have learned to continue to survive. We have become prisoners to forms other people have created without using our imagination to survive. If we had used our imagination, we could have rebuilt every boarded-up house in every metropolitan community where we live in the United States. We're good carpenters, imaginative planners, and great decorators, because we use color in situations so well. The question is, why haven't we used our cultural gift to save ourselves?

Let's look beyond the United States. Let's look at the Caribbean Federation (a great heartbreak to me). Let's look at the Civil Rights movement (another heartbreak), and let's look at the failure of the African Independence Explosion—the greatest of all the heartbreaks because that could have saved the two of us. All three of them failed because instead of using our imagination, we were using forms developed by someone else, not knowing that the slave master and the colonial master created nothing that we can use to save ourselves because his form was to keep him in control of us. When we use this form to control our own people, our situation is merely changing faces. We change our condition without changing our position. We have to understand the nature of the position in relationship to the condition.

There is a need now to examine the Caribbean concept of union and federation. The idea of Pan-Africanism was formulated by the Caribbean mind. How is it that the three great Pan-Africanists came from Trinidad: H. Sylvester Williams, George Padmore and C.L.R. James? They could never unify Trinidad. The great federalists mostly came from Jamaica. The great internationalists came mostly from the Virgin Islands, men like Edward Wilmot Blyden and Hubert Harrison, but mainly Blyden, who tried to build a three-way bridge between African-Americans, the Caribbeans and Africa. Today, in no part of the Caribbean Islands, does one find any nationalism of consequence.

Even the Rastas are confused. Many of them are actually rascals. Some are beachcombers, roaming the beaches of the Caribbean, serving the unfulfilled physical needs of female tourists. Is this on their road to Africa? It is at best a side road. Thus, there's some confusion, even by those who claim Africa in purity. And anybody who claims Haile Selassie as the incarnation of God on this earth is confused about the history of Haile Selassie.

I like the idea of the Rastas. I wish some Rastas weren't rascals. I wish there were something in the Caribbean Islands of pure black nationalism, because they've got something we don't have here—they've got a majority. They've got something else we don't have, a special kind of revolutionary heritage based on being a majority. Their slave revolts were the most successful of the slave revolts outside of Africa. They have forgotten their revolutionary heritage and become too dependent. Their slave revolts were successful because they had an African culture continuity. Our cultural continuity in this country was broken, almost destroyed, and yet we maintained a large degree of that cultural continuity. "Come to Jamaica!" Everybody in Jamaica wants to be something except an African person. They're willing to tell you about their Dutch uncles, Scottish grandfathers, etc. I have not found one who will say boldly, "I am an African person."

At a conference on Marcus Garvey in Jamaica in 1987, I raised a question: "Where would Marcus Garvey be safe in the Caribbean Islands? Where would he be safe in the world if, indeed, he were alive walking around? Where would he be safe?" If he were in Jamaica, I believe some politically deranged person would stone him to death; he failed twice in Jamaica. He's dead now; they'll make him a hero, bury him at King's Park. Everybody says, "Marcus Garvey's buried out there." They emphasize that he's buried there. When you're dead, you can't hurt anybody. Anybody who would elect Edward Seaga (a Lebanese con man from Boston) as their Prime Minister has placed their African loyalty into question.

There may be some hope. I haven't found it. Yet, if the Caribbean Islands are ever to be the seat of the rallying cry for the return to Africa, it will begin in Jamaica. It has the resource; it has the intellectual personnel; it has the technical personnel. Just as, if Nigeria becomes a truly African nation (and not a den of thieves), it can change all of Africa. Half of the lawyers, technicians, the African-trained engineers, school teachers and qualified professors in Africa are Nigerians. Nigeria could turn Africa around, if it would, but it would have to work as a collective and not as individuals.

Let's look at what we call the Civil Rights movement in the United States and why this failed to be a vehicle that we could use to save ourselves. Let's see if we can show you that when you do not understand the nature of the history behind an event, you're going to misinterpret the event, misuse the event and misuse yourself in relation to the event. These young people, brilliant, beautiful, and brave, got the illusion that they were making a revolution such as had never appeared before among their own people. They were totally ignorant of the early nineteenth century black revolution of the black freedmen in New England under Frederick Douglass; of the newspapers published by that group (*The Anglo-American*, Douglass' *North Star*, *Freedom's Journal*). They were ignorant to the relation of the brilliant Caribbean minds to that movement, ignorant of the great contribution of the Barbadian, Prince Hall, who founded our Masons (and didn't call it Masons; Black Masons or anything like that). He called it the African Lodge.

Why were we closer to Africa then than we are now? Why did we have a romance with the word "Africa" then and we're avoiding it now? Why do we want to be something else now, when we were comfortable being African then? When we lose our African connection, we lose our world connection. When we disconnect ourselves from Africa, we cease to be a world people. It is the African connection that makes us an important people of the world. Without the African connection, we are a disjointed people (just "hung out"), begging for entry into somebody else's house. As an African people, we've got a big house—12,000,000 square miles, full of riches. And people are begging to enter our house to enjoy its riches. We are on the outside, not developing the talent to master those riches and exploit them for the benefit of all African people of the world, or anybody other than European investors. If we stop talking about apartheid long enough, we would realize that the real issue in South Africa is not apartheid. It is European control over the mineral wealth of the world, with the headquarters of that control being in South Africa. Most of the countries that control the mineral wealth of the world are in support of South Africa.

In Cheikh Anta Diop's little book on Africa (written over ten years ago), *Black Africa: The Economic and Cultural Basis for a Federated State*, he outlined exactly how the mineral wealth of Africa was taken. He tells us exactly what we're going to have to do to take it back and to preserve it for African generations still unborn.

Cheikh Anta Diop's work, *Civilization or Barbarism*, his fifth and last book, has not been published in English. I have not met ten people who have seriously read his work. In this book, written before his untimely death (when a man is great, any death is untimely, even if he dies at 102), he takes off the gloves. He doesn't say "maybe" anymore; he doesn't hedge anymore; he doesn't say "the information points" or "it indicates." This is his final confirmation of the truth of African history and how African history relates to world history. We know for the first time our place in the history of the world.

My main point is that we have not heard our greatest messengers, and we interpreted as a fight a lot of things in our life which were not fights. Booker T. Washington's message was one of self-reliance, and we condemn him as being an Uncle Tom because he did not take public stands on many things. Yet, Booker T. Washington could have scratched his head when it wasn't itching, could have shuffled when there was nothing funny; he did achieve something we need to respect him for. He did keep Tuskegee open; he did train a generation of people; he did develop an education system that was good then and is good now. Had we followed that system and paid respect to him, you would never see a white plumber working in a black neighborhood, because we would have our own. If you live in a brick house, you should have a brickyard; if you wear leather shoes, tan your own leather and make them.

Kids used to walk to Tuskegee through three states; they didn't have any money. They would walk their way to school barefoot. Booker T. Washington used this as an opportunity to start a shoe repair shop and later developed courses for designing shoes. For years most of the blacks trained in design of orthopedic shoes—were trained at Tuskegee. It's all gone now; it's a liberal arts school (as though we don't have enough of those). We need more good technical training schools, schools where a man or woman will be trained to be a plumber, trained to lay tiles.

A good plumber makes more money than a good college professor.

If you can lay tile in a bathroom properly, you make more than a college president. There's nothing wrong with using your hands and your brain at the same time. If you put those two things together with skill, you go home with nice money. We have forgotten this in the smugness of looking at Hollywood and at the soap operas (the most unreal thing in existence, even unreal to the people who created them).

My point is that when we look at the Independence Explosion that began in Africa in 1957 (with the independence of Ghana), the real genesis of the explosion was a hundred years before. Throughout the whole of the nineteenth century most Africans did not negotiate anything with the Europeans. They did not go to Whitehall; they did not go to Europe and be dazzled with the chandeliers; the smiling ladies and the champagne. They picked up their spears and their shields and went to the battlefield. And they out-generaled some of the finest soldiers of Europe.

There is a good record of it in Edward Roux's book, *Time Longer Than Rope*. There is also a record left by the young Winston Churchill, one of the greatest war reporters since Caesar came home from Gaul, about the Sudan, *The River War*. The people that the Africans opposed and defeated wrote it down. We should read the record of the last of the Ashanti wars led by a woman, Yaa Asantewa, ably supported by men. This was the time of the siege of Kumasi, the great drama of Kumasi. Any history of Ghana includes the story of that war and this brilliant woman.

We keep comparing ourselves with Europeans, but we are not Europeans in temperament. No European would have followed a woman into a war for nine months, giving no quarter and asking none. She had that war won until a great contradiction in history appeared: the famous West Indian Regiment, that she thought was friendly.

She told her men, in effect: "Lay down your guns and go out and greet our brothers; they've come to help us at last." Those brothers were in the pay of the British and had come to do them in—and they did.

We should celebrate Yaa Asantewa's war. It shows that we have not looked at women in the same way as the European. Even in courtship, when we take the same approach as the European, we are dead wrong. When we take the same general attitude toward women as the European, we are dead wrong. The European fears women; if he enslaves ours, he enslaves his, too. The only difference, many times, is that the European woman's auction block, figuratively, is air-conditioned; but she's on the auction block, too.

When we look at this African Independence Explosion, we must take into consideration that not one African nation came to power using a conventional African structure of government. Every one used an imitation of parliamentary procedure taken from Europe. It's like wearing a coat that wasn't designed for your body and will never fit. The tailor has never seen your body, and, therefore, cannot cut a coat to suit it. This is something you have to do yourself, because you can't wear a tight-fitting coat. You need another kind of coat, politically and figuratively speaking. Africa will never succeed using European parliamentary techniques. It will never succeed using Christianity or democracy as designed by the European, because the Europeans theorized these concepts, while, in most cases, the Africans lived out these concepts without dogma or without making them into rationales for the conquest of other peoples. The African never used the word "democracy."

He never used the word, yet he had more democracy than the European ever dared to practice. This is where some lawyers need to study the African customary court system. When the late Pauli Murray, who was a brilliant lawyer, went to Africa, I asked her, "Why don't you study the customary court system in Africa?" She never got around to it, but had she studied it, she would have learned that it is democratic to the point of being cumbersome. For example, the accused can examine everybody in the court, including the judge. The case is not closed until the accused calls his last witness, and generally the last character witness is his wife, who will bear witness to his good character and whether he takes care of his family. If that fails to convince, he's guilty as hell.

It is a system that takes the man's total humanity into consideration. Now will we throw away all of that for a European system? "Where were you on the night of June 13th?" That's not the issue; besides I can't remember. In an African court the issue is whether you have violated the customary laws that govern the society and having done so, whether you have endangered the whole society. If you have endangered the whole society, then the entire society has a right to call for your punishment. The judge of the case (once you are proven guilty) asks you what sentence you think needs to be passed upon you now that you are proven guilty.

In most cases, the guilty party announces a sentence for himself more harsh than the court normally would put upon him. He participates both in his innocence and in his guilt. This is democracy to the point of being retarding. This kind of trial would last too long in America; but the spirit of what the Africans are doing is worth preserving.

In Botswana, among the Bamanwaita people, where the court is called the Kahatla, you bring your stool, your lunch, fresh water and diapers for the children. You sit under a tree. You might come back in three days and find the trial is still going on.

We must rescue these old values, even if we update them, and prune away the excess time involved (because we have to move faster now). We must talk to each other, as we never did before.

When I was growing up—because there was no such thing as illegitimacy—you didn't turn a girl out just because she had a child out of wedlock. The ladies in the community did gather around her and talk to her and let her know about the danger of this kind of thing, and that it wasn't exactly the right kind of thing to do. The men would gather around the man and want to know, "Inasmuch as you're not going to marry this girl, what are you going to do towards her support?"

Today, men are impregnating ladies and telling people, "None of your business, after all she should have kept her dress down." Girls have to learn how to check people out before they favor them, and if they're not dependable, not favor them. You're not going to die. You can go a long ways through life without it; he ain't going to die either. Some things can wait until you make a proper selection of someone who you can depend on or believe in.

We need to concentrate on the quality of people we bring into the world. There's no point bringing someone into the world who's going to be a burden to the society. We want everybody to be a contributor. To be a contributor, a child needs more than mothering; it needs fathering, too. A child needs socialization. If a child is without a father, he shouldn't be without the male image in his life.

If we are indeed going to save ourselves, we have to find out not only what we have done wrong, but the number of people among us that we have failed to make accountable to us. Everyone who calls himself or herself a leader must be accountable to us. If they are too sensitive to be accountable to us, then they don't go forth and call themselves a leader. Let us deny them.

Somewhere along the way all of us, in our fascination for foreign toys, political and otherwise, reach the fork in the road. We have seen many roads leading in many directions, and we read the signboards wrong. We went down roads that did not lead us home. We have to go back to the fork in the road and read those signboards again. We have to find a signboard that reads: Unity, African World Federation, Pan-Africanism, African Solidarity. When we see that on the board (the unification of all African people throughout the world, the self-interest of African people first, black and black unity, meaning more than black and white unity), after we go back to the fork in the road (meaning we might have to go back before we can go forward) we may have to recheck ourselves.

We might have to go back and make a principled decision. We might have to build great industries; we might have to start with our underwear. The reason I say start with underwear is because no one is looking at it. If we get our seams wrong, we've got time to get it straight. Then we go to our shoes and our suits. And we learn something that is basic to the re-emergence of modern Japan. There are two things the Japanese would not let their conqueror take from them: their self-confidence and their image of God as they conceived Him to be.

In slavery and in colonialism African people lost their self-confidence. You cannot worship a white spiritual image of authority on the weekend, beg the same image for a job the rest of the week and give full respect to the black father, as the authority image, in the home. You cannot turn viciously on yourself because you do not resemble that white image; you cannot look at that same image as the epitome of everything good and look at the image staring at you from the mirror as the image of everything bad. Psychologically, you cannot save yourself until you love yourself. And you begin with the mirror. You stand in front of the mirror until you like what's staring back at you. You speak to the person staring back at you and say, "You and I will start a revolution that will change the world. We will start our revolution right now." I often say that this is tomorrow's work, and the time to start tomorrow's work is today.

The International Congress for African Studies was held in Kinshasha, Zaire from December 12 to 16, 1976. The main theme of this conference was African dependency and its remedy. The conferees talked about the subject for days without coming directly to the point or asking the right questions, such as, "Who programmed African people into foreign dependency, and how will they overcome this dependency in their immediate lifetime?"

As one of the conferees, I called attention to the groundbreaking and useful work on the subject done by Cheikh Anta Diop, especially in his book, *Africa, The Politics of a Federated State.* Part of my brief intervention was as follows:

The theme of the congress, "The Dependence of Africa and the ways of Remedying Situation," has long historical roots and many dimensions and we have not touched on all of them. I think most of us know that our papers and our deliberations have not done full justice to the theme of this congress. At best we have located the surface of the theme and scratched it all too lightly. We have given many answers without asking the right questions. Who is to blame for the dependence of Africa, and who is responsible for finding a remedy? Most of us do not seem to be aware of the fact that African thinkers have already asked the question and thought out some answers that are worth serious consideration.

In 1960, *Présence Africaine* in Paris published a work by the Senegalese historian, Cheik Anta Diop, *Black Africa: The Economic and Cultural Bases of a Federated State.*

This book, first published nearly two decades ago, dealt with the theme of this Congress. With all due respects to our papers and deliberations this week, Professor Diop, in my opinion, brought more to the subject than our combined efforts.

In the English edition of the same book, recently published in the United States, he brought his information up to date by first dealing with the Energy crisis, now prevailing in Africa. He stated: "The days of the nineteenth century dwarf states are gone, our main security and development problems can be solved only on a continental scale and preferably within a federal framework before it is too late."

He calls attention to the drain of this nation's energy by the major Western powers in the following statement in his book:

> Belgian-American interests preparing for the political instability that would prevail in the colonies following World War II, working at maximum rate and beyond, mined all the uranium of the then Belgian Congo in less than ten years and stockpiled it at Oolen in Belgium. The Shinkolobwe mines in Zaire today are emptied having supplied the major part of the uranium that went into the Nagasaki and Hiroshima bombs. Until 1952, Zaire was the world's leading uranium producer; now it ranks sixteenth in reserves and has ceased to be counted among the producers. This one example shows how fast our continent can have its nonrenewable treasures sucked away while we sleep.

Professor Diop's book is about all the things that we have been talking about here this last week. The origins of African dependence and what can be done about it. His approach is Pan-Africanist and Socialist.

The African-American historian, William Leo Hansberry wrote a shorter work on this subject called *Africa, World's Richest Continent.* Professor Hansberry calls attention to the fact that the agricultural and hydro-electric potential of Africa is the greatest in all the world. His findings provoke the question: If Africa is so rich, why are most African people so poor? Who is managing the riches of Africa?

The Guyanian writer, Walter Rodney, wrote a history of the origin and growth of this dilemma in his book, *How Europe Underdeveloped Africa.*

The essence of the point that I have been trying to get across is: The problem of African dependency and the search for a remedy is not new. It is part of a crisis that started in the fifteenth and sixteenth century, with the second rise of Europe, the development of the slave trade and the colonial system that followed it.

The dilemma is both topical and historical. This dilemma will not be resolved until all Africa is completely liberated and freed from dependency.

This is not the problem only of the Africans who live in Africa. This is a problem, and a fight, that must be shared by African people everywhere. In this effort to complete the liberation of Africa and free Africa from dependency, we must extend the base of Pan-Africanism into a concept of an African World Union. This should be the mission of the present generation of Africans. It should also be the legacy that we leave for generations of Africans still to come.

In the search for our new place in the African sun and in the respectful commentary of world history, it is necessary that we look at the past in order to understand the present and probably prophesy the future. There are some critical questions we need to ask and answer, mainly, "Are African people ready for the twenty-first century?" Are we preparing to be free men and women, masters of our destiny or will we continue in the programmed dependency that has been our lot for the past 500 years? I maintain that it is the role of African thinkers, teachers and political leaders to ask the question, "How will my people stay on this earth?"

In order to survive, some of us have felt the need to live in a form of sick fantasy. Are we as a people ready for the consequences and the responsibilities of being free and self-governing in the next century?

Part of the answer to the question, "Are we ready for the twenty-first century?" is the statement: African people must first define themselves. They must decide who they are and understand their place in the world.

I have often said that history is the clock that people use to find their political time of day. It is also a compass that they use to locate themselves on the map of human geography.

We are a world people, a potentially powerful people without power and we need to know why. We have been a natural attraction for other people. That was the basis of the crisis in Africa 3000 years ago. This is the basis of the crisis in the African world right now.

African people, all over the world, have answered to too many names that they did not choose for themselves. In finding yourself, you have to find who you are, and what name you are to be called: (1) Negro; (2) Colored; (3) Black; (4) African; (5) Arab-African *(No)*;

(6) Black-African *(No)*.

The question is what people did the slave ships bring here?

African People at the Crossroads

When you want to lose a people from history, you first destroy their self-confidence and historical memory. This is the basis of our dilemma: Our enemy wants us to forget who we were so we will not know what we still can be. This statement is really about conflict in culture and self-confidence. Culture, conflict and self-confidence are reoccurring themes in our lives and in the lives of all people.

With our people, these themes take on a special meaning. We created the world's oldest culture, and we act as if we are not aware of this fact. We have a conflict within ourselves about how to use culture as an instrument of liberation. If we had confidence in our culture, the second rate cultures of other people would not fascinate us.

What we do not seem to know is that our oppressor, who created the crisis, in most cases is also having a crisis of self-confidence of a different nature. The rulers of the world are in trouble because they cannot continue to rule over us. They have developed some skill in taking advantage of our crisis, but we have developed no skill in taking advantage of theirs. We are following a people who do not know where they are going.

Among other things, whites are turning to African religions because Africa is the origin of Eastern religions. Europeans are losing confidence in the gods that they sold to us. European rule over the world has been, and still is, a con-game. We are its victims and we can now decide the game is over.

Today, many Europeans are turning toward Eastern and African religions and cults, while more blacks are turning to millionaire gospel peddlers like: Jimmy Swaggert and Billy Graham, who are racists.

We live in a world of fantasy, searching for someone to love us, when all we need to do is love ourselves.

We need to love ourselves so well that we will begin to make the shoes we wear and the rest of the clothes we wear. We should love to run the stores in our community, and we should do so with pride.

According to the Chicago poet, Haki Madhabuti, "We are the only people who turn our children over to the enemy to be educated. We should start educating our children ourselves."

Powerful people never educate powerless people in how to take their power away from them.

Education, as I have said before, has but one honorable purpose; that is to train the student to be a proper handler of power. At first power over himself or herself.

Our communities are small nations under siege. They are about to be taken away from us because we do not realize that we have no place to go and must now take a stand.

The Way Out

The answer to the question: "Are we ready for the twenty-first century?" is both complex and simple.

We need to look back at the early part of the twentieth century in order to estimate what we might have to do in the early part of the twenty-first century.

Between the United States, the Caribbean Islands, South America and Central America, there are over 200 million African people, not including those who are hiding the fact. Taking into consideration the newly discovered Africans on the islands of the Pacific and in other parts of Asia, there are at least 300 million people of African descent living outside of Africa. The Africans in Africa number at least 500 million. How did we get to be called a minority, anyhow? In the next century, there will be at least a billion African people in the world. We will be the second, if not the first, largest ethnic group in the world.

How do we deal with that?

We must look into education for nation-management. We cannot leave it to others to let us know about this. We need to listen to the black men that we have not listened to very well: Booker T. Washington, W.E.B. DuBois, Marcus Garvey. Pan-Africanism and African world unity is the real answer. The need is not just to unite against something—but to unite for something.

When we find ourselves, we will have to understand the role we as a people have played in history and still must play. Nation-management is our only hope.

As Professor Willard Johnson of Massachusetts Institute of Technology has said, "We can change the world—if first we change ourselves."

In a nation of immigrants, the black American is really unique. We are the immigrants who came to the Americas against our will. We are the only immigrants who were actually invited here. The nature of the invitation is too well known to be discussed here. Although we lost a great deal of our Africanness, we did not lose all of it.

After the middle of the nineteenth century, black Americans in the United States were no longer considered to be African. What to call them has always been a dilemma. W.E.B. DuBois reminds us that we were brought to America as temporary immigrants, with the assumption that we would eventually be returned to Africa. He also reminds us that our first institutions bore the name "African", such as The African Methodist Episcopal Church, and the African Lodge that became, in actuality, the first black Masonic order established in the United States. In the closing years of the nineteenth century, we began to refer to ourselves as "colored" or "negro." However, neither word has any meaning in reference to the national home base of a people. We did not begin to use the word "black" until the middle of the twentieth century, during the period of the Supreme Court's decision against segregated schools in 1954 and the rise of the Civil Rights movement after the Montgomery bus boycott of 1955.

The word "African" again became part of our conscious speech after the African Independence Explosion, starting with the independence of Ghana in 1957. With the rise of the Black Studies concept following the beginning of the decline of the Civil Rights movement, the word "black" became more acceptable to a larger number of Americans of African descent. With the same consideration being given to the Pan-African concept, the word "African" once more became a part of our vocabulary. What the Africans living outside of Africa began to understand, especially those living in the United States, is that we are a nation within a nation still searching for a nationality. Italian-Americans, German-Americans, Asian-Americans, and other hyphenated Americans do not seem to have any problems referring to the country and the land of their geography as part of their heritage.

Some of us are just beginning to be comfortable with the word "African." Numerically, in the United States, we are more than a nation, although we are sometimes lacking in nation-consciousness. Professor Ivan Van Sertima has said that we have been locked in a 500-year room tragically shielded by a curtain marked "Slavery." Our desire to look behind and beyond that curtain is what the concept of Black Studies was all about. We African people of the world, along with the Chinese, are the only people who might number a billion people on the face of the earth. African people are the most dispersed of all of the world's people. When you consider the fact that between the Caribbean Islands and the large number of African people in South America, especially Brazil, which has the largest number of African people living outside of Africa, there are at least 200 million African people in the Western hemisphere. When you consider the large number of African people in Asian countries and on the Pacific Islands, there are more than 100 million African people living in the Eastern hemisphere. This does not include the 100 million people living in India, referred to in a recent book as the *Black Untouchables*.

There is a need now to read or reread Sir Godfrey Higgins' book, *Anacalypsis*, originally published in 1833, which deals with the dispersion of African people throughout the world. Our presence and the culture that we have created have influenced the whole world. Because of racism and the colonization of the information about history, we are considered strangers among the world's people and called many different names in the many places where we live. The name that is applicable to all of us, wherever we live on this earth, is African.

What's in a name? Shakespeare said, in effect, "A rose by any other name is just as sweet." That is all right when you are dealing with roses, but when you deal with people you have to be more precise.

Jesse Jackson's announcement that black people in the United States should be called Africans caused me to sigh with some boredom and ask, "What else is new?" I, personally like Jesse Jackson and have no fight with him in this regard. His remarks and the numerous radio and TV talk shows that recently discussed the name prove to me that the public pays more attention to politicians than they do to scholars. Since the mass forced emigration of Africans outside of Africa in the fifteenth and sixteenth centuries, during the slave trade, which contributed to the economic recovery of Europe after the Middle Ages, African people in one way or the other have been searching for their African selves. What we need to learn here is that in the European conquest and colonization of most of the non-European world, they also colonized information about the world. They knew then what most of us don't seem to know now: You cannot successfully oppress a consciously historical people.

Once a people knows who they are, they will also know what they have to do about their condition. To make a people almost assume that oppression is their natural lot, you have to remove from them the respectful commentary of their history and make them dependent on the history of their conquerors. To infer that a people have no history is also to infer that they have no humanity that you are willing to recognize. African people the world over need a definition of history that can be operational in different places at different times and operational everywhere African people live. Because we are the most dispersed people on the face of the earth, our operational definition of history must be universal in scope, applicable to people in general, and to African people specifically.

This is my definition: I repeat, history is a clock that people use to tell their political and cultural time of day. It is also a compass that people use to find themselves on the map of human geography. The role of history is to tell a people what they have been and where they have been, what they are and where they are. The most important role that history plays is telling a people where they still must go and what they still must be.

No people can move into the mainstream of history and be respected when they answer to an ethnic name not of their choosing and worship a God-concept not of their choosing. All people develop within a culture container that includes their geographical background, their religion, and their method of surviving in their original habitat. When you take a people out of the cultural surroundings in which they originally developed, you take away part of their humanity. African people living outside of Africa are so obsessed with surviving under conditions that they did not create that they often lack a universal view of their condition and how it started.

The writer, Lerone Bennett, Jr., has said, "We have been named, we should now become 'namers'." In the process of reconsidering ourselves and our role in world history, our initial assignment is to find the proper name for ourselves. The name "colored" means nothing because all people are colored, one way or another. The name "negro" should mean nothing to us because there is no such race of people or person. Some Spaniard or Portuguese took a descriptive adjective and made a noun out of it. We as a people are neither a noun nor an

adjective. Those who responded, pro or con, to Jesse Jackson's suggestion that we use the name "African" also clearly indicated that they
had not read any of the reasonably large body of literature on the
subject. Among some of our scholars this debate has been going on for
almost 200 years with small audiences that obviously did not understand the nature of the debate. There are times that when a people
answer to a name that they did not choose for themselves they fall into
a condition that they also did not choose. If you answer to the name
"dog," in some ways you will become a dog.

Over 100 years before the abolition of slavery, our scholars were
addressing themselves to this situation. They were close enough to the
name "African" to have no compunction about using it. This is a late
seventeenth and early twentieth century debate. The Brazilian abolitionists of African descent argued among themselves whether they were
Brazilians or Brazilian-Africans. Paul Cuffe, the first black American
sea captain was very clear about his African name and his African
heritage. In the non-fictional historical writings of our first novelist,
William Wells Brown, the word "Ethiopian" was often used synony-
mously with "African" and black as though they were interchangeable.
I now refer to the book, *Search for a Place*, that contains Martin
Delany's report on the Niger mission and Robert Campbell's report on
the same mission under the title, "Pilgrimage to My Motherland."
When that small and dedicated group of New England blacks emerged,
they mainly used the name "African" in their writings and references
to African people. When the Barbadian, Prince Hall, founded the first
black Masonic order, he called it the African Lodge. When Richard
Allen and other black religious dissidents founded the independent
black church, they called this church The African Methodist Episcopal
Church. Our first stage comedians were often referred to as the African
clowns or the Ethiopian rascals.

Edward Wilmot Blyden, in his famous inaugural address at Liberia
College, in 1881, spoke of the images about ourselves that were created
by other people's interpretation of what we are and what we should be.
Dr. Blyden said in his address: "We shall be obliged to work for many
years to come without the sympathy or understanding we need to
have." He also said that we as a people are in revolt against the
descriptions of African people in travelogues, textbooks and in journals
by missionaries and mercenaries. He further explained that "we often

strive to be those things most unlike ourselves, feeding grist into other people's mills instead of our own." He concludes, "Nothing comes out except what has been put in and that, then, is our great sorrow." Professor Blyden continued this emphasis in other works like, *On African Customs*, and his greatest and best-known work, *Christianity, Islam and the Negro Race*.

In the closing years of the nineteenth century, when George Washington Williams was writing the first formal history of the African people in the United States, *The History of the Negro Race in the United States*, he introduced the book with an argument he seemed to be having with himself about the word "African" as opposed to "negro." He must have lost the debate with himself, because in spite of favoring the word "African" he used "negro" throughout the two-volume work.

The greatest intellect, in my opinion, that we have produced outside of Africa emerged in the closing years of the nineteenth century. His name is W.E.B. DuBois. His book, *The Suppression of the African Slave Trade to the United States* was published by Harvard University Press. Booker T. Washington and his educational theory of self-reliance emerged during the same period. These two minds, using different words and methods, guided the Africans in the United States into the twentieth century. We were now using the word "negro" or "colored" in order to distinguish ourselves from the Africans living in Africa and those living outside of Africa. However, the word "negro" was not extensively used in the Caribbean Islands nor in South America. In his famous *appeal* of 1829, David Walker had used the word "colored." In our publications and documents the name "negro" became our new mark of identity, as reflected in publications like the *Negro Year Book*, edited at Tuskegee Institute by Monroe Work. In 1915, when Carter G. Woodson founded the Association for the Study of Negro Life and History, and later the *Negro History Bulletin*, Africans in the United States were more or less settled on the word "negro."

The literary movement of the 1920s, sometimes called The Negro Renaissance or the Harlem Renaissance, had its emphasis in two different places: one in the reclaiming of the African past and the other in surviving the conditions that African people had to live under in the United States, the Caribbean Islands, and in South America. Interests merged at this point and some intellectuals began to think of a Pan-African movement that would encompass all the African people of the world. In 1927 the Jamaican, Raphael Powell, seriously questioned the use of the work "negro" in his book, *The Human Side of a People and the Right Name*. Mr. Powell dedicated his book to the "human race," especially "to those who have been taught to believe that they are other than what they are and to those who will think with a mind of reason, logic and common sense .... "

Mr. Powells' opinion was that "Ethiopian was co-ordinate with Mongolian, Malay, Indian and Caucasian as ethnic labels and that the word 'negro' was not only a superfluous term but one that carried with it a connotation of contempt, opprobrium and inferiority." Mr. Powell further stated, "Biblical literature has not a single reference to black men as 'negroes' although black men figure repeatedly in Bible lore." He said, "In Africa, as elsewhere, neither color nor language can serve as criteria of the homogeneity of race." From Willis Huggins' Forward to this book, I extract the following quotes:

> If not strange, it is at least unique, that American-born Africans became "negroes" in common parlance, while American-born Europeans, or Asiatics, remain Italians, Poles, Koreans, Japanese or Tibetans.

> Although it is too late for peoples of African descent to trace their lineage to any particular African tribe, yet for all that, they remain Africans.

> What is needed in this matter is new education; unbiased instruction which should lead to the recognition of particular African peoples for what they are, i.e., Basutos, Buandas, Nubians, Senegalese.

Dr. Huggins' summation of Raphael Powell's finding is that "this will require the preparation of simple texts in ethnology and anthropology by experts and there placed in the common schools and used in lecture forums." Mr. Powell continued his inquiry in other books, *No Black-White Church* and *The Common Sense Conception of the Race Problem*. Dr. Huggins further stated that, "Mr. Powell is on the right track in running down the word, 'negro' for he sees that just as the word 'Aryan' has come to plague Western Europe today; he predicts that the word 'negro' will rise in the future as a plague to America and the Western world."

Mr. Powell's book is the first extensive investigation into the semantics of race as it refers to African people. In the early 1960s a Harlem bookstore owner and political activist, Richard B. Moore, formed a committee to tell the truth about the word "negro." Mr. Moore and his committee were of the opinion that the word needed to be dropped from our vocabulary as having no relevance to the identification of a people. In his book, *The Name Negro, Its Origin and Evil Use*, he said, "Slaves and dogs are named by their masters. Free men name themselves." Mr. Moore further stated that the proper name of any people must relate to land, history and culture. He emphasized that black tells you how you look, but it does not tell you what you are. Africa is the home of a variety of people, of many shades and colors, but mainly they are black. Any person in Africa, he further stated, who cannot be referred to as an African, is either an invader or the descendant of an invader.

No disrespect for Jesse Jackson is intended, but I am of the opinion that he has not read one word of this literature of definition that black scholars have been creating for over 100 years.

In the 1968 challenge of black scholars to the African Studies Association, their main disagreement with the white-dominated organization was over the definition of African people in world history. Their explanation for the formation of a new organization, the African Heritage Studies Association, is detailed in their objectives as follows:

Introduction:
The African Heritage Studies Association (ASHA) is an association of scholars of African descent, dedicated to the preservation, interpretation and academic presentation of the historical and cultural heritage of African peoples both on the ancestral soil of Africa and in diaspora in the Americas and throughout the world.

Aims and Objectives:
1. Education:
    a. Reconstruction of African history and cultural studies along Afro-centric lines while effecting an intellectual

union among black scholars the world over.

b. Acting as a clearing house of information in the establishment and evaluation of a more realistic African Program.

c. Presenting papers at seminars and symposia where any aspect of the life and culture of the African peoples are discussed.

d. Relating, interpreting and disseminating African materials for black education at all levels and the community at large.

2. International:

a. To reach African countries in order to facilitate greater communication and interaction between Africans and Africans in the Americas.

b. To assume leadership in the orientation of African students in the United States and orientation of African-Americans in Africa (establish contacts).

c. To establish an Information Committee on African and American relations whose function it will be to research and disseminate to the membership information on all aspects of American relations with respect to African peoples.

3. Domestic:

a. To relate to those organizations that are predominantly involved in and influence the education of black people.

b. To solicit their influence and affluence in the promotion of Black Studies and in the execution of ASHA programs and projects.

c. To arouse social consciousness and awareness of these groups.

d. To encourage their financial contribution to Black schools with programs involving the study of African peoples.

4. Black Students and Scholars:

a. To encourage and support students who wish to major in the study of African peoples.

b. To encourage black students to relate to the study of the heritage of African people, and to acquire the ranges of skills for the production and development of African peoples.

c. To encourage attendance and participation including the reading of papers at meetings dealing with the study of African life and history so that the African perspective is represented.

d. To ask all black students and scholars to rally around ASHA to build it up as a study organization for the reconstruction of our history and culture.

5. Black Communities:

a. To seek to aid black scholars who need financial support for their community projects or academic research.

b. To edit a newsletter or journal through which ASHA activities will be known.

In the new interest in Pan-Africanism that is gaining momentum throughout the African world, the intent of the Africans is not only to change their definition in world history but to change their direction. Theirs is a hope that Pan-Africanism will spread beyond its narrow intellectual base to become the motivation for an African World Union. This will begin when we recognize that we are not "colored," "negro," or "black." We are an African people wherever we are on the face of the earth.

African people will have to take a three-way look at themselves, using the past to evaluate the present and using the present to prophesy the future. In our long journey on this earth, we have had few friends, if any. All non-Africans who have come among us or been associated with us have clearly shown that they would betray us any time it was in their self-interest. We have never made good alliances with other people. Properly counted, Africans may number a billion people on the face of the earth. With that many Africans in the world, and with some political astuteness, we are in a position to make either alliances that are to our benefit or none at all. We know that the most important alliance we need to make is among ourselves.

To be sufficiently argumentative on the subject of black-white alliances, I would have to speak for a week, and I would still barely exhaust the subject: If there is one thing that can be said about black people that has caused a lot of pain, and yet is historically true, it is that politically we are one of the most naive of people. We have been taken in by practically everything and everybody that has come to us. I think this taking in, this betrayal, has something to do with both our weaknesses and our strengths. If you find the strengths of a people, you will find their weaknesses, because the two are closely related.

In the first place, we have been an extremely humane people. We have been hospitable to strangers, and nearly always to the wrong strangers. Almost all of our relationships with non-African people began with gestures of friendship. More than anyone else in the world, we have repeatedly invited our future conquerors to dinner. There is a need to look at black-white alliances going back 2,500 years.

I think that the nature of our betrayal by people who come among us, who solicit our help and get it tells us something that is quite frightening, i.e., we are a totally unobligated people. We don't owe Christianity anything because we created the religion. The Europeans bought it, reshaped it, sold it back to us and used it as a basis for the slave trade. We created Islam; then the Arabs, after years of fruitful partnership with us, turned on us and used Islam to justify their slave trade. We created the concept called socialism: An African king 1300 years before the birth of Christ was preaching the same thing that Karl Marx thought he invented. When the newly-found socialism used us, it turned on us. In looking at alliances, we're taking a global view of the African and his humanity and the manifestations of his humanity in relationship to people in other parts of the world.

At one point, there was a disruption within Africa itself. The African Cushites invaded Egypt. The people of the Middle East (again, this tells you something about how we might miss certain points) were buying iron from a city called Meroe in Cush, from which they made iron-tipped weapons, while the magnificent army of Cush was using bronze-tipped weapons; bronze is softer than iron. With the iron bought from the Africans, they could drive Africans out of the Middle East and begin the decline of Egypt. Once again Africans had naively trusted an ally.

You will find this pattern consistent from the Shepherd King alliance to the alliance of American blacks with the American Communist Party. Africans are always a junior partner. If the alliance can be broken without your consent, then it is not an alliance. You are a servant of it instead of being a partner of it. If it is a genuine alliance and a genuine friendship, then collectively both of you decide how it should go and how it should not go. Why are so many of the alliances blacks make with other people dismantled to the detriment of Africans and Africans have nothing to say about them? These alliances aren't real alliances and blacks aren't partners in them in the first place.

Kohanna was the first African to attempt to drive the Arabs out of Africa. She called them interlopers and said they had no business there. Religiously she was Hebrew, but she advised her nephew and her son to join Islam because it was politic to do so. Her nephew, Tarik-binziad, was the leader of a group of Africans around Senegal and Mauretania who moved up to North Africa. Now this African, who came from inside Africa and who had joined Islam and made an alliance with it for political reasons, but who for other than political reasons was not even Moslem, knew that the Visogoths and the people controlling Spain were in serious trouble. He sent an army to test out and see what kind of resistance he would face in Spain, and following this, decided to take Spain. This conquest of Spain that is attributed to the Arabs was truly an African conquest. The Africans again began to make new alliances, and these were effective for 700 years. Why were these particular alliances so effective? (Let's talk about some of the good ones we made.) They were effective because the Africans had the muscle and they called the tunes. The alliances did not break until Africans lost that muscle, and they lost that muscle in arguments with the Arabs.

The Arabs are another overrated people in history, another people who have been both good and bad to the extent that black people don't even know how to make an assessment of them. They have manipulated both blacks and whites depending on the political climate. If the white political climate is good, they are white; if the black political climate is good, they are black. But they are mixed people and always have been. When Islam advanced in East Africa, it did so with a single missionary. He would come into an African village; he would render some service that was needed; he would marry an African woman; he would convert her and then convert her family. Then he would use that family to convert other families. As the Arab moved more and more into Africa, whatever color he was originally, he was getting blacker and blacker. He was "dissipating" his original physical being into the bloodstream of Africa. This went on for well over a thousand years and is still going on. By no stretch of the imagination can you call the Arabs white people, although there are many who prefer to called white and treated as such. Quite a few act no different from white people in their relationship to us. My point is that this African-Arab alliance was basically good in Spain, because the military arm that held Spain was African. The Africans entered Spain in 711; they sent another wave into Spain in 1076. The Almohads, in 1240, came from North Africa. The argument between the Almohads and the Almoravids weakened the African hold on Spain until about 1450, when Europe was rising again to its feet, thanks to an internal quarrel between the Africans and Arabs. When these Arabs were expelled in 1492, the year Columbus allegedly discovered America, instead of going back to Africa and building an African nation, these Arabs went down the East coast and began to trade arms with the Africans along the East coast of Africa and continued the Arab slave trade. Thus, the Arabs cannot be freed of any guilt of it. This Arab-African alliance was over now. It had gone bad, and the Arabs' encroachment on African countries weakened Africa to the point where Africa could not mount a successful resistance against the Atlantic slave trade. That was disaster. But more disaster would come later on. From 1591 to 1594 the North Africans, themselves black, the emperor of Morocco in North Africa, Yakud Almansur, would send an army across the desert, using an African trader to show the way. They would break up the kingdoms of inner western Africa. Timbuctoo would soon be gone. The great university, Sankore, would soon be gone.

This was in 1594 when the slave trade was 100 years old. These people in inner Africa had great universities. There are still four universities in Timbuctoo alone. Jenne was another city university, and all of this is totally left out of history. These North Africans came down and wrecked this. Now it was Moslem against Moslem. These Africans would tell these Moslems, using white mercenaries with modern arms of that day, "We are Moslems, we're Moslems, we're your kin," and Africans would just go ahead with their slaughter. The tragedy of the breaking up of the great independent states of Africa before the European slave trade could really move was the tragedy of this alliance. Islam and the Arabs will have to share the guilt in this, because at that same time they were breaking up the great African kingdoms in the Western Sudan and West Africa, the Arab slave trade had been intensified along the coast of East Africa. The partnership between Africans and Arabs of those great states had lasted for years. That partnership had now grown sour. Again the partner had turned on the African; the guest had turned on his host, as has happened so many times with us.

The African's role and influence in Spain collapsed, and the African tried to make new alliances. But none of them would work for very long. The Portuguese entered the Congo and stayed for 100 years. This was an alliance that the Africans could control, they would not allow the Portuguese to build those fortresses that they had built in Ghana to take out the slaves. The Africans would not even permit them to begin the slave trade. When the Portuguese decided to start the slave trade in the Congo, the Africans ordered them out; and they got out.

Why is it that in one part of Africa the Africans ordered the Europeans out, and they had to go, and in the other part of Africa they ordered them out and they refused to go? We're dealing with two kinds of structure; and if we could understand this, we could understand the fragmentation of black movement right now. The slave trade failed in every part of Africa that had a monolithic government, a solid government where one king said yes or no for everybody. When the king and the government said no and told the Portuguese to get out, they got out. They would move South, but there they would face another great African queen, Ndongo, today called Angola. She would fight them for fifty-two of her eighty-one years. The clearest picture of her as a political figure is in Chancellor Williams' book, *The Destruction of Black Civilization*. Her life begs for better treatment. Politically, she was straight on the mark every time. Can you imagine a woman opposing the Europeans fifty-two years and never making one bad decision? This woman wanted to consolidate all of South East and South West Africa and stretch her kingdom across to the other shore. Nzinga made whatever alliances she had to make, but she always controlled them, and got the best out of them until she died.

In the nineteenth century, certain African kings (I am not using the word chief, because it was invented to keep from addressing Africans as kings) were naive enough to make alliances with Europeans. Nothing came of these alliances, and when they were betrayed, they went to the battlefield and fought it out. The Africans won more than they lost and managed to frustrate the European presence in Africa for the whole of the century. These Africans who thought there was something to be gained in alliances with the Europeans were sadly mistaken. Along the east coast of Africa after the Portuguese came, certain Africans made alliances with the Portuguese and others with the Omani Arabs. The Africans would, tragically, go to the Omani Arabs and help them against the Portuguese and go to the Portuguese and help them against the Arabs. They did not know that the Portuguese and the Omani Arabs had gotten together against them. They were once again caught in the middle, and tragically naive.

The main point here is that we people really need to take a good look at ourselves and begin to exercise the essential selfishness of survival. I'm saying that *our first allegiance* is going to have to be *our* blackness or *our Africanness*. We will have to ask questions and make alliances that are based on our self-interest. If it is not to our self-interest, to hell with it, no matter how good it sounds. There are too many of us who think that we have to become international now. I think when there is an international motif in the politics of the world, our agenda must be looking inward to ourselves first. We have to take inventory of ourselves as a people. We must stop talking about multi-racialism. People in power do not talk about multi-racialism. They talk about their laws, and either you obey them or you get out.

I heard this saying recently in Jamaica: "We have no trouble here. We're multi-racial." But the same people who were on top when the colonists were overtly in charge are still on top. The status quo does not change. They spend so much time defending the right of a minority that lives among them without restrictions, that nobody talks about that man in the hills. "Do you mean in a country that is 98 percent black you want to discuss the white minority?" Yes. When you live in a European country, you have to obey European law or take the first train out. No argument—either you're in charge, or you're not in charge. You accommodate your people first and foremost, and if the laws you make to accommodate your people are not good enough for the outsider, then let the outsider go back outside! But we are so hung up with sentiment that we don't know how to handle power. The only way to handle power is to be powerful not to talk about it, but to exercise it. Because we're so non-racial, we do not produce that kind of safeguard to protect ourselves. We need some protection from our sentiment, because sentiment and power don't go together. And we can lose some of our naïveté and sentiment without losing our humanity, which is something I can't say for most of the powerful people in the world. In order to lose their sentiment and to deal with power, they lost their humanity and human feelings toward human beings. I don't think we have to do it.

I have to conclude this, though there really isn't a conclusion. What you have to understand is that you stand on the wings of power, and you stand in the wings, ready to come on to the stage of history. And whether you do badly or not, or whether you're ready or not, you can't even stop coming if you want to. It will be left with you to make this a world where no man will have to apologize for his color and no man will have to celebrate it. But, out of your essential Africanness, looking out for yourself and your children first and foremost, you might create an atmosphere where other people need not necessarily walk in fear. Understand me well, I said nothing about forgiving anybody. I'm talking about how your energy will be deployed in building *first*, a social order for yourself and your children and then using your new position to build a social order for the world. I'm saying that *only* out of your nationalism and our Africanness can this happen.

If African people the world over are to save themselves, they must find a way to reclaim some of the life sustaining things they lost in slavery, colonialism and through the massive anti-African propaganda dispensed by Europeans all over the world. It is basic that African people, and all people, regain their self-confidence and their image of God as they originally conceived Him or Her to be. In the conquest of most of the non-European world, Europe's greatest achievement was the conquest of the mind. The Europeans and the Arabs deprived the Africans of the right to call on God in a language of their own creation and to look upon Him in the image of their own imagination.

The total liberation of African people involves more than "flag independence." A country that is not economically free is not fully politically free. A people who cannot control or heavily influence the education of their children cannot control the future action of their children, because they are not in charge of their cultural and psychological direction.

The education of the African by this former colonial master is a contradiction in terms. Powerful people never educate powerless people in the strategy of taking their power away from them. Education, I have often said, has but one honorable purpose, one alone. Everything else is a waste of time. The role of education is to train the student to be a responsible handler of power.

In Africa, there is a need for a generation of Africans to be educated in Africa by other Africans for the express purpose of serving Africa. All Africans living outside of Africa should be committed to devoting at least part of their time and their talent to the preservation and the enhancement of Africa. The industrialization and the total reconstruction of Africa should not be left to the Africans who live in Africa alone. This should be a world mission of African people wherever they are on the face of this earth.

There is a need for a Pan-African mission that will transcend national borders, cultural and religious differences and political preference. The Africans living in the Western hemisphere should be sensitive to the fact that the slave ships coming from Africa to the so-called New World brought no West Indians, no black Americans, no South Americans. They brought African people who had to adjust to the conditions where the slave ships put them down. It is by sheer accident that some Africans away from home are called Jamaicans, some are called Trinidadians, Barbadians and some are called African-Americans. They are all African people reacting to different forms of oppression.

If Africans everywhere stopped being consumers of the products of other people, and began to produce everything we needed from toilet paper to locomotives, over half of the Africans of the world would be employed furnishing goods and services for each other. In doing this we would not only radically change our economic status, we would radically change the economic direction of the world. We need to remember that for most of the time of our existence on this earth, we did not know about Europeans. We fed ourselves then, and we clothed and housed ourselves. Now we need to adjust to the new condition in the world, regain our confidence in ourselves and announce with this new confidence that if we have changed the world before, we can do it again.

There is a need for an operational definition of Pan-Africanism and African nationalism that will be broad enough to include all Africans in the world. We have lived through the longest and most tragic Holocaust in human history. Every attempt has been made to dehumanize us and deny our humanity. I am of the belief that faith has preserved African people for a special purpose on this earth. We are the only people who can make universal promises and keep them, because we have no designs on the lands or the resources of other people. Part of our mission should be first and foremost to deliver Africa to African people. And from the vantage point of our Africanness, we can give the world a new definition of freedom and responsibility. If this is our mission, it is also the legacy that we can leave for our children and other children still unborn.

BIBLIOGRAPHY

▼

Alex-Hamah, John, *Farewell Africa: Life and Death of Nkrumah*, Lagos, Nigeria: Times Press Ltd., 1972.

Aptheker, Herbert, *American Negro Slave Revolts*, New York: International Publishers, 1970.

———, ed., *One Continual Cry by David Walker: Its Setting and Meaning*, New York: Humanities Press, 1965.

Asiwaju, A.I., ed. *Partitioned Africans: Ethnic Relations Across Africa's International Boundaries 1884-1984*, London: C. Hurst & Co., 1985.

Babatope, Ebenezer, *Nkrumaism Revisited*, 1978.

ben-Jochannan, Yosef, *Abu-Simbel-Gizeh, Guide Book/Manual*, New York: Alkebu-lan Books, 1986.

———, *We, The Black Jews*, Vol. I and II, New York: Alkebu-lan Books, 1983.

Bennett, Lerone, Jr., *Before the Mayflower: A History of Black America*, Chicago: Johnson Publishing Co., 1962.

———, *Confrontation: Black and White*, Baltimore, Md.: Penguin, 1966.

———, *Pioneers in Protest*, Baltimore, Md.: Penguin, 1968.

———, *The Shaping of Black America*, Chicago: Johnson Publishing Co., 1975.

Berger, Graenum, *Black Jews in America: A Documentary with Commentary*, New York: Federation of Jewish Philanthropies, 1978.

Beshir, Mohamed Omer, *Terramedia: Themes in Afro-Arab Relations*, London: Ithaca Press, 1982.

Betts, Raymond F., *The Scramble for Africa: Causes and Dimensions of Empire*, Boston: Heath and Co., 1966.

Billingsley, Andrew, *The Black Families in White America*, Englewood Cliffs, N.J.: Prentice-Hall, 1968.

Blyden, Edward Wilmot, *Christianity, Islam and the Negro Race*, Edinburgh: Edinburgh University Press, 1967.

———, *Inaugural Address at Liberia College, 1881*, New York: Young's Book Exchange, 1926.

421

———, *On African Customs*, London: African Publication Society, 1969.

Bradley, Michael, *The Iceman Inheritance: Prehistoric Sources of Western Man's Racism, Sexism and Aggression*, Toronto, Ont.: Dorset Publishing Co., 1978.

Breitman, George, ed., *By Any Means Necessary: Speeches, Interviews and a Letter by Malcolm X*, New York: Pathfinder Press, 1970.

———, *The Last Year of Malcolm X: The Evolution of a Revolutionary*, New York: Pathfinder Press, 1967.

———, *Malcolm X, The Man and His Ideas: A Speech Delivered to the Friday Night Socialist Forum at Eugene V. Debs Hall in Detroit on March 5, 1965*, New York: Pioneer Publishers, 1965.

———, Herman Porter, and Baxter Smith, *The Assassination of Malcolm X*, New York: Pathfinder Press, 1976.

Brenner, Lenni, *Zionism in the Age of the Dictators: A Reappraisal*, Westport, Conn.: Lawrence Hill, 1983.

Brotz, Howard M., *The Black Jews of Harlem, Negro Nationalism and the Dilemmas of Negro Leadership*, New York: Schocken Books, 1970.

Burkett, Randall K., *Garveyism as a Religious Movement: The Institutionalization of a Black Civil Religion*, Metuchen, N.J.: The Scarecrow Press, 1978.

Calder, Ritchie, *Agony of the Congo*, London: Victor Gollancz Ltd., 1961.

Campbell, Mavis C., *The Maroons of Jamaica, 1655-1796*, Trenton, N.J.: Africa World Press, 1990.

Carruthers, Jacob H., *The Irritated Genie*, Chicago: The Kemetic Institute, 1985.

Clarke, John Henrik, ed., *Marcus Garvey and the Vision of Africa*, New York: Random House, 1974.

Cleage, Rev. Albert and George Breitman, *Myths about Malcolm X: Two Views*, New York: Merit Publishers, 1968.

Cohen, Aharon, *Israel and the Arab World*, Boston: Beacon Press, 1976.

The Congo, A Report of the Commission of Enquiry Appointed by The Congo Free State Government, New York: G. P. Putnam's Sons, 1906.

Cronon, E. David, *Black Moses: The Story of Marcus Garvey and the Universal Negro Improvement Association*, Madison: University of Wisconsin Press, 1962.

———, ed., *Marcus Garvey*, Englewood Cliffs, N.J.: Prentice Hall, 1973.

Dann, Martin E., ed., *The Black Press, 1827-1890*, New York: G. P. Putnam's Sons, 1971.

Danquah, Joseph B., *The Akan Doctrine of God*, 2d ed., Frank Cass & Co., 1968.

———, "The Historical Significance of the Bond of 1844," *Transactions of the Historical Society of Ghana*, Vol. III, Part I, Achimota, 1957.

———, "Obligation in Akan Society," *West African Affairs*, No. 8, London.

Davidson, Basil, *Which Way Africa? The Search for a New Society*, Baltimore, Md.: Penguin Books, 1964.

Davis, Lenwood G., and Janet L. Sims, compilers, *Marcus Garvey: An Annotated Bibliography*, foreword by John Henrik Clarke, Westport, Conn.: Greenwood Press, 1980.

Delany, M. R. and Robert Campbell, *Search for a Place: Black Separatism and Africa, 1860*, Ann Arbor: University of Michigan Press, 1971.

Dickens, Charles, *A Tale of Two Cities*, New York: Viking Penguin, 1970.

Diop, Cheikh Anta, *African Origins of Civilization: Myth or Reality?* Westport, Conn.: Lawrence Hill and Co., 1974.

———, *Black Africa: The Economic and Cultural Bases of a Federated State*, Paris: Présence Africaine, 1960.

———, *Civilization or Barbarism*, Westport, Conn.: Lawrence Hill and Co., 1989.

———, *A History of Precolonial Black Africa* (in French), Paris: Présence Africaine, 1960.

———, "The Origin of the ancient Egyptians," in *The Peopling of Ancient Egypt and the Deciphering of Meroitic Script*, pp. 27-57, The General History of Africa Studies and Documents, I, General History of Africa, II.

DuBois, W.E.B., *The Gift of Black Folk*, Fawcett, 1965.

———, *The Negro*, New York: Oxford University Press, 1970.

———, *The Suppression of the African Slave Trade to the U.S. of America, 1638-1870*, New York: Schocken Books, 1969.

———, *The World and Africa ... An Inquiry into the Part Which Africa Has Played in World History*, New York: International Publishers, 1965.

Elmessiri, Abdelwahab M., *The Land of Promise: A Critique of Political Zionism*, New Brunswick, N.J.: North American, 1977.

Epstein, Howard, ed., *Revolt in the Congo, 1960-64*, New York: Facts on File, 1965.

Fax, Elton C., *Garvey: The Story of a Pioneer Black Nationalist*, New York: Dodd, Mead & Co., 1972.

Franklin, John Hope, *George Washington Williams: A Bibliography*, Chicago: University of Chicago Press, 1985.

Garvey, Amy Jacques, *Garvey and Garveyism*, Kingston, Jamaica: United Printers, Ltd., 1962.

———, compiler, *The Philosophy and Opinions of Marcus Garvey or Africa for the Africans*, With a New Introduction by E.U. Essien-Udom, Two Volumes in One, Frank Cass, 1967.

——— and E. U. Essien-Udom, eds., *More Philosophy and Opinions of Marcus Garvey*, Vol. 3, Frank Cass, 1977.

Goldman, Peter, *The Death and Life of Malcolm X*, New York: Harper & Row, 1973.

Goodman, Benjamin, ed., *The End of White World Supremacy: Four Speeches by Malcolm X*, New York: Merlin House, 1971.

Graves, Robert and Raphael Patai, *Hebrew Myths: The Book of Genesis*, New York: McGraw Hill, 1963.

Gutman, Herbert G., *The Black Family in Slavery and Freedom: 1750-1925*, New York: Pantheon Books, 1976.

Ha'am, Ahad, *Nationalism and the Jewish Ethic*, New York: Schocken Books, 1962.

Hansberry, William Leo, "Africa: World's Richest Continent," *Freedomways*, Winter, 1963.

Harris, Joseph E., ed., *Global Dimensions of the African Diaspora*, Washington, D.C.: Howard University Press, 1982.

Harris, Sheldon H., *The African Returns*, New York: Simon and Schuster.

Hempstone, Smith, *Rebels, Mercenaries, and Dividends: The Katanga Story*, New York: Frederick A. Praeger, 1962.

Hennessy, Maurice N., *The Congo: A Brief History and Appraisal*, New York: Frederick, A. Praeger, 1961.

Higgins, Godfrey, *Anacalypsis*, 2 vols., New York: University Books, 1965.

Hill, Robert A., ed., *Marcus Garvey Life and Lessons*, A Centennial Companion to the Marcus Garvey and Universal Negro Improvement Association Papers, Berkeley: University of California Press, 1987.

————, *The Marcus Garvey and Universal Negro Improvement Association Papers*, Vols. 1-6, Berkeley: University of California Press, 1983-1989 (a projected 10 volumes).

Irwin, Graham W., *Africans Abroad*, New York: Columbia University Press, 1977.

Jacobs, Steven, *The Hebrew Heritage of Black Africa*, Rose-Lee, Inc., 1971.

Jacobs, Sylvia M., *The African Nexus: Black American Perspectives on the European Partitioning of Africa, 1880-1920*, Westport, Conn.: Greenwood Press, 1946.

James, C.L.R., *Nkrumah and the Ghana Revolution*, Westport, Conn.: Lawrence Hill & Co., 1977.

Jansen, G. H., *Zionism, Israel and Asian Nationalism*, Beirut: The Institute for Palestine Studies, 1971.

Joseph, Benjamin M., *Besieged Bedfellows: Israel and the Land of Apartheid*, Westport, Conn.: Greenwood Press, 1988.

July, Robert W., *The Origins of Modern African Thought*, New York: Praeger Publishers, 1967.

Kaiser, Ernest, "The History of Negro History," *Negro Digest*, Chicago, February, 1968.

Legal Status of the West Bank and Gaza, New York: The United Nations, 1982.

Legum, Colin, *Congo Disaster*, Baltimore, Md.: Penguin, 1961.

Lehn, Walter, *The Jewish National Fund: An Instrument of Discrimination*, EAFORD Paper No. 18, London, Nov. 1982.

———, "West Bank Sojourn," *Journal of Palestine Studies* 36, Vol. IX, No. 4, Summer 1980, Institute for Palestine Studies and Kuwait University.

Lemarchand, René, *Political Awakening in the Belgian Congo*, Berkeley: University of California Press, 1964.

Lewis, Rupert and Maureen Warner-Lewsi, *Garvey, Africa, Europe, the Americas*, Kingston, Jamaica: The Hearald, Ltd., 1986.

Logan, Rayford, *The Betrayal of the Negro from Rutherford B. Hayes to Woodrow Wilson*, New York: Collier Books, 1965.

Lomax, Louis E., *To Kill a Black Man*, Los Angeles: Holloway House, 1968.

Lumer, Dr. Hyman, *What Are We Doing in the Congo?* New York: New Outlook Publishers, 1965.

Patrice Lumumba: Fighter for Africa's Freedom, Moscow: Progress Publishers, 1965.

Lynch, Hollis R., *Edward Wilmot Blyden: Pan-Negro Patriot, 1832-1912*, New York: Oxford University Press.

———, "The Meaning of Malcolm X," *The Black Collegian*, Vol. 11, No. 3, Dec. 1980/Jan. 1981, New Orleans.

McKenzie, Rennie, Rhoda, *Nkrumah: Greatest of Modern Philosophers*, New York: Vantage Press, 1977.

Madhubuti, Haki R. (Don L. Lee), *Enemies: The Clash of Races*, Chicago: Third World Press, 1978.

Majeke, Nosipho, *The Role of the MIssionary in Conquest*, Johannesburg Society of Young Africa, 1952.

Mallison, W. Thomas and Sally V. Mallison, "The National Rights of the People of Palestine," *Journal of Palestine Studies* 36, Vol. IX, No. 4, Summer 1980, Institute for Palestine Studies and Kuwait University, Beirut.

Mansour, Christopher and Richard P. Stevens, *Internal Control in Israel and South Africa: The Mechanisms of Colonial-Settler regimes*, Washington, D.C., 1983.

Martin, Tony, *The Pan-African Connection from Slavery to Garvey and Beyond*, Dover, Mass.: The Majority Press, 1983.

———, *Race First: The Ideological and Organizational Struggles of Marcus Garvey and the Universal Negro Improvement Association*, Westport, Conn.: Greenwood Press, 1976.

Mazrui, Ali A., *The Africans: A Triple Heritage*, Boston: Little, Brown and Company, 1986.

Meredith, Martin, *The First Dance of Freedom: Black Africa in the Post-War Era*, New York: Harper & Row, 1984.

Merriam, Alan P., *Congo: Background of Conflict*, Boston: Northwestern University Press, 1961.

Moleah, Alfred T., *Israel and South Africa: Ideology and Practice*, EAFORD Paper No. 9, Washington, D.C., 1979.

——, *Zionism and Apartheid: the Negation of Human Rights*, EAFORD Paper No. 24, London, 1981.

Moore, Richard B., *The Name "Negro": Its Origin and Evil Use*, New York: Afro-American Publishers, 1960.

Morel, E. D., *The Black Man's Burden*, London: National Labour Press, 1920.

N'goudi, Prosper N'gom, "The Israeli Experience and African Development," *Présence Africaine*, Vol. 23, No. 51, Paris, 1964.

Nkrumah, Kwame, *Africa Must Unite*, New York: Frederick A. Praeger, 1963.

——, "African Prospect," *Foreign Affairs*, New York, October, 1958.

——, *The Autobiography of Kwame Nkrumah*, New York: International Publishers, 1957.

——, *Axioms of Kwame Nkrumah*, London: Panaf Publications, 1967.

——, *Challenge of the Congo*, New York: International Publishers, 1967.

——, *Class Struggle in Africa*, New York: International Publishers, 1970.

——, *Consciencism*, New York: Monthly Review Press, 1964.

——, *Dark Days in Ghana*, New York: International Publishers, 1968.

——, *Neocolonialism: The Last Stage of Imperialism*, New York: International Publishers, 1965.

——, *The Struggle Continues*, London: Panaf Books, 1968.

——, *Towards Colonial Freedom*, London: The Windmill Press, 1962.

——, *Voice from Conakry*, London: Panaf Publications, 1967.

Novack, George, "Malcolm X, Black Nationalism and Socialism," *International Socialist Review*, July-Aug. 1967, New York.

Okumu, Washington, *Lumumba's Congo: Roots of Conflict*, New York: Ivan Obolensky, 1963.

Padmore, George, *Africa: Britain's Third Empire*, London: Dennis Dobson, 1949.

——, *How Britain Rules Africa*, London: Wishart Books, 1936.

——, *Pan-Africanism or Communism*, New York: Doubleday/Anchor Books.

Panaf Great Lives, *Kwame Nkrumah*, London: Panaf Books, 1974.

Patai, Raphael, *The Arab Mind*, New York: Charles Scribner's Sons, 1976.

——, *The Jewish Mind*, New York: Charles Scribner's Sons, 1977.

Powell, Raphael, *The Human Side of a People and the Right Name, 1927*, New York: The Philemon Co., 1937.

——, *The Common Sense Conception of the Race Problem*, Boston: Square Deal-Chronicle Publishing Company, 1927.

——, *No Black-White Church: A Plea for Change-Satire*, New York: Carlton Press, 1985.

Price, Willard, *The Negro around the World*, New York: George H. Doran, 1925.

Reddaway, John, *"Seek Peace, And Ensue It": Selected Papers on Palestine and the Search for Peace*, The Council for the Advancement of Arab-British Understanding, 1970-1980.

Rodney, Walter, *How Europe Underdeveloped Africa*, London: Bogle-L'Ouverture Publications, 1972, pp. 40-83.

Roth, Cecil, *A History of the Jews: From Earliest Times through the Six Day War*, New York: Schocken Books, 1961.

Routtenberg, Max J., *Decades of Decision* New York: Black Publishing Company, 1973.

Schuyler, Phillipa, *Who Killed the Congo?* New York: Devin-Adair, 1962.

Shepperson, George, "Notes on Negro American Influence on the Emergence of African Nationalism," *Journal of African History*, Vol. I, No. 11, 1960.

Skinner, Elliot P., "Africans and Afro-Americans, White Americans: A Case of Pride and Prejudice," *Freedomways*, Vol. 5, No. 3, New York.

———, *Afro-American and Africa: The Continuing Dialectic*, New York: The Urban Center, Columbia University.

Slade, Ruth, *The Belgian Congo*, 2d ed., London: Oxford University Press, 1961.

Smith, Gary V., *Zionism: The Dream and the Reality, A Jewish Critique*, New York: Harper & Row, 1974.

Staudenrous, P.J., *The African Colonization Movement, 1816-1865*, New York: Columbia University Press.

Stevens, Richard P., *Weizmann & Smuts: A Study in Zionist-South African Cooperation*, Beirut: The Institute for Palestine Studies, 1975.

——— and Abdelwahab Elmessiri, *Israel and South Africa: the Progression of a Relationship*, New Brunswick, N.J.: North American, 1977.

———, ed., *Zionism and Palestine Before the Mandate: A Phase of Western Imperialism*, Beirut: The Institute for Palestine Studies, 1972.

Stuckey, Sterling, *The Ideological Origins of Black Nationalism*, Boston: Beacon, 1972.

Tekiner, Roselle, *Jewish Nationality Status as the Basis for Institutionalized Racism in Israel*, EAFORD Paper No. 40, Dec. 1985, New York.

Thompson, Vincent Bakpetu, *The Making of the African Diaspora in the Americas, 1441-1900*, New York: Longman, 1987.

Time Magazine, "Quiet Man in a Hot Spot," August 22, 1960, New York.

T'Shaka, Oba, *The Political Legacy of Malcolm X*, Chicago: Third World Press, 1983.

Turki, Fawz, "The Passions of Exile: The Palestine Congress of North America," *Journal of Palestine Studies 36*, Vol. IX, No. 4, Summer 1980, Institute for Palestine Studies and Kuwait University.

Twain, Mark. *King Leopold's Soliloquy*, New York: International Publishers, 1970.

Van Sertima, Ivan, ed., *Journal of African Civilization*, Special Issues: 1. African Presence in Early Asia, 2. African Presence in Early Europe, New Brunswick, N.J.: Rutgers University, 1985.

Velman, Victor, *Martin Delany: The Beginning of Black Nationalism*, Boston: Beacon, 1971.

Vernon, Robert, "Wechsler's Attack on Malcolm X," *The Black Ghetto*, New York: Merit Publishers, October 1964.

Vincent, Theodore G., *Black Power and the Garvey Movement*, Berkeley, Calif.: The Ramparts Press.

David Walker's Appeal, introduced by David Wiltse, New York: Hill and Wang, 1965.

Walters, Ronald, "White Racial Nationalism in the United States," *Without Prejudice*, The EAFORD International Review of Racial Discrimination, Vol. I, No. 1, Fall 1987, Washington, D.C.

Weizmann, Chaim, *Trial and Error: The Autobiography*, New York: Schocken Books, 1966.

Welsing, Frances Cress, *The Cress Theory of Color-Confrontation and RACISM (White Supremacy)*, 1970.

Wesley, Charles H., *Prince Hall: Life and Legacy*, Philadelphia: The Afro-American Historical and Cultural Museum, 1977.

Williams, Eric, *Capitalism and Slavery*, New York: Capricorn Books, 1966, pp. 3-4.

Williams, Jean-Claude, *Patrimonialism and Political Change in the Congo*, Stanford, Calif.: Stanford University Press, 1972.

Williams, Joseph J., *Hebrewisms of West Africa*, New York: The Dial Press, 1931.

Work, Monroe, ed., *Negro Year Book*, Alabama: Tuskegee Institute, 1928.

X, Malcolm, *The Autobiography*, with the assistance of Alex Haley, New York: Grove Press, 1964.

———, "Malcolm X Talks to Young People," New York: A Young Socialist Pamphlet, Nov. 1966.

———, *On Afro-American History*, Expanded and illustrated edition, New York: Pathfinder Press, 1970.

Young, Crawford, *Politics in the Congo: Decolonization and Independence*, Princeton, N.J.: Princeton University Press, 1965.

INDEX

▼

429